The Reconstruction of Nations

The Reconstruction of Nations

Poland, Ukraine, Lithuania, Belarus,

1569–1999

Timothy Snyder

Yale University Press

New Haven & London

Published with the assistance of the Frederick W. Hilles Fund of Yale University.

Printed in the United States of America.

The Library of Congress has cataloged the hardcover edition as follows:

Snyder, Timothy.

    The reconstruction of nations : Poland, Ukraine, Lithuania, Belarus, 1569–1999 / Timothy Snyder.

      p. cm.

    Includes bibliographical references and index.

    ISBN 0-300-09569-4 (cloth : alk. paper)

    1. Europe, Eastern—History—20th century. I. Title.

DJK48.5 .S66   2003

947.084—dc21

                            2002066356

A catalogue record for this book is available from the British Library.

The paper in this book meets the guidelines for permanence and durability of the Committee on Production Guidelines for Book Longevity of the Council on Library Resources.

ISBN 0-300-10586-x (pbk. : alk. paper)

For
Marianna Brown Snyder and Guy Estel Snyder
and in memory of
Lucile Fisher Hadley and Herbert Miller Hadley

Contents

Names and Sources

The subjects of this book are the transformation of national ideas, the causes of ethnic cleansing, and the conditions for national reconciliation. One theme is the contestation of territory, and contested places are known by different names to different people at different times. Another theme is the difference between history and memory, a difference revealed when care is taken with names. The body of this book will name cities between Warsaw and Moscow according to the usage of the people in question at the relevant moment. This minimizes anachronism, recalls the importance of language to nationalism, and emphasizes that the disposition of cities is never final. The gazetteer provides toponyms in eight languages in use as of this writing.

The names of countries also require some attention. In this work, attributes of the medieval principality of Kyivan Rus' are denoted by the term "Rusian." The culture of East Slavs within the early modern Polish-Lithuanian Commonwealth is called "Ruthenian." The adjective "Russian" is reserved for the Russian empire, the Russian Soviet Federative Socialist Republic, and the Russian Federation. "Ukrainian" is a geographical term in the medieval and early modern periods, and a political term in modern contexts. The use of "Belarus" signals an orientation toward local traditions; "Belorussia" suggests a belief in an integral connection with Russia. "Lithuanian" and "Polish" refer to the appropriate polities and cultures in the period in question. The historical lands of "Galicia" and "Volhynia" will be named by these Latinate English terms throughout.

This book draws on archival materials; document collections; parliamentary records; ministerial memoranda; local, national, and national-minority newspapers of various countries and periods; diaries, memoirs, and correspondence; scholarly publications; other printed and unprinted sources; and interviews with civil servants, parliamentary deputies, ministers, and heads of state. Archives are cited by four-letter abbreviations, and document collections by short titles: a key is found at the back of the book. Books and articles are cited in full at first, and then by author surname and short title. Other sources are cited in full. Authors' names are spelled as they appear in the cited work, even when this gives rise to inconsistencies of transliteration.

Transliteration is the unavoidable practice of rendering words spelled in one alphabet legible in another. The Polish, Lithuanian, and Czech languages, like English, French, and German, use various orthographies within Roman script. Ukrainian, Belarusian, and Russian use various orthographies within Cyrillic script. Like translation, transliteration abounds in intractable problems: so critical readers will know that all solutions are imperfect. With certain exceptions for well-known surnames, Cyrillic script is here rendered by a simplified version of the Library of Congress system. Translations, except from Lithuanian, are my own.

GAZETTEER

English	Ukrainian	Polish	Belarusian	Russian	Yiddish	German	Lithuanian
Vilnius	Vil'nius	Wilno	Vil'nia	Vil'nius	Vilne	Wilna	Vilnius
Lviv	L'viv	Lwów	L'vou	Lvov	Lemberik	Lemberg	Lvovas
Kyiv	Kyiv	Kijów	Kieu	Kiev	Kiv	Kiew	Kijevas
Minsk	Mins'k	Mińsk	Minsk	Minsk	Minsk	Minsk	Minskas
Galicia	Halychyna	Galicja	Halitsiia	Galitsiia	Galitsye	Galizien	Galicija
Volhynia	Volyn'	Wołyń	Valyn	Volyn'	Volin	Wolynien	Volyne
Poland	Pol'shcha	Polska	Polshcha	Pol'sha	Poyln	Polen	Lenkija
Lithuania	Lytva	Litwa	Letuva	Litva	Lite	Litauen	Lietuva
Belarus	Bilorus'	Białoruś	Belarus'	Belorussia	Vaysrusland	Weissrussland	Baltarusija
Ukraine	Ukraina	Ukraina	Ukraina	Ukraina	Ukraine	Ukraine	Ukraina
Russia	Rosiia	Rosja	Ras'eia	Rossiia	Rusland	Russland	Rusija

Polish "w" is pronounced as English "v" in "vain"; Polish "ó" as the English "u" in "true"; Polish "j" as the English "y" in "yoke"; Polish "ń" as the first "n" in English "onion"; Polish "ł" as the English "w," in "wonder." The Russian, Ukrainian, and Belarusian toponyms would normally be spelled in Cyrillic characters, and the Yiddish in Hebrew.

The Polish-Lithuanian
Commonwealth, 1569

DENMARK

BALTIC
SEA

LIVONIA

COURLAND

Moscow

MUSCOVY

DUCAL
PRUSSIA

Wilno

Gdańsk

Minsk

LITHUANIA

Berlin

Vistula

HOLY ROMAN

EMPIRE

Warsaw

Bug

Volhynia

Dnieper

POLAND

Kijów

HABSBURG

Cracow

Lwów

Ukraine

DOMAINS

ROYAL

Galicia

Zbrucz

HUNGARY

Vienna

CRIMEAN
KHANATE

CROATIA

Dniester

OTTOMAN EMPIRE

ADRIATIC SEA

BLACK   SEA

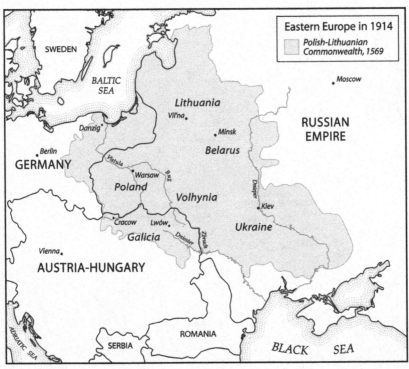

Eastern Europe in 1914

*Polish-Lithuanian
Commonwealth, 1569*

SWEDEN

BALTIC
SEA

Moscow

Lithuania

Vil'na

RUSSIAN
EMPIRE

Danzig

Minsk

Berlin

Belarus

GERMANY

Vistula

Warsaw

Bug

Poland

Volhynia

Dnieper

Kiev

Vienna

Cracow

Lwów

Ukraine

Galicia

Dniester

Zbrucz

AUSTRIA-HUNGARY

ADRIATIC SEA

ROMANIA

SERBIA

BLACK   SEA

Interwar Eastern Europe circa 1938

Polish-Lithuanian Commonwealth, 1569

SWEDEN

BALTIC SEA

Tallinn

ESTONIA

Riga · LATVIA

LITHUANIA

Kaunas

DANZIG · Wilno

GERMANY

Minsk

BELORUSSIAN S.S.R.

· Moscow

SOVIET UNION

· Berlin

GERMANY

Vistula

Warsaw · POLAND

Bug

Volhynia

· Kiev

Dnieper

Prague ·

CZECHOSLOVAKIA

Cracow · Lwów.

Galicia

Zbruch

UKRAINIAN S.S.R.

Dniester

Vienna ·

AUSTRIA

· Budapest

HUNGARY

ROMANIA

ADRIATIC SEA

Belgrade ·

YUGOSLAVIA

· Bucharest

BLACK SEA

Wartime Eastern Europe circa 1942

SWEDEN

BALTIC SEA

REICHSKOMMISSARIAT OSTLAND

Kauen

Danzig · Wilna

Minsk

· Moscow

SOVIET UNION

· Berlin

GERMANY

Vistula

· Warsaw

GENERAL-GOUVERNEMENT

Bug

Volhynia

Cracow ·

Lemberg

Galicia

Kiew ·

REICHSKOMMISSARIAT UKRAINE

Dnieper

Dniester

Zbruch

Vienna ·

SLOVAKIA

HUNGARY

CROATIA

SERBIA

ROMANIA

ADRIATIC SEA

BLACK SEA

Postwar Eastern Europe circa 1945

▨ *Polish-Lithuanian Commonwealth, 1569*

SWEDEN

BALTIC SEA

Tallinn
ESTONIAN S.S.R.

Riga LATVIAN S.S.R.

LITHUANIAN S.S.R.

Vilnius

Moscow

RUSSIAN S.F.S.R.

RUSSIAN S.F.S.R.

Gdańsk

Berlin

Minsk

BELORUSSIAN S.S.R.

SOVIET UNION

GERMAN DEMOCRATIC REPUBLIC

POLAND

Warsaw

Vistula

Bug

Volhynia

Dnepr

Prague

Kiev

CZECHOSLOVAKIA

Cracow

Galicia

L'viv

Dniester

Zbruch

UKRAINIAN S.S.R.

Vienna

AUSTRIA

Budapest

HUNGARY

MOLDAVIAN S.S.R.

ROMANIA

Belgrade

Bucharest

YUGOSLAVIA

ADRIATIC SEA

BLACK SEA

Eastern Europe, circa 1999

▨ *Polish-Lithuanian Commonwealth 1569*

SWEDEN

BALTIC SEA

Tallinn
ESTONIA

Riga LATVIA

LITHUANIA

Vilnius

Moscow

RUSSIA

RUSSIAN FEDERATION

Gdańsk

Berlin

Minsk

BELARUS

GERMANY

POLAND

Warsaw

Vistula

Bug

Volhynia

Prague

Kyiv

CZECH REPUBLIC

Cracow

L'viv

Dnieper

Dniester

Galicia

Zbruch

UKRAINE

SLOVAKIA

Vienna *Bratislava*

AUSTRIA

Budapest

SLOVENIA

HUNGARY

MOLDOVA

CROATIA

ROMANIA

BOSNIA-HERZEGOVINA

YUGOSLAVIA

Bucharest

ADRIATIC SEA

BLACK SEA

Introduction

When do nations arise, what brings ethnic cleansing, how can states reconcile?

This study traces one passage to modern nationhood. It begins with the foundation of the largest realm of early modern Europe, the Polish-Lithuanian Commonwealth, in the sixteenth century. The nation of this Commonwealth was its nobility, Catholic, Orthodox, and Protestant. United by common political and civil rights, nobles of Polish, Lithuanian, and East Slavic origin alike described themselves, in Latin or Polish, as "of the Polish nation." They took for granted that, in the natural order of things, the languages of state, speech, literature, and liturgy would vary. After the Commonwealth's partition by rival empires in the eighteenth century, some patriots recast the nation as the people, and nationality as the language they spoke. At the end of the twentieth century, as this study closes, the core lands of the old Commonwealth were divided among states named after nations: Poland, Ukraine, Lithuania, and Belarus. By then, the prevailing conception of nationality expected state borders to confine linguistic communities, and the languages of speech, politics, and worship to be the same. How did four modern national ideas arise from a single early modern one?

Our route through this passage follows the national ideas of the early modern Commonwealth (1569–1795), of the nineteenth-century empires that partitioned it (1795–1918), and of the independent states and Soviet republics that supplanted them (1918–1939). We will find that the early modern Polish nation survived partition and prospered under empire, its disintegration beginning in the late nineteenth century. Even then, modern national ideas emerged in intimate competition with this early modern vision, against a more distant backdrop of imperial rule. This close contest between traditional patriotism and ethnic nationalism continued in the new polities established after the First World War. Although statehood itself forced choices and closed options after 1918, the newly privileged idea of the modern ethnic nation was not yet hegemonic. Only the organized violence of the Second World War finally broke the historical integument in which early modern ideas of nationality could cohere. Deportations, genocide, and ethnic cleansing destroyed historical regions and emptied multicultural cities, clearing the way for modern nationalism. The mass murder and displacement of elites uprooted traditions. In advancing this claim, this study concentrates upon the wartime experience of Poles and Ukrainians, and inquires about the causes of their mutual ethnic cleansing. After four years of Soviet and Nazi occupation, Ukrainians and Poles ethnically cleansed each other for four more. These cleansings claimed more than 100,000 lives, and forced 1.4 million resettlements. How did this come to pass? Is ethnic cleansing caused by nationalism, or does ethnic cleansing nationalize populations?

Can nation-states come to terms with such history? Can the demands of modern national ideas, so brutally expressed by ethnic cleansing, find a peaceful articulation? These are the questions posed by the 1940s to the 1990s. In the years following the revolutions of 1989, every imaginable cause of national conflict could be found among Poland, Lithuania, Belarus, and Ukraine: imperial disintegration; frontiers without historical legitimacy; provocative minorities; revanchist claims; fearful elites; newly democratic politics; memories of ethnic cleansing; and national myths of eternal conflict. From these beginnings, a Polish eastern policy aware of modern nationality fashioned a stable geopolitical order. The collapse of the Soviet Union was anticipated, hastened, and turned to peaceful ends. The simplest evidence of Polish success was Western ignorance of the historical rivalries and wartime cleansings that this book will describe. Where there was armed conflict in the 1990s, as in Yugoslavia, the public learned of wartime precedents and supposedly ancient hatreds. Where peace and prosperity prevailed, as in Poland, the historical narrative of the "return to Europe" took center stage. Another proof of the success of Poland's eastern policy was precisely Poland's Western integration. 1999 witnessed a startling juxtaposition of success and failure in the new Europe: as NATO admitted Poland, it bombed Yugoslavia. As the world followed conflicts among Serbs and their neighbors, a joint Polish-Ukrainian peacekeeping battalion was dispatched to Kosovo. Why did northeastern Europe come together as southeastern Europe fell apart?

TIME

These three questions—when modern nations arise, why ethnic cleansing takes place, how nation-states make peace—suggest the chronological range of this study: 1569–1999. 1569 marks the creation of the early modern Polish nation. In that year, the Polish and Lithuanian nobility established their Commonwealth by an agreement known as the Lublin Union. Henceforth Lithuanian and Polish nobles were together represented in a single parliament, jointly elected monarchs, and increasingly shared a common civilization. The Polish Kingdom and the Grand Duchy of Lithuania retained separate codes of law and administrations, and an internal border. The Lublin Union altered this frontier to Poland's advantage, transferring Lithuania's more southerly East Slavic lands to Poland. This divided East Slavic nobles and peoples, creating a new border between what we now call Ukraine and Belarus. The Lublin Union, although issued in a spirit of religious toleration, coincided with ambitious church reform. Conversions of East Slavic gentry from Eastern to Western Christianity created a new difference between nobility and commoners in the lands we now call Belarus and Ukraine. Thus the unification of a Polish noble nation was accompanied by new divisions among other social orders. The rebellion in Ukraine that followed in 1648 provided the contours of Polish, Ukrainian, and indeed Russian national history.

1569 is an untraditional starting point. National histories of Poland, Lithuania, Belarus, Ukraine, or Russia usually begin with the medieval period, and trace the purportedly continuous development of the nation to the present. To recognize change, it is best to accept the unmistakable appearance of a single early modern nation in the vast territories of the early modern Commonwealth, then consider its legacies to modern politics. This early modern nation was called "Polish," but the term signified citizenship and civilization rather than language or ethnicity. Beginning with 1569 allows us to see the coherence and appeal of the early modern Polish nation, and to liberate ourselves from our own modern assumptions about what nationality must entail. Since this is a study of nationality rather than statehood, its intermediate caesurae are also unconventional. The nineteenth century was the "beautiful age" of Polish civilization, even though the Commonwealth had been partitioned in 1795. Rather than dwelling on 1795, as Romantic, national, and historiographical tradition all recommend, this book regards 1863 as the beginning of the end of early modern politics. In 1863, Polish nobles rebelled one last time against Russian rule; after 1863, the Russian empire began to challenge Polish cultural and economic dominance in its western domains. After the uprising, important sections of the traditional Polish elite turned against traditional definitions of the polity and the nation. They were joined by a few imperial administrators and folk activists, who proposed that nations were defined by religion and language. Only after 1863 do we see modern Polish, Lithuanian, and Russian nationalisms hostile to the early modern inheritance, and the hint of a Belarusian idea. There was no such rupture in the small portion of the old Commonwealth taken by Austria. Here we shall concentrate on 1876. In that year Ukrainian publications were banned in the Russian empire; henceforth, the Ukrainian idea in Austria began to gather force, and the conditions for the Ukrainian Polish rivalry in Austrian Galicia were put in place.

We shall see that the past does matter in the rise of modern nations, but not in the ways that these new modern nationalists would claim. Every modern nationalism we encounter will ignore palpable early modern traditions in favor of imagined medieval continuities. We will also find that modernization is linked to nationalism, even if theories of modernization cannot explain the essential particulars of national success and failure. The features of modern society—political ideologies, democratic politics, refined propaganda, mass media, public education, population growth, urbanization, industrialization—all take their place in this study. The centralized state is something of a fetish both of nationalists, who project it back into the past; and of social scientists, who properly emphasize its novelty and potential but sometimes exaggerate the success of state-builders. States, no less than nations, exist in time. State power is legitimate when people find it to be so. In this study, attempts to build modern centralized states are seen as projects with mixed and often unanticipated results. States are destroyed as well as created, the manner of their destruction often determining the national ideas of the next generation. When created, states often take ambiguous forms: for example, early Soviet republics with changing nationality policies, where national renaissance is followed by the mass murder of the intelligentsia thus exposed; an ambitious interwar Poland divided about the definition of the nation, able neither to assimilate the borderlands nor to build a federal structure; or a postwar Polish state legitimated by ethnic homogeneity but governed by communists. In its treatment of the first decades of the twentieth century, the book is concerned with state-building as one experience, among others, that helped or hindered national ideas.

In the middle of the twentieth century, centralized states of a particular kind, Nazi Germany and the Soviet Union, occupied all of the territories with which this book is concerned. The systems they imported were hostile to the peoples who fell under their domain, and foreign to traditional methods of local politics. While attending to the establishment (or not) of nation-states (or their simulacra) after the First World War, this study thus attaches more importance to the fate of peoples during the Second. The Second World War battered the remnants of early modern nationality, and spread modern nationalism far and wide. Although both are intermediate caesurae, 1945 is thus more important than 1918. After 1863 modern national ideas embraced the mass population; after 1945 mass populations embraced modern national ideas. For similar reasons, the study ends in 1999 rather than 1989. Although Poland regained sovereignty in 1989, and Belarus, Lithuania, and Ukraine gained independence in 1991, it is Poland's accession to NATO in 1999 that suggests the end of a stage of national history. NATO membership not only confirmed the success of a modern Polish nation-state, it rewarded Poland's handling of sensitive national questions. In supporting the new nation-states between itself and Russia, Poland succeeded in defining itself as part of the West. 1569 marked an early modern Polish commitment to eastern expansion that ended in the 1940s; 1999 marked a novel Polish commitment to a western security and political identity.

TERRITORY

Rather than follow the borders of twentieth-century nation-states or nineteenth-century empires, this study considers lands of the Polish-Lithuanian Commonwealth, as constituted in 1569. Part One concentrates on the city of Vilnius. Vilnius was the capital of the Grand Duchy of Lithuania, a provincial capital within the Russian empire, a Polish city in the 1920s and 1930s, and a Soviet Lithuanian city after the Second World War. It is today the capital of independent Lithuania. Before the Final Solution, Jews called Vilnius the "Jerusalem of the North"; until very recently the city was claimed by Poles, Russians, and Belarusians as well as Lithuanians. Within an early modern framework of political nationality, Vilnius is a Lithuanian city, since it was the capital of the Grand Duchy of Lithuania within the Polish-Lithuanian Commonwealth. Within a modern framework, Vilnius was anything but a Lithuanian city before the Second World War: very few of its inhabitants were Lithuanians, and it was part of the Polish state. Thus our concern here is how the city became Lithuanian in a modern national sense, in population and culture.

Part Two focuses on eastern Galicia and Volhynia. These East Slavic territories, inhabited by large Polish and Jewish populations, were heartlands of the old Commonwealth, and imperial hinterlands after its demise. In the partitions of the late eighteenth century, Volhynia fell to Russia, and Galicia to Austria. As in historic Lithuania, in Galicia and Volhynia Poles remained the dominant element throughout the nineteenth century. Only at century's end did Polish landlords give ground to Russian rivals in Volhynia, or compromise with Ukrainian political parties in Austrian Galicia. In both empires, Polish nationalists helped the Ukrainian cause by degrading Polish nationality. The early modern Polish nation was a matter of associating oneself with the impressive attainments of a civilization that operated in Polish. By relocating the nation in the people, Polish nationalists redefined the Poles as one ethnic group among others, and invited competition on the level playing field of the illiterate peasantry. After the First World War, both Galicia and Volhynia were absorbed by a new Polish state. Although interwar Poland's indecisive policies aided Ukrainian nationalists, the early twentieth century in Galicia and Volhynia was very similar to the nineteenth or even the eighteenth. Only the Second World War destroyed the historical integrity of Galicia and Volhynia, and brought the triumph of modern nationalism. These lands were joined in 1945 to Soviet Ukraine, and since 1991 have been the most patriotic regions of independent Ukraine. Today they are known as "western Ukraine."

A tight geographical focus on Vilnius (for Poland-Lithuania-Belarus) and Galicia and Volhynia (for Poland-Ukraine) over the *longue durée* is a means of clarifying these transformations. If we fix our gaze upon historical regions over the course of four centuries, we can register economic and social change, see armies pass back and forth, and, in the twentieth century, observe peoples exterminated, deported, and resettled. If we can stand to stand still, if we are moved without moving, we recognize painful and definite change. We can watch the political landscape shift, rupture, and finally resolve itself into something new. In recognition of the transformations of the 1940s, the third part of this book concentrates not so much on the Vilnius, Galicia, and Volhynia, as on the diplomatic problems they posed for newly sovereign nation-states after the revolutions of 1989. Part Three discusses a Polish grand strategy of the 1990s that accepted and confirmed the division of Eastern Europe into nation-states within present borders. That may appear straightforward, but it was an innovation in Polish political theory, and unusual in the practice of East European diplomacy after the end of communism.

JEWS, RUSSIANS, GERMANS?

When the statue of Lenin in the Galician town of Kolomya was dismantled, its pedestal was seen to be constructed from Jewish tombstones. Kolomya, today, is a town in southwestern Ukraine. In 1939–41 and 1945–91 it was a town in southwestern Soviet Ukraine, between 1941 and 1944 a town in the Nazi *Generalgouvernement,* before the Second World War a town in Poland's Stanisławów province, before the First World War a town in Austrian Galicia, before 1772 a town in the Polish Kingdom's Ruthenian province. Until the Final Solution of 1941–42, Kolomya was, whatever its rulers, a Jewish town. The absence of Jews, in Kolomya as throughout Eastern Europe, coincided for forty years with the presence of communist rule. The 1990s brought an explosion of national history in Eastern Europe, but new research often began from the national world inherited from the Second World War and codified by communists. Jewish history has been separated from the mainstream of East European history. Just as Israeli historiography emphasizes the successful Zionist project, neglecting the East European origins of Israeli politics, so East European historiographies concentrate on statehood, often failing to give the Jews their due place. There are numerous worthy exceptions, and a recent laudable trend to publish edited volumes featuring multiple national points of view. Although this is immensely useful, it does not resolve the problem of nationalism in history. It can lead to a politically correct multi-nationalism, in which parallel national canals are cut through historical ground that requires careful irrigation.

Given the scope of this work, why are Jews, Germans, and Russians omitted from its subtitle? This is a study of modern Polish, Ukrainian, Lithuanian, and Belarusian nationality, with no ambition to follow German, Russian, or Jewish nationality to contemporary conclusions. This is humility, not neglect. The main lines of German national history lead elsewhere. The Russian national idea is treated here in its connection with early modern Ukraine and Lithuania. For five reasons, the emergence of the Jewish national idea must await a separate treatment. First, the Jews are an older historical community than the Slavic and Baltic nations. Second, the communal autonomy of Jews in the old Polish-Lithuanian Commonwealth, the necessary introduction to this subject, escapes our structure here. Third, the Jews' gateway into modern political life was the abolition of community privileges and legal separation characteristic of the Commonwealth and the (slow and incomplete) extension of individual rights by the partitioning empires during the nineteenth century. This experience is sufficiently different from the restorationist national politics of Gentiles to require separate attention. Fourth, twentieth-century territorial nationalism aspiring to repartition the old Commonwealth into nation-states was never an option for the Jews. Finally, the relationship between the Shoah and the State of Israel, although it reinforces a major argument of this book, would draw us away from the East European territorial focus that serves as its method. There will be commonalities and convergences: and yet the periodization and argumentation of a proper history of Jewish nationality requires a different sort of reconstruction than this.

While it does not aspire to treat Russian, German, and Jewish national history, this study does contend that Polish, Ukrainian, Lithuanian, and Belarusian national history is unintelligible without the Russians, Germans, and Jews. A particular effort is made to present a unified history of the Second World War, subsuming what are sometimes treated as separate subjects. The Final Solution is integrated here into the wartime and postwar history of Eastern Europe. We shall see that the extermination of Vilnius Jews in 1941–44 and the expulsion of Vilnius Poles in 1944–46 were conditions for the postwar construction of a Soviet Lithuanian Vilnius. We will find that the Volhynian Holocaust of 1942 trained the young men who began the slaughter of Volhynian Poles in 1943. Soviet violence, too, finds its place. In the context of ongoing Ukrainian-Polish ethnic cleansing, Soviet nationality policy was changed by its application to Polish territories in 1944. Polish communists, aided directly by Soviet forces and indirectly by Polish nationalists, completed a project of national homogenization in 1947. Withal we observe the lines of continuity: from the Final Solution to partisan cleansings to communist cleansings to the establishment of communist rule.

This study draws gratefully upon contemporary East European historiography. It seeks, however, to present national history in a particular framework. It treats multiple national questions, rather than creating or revising a single national narrative. It moves forward rather than backward in time, seeking to avoid the projection of later political forms upon earlier periods. Its gaze is focused upon defined places, so that changes in national ideas, movements, and claims are seen for what they are. It defines early modern or hybrid ideas of nationality that a modern reader may find alien. It takes note of accidents, contingencies, and luck. It treats national failures (e.g. Belarus) as attentively as national successes, since they convey just as much about what modern nationality requires for political success. It portrays national heroes in the context of the early modern ideas of nationality they contemplated, adapted, or rejected. It reconsiders ideological oppositions, as between nationalism and communism. These general aims are accepted by a number of historians of and in Eastern Europe. I claim no originality in specifying them, only an ambition to write within the framework they define.

The debt to previous historiography is greatest in chapters 1–7, although they offer some new interpretations. The argument that Romanticism served both early modern and modern ideas of nationality under imperial rule, in nation-states, and in the Soviet Union may be an innovation. The systematic investigation of the Belarusian national failure in the context of the successes of other national movements is, as far as I know, unprecedented. The sustained effort to explain the Lithuanization of Vilnius is, to my knowledge, the first of its kind. Chapters 8–14 rely on archival and other primary source research, and present not only new arguments but little-known events. Chapters 8–10 provide the first scholarly treatment in English of the totality of Ukrainian-Polish ethnic cleansing between 1943 and 1947. Chapters 11–14 connect a Polish grand strategy elaborated in the 1970s, a Polish eastern policy implemented in the early 1990s, and Polish success in European integration. While there are numerous studies of the collapse of Yugoslavia and southeastern Europe, these four chapters present the first treatment of the stabilization by Poland of northeastern Europe. As a whole, this study unifies the early modern Polish nation and its multiple modern successors. Only by crossing conventional divides, such as that between Eastern Europe and the Soviet Union, or that between the Russian and Austrian empires, can we chart the passage from early modern to modern nationality.

MYTHS AND METAHISTORIES

In presenting a new view of East European history, this study rarely polemicizes with national myths. There are, for example, mature and hardened Lithuanian and Polish discourses about what happened when Polish troops seized Vilnius in 1920, just as there are opposed Ukrainian and Polish versions of the ethnic cleansing of Volhynia in 1943. Each party to such national disputes advances important arguments, but both sides taken together do not provide everything that an outsider would wish to know. Compromise among competing national myths is certainly important in diplomacy, but does not provide the historian a way forward. No amount of compromise can generate independence, and the historian must work within an independent framework. While no one would claim that any framework eliminates politics, there is a clear difference between building a scholarly apparatus and taking on national myths. Refuting a myth is dancing with a skeleton: one finds it hard to disengage from the deceptively lithe embrace once the music has begun, and one soon realizes that one's own steps are what is keeping the old bones in motion. It is easy to be captured by the choreography of mythmaking and -breaking, and hard afterwards to regain one's own rhythm. The musty smell lingers for some time, too.

By the same token, this book does not dwell on the great nineteenth-century national schemes of history that organize so much historical discussion in our own day. Poles, for example, colloquially refer to the early modern Common-wealth as "Polish," meaning that it was something like a modern Polish state. Russians imagine that the centuries that East Slavic lands spent within the Commonwealth are a meaningless prelude to their "reunification" with Russia. These views are metahistorical, a long word that here means "not even wrong." Their popularity inspires their opponents to turn them on their heads: Lithua-nians can "demonstrate" that medieval Vilnius was not Polish but Lithuanian, or Ukrainians can "prove" that they, not Russia, inherited Kyivan civilization. To argue with metahistory risks accepting its rules of engagement: and non-sense turned on its head remains nonsense. There are no syntheses to be found there, only theses and antitheses. Dialectics of myth and metahistory sharpen the minds of nationalists, and are thus properly a subject rather than a method of national history.

VOICE AND MODE

The voice of mythmakers and metahistorians is earnest and confiding; their claims depend upon what authors take to be self-evident. The voice of theorists of nationalism can be distant and ironic; they see that the apparently obvious is obviously mistaken, that the emperor has no clothes. The question is why naked emperors get to rule. Part of the answer is the deceptively soporific na-ture of irony. In the guise of a vivifying exposure of contradiction, irony can confirm our slumbering misconceptions about how the world works. Since the experience of irony depends upon what we take for granted, our complacency is the ground on which it gains traction. If we treat irony as the moment for closure, we might mistakenly conclude from the examples to follow that nationality is invented, or accidental, or too confusing to categorize. It is ironic, perhaps, that a great Ukrainian activist of the twentieth century, a Greek Catholic churchman, was raised in a Polish family and baptized a Roman Catholic. This irony should be seen as a proposal: that we consider the complexity of his native Galicia, and the modern transformation of the early modern inheritance of the Commonwealth. It might also seem ironic that the most famous Polish statesman of the first half of the twentieth century called himself a "Lithuanian," or that the one line of poetry every Pole can recite is "Lithuania! My fatherland!" If we experience irony as an invitation to investigate, we find that variants of the early modern nationality of the Commonwealth survived its demise by more than a century. In this study, irony is a way to ask questions, not a substitute for answers. The nation is here neither an object of faith nor an object of fun, but an object of study.

The chosen mode of expression is chronological historical narrative. This mode has been criticized, and rightly so, for its tendency to treat "the nation" as the literary protagonist of an epic of suffering, salvation, and suchlike. This introduction has proposed a topic about which, a period for which, a space in which, and a voice by which a critical narrative of national history might be written. Yet this has not been a defensive venture. Narrative history is indispensable to the important task of understanding nations and nationalism. Recent debates over theories of nationalism began from a handful of outstanding works of social science, all of them parasitical upon history. Parasitism has a bad name: what I mean is that social scientists discreetly consume historical narratives as they energetically analyze nationalism. As historiography lumbers forward to meet this challenge, parasitism becomes symbiosis. After all, the questions posed by the constructivist turn in the study of nationality require further historical research. And just as historical narrative can profit from sociological critique to gain distance from politics, so too can social science gain political perspective from history. Neither, after all, is innocent of political applications. There are people today with great vested interests in showing, for example, that Ukraine was the "construction" of Austrian (German, Polish, whatever) agents, just as others are committed to the view that an "essentially" continuous Ukrainian history justifies Ukrainian independence. After the Yugoslav wars, it is sometimes held that ethnic cleansers are motivated by essentialist views about blood and belonging; in fact, historical study reveals that the ones who matter employ a sophisticated constructivist view of nationality. The simple fact that nationality is a major foundation of political legitimacy implicates all of its students, and for that reason among others its study should be cooperative. To this enterprise, narrative offers chronology, comparison, and coherence: a historian's simple gifts. Yet how to tell, at the end of the day, if the historical narrative is critical?

Conventional wisdom is like a sheet of ice, covering the dark sea of the undiscovered. Does the narrative flow like water over the smooth surface? Water takes the path of least resistance, yielding to gravity and then to the cold. It seals promising cracks as it freezes, in the end adding its own mass to the ice. It proves to be of the same matter as that with which it deals. Or does the narrative move like an icebreaker: sailing under its own power, identifying problems, and confronting them? Is it sharp in front, does it welcome hard weather, can it survive heavy blows? Does it leave in its wake a view of the deep, a black line through white ice, a passage that others may follow?

Part I The Contested Lithuanian-Belarusian Fatherland

Chapter 1 The Grand Duchy of Lithuania (1569–1863)

Lithuania! My fatherland! You are like health.
Only he who has lost you may know your true worth.
—Adam Mickiewicz, *Pan Tadeusz* (1834 Paris)

Once upon a time, the Grand Duchy of Lithuania dominated medieval Eastern Europe. Since 1991, the Republic of Lithuania has been a small country on the Baltic Sea. Vilnius, once the capital of the Grand Duchy, is today the capital of the Republic. The apparent continuity conceals tremendous change. For half a millennium before 1991, Lithuanian was neither the language of power in Vilnius nor the language spoken by most of its inhabitants. Before the Second World War, the language spoken in a third of its homes was Yiddish; the language of its streets, churches, and schools was Polish; and the language of its countryside was Belarusian. In 1939, almost no one spoke Lithuanian in Vilnius. In that year, the city was seized from Poland by the Soviet Union. How, then, did "Lithuania" come to mean what it does today: a small independent nation-state with Vilnius as its capital? How did the past matter, if it mattered at all?

The present may be understood in terms of closed possibilities. From the middle of the sixteenth until the middle of the twentieth century, the city was a center of Polish and Jewish civilization. Before it became a modern Lithuanian city, Vilnius ceased to be Polish and Jewish. Vilnius was once the capital of a great multinational realm. For it to become the capital of a small state, modern proposals to revive the old Grand Duchy as a federation had to be defeated. The city also did not become Russian, despite being ruled from Moscow and St. Petersburg for most of the past two hundred years; nor Belarusian, despite the preponderance of East Slavic peasants in the countryside. A modern Lithuanian idea based upon history and language was victorious in Vilnius, even though we see that history and language themselves had little to offer Lithuanian nationalists who dreamed of the city. How does modern nationalism recover territory in such conditions? Why one modern nationalism rather than another?

Present national ideas arose in intimate contact with past rivals. Assertions of continuity and justice, mainstays of the national histories of established states, were once weapons in fierce and uncertain contests. The next five chapters discuss the fate of Vilnius not only in terms of Lithuanian success, but in light of the aims and plans of the city's Poles, Belarusians, Russians, and Jews. Henceforth, the capital of the old Grand Duchy will be called by the name the aspirant or inhabitant attaches to it: "Vilnius" for Lithuanians, "Wilno" for Poles, "Vil'nia" for Belarusians, "Vilne" for Jews, "Vil'no" (then "Vil'na," then "Vil'nius") for Russians. This nominal pluralism may appear awkward at first, but it allows us to see political disputes, and awakens our skepticism to settled "facts" of geography. In this way, we may see competing ideas, movements, and states for what they were: stages in the reconstruction of the elite early modern nation of the Grand Duchy into new modern nations. To avoid seeing these developments as inevitable, we shall concentrate on twists and turns, on contingencies, on misunderstandings, on unintended consequences. We shall attend to the successes, and to the failures.

Nothing is simple in the relationship between national ideas and political power. Different parts of a society subscribe to different forms of national loyalty, and these differences may prevent consensus on crucial questions. National ideas have a force of their own, and can be put to political use by calculating outsiders. National ideas arise in circumstances other than those when they gain force: when true to tradition they prove unwieldy in practice; when innovative they awkwardly call for change in the name of continuity. The more effective national ideas involve getting the past wrong; to understand their power to bring about the change they conceal, we must get the past right. Our goal is not to correct national myths, but to reveal the political and social conditions under which they gained life and force. This chapter and the next will help us to see the novelty of modern national ideas of Lithuania, Belarus, and Poland by defining the early modern nationality that preceded them. To get a sense of the legacies bequeathed to modern national activists in the twentieth century, we must consider the medieval Grand Duchy of Lithuania, and the early modern Polish-Lithuanian Commonwealth. The modern competition for Vilnius grew from an earlier idea of nationhood within historical Lithuania.

THE GRAND DUCHY OF LITHUANIA, 1385–1795

Lithuanian grand dukes were the great warlords of thirteenth- and fourteenth-century Europe. They conquered a vast dominion, ranging from native Baltic lands southward through the East Slavic heartland to the Black Sea. Picking up the pieces left by the Mongol invasion of Kyivan Rus', the pagan Lithuanians incorporated most of the territories of this early East Slavic realm. The Orthodox boyars of Rus', accustomed to Mongol overlordship, could regard Lithuania not as conqueror but as ally. As Lithuanian military power flowed south, to Kyiv, so the civilization of Rus'—Orthodox religion, Church Slavonic language, and mature legal tradition—flowed north to Vilnius. As Vilnius replaced Kyiv as the center of Orthodox Slavic civilization, two Catholic powers, the crusading Teutonic Knights and the Polish Kingdom, aspired to Lithuanian territories. Pagan Lithuanian grand dukes astutely bargained for their baptism. In the late fourteenth century, Lithuanian Grand Duke Jogaila traded Catholic conversion for the Polish crown. Polish nobles, keen to avoid a Habsburg on the throne, offered Jogaila eleven-year-old Princess Jadwiga and with her the Polish succession. Jogaila, as grand duke of Lithuania and Lord and Heir of Rus' ("dux magnus Litvanorum Russiaeque dominus et haerus naturalis"), accepted a merger of his domains with Poland at Krewo in 1385. He was baptized as Władysław Jagiełło and elected king of Poland the next year. Successive agreements preserved the personal union by restoring Lithuanian autonomy and linking the Polish and Lithuanian nobility. The Jagiełło dynasty ruled both Poland and Lithuania for almost two centuries, until 1572.

Even before the Krewo Union of 1385, Lithuania was in religion and in language rather an Orthodox Slavic than a pagan Baltic country. Jogaila's promise of conversion to Catholic Christianity applied to himself and remaining pagans: most of his realm, and many of his relatives, were already Orthodox Christians. The result of Jogaila's conversion was not so much the Christianization of a pagan country as the introduction of Roman Catholicism into a largely Orthodox country. The introduction of Catholicism established a cultural link between Lithuania and Europe, and created the potential for Polish influence. The baptism of the Lithuanian Grand Duke as a Catholic ensured that Lithuania was not an Orthodox state in the sense that Muscovy was being established as one. By the same token, Jogaila's baptism opened the way for Muscovy to pose as the protector of Orthodoxy. By the time Lithuania had incorporated Kyiv, the Orthodox metropolitan had vacated the city for Vladimir-on-the-Kliazma. The metropolitan's subsequence residence in Muscovy complicated Lithuania's claim to be the successor of Rus'. Jogaila did have the opportunity to resolve this tension, since in the 1380s he had a choice between Catholic Poland and Orthodox Muscovy. In 1382 he went so far as to agree to marry the daughter of Dmitrii Donskoi and accept Orthodoxy. This plan had two disadvantages: Orthodoxy would not defend Lithuania from the Teutonic Knights, who treated it as heresy; and Orthodoxy would favor the Slavic boyars in Lithuania, already more numerous and more cultured than Jogaila's Baltic Lithuanian dynasty. The Polish crown and Catholic cross were favorable in both domestic and international policy: they provided a reliable bulwark against the Teutonic Knights, a reliable basis for expansion to the east, and a new source of distinction for Jagiełło and his descendants.

Politics aside, medieval Poland and Lithuania had more in common than one might suppose. When we imagine Lithuanians and Poles negotiating the terms of their alliance in 1385, or planning the common assault on the Teutonic Knights at Grunwald in 1410, we must keep in mind that they could communicate not only in Latin but also in Slavic languages. Local recensions of Church Slavonic, introduced by Orthodox churchmen from more southerly lands, provided the basis for Chancery Slavonic, the court language of the Grand Duchy. Having annexed Galicia, a former province of Kyivan Rus' known in Poland as the "Rus' Palatinate" ("Województwo Ruskie"), Poland also had its share of Orthodox churchmen and Church Slavonic scribes. Having divided the lands of Kyivan Rus', Poland and Lithuania shared its cultural inheritances. Poles and Lithuanians were not divided by language to the same extent as were contemporary Poles and Germans. After 1386, the Polish-Lithuanian courts functioned in Latin and in two distinct Slavic languages: the Polish of the Polish Kingdom, and the Chancery Slavonic of the Grand Duchy. Lithuanian continued to be a spoken language of the Lithuanian Grand Dukes and their entourage for another century, but in the politics of Poland-Lithuania its role was minor.[1]

In the next chapter we shall see that the Baltic Lithuanian language provided the basis for a modern Lithuanian nation; here we must a fortiori record its irrelevance in the early modern Grand Duchy of Lithuania. The last grand duke to know the Lithuanian language was apparently Kazimierz IV, who died in 1492. When Kazimierz IV confirmed the privileges of Lithuania in 1457, he did so in Latin and Chancery Slavonic; when he issued law codes for the realm, he did so in Chancery Slavonic. During Kazimierz's reign the printing press was introduced in Poland: Cracow publishers published books in Polish and Church Slavonic, but not in Lithuanian. Frantsysk Skaryna, the first printer of the Grand Duchy of Lithuania, published much of the Bible around 1517, in a Belarusian recension of Church Slavonic.[2] In the early sixteenth century we also find biblical translations into the Slavic vernacular, Ruthenian, though not in the Baltic vernacular, Lithuanian. Unlike Skaryna's, these involved direct translations of the Old Testament from the Hebrew. These Old Testament translations were apparently executed by Lithuanian Jews, who knew Hebrew and spoke Ruthenian.[3] Since Ruthenian was spoken by local Christians and Jews in the early sixteenth century, intended readers may have been Christians, Jews, or both. One confirmation of the privileges of the Jews of Lithuania was issued in the year "semtisiach dvadtsat vtoroho"—the year 7022/1514 reckoned in both Eastern and Western Christian fashion, dating a decree in Chancery Slavonic of the King of Poland and Grand Duke of Lithuania.[4] The Grand Duchy's Statute of 1529 was composed in Chancery Slavonic. The statute was interpreted by Grand Duke and King Zygmunt August in his replies to the Lithuanian gentry in Vil'nia in the 1540s in a Chancery Slavonic riddled with Polish.

In Muscovy the state language of the Grand Duchy of Lithuania, which we are calling "Chancery Slavonic," was called "Lithuanian" or Belorussian." Although modern Russian historians sometimes call this language "Russian," at the time Muscovite scribes had to translate the Lithuanian statutes into Moscow dialect for them to be of use to their court.[5] Chancery Slavonic differed significantly from contemporary Polish, but in the context of dynastic union with Poland it provided a Slavic platform for the spread of the Polish language and ideas. As early as 1501 legal texts in Chancery Slavonic are penetrated by Polish terms and even Polish grammar. The introduction to the Grand Duchy's 1566 Statute records that the Lithuanian gentry was already using Polish in practice.[6] The acts of the 1569 Lublin Union, which created the Polish-Lithuanian Commonwealth, were recorded in Polish only. The position of the Polish language in Lithuania was not the result of Polish immigration, but rather of the gradual acceptance of a political order developed in Poland and codified for a new Polish-Lithuanian Commonwealth in 1569. That this was matter of political culture rather than of personal origin is emphasized by the Grand Duchy's 1588 Statute, which ennobled Jewish converts to Christianity. Poland also served to communicate larger trends in European law: whereas the medieval appropriation of Roman law never reached Muscovy, the Statutes of 1566 and 1588 demonstrate the growing importance of Roman (and Germanic) models in Lithuania.[7] During the Renaissance, much of what was conveyed to Poland from Italy in Latin was conveyed from Poland to Lithuania in Polish.

As the Polish vernacular was elevated to the status of a literary language in Poland, it superseded Chancery Slavonic (and vernacular Ruthenian) in Lithuania. The Polish and Lithuanian nobility came to share a language during the Renaissance, facilitating the creation of a single early modern political nation. That said, there was a pregnant difference between the Latin-to-Polish shift in Poland and the Chancery Slavonic-to-Polish shift in Lithuania. In the Polish Kingdom the vernacular (Polish) dethroned an imported literary language (Latin). The elevation of Polish to equal status with Latin was an example of a general trend within Latin Europe, which began with the Italian "language question."[8] In the Grand Duchy of Lithuania an import (Polish) supplanted the native language of politics and law (Chancery Slavonic), and forestalled the further literary use of the local vernacular (Ruthenian). As we have seen, the Baltic Lithuanian language had lost its political importance long before. The Renaissance "language question" was thus answered in an unusual way in Lithuania. In Italy after Dante, and then throughout Christian Europe, the vernacular was elevated to a language of literature and state. The Grand Duchy of Lithuania became a country in which the language of culture and politics was further from, rather than closer to, the vernacular. Polish as common high language well met the needs of the republican institutions and ideals of early modern Poland-Lithuania; it would not withstand the advent of modern democratic national ideas that bore these same names.

EARLY MODERN AND MODERN NATIONS

In pointing to legacies of early modern politics to modern politics, we must be clear about the differences. The early modern Polish nation which the Lithuanian gentry jointly created was far from the modern concept of the nation with which we are familiar. It was based on citizenship in a great republic where the gentry enjoyed extensive and codified rights. By the early sixteenth century, the Polish gentry had secured for itself protections against arbitrary action by the

Fig. 1. Frantsysk Skaryna (1490?–1552?), East Slavic Renaissance man. Self-portrait, engraving, 1517. At first, Lithuania partook in the Renaissance in its native Church and Chancery Slavonic languages. From about the time of Skaryna's death Polish was the language of civilization.

king, a major role in the conduct of foreign affairs, and the right to reject new legislation. The increasingly constitutional basis of the Polish polity allowed for the lasting inclusion of units with distinct traditions of local rights, such as Royal Prussia.[9] By the same token, the Polish system created a model for neighboring gentry who wished to formalize and extend their own privileges.[10] In deciding upon a constitutional union with Poland, Lithuania's gentry were pursuing such rights, privileges, and protections for themselves. During the period of dynastic union with Poland, Lithuania became an East Slavic realm in which the gentry enjoyed rights relative to the sovereign. By the terms of the 1569 Lublin Union, Lithuanian nobles joined their Polish neighbors in a single parliament, and in the common election of kings. Lithuania preserved its own title, administration, treasury, code of law, and army. The Commonwealth thereby created was a republic of the gentry, whose myth of Sarmatian origin included nobles of various origins and religions, and excluded everyone else.[11]

After 1569, the Polish identity of Lithuanian gentry was increasingly a matter of culture as well as politics, involving sometimes acceptance of the Renaissance charms of Polish letters, sometimes conversion from Eastern Orthodoxy to Roman Catholicism. The Reformation and Counter-Reformation followed a special trajectory in the Grand Duchy. Like aristocratic families across Europe, much of the Lithuanian gentry converted to Calvinism in the 1550s and 1560s. Orthodox converts were drawn to Protestantism not only by its methods and doctrines, but by its similarity to the Eastern Church in matters of practice: the marriage of clergy, the use of the vernacular in liturgy, and the chalice for laymen. Unlike nobles in Germany or France, who converted from one variety of Western Christianity to another, Lithuanian nobles usually partook in Reform by converting from Eastern to Western Christianity.[12] After a single generation as Protestants, formerly Orthodox Lithuanian families usually converted to the Roman Catholicism. In this way, Protestantism proved to be the unwitting ally of Catholicism in the Grand Duchy of Lithuania. It was not Catholicism itself, but Reform which drew Orthodox Lithuanian nobles to accept Western Christianity, first in its Protestant and then in its Catholic form. Of course, Counter-Reformation Catholicism adopted the tactics of its Protestant rivals. Its use of Polish as the vernacular (although Catholics published a few books in Lithuanian as well) reinforced the prestige of Polish culture among the Lithuanian nobility, and its new proselytism brought the Lithuanian-speaking peasantry into contact with the Polish language.[13] The Jesuits opened an academy in Wilno in 1579. Their propaganda against Protestantism could not be separated from their appeals to the Orthodox to accept the authority of Rome.[14]

Although Roman Catholicism was known as the "Polish faith," even after the Counter-Reformation the "Polish faith" was by no means necessary for "Polish" political loyalty. Like language, religion would be retrospectively understood by later nationalists as a marker or a carrier of national identity. Yet there had been no religious strife to force territorial resolutions on the German principle of "cuius regio, eius religio," nor to suggest the French solution of "un roi, une foi, une loi." The Grand Duchy's 1566 Statute was written by a committee of five Orthodox and five Catholics. Augustyn Rotundus, a Polish participant in the Counter-Reformation in Lithuania, was a friend of Mikołaj Radziwiłł (the Black, 1515–65), the palatine of Wilno and the main Lithuanian propagator of the Reformation (first in its Lutheran, then in its Calvinist, and finally in its Antitrinitarian forms). Rotundus, Pole and Catholic, wrote a long defense of Lithuanian law, which Radziwiłł, Lithuanian and Protestant, published. Rotundus also edited and translated the 1566 Lithuanian Statute (into Latin). Rotundus agreed with Radziwiłł that Lithuania was a "respublica bene ordinata."[15] Piotr Skarga (1536–1612), the greatest of the Polish Jesuits, dedicated the 1577 edition of his greatest work to the Orthodox palatine of Kijów, Prince Konstantyn Ostroz'kyi. In that case, the accord was less charming. Ostroz'kyi, a proud and ambitious man who wanted church union on his own terms, bought up and burned the edition. The Commonwealth's political order was predicated not only on toleration of varieties of Western Christianity, but upon toleration of Eastern Christianity as well. Religious toleration for the entire body of the Christian nobility was established by the 1573 Confederation of Warsaw. Although toleration of varieties of Christian faith within a limited sphere of society may seem like intolerance to our sensibilities, the Confederation of Warsaw had no parallel in the Europe of the time.

Early modern ideas of the Polish nation were at once more exclusive and more inclusive than the modern nationalisms which would succeed them. They were more exclusive, for while modern nationalism enlists all members of the putative nation, early modern Polish nationality distinguished a voting political estate from disenfranchised lower orders. The early modern nation was not an economic class. Magnates were always nobles, but very few nobles were magnates. Rich burghers were not citizens unless they were ennobled. The early modern nation was more inclusive than the modern nation in political terms, for while modern nationalism demands a centralized state, the Commonwealth retained separate Polish and Lithuanian law codes and administrations. The early modern nation was more inclusive in personal terms, for while modern nationalism tends to insist that national identity subsumes cultural origin and political destiny, early modern Polish identity presumed that gentry could be of one cultural affinity and of another political loyalty. Both the exclusivity and the inclusivity are reflected in the attitude to language. It was thought normal that a noble would use one language (Polish) with his peers or in politics, and another (what we would now call Belarusian or Lithuanian) in his household or with his serfs.

A nobleman could be "Lithuanian" by origin, "Polish" in politics, and "Rusian" (or "Greek") by religion. Since Lithuania for a very long time included a majority of Orthodox subjects and most of the Kyivan patrimony, it was called a "Rusian" realm. In unifying his domains with Poland in 1385, Jogaila acted as "Grand Duke of Lithuania and Lord and Heir of Rus'." In a 1449 treaty between Poland-Lithuania and Muscovy, the former was called "Rusian," the latter "Muscovite." After the fall of Constantinople to the Turks in 1453, Muscovy espoused spiritual and political claims as the seat of Orthodoxy, the heir of Byzantium, and the successor of Kyivan Rus'. These provided the justification for Muscovy's wars with their fellow East Slavs of Lithuania, whose grand dukes had regarded themselves for a century as the successors of Kyivan princes.[16] In practice, Muscovy's claim to be Rus' pushed Lithuania toward Poland. When Ivan IV (the Terrible, reigned 1530–1584, proclaimed tsar 1547) began the Livonian Wars in 1558, he hastened the Polish-Lithuanian Union of 1569. At that time, of course, Poland-Lithuania also claimed to be Rus': Zygmunt August's titles, as listed in the privilege of 1569, were "King of Poland, Grand Duke of Lithuania, Lord and Heir of Rus', Prussia, Mazovia, Samogitia, etc." (Król Polski, Wielki Książę Litewski, Ruski, Pruski, Mazowiecki, Żmudzki, itd. Pan i Dziedzic.") Ivan's treatment of boyar rivals also provided the telling contrast to the rights Lithuanian nobles formalized under Zygmunt August that same year.[17]

Although the Commonwealth enjoyed great successes in the wars with Muscovy of the seventeenth century, and King Jan Sobieski's famous rescue of Vienna from the Turks in 1683 brought glory to Poland, the eighteenth century witnessed failure after failure. As we shall see in chapter 6, rebellion in Ukraine fatally wounded the Commonwealth in the middle of the seventeenth century. The Commonwealth failed to establish the fiscal or military bases of modern power. After some initial good luck, the election of monarchs ill served the interests of the Commonwealth. Kings who could not establish dynasties were less willing to consider the welfare of the Commonwealth, and kings of foreign origin were less likely to immerse themselves in the difficulties of Polish politics. The expansive rights of Polish and Lithuanian gentry even provided the Russian empire (as Muscovy was called after 1721) with a way to hamstring the Commonwealth's polity. Since the Commonwealth's parliament functioned according to the principle of unanimity, one bribe was enough to prevent any reform. Tsar Peter I (the Great, r. 1682–1725) reached the Baltic and corrupted the Commonwealth. Polish anarchy was exploited by Muscovite despotism. Yet even as the Commonwealth disintegrated as a state in the eighteenth century, and as its cherished principles of toleration eroded, Polish civilization further penetrated the Grand Duchy of Lithuania. What was once a sign of nobility became a sign of status, and thus Polishness flourished in Lithuania throughout the eighteenth century, and indeed long after the Polish-Lithuanian Commonwealth was naught but a memory.[18] The Commonwealth's culture evolved as its institutions failed to adapt. The first partition of the Commonwealth by Austria, Prussia, and Russia was executed in 1772. The final attempt of the Polish-Lithuanian nobility to repair the Commonwealth's institutions was the Constitution of 3 May 1791. This constitution treated the Polish-Lithuanian nobility as a single political nation, did away with principle of unanimity in parliamentary voting, and sought to create a modern, centralized republic.[19] This provoked the second partition, by Prussia and Russia, in 1793. The 1794 Kościuszko uprising against Russia was defeated, and was followed by the third and final partition in 1795. The Commonwealth had been removed from the map of Europe.

The Russian empire of Tsaritsa Catherine II (the Great, r. 1762–96) progressively annexed almost all of the Grand Duchy of Lithuania: the cities of Polotsk in 1772, Minsk in 1774, and finally Vil'no in 1795. By incorporating Lithuania, Russia absorbed elites who spoke Polish, peasants who spoke (for the most part) what we would now call Belarusian, and towns inhabited in the main by Jews. The end of the Commonwealth meant the end of a political regime where, despite local prejudice, the Jews enjoyed an institutionalized regime of communal toleration.[20] At a stroke, Russia held the largest part of world Jewry. After the Russian share of the old Commonwealth was enlarged to include Warsaw at the Congress of Vienna (1815), the empire included most of the world's Poles. From the Grand Duchy of Lithuania alone—to speak neither of what was established as the Congress Kingdom of Poland, nor of Ukraine—Russia absorbed more nobles of Polish culture than there were nobles of Russian culture in the entire Russian empire. In the early nineteenth century, far more sub-

jects of the tsar could read Polish than Russian. Some Polish-Lithuanian nobles, such as Prince Adam Czartoryski, attained enormous influence in the
court of Tsar Alexander I (r. 1801–25). Czartoryski, for example, was partially
responsible for the terms of the Russian empire's 1804 Jewish statute.[21]

The destruction of the Commonwealth, and the concomitant establishment
of the Pale of Settlement in Russia, were accompanied by radical attempts to reform Judaism and Jewish social practice. We shall return to these in chapter 3.
Here we may only note that they involved historical myths that were not territorial (as in Hasidism, which arose in Ukraine after the death of the Ba'al Shem
Tov in 1760) or trends that were pan-European (as in the Haskalah, the Jewish
Enlightenment). These trends, though they met at Vilne, were something
other than a variant of the traditions of the Grand Duchy. Only at the end of
the nineteenth century did something like secular Jewish politics arise. Among
the tsar's Christian subjects, the early modern gentry nation was slowly and
partially replaced by modern conceptions of the nation as the sum of speakers
of a vernacular tongue. The nineteenth-century national divergence among
Christians in Lithuania was a long and complicated process, itself denying the
crisp, retrospective categorizations of the modern nationalists it produced. A
prism through which to observe the refraction of early modern Lithuanian patriotism into distinctly colored national ideas is a poem: "Pan Tadeusz," or
"Lord Thaddeus," completed by the great Romantic poet Adam Mickiewicz in
1834.

RUSSIAN EMPIRE AND LITHUANIAN FATHERLAND

Mickiewicz (1798–1855) was born on Christmas Eve, three years after the final
partition of the Commonwealth, in Nowogródek, a Yiddish- and Polish-speaking town. The local Lithuanian Tatars had just built a new mosque. Although
there were Lithuanian villages nearby, most local peasants spoke Belarusian.
Mickiewicz was raised by an upstanding Polish gentry family, although his father was probably of Orthodox and his mother perhaps of Jewish descent.[22]
Mickiewicz attended the imperial university at Wilno, an institution that
nicely illustrates the dilemma of an illiterate empire that has absorbed large
numbers of literate families. In the early nineteenth century, Russian policy
aimed to preserve educational attainment in Polish rather than Russify potentially useful subjects. In 1803 Tsar Alexander I (r. 1801–25) had revived the
Vil'no school (founded by the Jesuits in 1579) as a university, with Polish as the

language of instruction. The university and the entire Vil'no school district were directed by Tsar Alexander's friend, advisor, and mentor, the Polish-Lithuanian Prince Adam Czartoryski (1770–1861). Vil'no University, an inheritance of the Commonwealth, was the largest university in the Russian empire. For a full generation it confirmed local elites, such as Mickiewicz, in their belief that the language of culture and politics was Polish. The university and its associated schools educated men who codified in history, literature, and poetry the legacy of the recently defunct Grand Duchy of Lithuania.[23] (Incidentally, for a time Czartoryski's secretary and his immediate superior were both Ukrainians. Just as the partitions brought Poles into Russian service in the late eighteenth century, so a century earlier the partition of Ukraine by the Treaty of Andrusovo had brought in Ukrainians.)

Without a university education in his native Polish in his native Lithuania, Mickiewicz's poetic career is difficult to imagine. This can be seen clearly on the example of his masterpiece, *Pan Tadeusz,* which Mickiewicz finished in Parisian exile in 1834. Its story of the quarrels and loves of Lithuanian gentry families concludes in spring 1812, as Napoleon and his armies marched across Lithuania toward Moscow. In the poem, Lithuanian noblemen have joined the French armies, which was certainly accurate. Mickiewicz observed this himself as a boy of thirteen. In fact, the gentry who joined Napoleon in 1812 included a third of the students of Vil'no University. Tsar Alexander won the war. When Alexander regained Lithuania, he declined to close Vil'no University, so its gates were open to Mickiewicz in 1815. Registering as a student with a government scholarship, the young man even gave his name as Adam Napoleon Mickiewicz. The patience of a Russian tsar, after his empire was attacked by the Lithuanian gentry his university was educating, allowed Mickiewicz to gain higher education in Polish. Mickiewicz then matured to create a nostalgic masterpiece that connected the tragedy of Poland with that very attack on Russia.[24]

At the time of Mickiewicz's university studies, Polish Lithuanians presumed that the inevitable Lithuanian revival would hasten a new Polish-Lithuanian Commonwealth. The putative enemy of this idea was not rival nationalisms, which did not then exist, but the imperial Russian state. These motives of renewal animated Mickiewicz and his student friends, who called themselves the Philomaths. After graduation, Mickiewicz was rescued from the drudgery of teaching school in Kowno by arrest, imprisonment, and exile in Russia. His years in exile in Odessa, Petersburg, and Moscow, and then in emigration in Dresden and Paris, were fantastically productive of the best Polish poetry yet written. Mickiewicz did not join the Polish rising against Russian rule of 1830–

31, the failure of which began the Romantic period of Polish political thought. It also led directly to the closing of Vil'no University. The university's students lived on, in Lithuania, in Poland, in Russia, and in Europe. Mickiewicz's own poetry was composed in a harmony of human and national longing. The Commonwealth would not be restored, and he never again saw his native Lithuania. His masterpiece *Pan Tadeusz* was written between 1832 and 1834, immediately after the rising had been crushed. As every Polish and Lithuanian schoolchild knows, the poem begins: "Lithuania! My fatherland! You are like health! Only he who has lost you may know your true worth."[25]

Since his creations proved so adaptable to succeeding ages, Mickiewicz must be placed in his own time. Like other European Romantics, Mickiewicz wished to "create a new world on the ruins of the old."[26] For Romantics in Western and Central Europe, the French Revolution and Napoleon had destroyed classical Europe, and the task was to establish new political and cultural principles. For Mickiewicz and the Polish Romantics, the partitions of Poland had destroyed the old order, and the French Revolution and Napoleon had provided some hope that it might be restored. After Napoleon's defeat, the gentry of the Grand Duchy had no possible allies but the peasants who surrounded them, and Mickiewicz's poetic Romanticism created a political dilemma. Whereas it was relatively simple for Romantics of other stateless nations such as Italy or Germany to conflate the "common people" with the rising "political nation," in historic Lithuania the matter was far more complicated. The Herderian idea that each people had its own distinct genius was hard to apply in a region where

Fig. 2. Adam Mickiewicz (1798–1855), European Romantic poet of the Polish language. Frontispiece of the 1834 edition of his masterpiece *Pan Tadeusz.*

various localities, languages, and religions had long been held compatible with membership in a single political nation. The problem lay in not only in variety of culture, but in living memory of political institutions. In the middle of the nineteenth century, the idea of unified Germany or Italy left plenty of room for the imagination, since no such entities had existed before. The idea of a unified Poland automatically raised the specter of the recently defunct Commonwealth—the more so as the Commonwealth had promulgated Europe's first constitution just before its demise. In Mickiewicz's vision, Lithuania was at once part of this political tradition, and home to Romantic virtues such as harmony, beauty, energy, and pleasure. Whereas Herder had believed that Slavs might bring youth and energy to Europe, Mickiewicz believed that Lithuania would revive the entire Commonwealth.[27]

Mickiewicz's early modern idea of "Lithuania" as a land of many peoples but of an ultimately Polish destiny suffered the contradictions immanent in durability in a century when the sense of nationality radically changed. Although he was not himself a folkish Polish nationalist, and never set foot in Warsaw or Cracow, his lovely poetry created the medium for a folkish Polish nationalism after his death in 1855. Although he never imagined a Lithuania separate from Poland, his images were used by Lithuanian activists ever more confident in their distinct ethnic and national identity. In the late nineteenth century, in the northwestern corner of the former Grand Duchy, the Lithuanian language provided the basis for a cultural distinctiveness that new national activists of an ethnic Lithuania would eventually exploit. This involved transforming Mickiewicz into a Lithuanian national poet. Ironically, the ethnic definition of nationality that emerged in central Poland and northwestern Lithuania, if a good description of historical trends, would have made Mickiewicz neither Polish nor Lithuanian but Belarusian. After all, Mickiewicz was born, and "Pan Tadeusz" was set, among East Slavic peasants we would now call Belarusians. Perhaps it is more ironic still that the Belarusian gentry and writers were most faithful to Mickiewicz, and did not seize upon their "ethnic" advantages by making exclusivist claims upon him as a "national" poet. A modern ethnic nationalism that encompassed Mickiewicz's Lithuania, the old Grand Duchy, would have been based upon the majority "language," dialects we would now call Belarusian. This is what did not happen. Ethnic nationalism is a political idea, and its success or failure has little to do with the size of what we now see as "ethnic groups." As we shall argue in the next chapter, politics granted the greatest possibilities to interpretations of *Pan Tadeusz* that were furthest in spirit from the original (Lithuanian and Polish ethnic nationalism), and mar ginalized its most faithful translations into politics (Belarusian and Polish federalism).

The test of early modern Lithuanian patriotism as articulated by Mickiewicz was the 1863 rising against Russian rule. Certain exceptional people believed that the Grand Duchy and the Commonwealth could be revived by way of an alliance of the (Polish-speaking) gentry with the (Lithuanian- or Belarusian-speaking) peasantry. Between the Russian defeat in the Crimean War (1856) and Tsar Alexander II's abolition of serfdom (1861), some Lithuanian Polish nobles had conspired to resolve the question of serfdom in a way that would satisfy landlords and peasants.[28] Jakób Gieysztor (1827–97) campaigned to convince Lithuanian nobles to free their peasants before the tsar did. Although Gieysztor was successful in his locality, in Lithuania as a whole the gentry missed the opportunity to take credit for the inevitable. Gieysztor, who thought himself a Polish noble building an alliance with the Polish people, ran a school in which Lithuanian was the language of instruction. He saw no contradiction.[29] In the 1863 rising against Russian rule, which he had opposed as premature, Gieysztor conspired with the radical Konstanty Kalinowski (Kastus' Kalinouski, 1838–64). During the rising, Kalinowski promised peasants land in their own language (Belarusian).[30] Antanas Mackevičius, although now seen as a proto-Lithuanian nationalist, fought to reestablish the Grand Duchy of Lithuania in a provisional association with Poland.[31] In 1863, all three sought to persuade peasants to fight for their own good, without really believing that peasants understood the importance of restoring the republic. These and other leaders of 1863 were no longer early modern patriots, keen to restore a gentry republic; but they were not yet modern nationalists, fully prepared to define the nation as the people. Their attempt to defeat the Russian empire with the help of the people revealed two incipient dilemmas. The use of languages other than Polish foreshadowed a new type of national politics. If peasants could be called to risk their lives in their own languages, surely they would expect to hear and read those languages in calmer times as well. The nobles' need to give land to the peasants to gain their support posed a hard choice between personal security and national liberation.

Mickiewicz's nostalgia after the failure of 1830 was for an early modern political nation. What emerged after the failure of 1863 were modern national ideas.

Chapter 2 Lithuania! My Fatherland! (1863–1914)

As butterflies drown in golden amber
Let us remain, dear, as we once were.
—Adam Mickiewicz, *Konrad Wallenrod* (St. Petersburg, 1828)

Modern politics after 1863 meant shrugging off the Commonwealth as a burden and embracing the peasant and his language as the nation. This first became clear in the extreme northwest of the old Grand Duchy of Lithuania, where the failure of the 1863 uprising hastened a modern, linguistic Lithuanian nationalism. The drastic nature of peasant emancipation accelerated the modernization of agriculture, and eventually created a new class of prosperous Lithuanian peasants.[1] The Russian imperial decision to draw Lithuanian students to St. Petersburg rather than Warsaw created a new secular elite. The uneven de-Polonization of schools had a similar unintended nation-building effect, as Russian culture proved far less attractive to Lithuanian students than Polish had been. In the decades to come, rising peasants of Lithuanian origin who learned to read their mother tongue in school, déclassé Polish-speaking gentry who relearned Lithuanian, socialists

31

and doctors educated in Russian universities, and Roman Catholic priests formed the Lithuanian national movement.[2] Lithuanian national activists saw the failed national rising of 1863 as a Polish blunder, and believed that they could develop a better national strategy for themselves. Rather than armed revolts, this new generation paid attention to national culture. In this they were in fact similar to the main current of post-1863 Polish patriotism, positivists who prescribed practical "organic work" to build a national society.[3] While for Poles such "work at the foundations" meant strengthening the mass basis for an elite national society, Lithuanians found that it required nationalizing themselves first.

The Lithuanian foundations were buried under a good deal of history. The Lithuanian language had not been considered a language of politics for centuries. The Lithuanian grand dukes had never published Lithuanian books. The last Lithuanian grand duke who even knew the Lithuanian language died the year Columbus discovered America. Not only were the traditions of the old Grand Duchy recorded in Polish and Chancery Slavonic (similar to Belarusian), the Lithuanian peasantry seemed fearfully keen to follow the historical example of its priests and lords. Throughout the nineteenth century, Lithuanian-speaking peasants were assimilating to the Belarusian language, which provided the Slavic platform for a further assimilation to Polish or Russian. In some peasant families, grandparents spoke Lithuanian, parents Belarusian, and children Polish: thereby in a single household encapsulating the historical trend that Lithuanian activists wished to reverse. Prosperous peasants Polonized their children directly by sending them to schools where Polish was the language of instruction (or at least schoolyard prestige). Open insecurity about the loyalty of the nation lent a certain insistency to the rhetoric of Lithuanian activists. Silent knowledge that they themselves spoke and wrote Polish better than Lithuanian lent an urgency to the task of national renaissance.

ETHNIC LITHUANIA AS FATHERLAND

Lithuanian activists referred to an imagined Grand Duchy that fit their present predicament. They discounted tangible continuities from the early modern traditions of 1569–1795 in favor of a mythical vision of medieval Lithuania and Vilnius before the 1569 Lublin Union with Poland. Activists privileged a language that was all but irrelevant in the early modern Grand Duchy (Lithuanian), promoted a social group that was marginal in the polity of the old Grand Duchy (Lithuanian-speaking peasants), and yielded to a Romantic nostalgia for paganism. They portrayed the 1569 union with Poland as a tyranny of lords over peasants, and contemporary "lords" (Polish-Lithuanian gentry) as traitors to the nation. Just as interpretations of national history corresponded to real problems with the putative nation, so this sense of injustice flowed from the social predicament of many Lithuanian national activists.

If Lithuania was to be a modern nation, it had to be a peasant nation. Leaders of a peasant nation must challenge their social superiors on the treacherous ground of language and history. The abolition of serfdom and the opening of schools to peasant children provided the political opportunity, if not immediately the requisite confidence. The Lithuanian movement originated in the Suvalkai region, where serfdom had been abolished by Napoleon in 1807. The "Russification" of what had been Polish schools after 1863 was another crucial step. The Mariampol high school, an agent of Polonization through 1863, became an imperial state school in 1867. Polish was banned, and Lithuanian was added to the curriculum. Mariampol high school produced the two most important Lithuanian national activists, Jonas Basanavičius and Vincas Kudirka. Both were bright children of prosperous peasant parents, both were expected to become Catholic priests, both found better possibilities in the Russian educational system. In this way the attempt by Russian authorities to limit Polish influence in Lithuania after 1863 unwittingly created the social space for a modern Lithuanian national movement, based upon the Lithuanian language.

The historical and linguistic formulae applied after 1863 had long been available. They were provided most convincingly by Teodor Narbutt (1784–1864), whose enormous Polish-language history of Lithuania was published between 1835 and 1841. Narbutt concluded after four thousand pages that the history of Lithuania "ceased" in 1569, and figuratively broke his pen on the grave of the Polish king and Lithuanian grand duke who then reigned.[4] Narbutt's massive achievement provided the scholarly foundation for the political view that modern Lithuanian should draw from medieval rather than early modern legacies. In the nineteenth century, it was cited more often than any other work of Lithuanian history.[5] Modern Lithuanian nationalism was actually articulated somewhat earlier, and in Lithuanian, by Simonas Daukantas (1793–1864). A classmate of Mickiewicz at Vil'no University, Daukantas shared Mickiewicz's fascination with medieval Lithuania. Daukantas was, it seems, the first to treat the 1569 union with Poland as a capitulation, and to see the spread of Polish language as the destruction of a superior local culture. In 1822 he presented these claims in the first scholarly history of Lithuania in Lithuanian. Although this book was not published until 1929, another influential study appeared in 1845.

As Lithuanian historians created this new periodization, in which the medieval was glorious and the early modern was shameful, Mickiewicz's poetry provided the color of the glory. His epics *Grażyna* (1823) and *Konrad Wallenrod* (1828) were both set in medieval Lithuania. Amusingly, another basis for the idealization of the medieval period emerged from an unwitting collaboration between Daukantas and Mickiewicz. In 1822 Daukantas translated a youthful literary exercise of Mickiewicz from Polish into Lithuanian, apparently mistaking it for an authentic excerpt from an ancient chronicle. Daukantas later incorporated Mickiewicz's story of the Lithuanian princess Żywila into historical writings. By the time Mickiewicz's authorship of the Żywila story was established in 1884, the tale had taken a significant place in Lithuanian national culture.[6] The "unmasking" of Żywila made little difference. Grażyna, another mythical princess and by the end of the nineteenth century a common name of Lithuanian girls, was also invented by Mickiewicz. Yet there was an important difference between the Romantic poet and his modern Lithuanian readers. Mickiewicz's preface to *Konrad Wallenrod* closed with a citation of Schiller: "What song makes immortal must perish in actual life." In Mickiewicz's view, ancient Lithuania had indeed perished, and the proper object of nostalgia, as in *Pan Tadeusz,* was the early modern Lithuania joined to Poland in a Commonwealth. Lithuanian activists, however, followed the line drawn by Narbutt and Daukantas: that Lithuanian history had ended in 1569, and therefore it was medieval Lithuania that must be revived. This was the model of history communicated by the first modern Lithuanian publications.

In 1883, Jonas Basanavičius (1851–1927) decided to establish a Lithuanian-language newspaper. Basanavičius was a graduate of the Mariampol high school, which during his time of studies changed from Polish to Russian as language of instruction, and added language classes in Lithuanian. He was among the young Lithuanians allowed to study in imperial universities, an experience that rendered more abstract and hence clarified his notion of Lithuania. In Moscow he studied under French professors, befriended Bulgarian national activists, and published on Lithuanian history (in Polish). In 1879 he completed his studies in medicine and emigrated to Bulgaria, where he worked as a doctor and continued his studies of Lithuanian history. These led him to Prague in 1882, where he encountered activists of the Czech national movement. Like his Bulgarian friends, his Czech acquaintances emphasized medieval grandeur, and explained away early modern failure. It was in Prague that Basanavičius decided to found a Lithuanian-language review. Seizing an image used in Prague to sug-

gest a nation awakening from darkness, Basanavičius decided to name the review *Aušra* (The Dawn).[7]

In 1883 Basanavičius made plans with compatriots in Germany to print his
newspaper. Although the Lithuanian language was legal in the Russian empire,
it had to be printed in Cyrillic characters. In Germany, Lithuanian activists
could publish in the Lithuanian language and Latin script, then smuggle their
work into the Russian empire. Basanavičius edited the first numbers from
Prague, entrusting the publication in Germany to Jurgis Mikšas. Mikšas had to
leave Germany after an amorous adventure, and was replaced by Jonas Šliupas,
who had earned his spurs in conspiratorial politics with the Polish socialist
party Proletariat. Šliupas (1861–1944) was in his turn expelled from Prussia.
Aušra's forty numbers popularized the search for continuities with the period
before 1569 and a Grand Duchy of Lithuania distinct from Poland. It relied on
the research of Daukantas and Narbutt and the poems of Mickiewicz.[8]

Not surprisingly, *Aušra*'s decision to skip the early modern period—to go
straight from the medieval to the modern—followed the framework developed
by Czech activists at the same time. The 1569 Lublin Union was for Lithuanians what the 1621 battle of the White Mountain was for Czechs: a clear marker
of the end of national life, allowing the foreigner to be blamed, the medieval
past to be cherished, the social origins of activists to be explained, and the common people to be exalted.[9] Just as the Lublin Union had (supposedly) deracinated the Lithuanian nobility, so the defeat at White Mountain (supposedly)
transformed the Czech nobility into a coterie of foreign adventurers. Thus the
national revival required new blood, and the national traditions to be revived
could be found only among the simple folk. In both cases, this medieval-mod-
ern synthesis was first developed in an early modern language of high culture:
German for the Czechs, Polish for the Lithuanians. To convey it back to the
people in their own language was the crucial step, but this too was fraught with
a raft of contradictions.

AGE, BEAUTY, AND POWER

In the 1880s *Aušra* publicized this scheme in the vernacular, in Lithuanian. As
we have seen, *Aušra*'s title—"The Dawn"—reveals the universal conceit of nations with weak state and cultural traditions: what seems to be death is only
sleep, and the sleeper will awaken as the world turns and night becomes day. Yet
the simple attempt to render this idea in writing in the Lithuanian language re-

veals a deeper possibility within this conceit. Within the idea of national awakening is the tempting possibility of exploiting backwardness by improving upon the achievements of others. The alphabet, for example, was really only invented once.[10] It must however be re-created by national activists who wish to reach the common people by codifying their vernacular speech as a literary language: a practical necessity full of national virtue. This we observe not in the meaning, but in the spelling of "Aušra." In history books, it is spelled with an "š", whereas in 1883 it was usually spelled "Auszra." The difference is between the Polish orthography ("sz" pronounced as "sh" in English) in which the Lithuanian language was usually spelled at the time, and the Czech orthography ("š" as "sh") the newspaper's editors tried to introduce to make their language look less Polish. This shift had nothing to do with publishing in the Russian empire: both spellings used Roman characters, and both were therefore illegal. The Russian police would confiscate a journal called "Aušra" and one called "Auszra": only something called "Аушра" would have been permitted. Lithuanian activists were only concerned to extract a Lithuanian culture from the Polish inheritance.

The ironies of the Lithuanian borrowing from Czech are four. (1) In the Middle Ages, before the association of Poland and Lithuania, Polish had become a written language under the influence of precisely Czech.[11] The Polish that entered the Grand Duchy of Lithuania in early modern times was thus written after the fashion of Old Czech. Centuries later, the phonetic symbols modern Lithuanian activists copied were designed by modern Czechs keen to avoid the presence of consonant compounds as well as certain letters that they associated with German. After this reform, modern Czech also began to look less like Polish, since Polish preserved elements of Old Czech spelling and used compound consonants to represent single sounds. This unintended side effect of Czech reforms, which some Czech Pan-Slavs themselves regretted, was what attracted Lithuanians, since their main rival was Polish culture. To give an example: traditionally, Czech, Polish, and Lithuanians represented the "v" sound with "w," like German. After reform, Czech and Lithuanian used "v" instead. Similarly, all 3 languages traditionally used "cz" to represent "ch". After reform, Czech and Lithuanian used "č" instead. Lithuanians thus turned a new Czech orthography against an older one in their struggle with Polish.

(2) But because Russia banned the use of Latin characters in Lithuanian writing, Lithuanians could use neither system in Vilnius. Lithuanians therefore used the Czech letters to write in their (more or less) reformed Lithuanian across the border in German East Prussia. In this roundabout way a script de-

signed to limit the spread of German culture made its way into Germany. (3) Yet this particular irony runs deeper. Part of the Czech solution for Lithuanian orthography was to replace "sz" and "cz" with "š" and "č." Another part, advocated years before by the German linguist August Schleicher, was to drop the Polish "ł" and use "v" instead of the Polish "w." So, in the end, a German supported the part of the Czech solution by which Polish influence upon the Lithuanian language could be shrouded in Russia. (4) The German philological interest in the Lithuanian language was itself part of the Romantic turn in German scholarship, which was partly an attempt to emancipate German culture from French influence. If we can keep our feet in this house of mirrors, we see that ideas of nationality reflected at odd angles around late nineteenth-century Europe, even as local nationalists were absorbed in an image they desired to see as distinct, pure, and beautiful. We also find the original image of nineteenth-century nationalism in France, seen by many east of the Rhine as both the home of political philosophy and a model national state.[12]

In a Europe where literature was universally regarded as a condition of nationhood, the nearly total absence of Lithuanian literature was obscured by redoubled attention to the inherent virtues of the language. Basanavičius contended that the formal perfection of the language proved that ancient Lithuanians had been civilized. Since nothing much in the way of secular literature survived to substantiate such claims, the age of the language substituted for attainments. Like Tuscan towns whose medieval towers survive not despite, but thanks to, early modern economic decline, the Lithuanian language preserved antique virtues not despite, but thanks to, its lack of early modern literary use. Polish rather than Lithuanian bore the brunt of Latin, German, and French neologisms; and Lithuanian's extraordinarily complicated grammar survived as an obscure speech of peasants. Mickiewicz had himself called Lithuanian "the oldest language spoken on the European mainland." In 1843 he linked Lithuanian to Sanskrit (and the Lithuanians to a lost tribe of Hindus). Eight years earlier the Lithuanian historian Narbutt had illustrated the connection between Lithuanian and Sanskrit in the first volume of his massive Polish-language history of the Lithuanian nation. Narbutt called upon German authorities such as Jacob Grimm (1785–1863): grammarian and philologist as well as collector of folk tales. Daukantas, in his 1845 study, drew on the philological work of Schleicher.[13] Mickiewicz's image of ancient Lithuania was also built in part from German sources, such as the history of Prussia of August von Kotzebue (1761–1819).[14] In making special claims for the Lithuanian language,

Daukantas, Narbutt, and Mickiewicz all drew from the folkish side of German Romanticism, and the achievements of German scholars. Moreover, Mickiewicz in his Paris exile communicated easily with French historians such as Jules Michelet. His claims about the ancient status of Lithuanian were made in lectures he gave in French as a professor of the Collège de France.[15] For us, it may seem ironic that conclusions about the Lithuanian language drawn or publicized in Germany and France later became a central element of Lithuanian nationalism. Yet these scholarly conclusions could not have been reached if not for the brute fact that Baltic Lithuanian dialects had survived centuries of nearly complete isolation from high culture.

In the twilight moment of the nineteenth century, when numbers were not yet seen to be enough to make a nation, when activists were still in contact with early modern cultures, they felt the need to prove that the new could match the old. Romantic nationalists throughout nineteenth-century Europe accepted common standards of nationality: high culture was necessary, literature proved high culture, but ancient culture was better than none at all. Age before beauty, when there is no beauty to be had. Accepting Grimm's, Narbutt's, and Mickiewicz's claims on behalf of the age of the Lithuanian language, Lithuanian activists of the *Aušra* generation simultaneously sought to show that the language could bear the weight of modern letters. Accepting Mickiewicz's premise that high culture is linked to political destiny, Lithuanian writers translated Mickiewicz's poetry into Lithuanian to disprove his presumption that Polish was the high language of Lithuania. If the Lithuanian language could convey Mickiewicz's extraordinary poetry, they thought, then Lithuania could be regarded as a separate nation with a distinct future. The apparent homage to Polish culture, by the literary judo of national revival, was to reveal the equality of Lithuania as a nation. Enormous efforts were expended so that a stage could be skipped, and age could become beauty.[16]

The beauty was largely to convince the Poles around them, and the Poles in themselves. For a national movement to arise, for beauty to become power, someone besides the activists had to be convinced. The poet Vincas Kudirka (1858–99), slightly younger than Basanavičius, found a way between age and beauty to the people. His was a complicated story, involving the appropriation rather than the rejection of the early modern Polish legacy. Although Kudirka, like Basanavičius, studied the Lithuanian language at the Mariampol high school, the school's main effect was to Polonize him. Consider his recollections of his years in school. "My self-preservation instinct told me not to speak in Lithuanian, and to make sure that no one noticed that my father wore a rough peasant's coat and could only speak Lithuanian. I did my best to speak Polish, even though I spoke it badly. When my father and other relatives visited me, I stayed away from them when I could see that fellow students or gentlemen were watching; I spoke with them in peace only when we were alone or outside. I saw myself as a Pole and thus as a gentleman, I had imbibed the Polish spirit."[17] One might ask why the Mariampol high school had such different effects on Basanavičius, who became self-consciously Lithuanian as a student, and Kudirka, who came to regard himself as a Pole. The answer reminds us of the importance of the smallest details of Russian imperial policy. A few years older than Kudirka, Basanavičius had studied at Mariampol during the period of martial law, when Russian bayonets enforced the ban on Polish. When martial law was lifted in 1872, during the second year of Kudirka's studies, Polish crept back into curricula across Lithuania. Even Mariampol, as we see, once again became an agent of Polonization.

Like Basanavičius, Kudirka left Lithuania to obtain university education in a Russian imperial university. Kudirka, however, studied in Warsaw, where he considered himself a Pole, and where his baptism into politics was in the company of Polish socialists. In the end, his long encounter with Poland served the Lithuanian cause. Whereas Basanavičius had learned from Bulgarian and Czech national revivalists, Kudirka was in a position to appropriate rather than simply reject the Polish inheritance. The brilliant stroke of Basanavičius was to ignore the complexities of early modern history, and like Czechs and Bulgarians glorify the medieval past. Kudirka harnessed the early modern Polish idea to the modern Lithuanian purposes he accepted after his return from Warsaw in 1889. His contribution was to present Lithuania not only as historically distinct from Poland, as had Basanavičius, but as a national equal in the present. Despite the twists, turns, and attempts at transcendence, the concern with status was consistent throughout. The sense that culture was to be attained and displayed motivated Kudirka's youthful attempts to pass as a gentleman; in his maturity, it underlay a larger project to dignify himself and his origins by raising the peasantry into politics. From his fascination with Polishness in the 1870s came the energy for his challenge of the 1890s. From his deep knowledge of Polish came his ability to turn Mickiewicz to the new purpose of building a peasant nation. As Kudirka saw in Warsaw, Polish national activists were turning Mickiewicz into a modern Polish patriot. Kudirka responded by transforming Mickiewicz's masterpiece into contemporary Lithuanian patriotism. From Mickiewicz's lonely opening "Lithuania! My fatherland!" came Kudirka's hopeful rendering "Lithuania! Our fatherland!" In 1898, Kudirka incorporated the first line of Mickiewicz's *Pan Tadeusz*, so modified, into a poem that became the national anthem of Lithuania.[18]

Two generations after Mickiewicz, the terms meant something new. Unlike Mickiewicz, Kudirka believed that the fatherland in question was home to a nation of Lithuanian speakers destined for statehood. In this understanding, alien to the sense of the original, if compatible with its wording, Mickiewicz's words, translated and slightly modified, became the motto of the Lithuanian national movement. This is something more than irony: it is the transformation of durable Romantic ideas of an early modern Commonwealth into one of many possible modern national forms. The failed rising of 1830 gave rise to the Romanticism of the mature Mickiewicz of *Pan Tadeusz;* the failed rising of 1863 divided its stream into several national currents. Like Mickiewicz and Polish Romantics after the rising of 1830, Kudirka and Lithuanian Romantics after the rising of 1863 wished to "create a new world on the ruins of the old." For them, the old Polish-Lithuanian Commonwealth was among the ruins.

THE GRAND DUCHY AS FATHERLAND

1863 is a caesura for Lithuanian nationality. In the Polish and Belarusian cases, it is harder for us to distinguish the dawn of modern nationalisms from the twilight of the early modern Grand Duchy. Even as a new generation of modern Lithuanian activists of the 1880s and 1890s defined a separate Lithuanian history and folk nation, Lithuanian Poles and Belarusians regarded "Lithuania" as a geographical and political notion. To be Lithuanian, in their understanding, was to preserve the traditions of the Grand Duchy. Many found the national question beside the point. The "tutejszość" ("localness", or more accurately if less literally "local-mindedness") of much of the gentry was often a conscious rejection of ideologies which seemed to ill fit the contours of local reality and tradition.[19] The "local-mindedness" of peasants near Vil'nia was a practical response to the complicated patterns of linguistic assimilation and a diplomatic way of avoiding the obligation to side with either Polish-speaking gentry or Russian imperial officials.[20] In the late nineteenth century, the superiority of Polish as a means of communication was as widely accepted in these lands as it had been in Mickiewicz's student days.[21]

Even after the failed uprising of 1863, gentry with political aspirations could try to adapt the traditions of the Grand Duchy to the demands of modern politics. The most important example of this trend was the Polish revolutionary and statesman Józef Piłsudski (1867–1935), heir on both sides to distinguished

Lithuanian noble families.[22] Piłsudski studied and matured in Russified schools in Wilno. After exile in Siberia, he returned to Lithuania, beginning his career as a Polish socialist in Wilno in the 1890s. As we shall see, he would be the individual most responsible for the creation of a Polish state in 1918, and its incorporation of Wilno thereafter. His patriotism was founded not upon a modern ethnic or linguistic definition of Poland, but upon nostalgic republican ideas of the Grand Duchy of Lithuania, which he opposed to a historical notion of an autocratic Russia. Piłsudski, who called himself a Lithuanian, spoke the literary Polish of his home, the folk Belarusian of the countryside, and the rough Russian of his Siberian exile. As we shall see, his failure as a Lithuanian was guaranteed by the very allies who allowed his success as a Pole.[23]

The appeal of Belarusian activists to the Grand Duchy of Lithuania, and their socialist federalism, were similar to Piłsudski's. Yet people who sought to revive the Grand Duchy of Lithuania under the new name "Belarus" were themselves constrained by their identification with an early modern Polishness. The Polish language had been the local language of culture for three hundred years, it was protected locally by elite Roman Catholic families and the Roman Catholic Church, and was supported by millions of speakers to the west. Lithuanian, although by no means comparable in status with Polish, was easily distinguished by its impenetrability as a Baltic language. Its speakers, although their number was shrinking, were better sheltered by geography than speakers of Belarusian. Belarusian was in the most delicate position: an uncodified low-status Slavic dialect located morphologically between Polish and Russian, whose speakers were located socially between Polish culture and Russian power. Belarusian peasants regarded Polish (and, as time passed, Russian) as languages of attainment, and what we call Belarusian as the simple speech of honest folk. To advance from the peasantry into society was to speak and to become Polish or Russian.[24] The linguistic flexibility so valuable to the early modern Polish-Lithuanian Commonwealth and Grand Duchy of Lithuania was a burden upon anyone who might have wished to advance a modern Belarusian linguistic nationalism.

Why then press into this cramped space? Why pay attention to Belarusian speakers and Belarusian national activists, given that their claim to Vil'nia would rarely be taken seriously, and given that a modern Belarusian nation has yet to emerge? The Belarusian branch of the traditions of the old Grand Duchy alerts us to the dangers of assuming that past linguistic or "ethnic" groups are simple predecessors of existing national groups, golems to be animated by the magic of modernity. When there are already modern nations, their historians find it easy to "prove" descent from "ethnic groups." The Belarusian failure therefore provides a useful test. Here we have an "ethnic group" which is the largest by far in the area in question. According to the Russian imperial census of 1897, more people spoke Belarusian in Vil'na province than all other languages combined. In Vil'na, Minsk, Grodno, Mogilev, and Vitebsk provinces, contiguous territories of historic Lithuania, speakers of Belarusian were three-quarters of the population. In the twentieth century, this "ethnic group" did not become a modern nation. In combination with Lithuanian and Polish successes, this Belarusian failure helps us to perceive what national movements actually need. If their success were actually determined by fidelity to the traditions of Grand Duchy of Lithuania, or by numbers of people speaking a given language, the Belarusians would have had more reason to hope than anyone else. The Belarusian failure is the result of social and political contingencies which escape national reasoning, and thus deserve historical attention.[25]

A BELARUSIAN LITHUANIAN FATHERLAND?

The hope for a Belarusian Lithuania was beautifully expressed by the poet Vincent Dunin-Martsinkevich (1807–1884). Dunin-Martsinkevich, heir of a petty noble Lithuanian-Polish family, was educated in Petersburg. He debuted in Vil'nia in 1840 with a Polish-Belarusian comic opera he wrote with Stanisław Moniuszko.[26] He ceased work on a Belarusian translation of Mickiewicz's "Pan Tadeusz" in 1859. Like the Lithuanian activists we have discussed, Dunin-Martsinkevich took for granted that the best sign of the dignity of the folk language was a proof of its equality with Polish, and that the most convincing demonstration of that equality was the translation of Polish literature. He keenly felt the pressure of Slavic literary languages on both sides: by his own account, it was the Russian translation of *Pan Tadeusz* rather than the Polish original that brought him to take up the project of a Belarusian translation. Like the Lithuanians, Dunin-Martsinkevich enjoyed what could be construed as support from the poet himself. Mickiewicz called Belarusian "the richest and purest speech of ancient origin"; Dunin-Martsinkevich intended to prove it by translating Mickiewicz's story "of Belarusian gentlemen" into a language that could be read by "Belarusian peasants."[27] This was extraordinarily ambitious, since the original poem is extremely long, complex, and beautiful, and Belarusian dialects had not been codified. Although a Belarusian-Ruthenian vernacular was used as a literary language in the sixteenth century, after the triumph of Polish after 1569 very little had been written.

A preliminary step had taken place: Belarusian folk culture had been translated into Polish by Jan Czeczot (Chachot, 1796–1847). Czeczot studied with
Mickiewicz in Wilno, was a member of the same secret society, and was a life-
long friend. While Mickiewicz adapted Belarusian folk customs in *Forefathers'*
Eve (two collections, 1822 and 1832) and wrote about the Polish-speaking gentry in Belarusian-speaking lands in *Pan Tadeusz,* his friend Czeczot collected
folk songs and adapted them to colorful but literary Polish.[28] Czeczot's project
was, in practical terms, far easier than that of Dunin-Martsinkevich. In a society still overwhelmingly concerned with status, translating folk culture into a
literary language is one thing; translating literary masterpieces into the speech
of the peasants is quite another. The cultured may be charmed when someone
brings back a muddy pearl from the sty, but it does not follow that they like seeing their own pearls thrown before swine.

These status difficulties lay within the Belarusian patriots themselves. Few of
them had any very high regard for the Belarusian peasant. Dunin-Martsinkevich, like Czeczot and Mickiewicz, still imbibed the early modern patriotism of
the old Commonwealth, in which Polish was the language of politics and culture. At the same time, Dunin-Martsinkevich was aware that Polish itself was
beginning to play a new political function in a new sort of politics. Despite
Mickiewicz's intentions, the fact that his poems were written in Polish was
helping to consolidate a linguistic (ethnic) Polish nationalism.[29] As Polish
moved "down" in Poland, Belarusian patriots hoped to move Belarusian "up" in
Belarus. As Dunin-Martsinkevich knew, the dialects spoken where the action
of *Pan Tadeusz* was set were Belarusian, and he hoped to elevate that language
to aid the Belarusian people in Mickiewicz's Lithuania.

A second set of problems lay within the politics in which such writers had to
live and work. At a time when Poles could publish *Pan Tadeusz* in the original,
and a Russian translation was available, the Russian censor confiscated Dunin-
Martsinkevich's translation on the grounds that the work used Latin rather
than Cyrillic script.[30] The Belarusian language was not banned at this time: it
simply could not be written in Latin (Polish) letters. The problem for Dunin-
Martsinkevich was that his Belarusian title page read *Pan Tadeusz,* exactly as it
would have in Polish, rather than "Пан Тадеуш," which would have looked
exactly like the Russian. Lithuanian activists dodged this problem by working
among compatriots in Germany; Dunin-Martsinkevich had no such expedi-
ents, since all Belarusians lived in the Russian empire. There were courageous
Belarusian activists; there were dialects that could have become a written language; there were millions of people who could have learned to read it. Yet in

the middle of the nineteenth century almost no one was literate in Belarusian only, there was no place to publish among Belarusians, and there was no market for Belarusian books.

POLAND, LITHUANIA, RUSSIA: BELARUS?

Problems apparently arising from Russian imperial policy were often rooted in the Polish and Roman Catholic inheritance of the Grand Duchy of Lithuania Belarusians wished to revive. At first, Russian power had actually supported institutions of the Grand Duchy of Lithuania. The Jesuit order, suppressed by Pope Clement XIV in 1773, was allowed to continue its activities in the Russian empire. Until its abolition in Russia in 1820, its academies, schools, and printing press operated mainly in Polish. Vil'no University (founded as a Jesuit academy in 1579) and the Vil'no school district, which used Polish, survived until 1832. The 1588 Statute of the Grand Duchy of Lithuania remained in force until 1840. Although the Statute was written in Chancery Slavonic, which is similar to Belarusian, dietines (local assemblies of nobles) and trials were held in Polish. In religion, schooling, and law, Russian rule initially preserved Polish civilization in what had been the Grand Duchy of Lithuania. This is not as odd as it may seem. Tsar Alexander's reign was far from the modern nationalism through which Polish-Russian history is recalled today. That prism was inserted after 1863. At the beginning of the nineteenth century, government was still thought to be a matter of co-opting local elites rather than mobilizing masses, and Alexander believed that general principles of Enlightenment—as taught by his Polish friend Czartoryski—were the most solid basis upon which to join new elites to the Russian state.[31]

In old Lithuania the nineteenth century very much resembled the eighteenth: Polish political ideas failed again and again, while Polish culture continued its steady march forward. This is what the Belarusian historian Mitrofan Dovnar-Zapolski (1867–1934), himself from a petty noble family from the Vil'nia area, meant when he referred to Russian policy under Alexander as "Polonization."[32] Dovnar-Zapolski, who was born after 1863, saw these events in crisp national terms that were not quite relevant at the time, but he rightly emphasized the continuity of Polish culture in Belarusian lands before 1863. Even after the failed rising of 1830–31, nobles now referred to as Belarusians could function without difficulty in Polish and Russian politics, without attending to the language or customs of the peasants around them.[33] To be sure, nobles in Belarus lost much of their traditional position when the Statutes of the Grand Duchy

were annulled in 1840, and much of their social position after the abolition of
serfdom in 1861. Just as certain nobles turned to Lithuanian folk nationality after 1863, others then turned to Belarusian folk nationality. Here again they
faced an institutional problem, once again only superficially a result of Russian
rule.

In the half-century that Russian policy allowed the Belarusian gentry to drift
toward Polish high culture, it removed the religious basis for a popular notion
of a distinct Belarusian nation. When the Commonwealth was partitioned for
the last time in 1795, perhaps four-fifths of the peasants in the Grand Duchy of
Lithuania were Uniates.[34] In 1839, the Uniate Church in these lands had been
absorbed by the Orthodox Church. Whereas Lithuanian activists could use
Roman Catholicism as a mark of distinction from Russia, Belarusian activists
could only regret the loss of "their" Uniate Church. After the 1863 rising, and
ever since, Belarusian patriots have bemoaned the fate of the Uniate Church.[35]
Yet the Uniate Church was far from a Belarusian national institution in 1839.
Created for the Commonwealth, it operated in Polish. Its hierarchy had not really used the local vernacular for almost two hundred years. Although the shift
from Polish to Russian was initially painful and difficult, it amounted to the exchange of one imported literary language for another. To be sure, the Uniate
Church did become a national institution in Austrian Galicia, but this required
more than a century of state support, and an international environment of competition with Russia. The Uniate Church, had it survived in Belarus, might have
become a Belarusian national institution: but this would have required a break
with, rather than a continuation of, its early modern traditions (see chart 1).[36]

AN ETHNIC OR HISTORIC LITHUANIA?

The aftermath of 1863 opened some social space for a Lithuanian national
movement; it closed the limited space available to Belarusians. Activists who
promoted an ethnic notion of Lithuania based on the Lithuanian people and
their spoken tongue enjoyed certain advantages in the Russian empire after
1863; activists who promoted an elite notion of Lithuania based on the traditions of the Commonwealth combined with the promotion of Belarusian dialects were at a distinct disadvantage. Whereas the aftermath of 1863 created a
new generation of modern Lithuanian activists, it kept Belarusian patriots right
between attractive Polish culture and increased Russian power. Recall Konstanty Kalinowski, the Polish-speaking Lithuanian nobleman who rallied peasants in 1863 with pamphlets in Belarusian. His appeal to the common people

had a bright future in the post-1863 era of mass politics: but the Belarusian language as a means of such appeals did not. After the 1863 uprising, Belarusians could not publish in Belarusian in the Russian empire. Before 1905, the rest of the Belarusian national revival had to take place in faraway Cracow, Posen, and Vienna.[37] Frantsishak Bahushevich, yet another son of minor gentry from the Vil'nia region, published his Belarusian poems in Cracow in the 1890s—in Belarusian language, and Polish orthography. The Polish alphabet was still widely used for Belarusian publications, even (after 1905) when they were legalized in the Russian empire. The first important Belarusian periodical, *Nasha niva* (Our Soil), published both Roman and Cyrillic editions. Although Bahushevich is now regarded as the father of Belarusian literature, his poetry had limited influence in the Russian empire. It was banned in 1908: not for its Belarusian language, but for its nostalgia for traditions that preceded Russian rule.[38]

It might seem that Lithuanian activists faced similar problems. From the 1860s Lithuanian publications illegal in Russia were produced in Germany, and the Lithuanian national movement was led by men as far away as Bulgaria and the United States. Why then did the Lithuanian national movement attain coherence after 1863 when the Belarusian national movement did not? What may seem at first glance to be disadvantages turned out to be advantages. Take, for example, the need of Lithuanians to break with the past. Although the Lithuanian national idea involved extraordinary feats of historical imagination, it is much easier to invent history by writing massive tomes than it is to change tradition by changing elite behavior. Tradition involves what people actually do now, whereas history narrates what people supposedly once did. Where tradition stops and history begins appears to depend a great deal upon the social origins of national activists. Here again the Lithuanians enjoyed an unexpected advantage over the Belarusians. Activists of humble social origins, whose families never played any role in early modern politics, found it easier to treat the entire past as history. Lithuanian activists, often Russian-educated peasant sons, happily skipped over several centuries and spoke of rebirth. Belarusian activists, Polish-speaking Roman Catholic gentry, were bogged down in the received truth of the actual tradition they learned from their parents and grandparents. The idea of creating an ethnic Belarus based on the people and the language came much harder to them than did the idea of an ethnic Lithuania to the Lithuanians. At the very moment Lithuanian activists sought to show their break from Poland by inventing new orthographies, Belarusians sought to show their distance from Russia by using Polish script and spelling.

This reminds us that Belarusian is a Slavic language similar to both Polish and Russian, whereas Lithuanian is a Baltic language very different from both. The Russian ban on Lithuanian publications in Roman script was felt by some Lithuanian-speaking peasants, and was thus useful to Lithuanian activists. If the state deprives society of something it values, organizations can gain support by providing what is desired. Here Belarusian activists were again in a worse position. In the Russian empire, no one learned to read in Belarusian in church or in school. Belarusians who were literate could already read Polish and Russian. The ban on Belarusian publications was thus of little use to Belarusian activists. No one missed Belarusian as people missed Lithuanian. As a result, Lithuanian activists or priests who dealt with Lithuanian peasants in their own language had an advantage over Russian-speaking officials or Polish-speaking gentry. A Belarusian activist, on the other hand, enjoyed a much smaller relative advantage over a Russian or Polish rival. In these ways a contingent fact of philology determined the range of influence of national activists.

This brings us back to the emigration of national activists, apparently an equally painful problem in both cases. Although emigration plays a prominent role in all national martyrologies, émigrés can be very useful to the national cause. Although Mickiewicz beautifully and no doubt sincerely pined for the trees of his native Lithuania, in fact he was bored stiff as a school teacher in Kowno (Kaunas). Imprisonment, exile, and emigration allowed him to be the great poet he became. The great poems cited here were published in St. Petersburg, Dresden, and Paris. Of course, wherever he was, he found Polish company. This is crucial. The Lithuanians who left Russia to publish *Aušra* in German East Prussia were, like Mickiewicz, Romantics who longed for a lost homeland. Yet they too, like him, could draw upon the resources of compatriots. There were about 100,000 Lithuanians in Germany. The book smugglers who brought Lithuanian materials into Russia from Germany performed remarkable feats of organization, but their task was at least a sustaining and plausible one. Belarusians, on the other hand, were entirely contained within the borders of the Russian Empire. It was simply impossible to cross the border and work with other Belarusians. Belarusians trying to sustain the national project from distant Cracow could find few local collaborators, and were liable themselves to drown in a sea of local Polishness. Whatever they published in Belarusian had to be transported great distances to have any effect. Partition, we see, has its advantages.

These factors—the social origins of national activists, the character of the national language, and the location of imperial borders—fit ill into master narratives about nationality. First, they are generally absent from the explanations

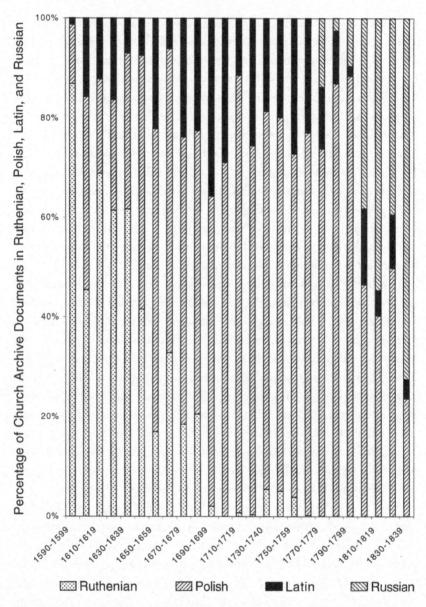

Source: Page count of Opisanie dokumentov Arkhiva zapadnorusskikh uniatskikh mitro-
politov, 2 vols., St. Petersburg, Synodal'naia, 1897–1907.

that successful national activists give for their success or failure. Second, an appreciation of these factors undermines the common notion that "ethnic groups" serve as "proto-nations." The "ethnic group" of Belarusian-speaking peasants was ten times larger than, and growing at the expense of, the "ethnic group" of Lithuanian-speaking peasants, yet a Lithuanian movement crystallized while a

Belarusian one did not. Third, these factors qualify the view that modernizing states create nations. After 1863, Russian policy contributed in unforeseen ways to other national movements, but never under Russian rule did any very large proportion of inhabitants of the capital of the old Grand Duchy call themselves "Russians."[39] The "Russianness" of some of the most famous ones is inseparable from the traditions of the Grand Duchy of Lithuania.

LITHUANIA AS GREAT RUSSIAN FATHERLAND

After 1863, Russian authorities generally regarded Polish elites as the enemy of consequence, the Lithuanian national movement as a way to weaken that enemy, and Belorussian peasants as part of the Russian nation. Local gentry elites lost more of their authority, due partly to a centralizing state which punished them after 1863, and partly to the people who received their land after 1861. The Russian state began for the first time to attend to the nationality of those mass populations. Although the process was slow and complicated, the 1860s were a turning point in the Russian approach to historic Lithuania, its Northwest Territory. Rather than relying upon local elites to govern local populations, Russia began to turn local populations against local elites, and to treat nationality as a tool of the state.

The oppression of the Polish gentry that followed the 1863 rising is associated with M. N. Muraviev, the governor general of Vil'na dispatched to crush the rising. His brutality earned him the sobriquet "The Hangman" in Russian, Polish, and Lithuanian. Muraviev saw the uprising as a national war between Russians and Poles for Vil'na. His idea that Poles were born rebels was confirmed by the rising, as was his view that Russia was something like a national state. Muraviev was popular in Petersburg not only for his reliable brutality, but for his ability to operationalize this national paradigm. In treating Lithuania as the theater of a national war between Poles and Russians, he helped to make it so. His policies forced aside historic ideas of the Grand Duchy of Lithuania. Konstanty Kalinowski, we recall, wrote in Belarusian, supported the Uniate Church, and thought of the Grand Duchy of Lithuania as his fatherland. Muraviev had him hanged in Vil'na in 1864 as the ringmaster of a Polish and Catholic plot.

This approach unexpectedly created the conditions for a new national alignment, at all levels of society. Before 1863, the most common self-appellation of the largest group in Russia's Northwest Territory—Belarusian-speaking peasants—was apparently "Lithuanian." After 1863, Russian religious policy, Russian repression, and Russian classifications forced this traditional idea to the periphery of social awareness. By treating the Orthodox as "Russian," the empire forced a choice between national labels. By century's end, such Belarusian speakers called themselves "Russian" if they were Orthodox, "Polish" if they were Roman Catholic, and "local" if they were watching out for themselves. By removing the historical sense of the term "Lithuanian" in the popular mind, Russian power cleared the way for a modern, ethnic definition of Lithuania, and simplified the task of Lithuanian activists.[40] Like Lithuanian activists after 1863, Russian historians likewise rediscovered the Grand Duchy of Lithuania, the latter treating it as a fledgling Russian state. The failure of the 1863 rising was presented, in the national idioms then emerging in Russia, as the end of alien Polish and Catholic influence in Russian and Orthodox lands.

In 1898, when Poles elsewhere in the Russian empire were raising statues to commemorate the centenary of Mickiewicz's birth, Russians and loyalists in Vil'na erected a statue to Governor General Muraviev. Mickiewicz had inspired patriotic aspirations to free Wilno from Russia; Muraviev accelerated the process by which these aspirations became modern nationalism. Still, something had changed since 1863, as we can see from the career of Prince P. D. Sviatopolk-Mirskii, governor general of Vil'na from 1902 to 1904. Whereas Muraviev was a brute the tsar needed to crush a rebellion, Mirskii was a delicate soul favored by the empress. Whereas Muraviev governed strictly on the basis of traditional principles, Mirskii harbored grand plans for reform. Like Muraviev, Mirskii took for granted that the Poles (and their Jewish allies) were the great enemy in Vilnius and historic Lithuania. Unlike Muraviev, Mirskii distinguished Polish-ness from Catholicism. He argued that imperial policy had driven non-Polish Catholics to Polish nationality, and that a more subtle approach could build loyalty among Lithuanians and Belorussians. One of Mirskii's last acts as governor general, in 1904, was to persuade the tsar to allow the Lithuanian language to be published in Latin script. As interior minister in 1905, he went so far as to support Belorussian nationality. Of course, Mirskii believed that these national movements had no future in the grand historical contest of Poland and Russia. In his view, they would slow assimilation to Polish nationality, buying time for the inevitable Russian victory.[41]

As some grateful Lithuanian activists realized, Mirskii was no intruder upon the lands he governed. Like dozens of Russian imperial officials who administered Poland and Lithuania for the tsar, he was the scion of an old Lithuanian gentry family. In the Grand Duchy, where most noble families were in fact of Orthodox origin, the Mirskiis and others "reconverted" to Orthodoxy under Russian rule. Literate Polish-Lithuanian gentry families provided not only much of the bureaucracy of the Russian empire, but some of its conservative thinkers.[42] In the early twentieth century, when Mirskii governed Vil'na, the Great Russian idea was imperial with a modern national element. The new national component was inclusive, in that it provided for the "return" of "lost" Slavic lands and peoples to the Russian fold. The Grand Duchy of Lithuania was seen in this narrative as a Lithuanian-Russian state, torn away by Poland and Catholicism, now returning to Russia and Orthodoxy.

This Great Russian view of history is startlingly similar to that promoted by modern Lithuanian activists after 1863. Both the modern Lithuanian and the modern Russian perspectives cast away early modern history, the two centuries of the Commonwealth, in favor of a medieval Lithuania that met the needs of modern politics. In the Lithuanian case, ancient history meant the history of ethnic Lithuanians in their own realm. In the Russian case, it meant one branch of a Great Russian narrative. After 1863, both Lithuanians and Russians returned to medieval names for the capital of the old Grand Duchy. Lithuanians began to call the city "Vilnius," and Russians began to call it "Vil'na": yet both were rejecting the same Polish form, "Wilno," heretofore universal. Both the Lithuanian and the Russian national historiosophies are syntheses of medieval and modern which omitted the early modern. In the name of supposed continuity with the medieval past, both recommended radical changes in the present to do away with early modern inheritances. Both views justified dramatic changes in family allegiances in the name of a deeper historical logic. Lithuanian activists were often Polish-speaking gentry who "returned to their roots" by associating themselves with the people. Tsarist officials were often Polish-speaking gentry who "returned to their roots" by converting to Orthodoxy and helping the tsar gather in the East Slavs.

Such Russians not only believed in the fusion of East Slavic elements into a Russian nation, they were examples of its reality as a historical process. In all likelihood Mirskii saw no irony in his return to Vil'na. Lithuania was his fatherland, too.

Chapter 3 The First World War and the Wilno Question (1914–1939)

Death, perhaps, will heal his wounds.
—Adam Mickiewicz, *Forefathers' Eve* (Dresden, 1832)

By 1914, the old capital of the Grand Duchy of Lithuania was a desired political capital to Lithuanians, Belarusians, and Poles wishing to lead nations; a spiritual capital to the Jews who were the city's most distinctive group; and an ancient Russian city to the officials who exercised power. Most of the city's schools taught in Russian, most of its churches were Roman Catholic, more than a third of its inhabitants were Jews. The population of the Vil'na province of the Russian empire had more than doubled since 1863; the percentage of city dwellers within the province nearly tripled; the population of Vil'na itself more than tripled.[1] In an era of industrialization and urbanization in the western Russian empire, each generation after 1863 had been more urban and educated than the last. The city was still known by a variety of names—"Vilnius" in Lithuanian; "Wilno" in Polish, "Vil'nia" in Belarusian, "Vil'na" in Russian and "Vilne" in Yiddish. After the Revolution of 1905, when ethnic claims to the city were mooted for the first time, this variety of language increasingly represented irreconcilable points of view.

Vilnius was for Lithuanian activists the capital of the Grand Duchy, built by Grand Duke Gediminas at the dawn of Lithuania's glory. Increasingly, they saw the medieval Grand Duchy as the antecedent of an independent Lithuanian state within something like ethnic frontiers. Although Lithuanian activists preferred to work in Vilnius, speakers of Lithuanian were but a tiny minority in the city (perhaps 1 to 2 percent).[2] Although the practical basis of Lithuanian distinctiveness was language, Lithuanian activists claimed Vilnius on historical grounds. This ambiguity was covered by formulations such as the 1902 program of the Lithuanian Democratic Party, which spoke of an independent Lithuania within "approximate ethnographic frontiers." During the Revolution of 1905, a Lithuanian national assembly organized by left and center parties called for a an autonomous Lithuania "formed from a nucleus of the present ethnographic Lithuania," to include Vilnius and surrounding lands. The word "present" modifying "ethnographic" was no accident. Like Polish National Democrats and other nationalists of the day, Lithuanian activists treated ethnography as both established by science and subject to political change. On their view, people in and around Vilnius who seemed to be Poles or Belarusians were Lithuanians who happened to speak Polish or Belarusian. In the right circumstances, "ethnographic Lithuania" could expand.[3] As we shall see, they were right about that.

Belarusian national activists were as present in Vil'nia as their Lithuanian rivals. They too harkened back to the Grand Duchy, regarded themselves as its heirs, and claimed Vil'nia as their capital.[4] Unlike Lithuanian activists, who were convinced that the 1569 union with Poland had destroyed Lithuanian independence, Belarusian activists favored a revived Polish-Lithuanian Commonwealth. This reflected, as we have seen, an important difference in historical interpretation. The Lithuanian critique of the Polish connection began in the 1840s, and was publicized in the 1880s; it appears that no Belarusian thinker even questioned the value of the old Commonwealth before 1910.[5] In the early twentieth century, the Belarusian claim to Vil'nia was advanced by socialists, sons and daughters of Polish-speaking Roman Catholic gentry families, who thought that socialist internationalism was consistent with traditional federalism.[6] The Revolution of 1905, during which Polish and Lithuanian parties showed new decisiveness and mass support, was a much more modest proving ground for the Belarusian movement. In its aftermath, the Belarusian idea began to seriously compete with the imperial idea of Belarus as "West Russia."[7]

The first important Belarusian periodical, *Nasha Niva* (Our Soil), appeared in 1906. Before 1914, no one thought in terms of a Belarusian nation requiring state independence. As we see, there was no simple connection between "ethnicity" and nationalism in politics. In Vil'nia city, Belarusian speakers far outnumbered Lithuanian speakers. In the Vil'na province as a whole, speakers of Belarusian were more than half the population. In Vil'na, Minsk, Grodno, Mogilev, and Vitebsk provinces, contiguous territories of historic Lithuania, speakers of Belarusian were three-quarters of the population. Nowhere, however, did Belarusian peasants much benefit from industrialization, and nowhere did Belarusians dominate urban life. In every city in which Belarusian speakers were a significant fraction of the population, they were less literate as a group than the rest of the population.[8]

Although Vilnius/Vil'nia was important for Lithuanian and Belarusian activists, these activists were not really important to Wilno. In 1914, Polish dominated public life, although it was not the same Polish spoken in Warsaw. Under Russian imperial rule, a special sort of Polish culture consolidated its hold on Wilno and the Wilno region (*Wileńszczyzna*). Despite a series of laws aiming to transfer land ownership to Russians and Orthodox, in the early twentieth century Poles still owned most of the land in Vil'na province.[9] In 1914, the Poles were probably, by a small margin over the Jews, the city's plurality. Depending upon one's point of view, Polish was either the dominant nationality in and around Wilno or not a nationality at all: assimilation to Polish language was regarded not so much as joining a distinct national society as joining respectable society.[10] In historic Lithuania, there was little thought of "awakening" speakers of Polish to their "true" national identity, since the culture was attractive anyway, and since mastery of the language itself signaled social position. Polish culture in the old Grand Duchy was not seen as an "ethnic" reality to be translated into political power by the energetic work of activists, but rather as a human quality whose representatives (whatever their "ethnic" origins) set the terms of cultured conversation.

Elite participants in this version of Polishness, known after 1905 as the "krajowcy" ("natives"), regarded it as distinct from the Polishness of the Polish crownlands to the west. Aware of their families' roots in the Lithuanian nobility, and often bilingual or trilingual themselves, they regarded the Grand Duchy as the most beautiful part of the Polish inheritance. For such Poles, Wilno was the center of the civilization they had formed, sustained, and wished to represent in a reborn Poland. Far from seeing Wilno as an "ethnically" Polish city in the northeastern corner of a future "ethnic" Poland, they regarded it as the capital of a historic Lithuania whose association with the Polish crownlands was a central question of politics. All of them saw Lithuania, in its post-1569 historical definition, as their political homeland. Most of them assumed that historical Lithuania would form a common entity with the Polish crownlands, although some preferred to leave this question to a future parliament in Wilno.[11] The "krajowcy" were more faithful students of Mickiewicz than either modern Polish or Lithuanian nationalists. In the early twentieth century, their political views were given a federalist structure by patriotic socialists such as Józef Piłsudski.

Such Lithuanian Poles presumed that their Polishness was superior to others' by virtue of the traditions of the Grand Duchy of Lithuania, and that Polish culture in general was of a higher quality than that available in the Lithuanian or Belarusian languages. As modern ideas of nationality spread, this double confidence set a trap. On the one hand, because the sense of superiority vis-à-vis the Polish crownlands was based upon local tradition, it could not be accepted by Poles in Warsaw or Cracow. The ongoing appropriation of Mickiewicz as simply Polish was proof of this. On the other hand, cultivation of those very local traditions risked a bitter harvest. There was no censure of those who carried out the first stages of the Lithuanian and Belarusian national revival in Polish, since folk culture was seen as part of the heritage of the Grand Duchy.[12] Yet the images and tropes of these works were available to modern challengers of the dominant culture, who reproduced them in Lithuanian and Belarusian. As some members of elite Roman Catholic families "defected" to the Belarusian and Lithuanian national movements after 1905, and as Lithuanian activists emerged from the countryside, Polishness slowly became a choice which had to be defended.[13]

During the Revolution of 1905 the Lithuanian assembly won meaningful concessions from the tsarist administration. Some Polish Lithuanians, such as Michał Römer (later Mykolas Römer'is, 1880–1945), drew the lesson that Lithuanian nationality was a force to be taken seriously. Römer believed that historic Lithuania should be created as a multinational state of Lithuanians, Belarusians, Jews, and Poles, in which Lithuanians could play the leading role, and in which Poles would mediate among cultures. This imaginative solution, faithful to the traditions of the Grand Duchy and alert to the new Lithuanian movement, was not easily acceptable to modern national activists. True, leading Lithuanian activists such as Basanavičius and Šliupas had flirted with something similar.[14] As we have seen, such Lithuanian national activists faced practical problems in the appropriation of this multinational legacy, problems which led them to define Lithuania in ethnic terms. By the time some Lithuanian Poles were ready for such a compromise, Lithuanian activists were determined to replace Polish culture with Lithuanian within a more or less ethnically defined Lithuanian state.[15]

Jews, whose connection to an ancient civilization was unquestionable, and whose distinctiveness was palpable, escaped such dialectics. The Jews, who represented 40 percent of the city's population and perhaps three quarters of its traders in 1914, had inhabited the "Jerusalem of Lithuania" in large numbers for four hundred years.[16] The "Lithuania" in question was the old Grand Duchy, which had included cities such as Minsk (by this time about 51 percent Jewish), Homel (55 percent Jewish), Pinsk (74 percent Jewish), and Vitebsk (51 percent Jewish). The Vitebsk of this era is best known from the paintings of its native son, Marc Chagall (1887–1935). Vilne had been one of the great centers of Talmudic scholarship, home to scholars such as Elijah ben Solomon (1720–97), known as the Gaon of Vilne and recalled as great opponent of the Hasidic movement. These oppositions should be kept in perspective: the Gaon, like the Hasidim, tried practical Kabbalah, and learned herbal medicine from Christians. He even tried to make a golem. In the nineteenth century Vilne was the major center of the Haskalah, or Jewish Enlightenment, in the Russian empire. The children of the Haskalah tended to become the founders of modern Jewish political parties. Although participation in politics was limited to a secularized (or secularizing) minority of young people, the atmosphere of the city was productive of Jewish political organization within historically viable possibilities. What was absent was a political assimilationism, which (as in contemporary Vienna or Lwów) linked public use of the dominant language to loyalty to the political regime. In Vilne the dominant Christian culture was Polish and Roman Catholic but the political regime was Russian and Orthodox, and there was no hope among Lithuanian Jews at the end of the nineteenth century that Polish culture could liberalize a Russian regime.[17] This great distance from Polish politics made Vilne (Wilno), unlike Lemberik (Lwów), the source of visions of alternative forms of modern Jewish politics.

Although Zionism was a form of nationalism and Marxism a form of internationalism, both posed problems for Polish culture in Vilne. Zionists and Jewish socialists alike were more hostile to Polish than to Lithuanian national aspirations, on the logic that a Lithuanian state would be multinational and weak, whereas a Polish state might be national and strong. Zionism was a reactive nationalism, a means to preserve and dignify the Jewish people by promising them their own territorial homeland. Since Jews were concentrated in cities and towns throughout the old Polish-Lithuanian Commonwealth (most of which had become the Russian Pale of Settlement), this was a special sort of national project. Zionists could not lay claim to a European territory on grounds of past statehood or present demography: their putative homeland lay in Asia (or, in some variants, Africa). Zionists could not compete for the territory of the old Grand Duchy, but in their use of Yiddish and their advocacy of Hebrew they could further distance Jewish culture from Polish. Jewish socialists in historic Lithuania, by contrast, conceived the future in terms of a European or international revolution. Legacies of the Grand Duchy of Lithuania and the strivings of modern nationalists would be mooted by this great transformation. In the meantime, however, it was necessary to organize the revolution, and the language of politics for such Jews was Russian or Yiddish. Jewish socialists in Vil'na annoyed Polish political activists by using Russian rather than Polish: in one instance Piłsudski proposed Yiddish as a compromise.[18] Russophone socialists of Jewish origin from historic Lithuania formed the Bund in Vil'na in 1897, and played a local part in the Revolution of 1905, and then a major part in the Bolshevik Revolution of 1917.

WORLD WAR AND NATIONAL CLAIMS

The Bolshevik Revolution and the First World War allowed the creation of new states in historic Lithuania. The defeat and collapse of the Russian empire opened the way for the creation of Lithuanian and Polish states, and for their contest for Vilnius/Wilno. After the Polish-Bolshevik war of 1919–20 and skirmishes between Polish and Lithuanian armies, Poland seized Wilno in 1920. Although this operation was organized by Polish federalists, it served the cause of Polish nationalists.

Although we have concentrated upon the Polish federalism of the Wilno region, the dominant trends in Polish nationalism were decided in Warsaw, Łódź, Cracow, Poznań and the central Polish countryside. In the old Polish crownlands, historical and social differences ensured that the Polish idea took a modern turn. Here Polish-speaking elites were confronted not with peasants who spoke another language, but with peasants who spoke Polish; Jews and Germans in the cities and towns; and Russian, German, or Austrian agents of empire. That some areas where peasants and workers spoke Polish had not been part of the Polish crownlands only strengthened a linguistic over a historical definition of nationality. In the late nineteenth century, linguistic (ethnic) nationalism could unite elites and masses in central Poland: it was no source of shame to use a language the people could understand, and that language was already codified and rich. Indeed, in central Poland the preservation of Polish culture became the first priority of patriots; and Polish language, Roman Catholic religion, and familiarity with Romantic poetry became markers of Polish nationality.[19] Whereas the Polish patriotism of Wilno was located in elite families who referred to the historical statehood of the Grand Duchy of Lithuania, the Polish nationalism of the crownlands—the National Democratic movement of Roman Dmowski (1864–1939)—was concerned with preparing Polish peasants and workers for a modern national state.

Dmowski and Piłsudski represented different sorts of Polishness and imagined different sorts of Polands. Piłsudski's socialist federalism was an exemplary reaction of Lithuanian Poles to modern politics. His conspiratorial socialist agitation in the Russian empire flowed naturally from the eastern Polish self-image as cultured elite with superior knowledge of the order of things. The 1892 program of his Polish Socialist Party (PPS) envisioned a federation. This socialist federalism, a halfway house between early modern patriotism and modern mass politics, can be distinguished from Dmowski's National Democracy in three ways. First, it was inherited tradition rather than invented history. Elite families who wished to restore the Grand Duchy were operating within generationally continuous conceptions of nationality. Second, socialist federalism was advanced not by enlightening the masses but by conspiring with trusted comrades. National issues were hotly disputed within Piłsudski's PPS, but until the party split in 1905 the party leadership never considered following the masses rather than leading them. Third, socialist federalism presumed that the nation was not a linguistic but a status group. The point was not to imagine that everyone on a given territory was of the same ethnic group and therefore deserved a national state, but to recognize differences and channel them within a republican idea of Polish citizenship. Sons and daughters of eastern Polish gentry families, confident of their superiority to local Lithuanian or Belarusian peasants and Jews, could believe that such a republic would be Polish in culture. Such people were quite numerous in the conspiratorial politics of imperial Russia before 1914, and there is reason to think that Polish gentry in the Wilno region voted for the federalist Left in democratic Poland after 1918.[20]

Dmowski, a stonecutter's son from a central Polish backwater, drew different political conclusions from a different historical situation. Whereas Piłsudski envisioned a Polish political nation floating above the multinational borderlands he called home, Dmowski saw a Polish folk nation in fierce competition with wily Jews and disciplined Germans. From the putative folk nation he drew the criteria by which Poles could be distinguished from others: language and religion. Dmowski added fashionable Social Darwinian arguments as to why such groups must consolidate around such features and defend themselves from others. Whereas Piłsudski was nostalgic, Dmowski called himself "a modern Pole." Dmowski openly sought to destroy the legacy of the Polish-Lithuanian Commonwealth, and replace it with a modern Polish identity. Although Piłsudski was the socialist, Dmowski was more concerned with social change and with the ideological content of mass politics. Before the First World War, Dmowski's social achievements were less dramatic than the spectacular coups of Piłsudski and his socialists, but did more to determine the content of Polish nationality. Dmowski's definition of Polishness was all but hegemonic by 1914, and his National Democratic movement the most important in Polish lands.[21] It was his party that won the most votes in Poland as a whole in elections held after 1918.

Piłsudski's and Dmowski's ideas mattered not simply in the long run of social history, but at crucial moments when it might seem, at first glance, that only military force decided the course of events. At the end of the First World War, Wilno was the scene of three overlapping contests: (1) between representatives of these two ideas of Polishness; (2) among believers in internationalist, multinationalist, and modern nationalist definitions of "Lithuania"; (3) among Bolshevik, Polish, Lithuanian, and Belarusian activists for physical control of the city. By 1918, all the groups mentioned thus far—internationalist children of the Grand Duchy (Slavs, Jews, and Balts alike) who became Bolsheviks, loyal children of the Grand Duchy who became Polish or Belarusian socialist federalists, Lithuanian national activists, and Polish modern nationalists—had firm ideas about the proper form of state organization and the proper arrangement of state borders. The Bolsheviks expected communism to embrace Vil'na; Polish and Belarusian socialist federalists agreed that Wilno/Vil'nia would be a capital of a multinational state; Polish and Lithuanian nationalists agreed that Wilno/Vilnius would be included within a nation-state (while disagreeing about which one). As we shall see, federalism was more demanding than nationalism or internationalism. Federalist solutions required well-chosen borders, compromises among local elites, and the consent of the governed. They were inherently more complex than the annexation of Wilno by either Bolshevik Russia or a national state.

Polish and Lithuanian nationalists proved correct that Wilno/Vilnius would be annexed by a national state, with the Polish nationalists right about which national state this would be. The prophets and victors, Polish nationalists, were far from the strongest group. Locally, they may have been the weakest. Unlike

Lithuanian nationalists and Belarusian federalists, they did not even expect mass support in the lands of the Grand Duchy of Lithuania. Unlike the Bolsheviks and the Polish federalists, they never fielded armies that occupied Wilno. Unlike every other single group (including the Bolsheviks), they made no reference to the legacy of the Grand Duchy of Lithuania. The triumph of both their preferred idea of the state and their preferred arrangement of borders reveals the advantages of modern nationalist ideas at moments of imperial collapse. Piłsudski had material advantages, but was trapped by inherent complications of the federalist project. When other parties rejected a federation, Piłsudski found himself with no choice but to throw his forces behind what was effectively Dmowski's policy. This was not so much a victory for Poland, as for one vision of Poland. It was not so much an example of postwar self-determination, as the triumph of modern nationalism over the traditional multinational patriotism of the Grand Duchy of Lithuania (and in some measure over the internationalism of the Bolsheviks).

By 1918, Mickiewicz's poetry, the fruit of nostalgia for the Grand Duchy of Lithuania, had entered the canons of modern Polish and modern Lithuanian nationalism. In 1920, Piłsudski's federalism, the hope to revive the Grand Duchy of Lithuania, motivated the soldiers who took Wilno and brought it within the borders of a Polish national state. Let us retreat from the realm of irony to the world of war, to see how this happened.

THE FIRST WORLD WAR AND THE
POLISH-BOLSHEVIK WAR

The Bolshevik Revolution of November 1917 and the end of the First World War in November 1918 created a very confusing situation in Russia's Northwest Territory, the former Grand Duchy of Lithuania. The German army would submit in the West to Britain, France, and the United States, but it was undefeated in the East. Meanwhile Soviet Red and Russian White Armies battled each other, and local politicians in historic Lithuania declared national independence and tried to raise armies of their own. The Entente powers' support for self-determination provided the normative basis for Polish independence, but Western states lacked the military power to determine or enforce outcomes in the East. German troops withdrew fitfully, and in many cases found reasons to stay and fight the Bolsheviks.[22]

Lithuanian and Belarusian activists hoped to use the presence of German troops as cover for the creation of their own new states before the Bolsheviks arrived. The Belarusian claim to Vil'nia was the first to fail. The Belarusian National Council, led by Anton Lutskevich (1884–1946), had proclaimed Vil'nia part of an independent Belarus in March 1918. The Belarus they had in mind was to be multinational, and their territorial claims were combined with a statement on toleration. Lutskevich wished to recreate the old Grand Duchy of Lithuania as a modern socialist federation stretching from the Baltic to the Black Sea. The declaration was made under German occupation, although it enjoyed no German support. In any event Lutskevich and most of the Council fled Minsk before the arrival of the Red Army in December 1918. In Vil'nia, they proposed a Belarusian-Lithuanian confederation. Belarusian socialists believed that federation would save Vil'nia from a "clerical bourgeois" Lithuanian national state.[23] Lithuanian leaders, in dire straits themselves by this time, were uninterested in that form of salvation. Thus ended, for the time being, the project to re-create historic Lithuania under the name Belarus. From this failure came a quiet success. Although the Bolshevik Party was centralized, it promised a Belorussian Soviet Socialist Republic to the Belarusian activists who stayed in Minsk.[24] Although initially but a sliver of territory around Minsk, the Belorussian SSR would expand enormously after the establishment of the Soviet Union in 1922, and survive for seventy years.

The Bolshevik Revolution had removed loyalism to Russia from Lithuanian political life, and the experience of war had clarified the goals of Lithuanian nationalists. The war's final year had whetted appetites for full independence. In September 1917, a Lithuanian national council (*Taryba*) enjoying the protection of the German army declared in Vilnius the necessity for an independent Lithuanian state "within ethnographic frontiers." Having endorsed the proclamation of a Kingdom of Poland, the Germans wished to prevent Polish claims to Wilno and Lithuania. Lithuanian activists were perfectly aware of such German strategic considerations, and sought to make the most of them.[25] On 11 December 1917, the *Taryba* declared independence in Vilnius, at the same time accepting the status of a German protectorate. Lithuanian activists watched anxiously as German and Bolshevik negotiators at Brest-Litovsk both used arguments of self-determination to secure their own claims to Lithuania. In February 1918 the *Taryba* once again declared independence, this time without the pledge of loyalty to Germany. Berlin paid little attention, as its troops advanced deep into Russia. It was German defeat in the West that allowed the *Taryba* in October 1918 to plot a new course.[26] There was no time for celebration. The Red Army began a quick advance. Hasty negotiations for Polish troops to protect Lithuania broke down in December 1918. The Lithuanian government, having failed to raise an army, evacuated exposed Vilnius for more westerly Kaunas. Local Polish volunteers were no match for the Red Army, which took the city on 5 January 1919. Vilnius then became the capital of the Lithuanian Soviet Socialist Republic, led by two Lithuanian communists. This creation was shortly merged with the new Belorussian Soviet Socialist Republic, and Vilnius became the capital of the "LitBel" Soviet Socialist Republic. For Piłsudski, Lithuanian patriot, Polish federalist, and republican socialist, this was the worst possible outcome. In Warsaw, he wept.[27]

Yet neither in Warsaw nor in Kaunas was this outcome seen as final. In early 1919, the presence or absence of military forces little affected how Lithuanians and Poles thought about Vilnius/Wilno. Lithuanian leaders saw Vilnius as their national capital, and from a position of extreme weakness they demanded that Poland renounce its claims. Piłsudski, now Polish head of state, was prepared to grant Wilno to the Lithuanians, on the condition that Lithuania join Poland in a federation. The idea of joining a Polish state was anathema to Lithuanian politicians, who feared Polish high culture and numerical predominance, and by now desired full independence.[28] These fears and aspirations were not fully grasped by Piłsudski and Polish federalists, although theirs was more liberal than the other Polish position. Their rivals in Poland, Dmowski's National Democrats, assumed that tiny Lithuania (if it survived at all) had no choice but to become a Polish satellite.[29] Polish and Lithuanian nationalists were in accord on the main issue: that the Polish-Lithuanian Commonwealth was dead, that no multinational federation could arise.

The practical issue of Bolshevik power was seen within the framework of such moral imperatives. In February 1919 Polish troops marched east to engage the Red Army. The Polish parliament was divided as to the territorial aims of the undeclared war, but could proclaim that "the northeast provinces of Poland with their capital in Wilno" should be liberated.[30] Piłsudski's army drove the Red Army from Wilno on 21 April 1919. Lithuanian and Belarusian communists fled to Minsk, blaming each other for the fall of the "LitBel" SSR. Before the attack, Piłsudski had sent fellow Polish Lithuanian Michał Römer to Kaunas to try to form a Polish-Lithuanian government, but no Lithuanian minister had been interested. On 22 April, Wilno heard Piłsudski promise, in his "Proclamation to the Inhabitants of the Former Grand Duchy of Lithuania," that the local population would be allowed to choose its own government. Polish and Lithuanian nationalists both condemned the oration. In Warsaw, Polish National Democrats thought it absurd to treat Wilno as anything but a Polish city;

in Kaunas, the Lithuanian government treated Piłsudski's appeal to the Grand Duchy as a facade for Polish imperialism.

During summer 1919, as the Entente powers tried to decide on a final territorial dispensation in Paris, Polish and Lithuanian troops fought a series of inconclusive skirmishes. In August 1919 Piłsudski proposed two plebiscites, one in the lands occupied by Polish troops, and another in the rest of Lithuania. Lithuanian leaders rejected this proposal on the grounds that Vilnius was Lithuanian ethnic territory regardless of the expressed opinions of its inhabitants. Foreign Minister Augustinas Voldemaras believed that "a nation is composed more of the dead than the living," which presumably raised practical problems in terms of counting votes.[31] Piłsudski then tried in August 1919 to overthrow the Lithuanian government in Kaunas, but his plotters found no Lithuanian collaborators and soon found themselves under arrest. If there had been any supporters of alliance with Poland among leading Lithuanians, this fiasco would have silenced them.

In winter 1919–20, Piłsudski believed that Russia could be defeated on the battlefield, and that the Wilno question would then answer itself. In April 1920, Piłsudski's Poland in alliance with Symon Petliura's Ukraine mounted an offensive against Bolshevik Russia; Bolshevik-Lithuanian treaty negotiations opened at about the same time. By the time Lithuania and Bolshevik Russia were ready to sign their bilateral treaty, in July 1920, the tide of battle had turned against Poland. Anticipating the coup de grâce, Bolshevik Russia offered Vilnius to Lithuania, in return for free passage of the Red Army through Lithuania into Poland. Lithuania agreed to attach a secret protocol to this effect to the Treaty of Moscow of 12 July 1920; and the Red Army quickly occupied Vilnius, later turning it over to Lithuania. Then, in August 1920, the Polish Army reversed the Red Army's advance at the edge of Warsaw, and drove the Red Army from Poland.[32] Had the Poles been defeated in summer 1920, Bolshevik Russia would have certainly absorbed the tiny Lithuanian state. The Lithuanian government, preoccupied with Poland, believed that a Bolshevik victory would both preserve Lithuanian independence and grant Vilnius to Lithuania. This was surely mistaken.[33]

As Polish and Bolshevik delegations began to talk peace at Riga in September 1920, the Entente powers pressed Poland and Lithuania to resolve their differences. The two sides reached a political agreement on 7 October 1920, providing for an armistice line that left Vilnius on the Lithuanian side. In secret, Piłsudski had already planned the military operation which would return

Wilno to Poland and revive hope for a renewed Grand Duchy of Lithuania. He entrusted the mission to General Lucjan Żeligowski (1865–1947), another Polish Lithuanian. Żeligowski was a former officer in the Russian army, husband to a Russian wife, speaker of a form of Polish we would hear as Belarusian: a child, in other words, of the Grand Duchy. In Piłsudski's address to the other officers of the "Lithuanian-Belarusian" division on their way to Wilno we can hear the appeal to a very local patriotism: "You're from these parts, you've been armed, so go on home."[34] On 9 October 1920 Żeligowski marched about 15,000 troops into Wilno. The Lithuanian army offered no resistance, and the city's Polish population welcomed the troops. On 12 October Żeligowski proclaimed "Central Lithuania," which was to be one canton of a Lithuania joined to Poland in a federation.

The other two cantons were to be an ethnic Lithuania with a capital in Kaunas, and a Belarusian Lithuania with a capital in Minsk. The idea of a Lithuania of cantons attached to Poland in a federation did not arise from the moment. It had been proposed during the uprising of 1863, and was discussed for decades by socialists. In the context of 1920, however, it was impossible to implement. A revived and federated Grand Duchy of Lithuania required at the very least all three cantons, and Żeligowski and Piłsudski could create only one. The Lithuanian government in Kaunas, of course, had no wish to be cantonized; and an invasion of Kaunas would not only have violated the spirit of federalism, it would have provoked the European powers. The Polish National Democrats made sure that no Belaruso-Lithuanian canton ever arose. The very day Żeligowski proclaimed "Central Lithuania," the Polish delegation at Riga declined the Bolshevik offer of Minsk and other lands then occupied by the Polish army. Everyone understood that this doomed the federalist program. This Polish delegation was dominated by the National Democrat Stanisław Grabski (1871–1949), who wished to create a Poland in which Poles could predominate. He overcame the federalist line represented by Piłsudski's ally Leon Wasilewski.[35] The delegation represented the democratic Polish government and constituent assembly, and not Piłsudski, the head of the Polish state. Behind Piłsudski stood the army and its officer corps, but behind Grabski stood the assembly, dominated by National Democrats.

The idea of a federation was doomed by the reinforcing refusals of Polish National Democrats in Warsaw and the Lithuanian government in Kaunas, who prevented the Belarusian and ethnic Lithuanian cantons from arising. This was a silent alliance of modern nationalists to create new national states, and to bury the early modern traditions of the Polish-Lithuanian Commonwealth. Lithuania, to avoid any ambiguity, had formally renounced the 1569 Lublin Union.

NATIONAL CONSEQUENCES OF
RIGA, 1921–1939

Belarus. Belarusian activists regarded the Riga settlement as treason and tragedy. Although other blows would follow, after Riga it was hard to see Warsaw as an ally of Belarusian aspirations. Although the Polish state kept Wilno and some west Belarusian territories, this was not enough to make the idea of a federation credible. The Riga borders left the Belarusian-speaking minority in Poland small and rural, as the National Democrats intended. Without Minsk, the Belarusian intelligentsia was too small to serve as an ally for any Polish political formation; once Minsk became Soviet, Belarusian national aspirations within Poland were seen as crypto-Bolshevism.[36] The Soviet Union did indeed exert a powerful attraction on Polish Belarusians. After the Riga settlement of 1921, the Soviet Union was established as a nominal federation of republics in 1922. One of these was a Belorussian Soviet Socialist Republic (SSR) with a capital in Minsk. Soviet policy, enforced on the Communist International, was that the Belorussian SSR should be extended westward to include ethnically Belorussian lands within Poland.

In the 1920s, the communism exported to Poland exploited antistate nationalism as well as peasant land hunger. In these early years of the Soviet Union, two of Lenin's tactical innovations—the alliance with the peasantry and the exploitation of national self-determination—were used to foment revolution in Poland. Agitation abroad was supported by action at home. The ethnic principle, the basis for the revanchism of the Belarussian SSR and the Communist Party of Western Belorussia established in Poland, was actually implemented within the Soviet Union. In 1923, 1924, and 1926 the territory of the Belorussian SSR was extended to the east at the expense of the Russian republic. In the 1920s Moscow supported Belarusian culture. While there had been no schools teaching in Belarusian in tsarist times, Soviet Belorussia in the 1920s boasted an Academy of Sciences, a State University, an Institute of Belarusian Culture, a Belarusian State Library, and four thousand Belarusian schools. It was in Soviet Belorussia that the first serious textbook of Belarusian history was written: but it was not published, and its author was exiled to Moscow.[37]

Polish policy remained repressive throughout the 1920s and 1930s, closing all remaining Belarusian schools and jailing opponents. The Belarusian movement stagnated in Vil'nia. Belarusian activists had little opportunity to speed modern national ideas beyond Vil'nia to proverbially backward regions such as Polesie. Polish policy never allowed for the creation of a Belorussian national society. Stalin's Soviet Union, on the other hand, destroyed during the 1930s the Soviet Belarusian society that had arisen in the 1920s. The contrast is well seen in the fate of the Belarusian politician and writer Branislau Tarashkevich (1892–1938). Tarashkevich, who was born near Vil'nia and educated in the city, in his youth took part in both Polish and Belarusian organizations in the Russian empire. In interwar Poland, he was a prominent advocate of the Belarusian cause, as a deputy in Parliament, as a director of Belarusian schools, and as founder and head of the peasant organization Hromada. He joined the Communist Party of Western Belorussia in 1925, and was imprisoned in Poland. In his prison cells, over the course of four years, Tarashkevich translated the entirety of *Pan Tadeusz*. He took the manuscript with him to the Soviet Union after a prisoner exchange of 1933. He could not publish it there. Indeed, he was not allowed to reside in Soviet Belorussia. He was arrested in Moscow in 1937, and

Fig. 3. The Prypiet Marshes, near Pińsk, Polesie region, Poland, 1934. Today in Belarus. These are the territories where people proverbially had difficulty ascertaining the nationality of the locals.

Fig. 4. Two old men of Chodynicze,
Polesie, Poland, 1934.

Fig. 5. A wanderer between Ratno and
Kobryń, Poland, 1934. The former is
today in Ukraine, the latter in
Belarus. At the time, the
photographer was in the middle of
marshy Polesie, Poland.

executed in 1938. Thanks to his widow, the manuscript of his translation survived.[38]

Poland. The Treaty of Riga, the partition of Belarus, and the violent seizure of Wilno marked a defeat of Mickiewicz's idea of the Grand Duchy in Polish political life. Piłsudski, representative of this federalist tradition, was ultimately defeated by Dmowski, advocate of integral nationalism. The National Democrats triumphed in foreign relations, as in domestic politics, because their approach was simple. They also enjoyed a basic advantage of political geography. The constituent assembly elected in February 1920 represented central Poland, since what became eastern Poland was at the time occupied by the Red Army. It was therefore disproportionately National Democratic, and thus disinclined to absorb enough eastern lands to create a federation. Its support of the Riga settlement created a Poland which was too westerly to be a federation, but not westerly enough to remain a national state. The National Democrats' gift of Minsk, Kamieniec Podolski, Berdyczów and surrounding lands to the Bolsheviks at Riga in 1921 left hundreds of thousands of Poles, many of them friendly to the idea of a federal Polish-Lithuanian-Belarusian state, in the tender care of Moscow. Most Soviet Poles would be deported to Siberia or Kazakhstan in the 1930s. The National Democrats' renunciation also reduced Poland's potential East Slavic populations by perhaps two million and potential Jewish populations by hundreds of thousands.[39] The National Democrats knew what they were doing. Had Poland's borders stretched any further to the east, the party would never have won an election. As the 1922 parliamentary elections demonstrated, Poland in its Riga frontiers was evenly split between the National Democrats and the Right, on the one side, and socialists and national minorities on the other. On 9 December 1922 the votes of the Left, the Center, and the national minorities elected Poland's first president, Gabriel Narutowicz. He was assassinated one week later by a right-wing fanatic. Like Piłsudski, Narutowicz was a Pole of Lithuanian descent who favored equal rights for the national minorities. The assassination of Narutowicz was a heavy blow to Piłsudski, who soon withdrew (for the time being) from politics.

Piłsudski's incomplete success in Wilno collapsed ineluctably into the National Democratic vision of Poland. With Piłsudski's idea of a reborn Grand Duchy of Lithuania buried by Polish and Lithuanian nationalists, Wilno was absorbed by a Polish national state. The civilian authority installed in Wilno by Żeligowski held elections to a local parliament on 8 January 1923. These were carried out under military rule by Poles, boycotted by the Jewish, Belarusian, and Lithuanian populations, and marred by various irregularities. Nevertheless, the 54.4 percent participation in Wilno city was a powerful political message, and the boycotts by non-Poles meant that Polish annexationists dominated the local assembly. In retrospect, it may appear that Poland annexed Wilno because Wilno was an "ethnically" Polish city. It was rather the other way around: the annexation of Wilno was the first step toward the elimination of traditional patriotism and the sharpening of Polish and Lithuanian ethnic nationalism. After the referendum, Poland annexed Wilno and surrounding territories, and the Entente powers recognized these frontiers.

Lithuania. How might Lithuanian nationalism have developed if Poland had granted Vilnius/Wilno to Lithuania? Piłsudski and Żeligowski, like many of the Polish-speaking residents of Wilno who voted for annexation, called themselves Lithuanians. The difference between Piłsudski's faith in a historical vision of Lithuania and Dmowski's desire to annex a "Polish" city is real and important, reflecting Piłsudski's traditional patriotism and Dmowski's ethnic nationalism. Nevertheless, by occupying Wilno, Piłsudski solidified a territorial order in which Polish and Lithuanian nationalists could flourish—a point made by his former comrade-in-arms, the Polish Lithuanian Michał Römer. Regardless of Piłsudski's motives, the seizure of the city could not be seen by Lithuanians as consistent with the traditions of the Grand Duchy. As we have seen, the link between Lithuania and Vilnius was historical. Whatever Piłsudski thought he was doing, taking the city by force of arms was bound to drive Lithuanian nationalists away from a political and toward an ethnic understanding of the nation. Moreover, and as Römer also pointed out, the annexation of Vilnius deprived the new Lithuanian state of the very people, Polish Lithuanians and Jews, who might have rendered its society more prosperous and its polity more practical. As Römer knew, Jews had been generally sympathetic to the Lithuanian claim, believing that a large multinational Lithuania with Vilne as its capital would be more likely to respect their rights. Their reward in 1919 had been the first pogroms in modern Vilne.[40]

Whatever their borders, any national states on the territory of the Grand Duchy would have forced choices on individuals. After 1920, secular Jews drew the conclusion that only a distinct Jewish political life could serve their interests in a Polish Wilno. Having declared their loyalty to a national state, Christian elites were confirmed in the corresponding national identity by the problems of a given national society, the milieux in which they functioned, and the availability of state power. Most Polish Lithuanians went one way or the other. Römer himself, once Piłsudski's comrade, then his envoy, and finally his critic, chose Lithuania for good in 1920, Lithuanizing his name to Römer'is. He served the state and the society well as a judge, professor of law, and rector of the University of Kaunas; and consistently opposed radical nationalism and worked for reconciliation with Poland. Other choices were equally dramatic. Gabriel Narutowicz, the assassinated first president of Poland, was the brother of Stanislavas Narutavičius, a member of the presidium of the Lithuanian *Taryba* and of the first Lithuanian government.

"Lithuania! My fatherland!"

Unlike other Polish Lithuanians, Piłsudski never quite chose between Poland and Lithuania after the First World War, never quite accepted that the world was composed of national states populated by citizens of the appropriate ethnicity. Having seized Wilno and ensured poor relations with the Lithuanians for at least a generation, Piłsudski said that he "could not help but regard them as brothers." Having realized the impracticality of federalism, he could not accept nationalism. His republican beliefs were not shared by most of his fellow Poles, and in the end he relied upon military force and personal charisma to keep majority views at bay. Having achieved power by military coup in 1926, Piłsudski neither trusted Polish citizens to replace him nor imagined absolute rule for himself. For nine years Piłsudski governed a Poland which he found disappointing and alien. When he died in 1935, he was buried in Wawel Castle in Cracow, in the company of Poland's kings, including the Lithuanian Jogailas. His heart was cut from his chest and buried in the Rossa cemetery in Wilno, in the family plot, next to his mother's grave.

"You are like health. Only he who has lost you may know your true worth."

Piłsudski had lost Lithuania, as he well knew, in the sense conveyed by Mickiewicz. If anything is more suggestive of the rupture between historical Lithuania and modern Poland than the separation of Piłsudski's heart from his body, it is the lack of a monument to Mickiewicz in Wilno in Piłsudski's Poland.[41] Mickiewicz was present in monumental form in Polish cities where he had never set foot, such as Warsaw and Cracow, but the city where the poet was educated and whence he was exiled failed to honor him in any permanent way. Under the tsars it had not been permitted, since the significance of Mickiewicz was then all too clear: an enduring Polish civilization in East Slavic lands, a Roman Catholic culture that continued to draw converts, a rival conception of the nation that Russian force and Russian education had not eradicated. In independent Poland, however, Wilno Poles found that they could not agree about

Fig. 6. Burial of the heart of Józef Piłsudski (1867–1935), Polish revolutionary and statesman of Lithuanian heritage, in Wilno (today Vilnius) on 12 May 1936.

what Mickiewicz meant and how he should be represented. Wilno was won by bullets and ballots: what place then for the poems and the prophecies?

"As butterflies drown in golden amber . . ."

In Wilno as throughout interwar Poland, the appealing obduracy of modern nationalism fossilized Romantic images, but could not grant them life. Nothing illustrates this better than Polish attempts to build a monument to Mickiewicz after the seizure of Wilno. General Żeligowski convened a committee to build a monument, but failed to gain support for any project. The local garrison of the Polish army then took the initiative to build a statue on its barracks, across the River Wilia and beyond the jurisdiction of municipal authorities. The soldiers accepted a hulking formalist design by the avant garde artist Zbigniew Pronaszko. Its wooden substructure, once unveiled, was mocked by the city's residents. The leading newspaper complained that the greatest Pole of all time was presented as a "gray wraith."[42] The model, four stories tall, was never set in concrete. Struck by lightening in summer 1939, its pieces rolled down the hill, beyond the grounds of the army base, and into the river. Pronaszko's design had been inspired by a verse of Mickiewicz's great rival, Juliusz Słowacki, comparing Mickiewicz to a Lithuanian god. The monument shared the fate of the idols of pagan Lithuania after the conversion to Christianity.

By 1939, another monument to Mickiewicz in Wilno was under construction. After the army unveiled its project, the city continued its search for more graceful alternatives. Henryk Kuna, the Polish-Jewish sculptor chosen for the municipal monument, was completing the granite bas-reliefs that summer. His unfinished work was hit by a German bomb that September. If there could be a more suggestive destruction of monument than by lightning in July 1939, it was by blitzkrieg in September 1939. Poland was invaded and divided by Nazi Germany and the Soviet Union that month. Stalin granted Wilno to Lithuania in 1939, then incorporated Lithuania into the Soviet Union in 1940. Then Nazi Germany invaded the Soviet Union in 1941, and exterminated Wilno's Jews in 1941–44. Under Nazi occupation, the granite slabs remaining from Kuna's monument were used to widen the main pathway of a cemetery.[43] The Red Army returned in 1944, and Soviet rule was reestablished in Lithuania. Between 1944 and 1946, Wilno Poles were deported.

"Let us remain, dear, as we once were."

In Soviet Lithuania, these granite slabs were (it seems) raised from the cemetery and given to the local art academy. Surely the country was Russified, the art catalogued, and the poet forgotten? Far from becoming a Russian Vil'na, the city became a Lithuanian Vilnius. Far from disappearing from view, Mickiewicz became a Lithuanian national poet. In 1984, in Soviet Lithuania, Lithuanians succeeded where Poles had failed: a statue of Mickiewicz (or rather Mickevičius) by Gediminas Jokubonis was unveiled in Vilnius. In 1996, in independent Lithuania, some of the original granite slabs were incorporated into the setting of this new monument. From Polish monument, to rubble, to cemetery pathway, to artistic fragments, to Lithuanian monument: this is chaos ordered by a Romantic cast of mind, indeed the Romantic idea of national resurrection improbably enacted in public art and political life. Lithuanians gained Vilnius during the Second World War, Lithuanized its public life under Soviet rule, reclaimed the great poet from the Poles, and in the end won national independence. How this came to pass is the subject of the next two chapters.

Chapter 4 The Second World War and the Vilnius Question (1939–1945)

Kuszelowo, Świteź, Ponary, Białowieża!
Forest friends to grand dukes of Lithuania!
Your shade once cooled the fearsome crowns
Of the dread Vytenis, of the great Mindaug.
And of Gediminas, who on Ponary's crest,
Warm in hunter's bearskin, lay down to rest.
Soothed by the songs of the wise Lizdejko,
Lulled by the rush of the sweet Vilejko,
He saw a wolf of iron in his dreams.
At the gods' clear command it seems
He built the city of Wilno in the forest
A brooding Wolf midst bisons, bears and boars.
From Wilno, as from the she-wolf of Rome,
Came Kęstutis, Algirdas, and Algirdas's sons.
Great hunters were they, and famous knights,
Whether chasing a foe, or a beast in flight.
The hunter's dream must be understood:
Lithuania needs her iron, and her woods.
—Adam Mickiewicz, *Pan Tadeusz* (Paris, 1834)

> To Israel, our elder brother: respect, fraternity,
> Help along the road to his earthly and eternal welfare.
> Equal rights.
> —Adam Mickiewicz, "A Set of Principles" (1848)

In September 1939, when Nazi Germany and the Soviet Union invaded Poland, Wilno was in a profound sense a Jewish city: Vilne. Vilne Jews were characterized by many of the traits local Christian patriots wished their groups to manifest. They were more distinguishable as a group than Belarusians, Lithuanians, or even Poles. Although outnumbered by Poles in Vilne, Jews were reckoned a third of the city's population. They also counted generations of settlement in the city itself, and centuries of recorded history in the region. Older Jews spoke Russian rather than Polish, a legacy of the Russian empire. Yet in general the literacy and historical sense of Jews was the envy of national activists from all sides. Most Jewish children were educated in Yiddish or Hebrew. Vilne remained a center of Jewish cultural life on an international scale. Jews separated by the Polish-Soviet border from Kiev and Odessa studied in Vilne, thereby restoring to the city some of the status it had enjoyed under the Commonwealth. YIVO, the Institute for Jewish Research, was founded in Vilne in 1925. Outstanding poets of Yiddish such as Abraham Sutzkever (1913–) comprised the *Yung Vilne* circle. As this suggests, educated Jews in interwar Vilne were engaged in not one but three competing "national revivals": the dispersion of Jewish folk culture in Yiddish within Poland; the spread of literacy in Hebrew in anticipation for the move to Palestine; and the attempt to master the state language and assimilate into Polish life.

Jews of all ages, and especially Jewish youth, were far more politicized than other inhabitants of the city. Lacking both gentry and peasantry, Jews avoided the class conflicts and status complexes that hounded other political groups of interwar Poland as they tried to apply unifying mass ideologies. On the other hand, Jews disagreed about whether Poland or Palestine was the proper theater of politics, and whether or to what extent religious believers could take part in politics at all. Jewish political life within the city was, if possible, even more fragmented than Polish. Although this energy and fragmentation reflected the social isolation and precarious position of Jews within a Polish city, Jewish life presented an imposing achievement. Just as the continuities of the Jewish culture exceeded even the most creative feats of national historians, so the plunge into modernity of Jewish politics in the twentieth century outshone the best efforts of any Christian nationality. That Vilne was the Jerusalem of Lithuania,

Fig. 7. Plac Ratuszowy in Wilno (Vilnius).

or indeed the Jerusalem of the North, required no special effort to ascertain. It was one of the capitals of a second Europe, a Yiddish-speaking Ashkenaze Jewish civilization, a particular unity following its own logic of development until 1941.[1]

There was another Wilno, a Polish city. Along with Warsaw, Lwów, and Cracow, Wilno was one of four centers of Polish civilization. In Wilno in 1939, Polish was the language of power and of culture, of most neighborhoods and most homes, and increasingly of the countryside. Józef Piłsudski had revived Adam Mickiewicz's Wilno University in 1919, exactly one century after the poet's graduation. As between 1803 and 1830, between 1919 and 1939 Wilno University provided higher education in Polish to Poles, Russians, Belarusians, and Lithuanians. This time it also accepted and sometimes acculturated Jews. Migration and Polish state power ensured that a majority of Wilno's 220,000 or so residents self-identified as Polish. Some of those calling themselves Poles were Jews who treated Polish identity as a matter of loyalty to the republic, affection for Polish culture, or simple self-interest; a larger number had been born to families that spoke Belarusian, and had learned Polish in school, in the army, or as adults (if at all). The Jews excepted, there was no national rival to Poland within the city. National tension in Wilno was mainly a matter of the Polish state, and Polish institutions, constraining the freedoms of Jews after Piłsudski's death in 1935. Polish rule was not necessarily popular among Jews and other minorities, but it was the order of the day and seen as such until the Polish state was destroyed in 1939.

Fig. 8. A peasant woman at a market in Wilno (Vilnius), interwar. Wilno was the central concern of those who laid claim to the heritage of Lithuania, all of whom imagined that peasants would finally choose a language and a nation.

Fig. 9. A Polish mansion in historic Lithuania (Łunna Wola, today Lunna, Belarus). In the sixteenth, seventeenth, eighteenth, and nineteenth centuries, social advance in historic Lithuania involved Polish culture.

By comparison, the Lithuanian and Belarusian presence in interwar Vilnius was negligible.[2] Jonas Basanavičius, the founder of *Aušra*, led a Scholarly Society in Vilnius until his death in 1927. The city's Roman Catholic bishop between 1918 and 1925 was a Lithuanian, Jurgis Matulaitis. All the same, there were simply too few Lithuanians in the city to sustain much in the way of visible culture. Vil'nia was the center of Belarusian life in Poland, but this was only a relative distinction. Polish local authorities gnawed at the foundations of Belarusian society, refusing to deliver telegrams in Belarusian, confiscating Belarusian newspapers, and closing Belarusian schools. Belarusian culture was permitted, if not supported, for a time. Vil'nia was the center of Belarusian literature in Poland, and for practical reasons Orthodox and Catholic churchmen alike began to use the Belarusian language. The Uniate Church, revived in Poland after having been liquidated in the Russian empire, was now seen as a possible Belarusian national institution. The Jesuits, so important in the replacement of Chancery Slavonic with Polish in the early seventeenth century, found it convenient to use Belarusian in the 1920s. As we have seen, a factor in the emergence of early modern Polish nationality in the Catholic-Orthodox borderlands was the adoption of Polish as the vernacular by the Jesuits and the Uniate Church. The emergence of Belarusian as a vernacular useful to modern churchmen hinted at the beginnings of the possibility of a modern Belarusian nation.[3]

Vilnius lived a separate diplomatic life. Lithuania and Poland remained officially at war over Vilnius/Wilno between 1920 and 1938. Lithuanians in interwar Lithuania were isolated from their nominal capital. The Lithuanian government had cut phone and rail lines when it had left for Kaunas, and the prevailing state of war precluded much human contact (although of course some people had both passports).[4] The nationalizing project of the Lithuanian state treated Vilnius as an object of immediate political concern, while mystifying its history and demography. The army played an important role in the education of young men, and male illiteracy fell from 15 percent to 1 percent on its curricular diet of nationalist history. For two decades Lithuanian schoolchildren learned that Vilnius was ethnically Lithuanian.[5] They read Mickiewicz's *Pan Tadeusz* in school in an abridged translation which expunged all references to Poland and to Poles.[6] Ancient legends Mickiewicz had helped sustain, such as Gediminas's dream of the iron wolf, found modern political life in independent Lithuania. The Iron Wolf was a conspiratorial fascist organization, banned in 1930. The Union for the Liberation of Vilnius, the Vilnius Foundation, and the newspaper *Our Vilnius* were pillars of Lithuanian civil society. October 9, the day Żeligowski took Vilnius in 1920, was a day of national mourning. Throughout the interwar period, the Vilnius question played an extraordinary role in Lithuanian domestic politics, as rivals attacked each other for being too soft on the Poles or too yielding to the League of Nations.

In international fora, Lithuanian leaders announced that Poland was the greatest danger to peace in Europe. Prime Minister Augustinas Voldemaras, following his self-proclaimed principle that "the enemy of my enemy is my friend," counted on Soviet antagonism to Poland to bring Vilnius to Lithuania. The legal foundation of the Lithuanian claim to Vilnius was a treaty signed with Bolshevik Russia in 1920. The 1926 nonaggression pact with the Soviet Union was attractive in part because the Soviets recognized the Lithuanian claim to Vilnius. In 1927 Voldemaras refused the request of British, French, and Italian envoys that Lithuania establish diplomatic relations with Poland. Later that year Voldemaras assured his Latvian counterpart that Poland was a greater threat than Germany and the Soviet Union, and in 1928 told British Foreign Secretary Austin Chamberlain that while the Soviet threat was "purely theoretical" the Polish threat was "entirely real."[7] This Lithuanian position, incidentally, was not based upon strategic miscalculation. Lithuanian leaders believed that their culture, and therefore their nationhood, was under threat from Poland. They felt no such threat from Russia. Despite appearances, this was a reasonable view. Lithuanian culture had never won a contest with Polish culture; it would never lose one with Russian.

When Voldemaras later made peace overtures to Warsaw, he found that public opinion and the Lithuanian army were keen to prevent concessions.[8] This problem visited the authoritarian regime of Antanas Smetona throughout the 1930s, as it became clear that neither of Poland's enemies—the Soviet Union and Nazi Germany—were Lithuania's friends. (Incidentally, Smetona had a Polish wife and, like his generation of Lithuanian activists, spoke good Polish). Smetona and much of the Lithuanian political elite eventually came to see that hostility toward Poland would not protect the Lithuanian state, and that Vilnius was not the only important question of foreign relations. But the very success of Lithuanian nationalism rendered the reversal of Lithuanian foreign policy exceedingly difficult. The idea of reconquering Vilnius was the most inspiring part of Lithuanian nationalism for the youth educated or conscripted after the First World War. Smetona's rule came to be seen by much of the next generation as cowardly because it did not retake the city by force.[9] The demand for Vilnius became so integral to the Lithuanian national idea that it threatened the very leader who called himself "the father of the nation." Relations were finally established with Poland in 1938, but only after a Polish ultimatum. Even this concession, which concerned only the formal establishment of relations, brought down the government and exposed Smetona himself to the opposition of much of society.

THE TRANSFER OF 1939

The destruction of the Polish state by Nazi Germany and the Soviet Union in September 1939 returned the Wilno question to international politics. In the secret annex to the Molotov-Ribbentrop pact of 23 August 1939, the Soviet Union and Nazi Germany had agreed that "the interest of Lithuania in the Vil'na area" was to be respected. Both sides hoped to use the city to manipulate the Lithuanian government. The rapid advance of the German army through Poland after 1 September 1939 signaled that Vilnius was once again on the table. The Lithuanian government declined a German offer of the city and a joint attack on Poland. Britain and France would have opposed such a move, and the attitude of the Soviet Union was as yet unknown.[10] Smetona and the government also calculated that, in the short run, German rule would be worse than Soviet; in the medium run, that the Soviet Union would be the victor in the

German-Soviet war they expected; and in the long run, that if independence was to be the price of Vilnius, it was better to make such a deal with the Soviet Union.[11] This was realism of the most clear-eyed sort, from a position of basic powerlessness. On 19 September 1939, the Red Army occupied Vil'na, and the Lithuanian representative in Moscow petitioned for the city. On 27 September, Stalin and Ribbentrop revised the previous Nazi-Soviet arrangement, this time leaving Lithuania and Vil'na within the Soviet sphere of influence.

Like Lithuanian diplomats, Belarusian activists hailing from both interwar Poland and the Belorussian Soviet Socialist Republic also pressed their claim to the city. The German-Soviet partition of Poland had granted to Stalin all of the territories of interwar Poland inhabited by speakers of Belarusian. This was welcomed, at least initially, by many of the Belarusian activists who claimed to speak for a three-million-strong Belarusian community in Poland. Among other things, they were convinced that Soviet expansion would bring Vil'nia into an enlarged Belorussian SSR. This was not merely wishful thinking inspired by their understanding of Belarus as the successor of the Grand Duchy of Lithuania, their experience of Polish opposition to Belarusian culture, and their attachment to Vil'nia. Belarusian leaders from interwar Poland were encouraged in this belief by Belorussian communists from the Soviet side, who themselves anticipated that the Belorussian Soviet Socialist Republic would include Vil'nia. After all, the Comintern had defined "Western Belorussia" to include Vil'nia and the Vil'nia region. The 1919 "LitBel" SSR, with its capital in Vil'nia, was only twenty years in the past.

Preparations for the Soviet occupation of Vil'na in September 1939 gave every sign of plans to include the city within Soviet Belorussia. Ivan Klimov, charged with the Soviet administration of western Belorussia, was authorized in early September to declare Vil'nia the capital of a West Belorussian Soviet Socialist Republic. The Belorussian NKVD, at a 15 September meeting, treated Vil'nia as part of the formerly Polish territories it was to incorporate within the Belorussian Soviet Socialist Republic. In the Wilno region, Belarusian, Jewish, and Polish communist activists aided the Soviet occupation of 17 September in the destruction of Polish state institutions. When Soviet troops reached Vil'na on 19 September, plans for the city were put into effect. Soviet occupying authorities used Belarusian in propaganda. The Soviet-sponsored newspaper justified the historic Belarusian claim to Vil'nia and explained the Belarusian character of the Grand Duchy of Lithuania. On 24 September, Klimov proclaimed to a meeting of leading Belarusians that Vil'nia would be joined to Soviet Belorussia.[12] The message was warmly received by a community which had devoted much to the idea of a Belarusian Vil'nia. That both Vil'nia and Belarus would be Soviet was perhaps forgotten in the enthusiasm of the moment.

Anton Lutskevich, the organizer of the ill-starred Belarusian republic of 1918, and the leading Belarusian activist in interwar Poland, was among those convinced. Lutskevich's considerable personal achievements and his consistent political failures were all connected to Vil'nia. In Vil'nia he had begun his political career as a democratic, patriotic socialist; in Vil'nia he had helped found and edit the first legal Belarusian newspaper before the First World War; in Vil'nia he had led the National Council that declared Belarusian independence in 1918; in Vil'nia he had published his protest of the Polish incorporation of Belarusian territory after 1921; in Vil'nia he had taught at the Belarusian high school (until he was fired by Polish superiors); in Vil'nia he had led Belarusian educational circles (until he was arrested by Polish authorities); in Viln'ia he directed the Belarusian museum for nearly twenty years; in Vil'nia he completed the first modern Belarusian translation of the New Testament. This former proponent of a renewed Grand Duchy, this translator of the Bible, was heartily disgusted by two decades of Polish rule—and ready to believe that a Soviet Belorussia and a Soviet Vil'nia were acceptable solutions to his people's historic woes.[13]

In late September 1939 Stalin apparently decided to grant Vil'na to Lithuania, and establish military bases on Lithuanian soil. Lutskevich and other Belarusian leaders in Vil'nia, led to believe that they would receive the city, instead found themselves behind bars. Lutskevich died in Soviet detention. Belarusians are early and forgotten victims of Stalin's decision to grant Vil'nia to Lithuania. Above and beyond the arrests and deaths of leading Belarusian activists, the denial of Belarusian aspirations to Vil'nia seriously encumbered the Belarusian cause. First, it meant that the Belarusian-speaking population surrounding the city of Vil'nia was lost for the time being to the Belarusian national idea. Second, the inclusion of Vil'nia within Lithuania (and soon within the Lithuanian SSR) confirmed the general belief that Lithuania and not Belarus was the successor of Grand Duchy of Lithuania. The conflation of an old politonym with a new ethnonym ("Lithuania") prevented non-Belarusians from seeing the connection between modern Belarus and the early modern Grand Duchy of Lithuania. The Belarusian communists who entered Vil'nia with high hopes in September 1939 were also disappointed. Like Uniate priests of the nineteenth century, Belarusian communists spent their time in the city of their dreams gathering archival documents of the Grand Duchy. Forced to depart when Stalin gave the city to Lithuania, Belarusian communists took the files they stole from Vil'nia archives to Minsk.[14]

On 1 October 1939 Lithuanian Foreign Minister Juozas Urbšys learned that the price for Vilnius was Soviet troops in Lithuania, and that the Nazi-Soviet treaty of 28 September had placed Lithuania within the Soviet sphere of influence. On 2 October the Lithuanian government demobilized its army. On 10 October 1939, nineteen years and one day after Żeligowski's troops had taken Wilno for Poland, Urbšys signed an agreement with the Soviet Union granting Vilnius to Lithuania. The price of Vilnius and other formerly Polish territories (2,750 square miles, 457,500 people) was basing rights for twenty thousand Soviet soldiers in Lithuania.[15] The main response of Lithuanian leaders and Lithuanians generally to the agreement was joy at the incorporation of Vilnius, accompanied by an outburst of pro-Soviet feeling. Fear of Soviet power was softened by the belief that, no matter how the war ended, Moscow would preserve Vilnius for Lithuania. Lithuanians thought that the arrival of Soviet power would cut the link between Vilnius and Poland, thus allowing for the region's Lithuanization.[16] As we shall see, these apparently odd predictions, based upon fear of Polish but not Russian culture, proved rather accurate. Although this seems strange to us today, many Lithuanian intellectuals even nurtured some sympathy for the Soviet regime. Mykolas Römer'is, the nation's outstanding jurist, was an example. As he wrote in his diary, "I myself had considerable Soviet sympathies before I encountered the Soviets, and in any event of the two I preferred the Soviet Revolution over Hitler's national socialism."[17]

Thus a particular conjunction of Soviet and Lithuanian interests brought Vilnius, for the time being, into independent Lithuania. Local Belarusians who protested were deported from what was still independent Lithuania by the Soviet NKVD; the Polish government in exile was told by Lithuanian authorities that Vilnius had been legally Lithuanian throughout the interwar period.[18] Demographic realities were harder to deny. When Lithuanian troops marched into Vilnius on 28 October 1939, they were shocked to find "instead of the princess of their fairy tales, the streets of alien Wilno, unknown, speaking a foreign language."[19] Such experiences only confirmed intellectuals' belief that speakers of Polish were "Polonized Lithuanians" who must be Lithuanized. This became the intellectual basis of Lithuanian policy. As Vilnius administrator and prime minister Antanas Merkys put it, the aims were "to make everybody think like Lithuanians" and "comb out the foreign element from the Vilnius region."[20] Poles and Jews, even those born in the city, were often denied Lithuanian citizenship. As Römer'is recorded in his diary, the application of ethnic rather than geographic or political classifications precluded the formation of any sort of Lithuanian state loyalty in Vilnius. The local Lithuanian-language newspaper "exposed" politicians who had accepted Polish rule in 1920, thereby closing off the possibility that these elites could be seen as loyal Lithuanians in the new circumstances of 1940.[21] The margin of hypocrisy necessary in mature polities was quickly closed by representatives of an earnest young nation, who in their enthusiasm lost sight of the world around them. As the Wehrmacht occupied Paris, Poles and Lithuanians quarreled over Polish theatres in Wilno/Vilnius. As Soviet troops poured into Lithuania in early 1940, the national debate in Kaunas concerned the threat from defeated and dismembered Poland.[22]

In June 1940, the Soviet Union extinguished Lithuanian independence. Soviet Foreign Minister Vyacheslav Molotov issued an ultimatum calling for a new government on 14 June; the Red Army entered Vilnius the next day. In conditions of general terror, elections were held in July to "legitimize" a new regime. The Communist-led Lithuanian People's Bloc announced that it had won 95 percent of the vote. Lithuania's "application" to join the Soviet Union was granted on 3 August. By 6 August 1940 the Red Army had taken up new positions, in greater numbers, in what had become the Lithuanian Soviet Socialist Republic. Between June 1940 and June 1941, the Soviet NKVD deported twenty to thirty thousand Lithuanians, Poles, and Jews to Siberia and Kazakhstan.[23] Former Prime Minister Merkys and Foreign Minister Urbšys were deported in July 1940. President Smetona had fled.

Smetona's Lithuania, like interwar Poland, had been a nationalizing state. Both Lithuania and Poland educated their populations in the spirit of nationalism, both sought to minimize the influence of national minorities in national politics and culture. Both states resorted to physical repression of minority activists deemed a danger to the state, and both (although Poland more than Lithuania) were characterized by official anti-Semitism by the late 1930s. Nevertheless, the destruction of Poland and Lithuania in 1939 and 1940 by Nazi Germany and the Soviet Union created the conditions for an entirely new sort of national and racial policies on their territories. The Nazis and the Soviets did what independent Poland and Lithuanian states did not: they deported and murdered individuals on the scale of hundreds of thousands, and even millions, on the basis of ascribed national or racial definitions. The practices of the Nazi and Soviet regimes were of a completely different quality than those of Poland and Lithuania.

This would be obvious just on the example of Polish-Lithuanian relations under Nazi and Soviet rule. In 1940–41 Soviet policy had aimed to decapitate

Polish and then Lithuanian society by deporting its elites. After 1941 German policy regarding Poles in Lithuania was comparable in brutality if different in form.[24] The Nazi regime allowed Lithuanians to serve as security police (*Saugumas*), which legitimized Lithuanian attacks on Poles in Wilno.[25] Whereas in 1939–1940 independent Lithuanian state discriminated against Poles in Wilno, and in 1940–41 the Soviet Union deported Poles from Wilno, in 1941–44 the Lithuanian security police and its German masters killed Poles in Wilno. The Lithuanian-Polish contest for Vilnius/Wilno, sporadically violent between 1939 and 1941, deteriorated into low-level civil war under German rule. From autumn 1943, the Polish underground Home Army attacked and disarmed collaborating Lithuanian police units in and around Wilno. Lithuanian policemen responded by executing Polish civilians. This was followed by retributive attacks on Lithuanian villages by Poles.[26]

THE END OF JEWISH VILNE, 1941–1944

The major novelty of the Nazi occupation of Vilnius from 24 June 1941 was the extermination of the Jews. Nazi policy in Lithuania was to kill every Jewish individual, and it very nearly succeeded.[27] Indeed, Lithuania was the first place in German-occupied Europe where Jews were executed on a mass scale. Within Lithuania, Vilnius was unusual in that here Lithuanians paid much more attention to Poles than to Jews once the Germans arrived. Lithuanian elites tried to convince the Germans that they, rather than the Poles, deserved to run the city. Unlike Lithuanians in Kaunas and elsewhere, those in Vilnius thought pogroms would destabilize their precarious hold on local authority. For Lithuanians in Vilnius the Polish question was more important than the Jewish question.[28]

The Final Solution began on lands that had been occupied by the Soviet Union for two years. As elsewhere on the Eastern Front, in Vilnius and in Lithuania the Nazis diverted the anger and shame of peoples occupied by the Soviets against the Jews.[29] In July 1941 the Germans began direct military rule of all of Lithuania. *Einsatzkommando 9* of the German Reich arrived in Vilnius on 2 July 1941. Having incorporated thousands of Lithuanian volunteers into its ranks, it began to eliminate Vilnius's Jews. In July and August 1941, hundreds of Jews were abducted by German and Lithuanian *Einsatzkommando* soldiers. These Jews were murdered by Germans and Lithuanians in the sand pits of the Paneriai (Ponary) forest. Much of the actual killing at Paneriai was carried out by Lithuanian volunteers known as the Special Platoon (*Ypatingas Burys*). In September 1941 3,700 Jews were rounded up and shot in the sand pits. On 6

Fig. 10. A Nazi propaganda poster in the Lithuanian language, probably of 1941, equates Stalinism and the Jews. When Germany invaded the Soviet Union in 1941, the SS first encountered populations weary of Soviet power.

September, 38,000 Jews were crammed into two small ghettos; another 6,000
or so were taken to the sand pits and shot. In October and November 1941, in
seven actions, more than 12,000 Jews were taken from the two ghettoes to the
sand pits and shot. By the end of 1941, after only six months of occupation, the
Germans (with Lithuanian assistance) had killed approximately 21,700 Vilnius
Jews. The pace slowed after November 1941, as the Wehrmacht won a reprieve
for the slave laborers it needed. The ghettoes were liquidated in September
1943. Of the 10,000 or so Jews taken from the ghettoes at this time, 5,000 were
murdered in the gas chambers of Majdanek. Several hundred more were shot in
the sand pits.[30] The rest were sent to labor camps in Estonia, where most were
killed as the Soviet army approached Lithuania in 1944. Of the 70,000 or so
Jews who were living in Vilnius in 1939, perhaps 7,000 survived the war.[31]

Some Jewish institutions survived. YIVO, rather miraculously, moved to
New York. But the Jewish civilization of Vilne had been utterly destroyed, and
its destruction over the course of years rather than its survival over the centuries
has become the central theme of its memorialization. Of the dozens of writers
associated with *Yung Vilne,* three survived. One of them, the poet Abraham
Sutzkever, came to symbolize the transfer of Jewish traditions to Israel, moving
as he did from the ruins of the Jerusalem of Lithuania to Jerusalem itself.[32] The

Fig. 11. The murder of Vilnius Jews in the Ponary forest, probably July 1941.

Fig. 12. Ruins of the Gaon Temple in Vilnius, 1944. The Final Solution ended ancient Jewish settlement in Vilnius, once the "Jerusalem of Lithuania."

destruction of the Jerusalem of Lithuania meant the end of historic Lithuania. The Paneriai forest, where the Final Solution began, was the Ponary forest Mickiewicz praised in *Pan Tadeusz*. In Mickiewicz's poetic vision, Lithuania was unimaginable without the Jews.

THE END OF POLISH WILNO, 1944–1946

As the Germans liquidated the ghettoes, the Wehrmacht was forced back across the entire front. When the Red Army returned to Vil'na in 1944, the claimants to the city were three: Poles, reduced in number but easily a national majority in the city; Lithuanians, fired by their faith that they had been victims of Polish, Soviet, and Nazi occupation in Vilnius; and Soviets, who once again held the levers of power. Unsurprisingly, Poles and Lithuanians were unable to form a common front against the Soviets.[33] The Polish Home Army had been fighting not only for Polish independence, but also for the return of Wilno to Poland. Most of its soldiers could not have imagined the one without the other. The Polish Home Army was therefore regarded by Lithuanians as an agent of Polish imperialism.[34] When the Red Army approached Vil'na in July 1944, the Polish Home Army had already secured the territories surrounding the city. A Polish attack on German positions in Wilno was indecisive; the Red Army retook Vil'na with Polish help on 13 July 1944. The Soviets then interned the Polish soldiers, and Stalin reestablished the Lithuanian SSR with its capital in Vilnius. Although Polish politicians came to Moscow to plead for Wilno, Stalin understood that he had more to gain by giving the city to the Lithuanians.[35]

Stalin knew that the city was Polish in culture. Indeed, after the Final Solution, it was more "ethnically" Polish than it ever had been. He also knew that local Poles preferred anything to Lithuanian rule. Lavrentii Beria (1899–1953), head of the NKVD, reported as much to Stalin. The terms he chose are revealing: "The mood of the population of Vil'na to the liberation of the city from German rule is positive. The population expresses its satisfaction that masses in church will now be said in Polish and not in Lithuanian. The population also hopes that Vil'na will be incorporated by Western Ukraine or Belarus, anywhere but Lithuania."[36] Although Beria never used the word "Poles," it is clear that the city's population at this point, after the extermination of the Jews, was almost entirely Polish. Yet Stalin's policy had nothing to do with self-determination, so the opinion of Wilno residents was by no means determinative. Once Stalin had decided that Vilnius was to be Lithuanian, he determined that the city would no longer be contested between Poles and Lithuanians. Here as elsewhere along the Soviet frontier, in territories that had been Polish before the war, Stalin resolved national questions by ethnic cleansing.[37] Once the new, more westerly, Soviet-Polish border was informally established in July 1944, the Soviet Union began a new policy of "population exchanges" between Soviet Lithuania and Poland. In 1939–41, Soviet policy had been to deport elites east, deep within the Soviet Union; in 1944–46 the Soviets deported the Polish nation as such from the western Soviet Union to Poland. About one hundred thousand individuals registered as Poles and left Vilnius for communist Poland between 1944 and 1948. As Römer'is noted in November 1944, within a few months the Polish question in Vilnius had "ceased to exist."[38]

Stalin chose not to create a Polish Soviet Socialist Republic or Polish Autonomous Republic after the Soviet Union reabsorbed Vilnius; he chose to push the border of Poland west in 1945; he chose to create a Lithuanian Soviet Socialist Republic and make Vilnius its capital; he chose to send Poles to communist Poland. The destruction of the Polish intelligentsia in Wilno undermined what remained of the federal tradition of Polish patriotism. The federal idea had always presumed the assimilatory force of the elite Polish culture centered in Wilno, an appeal that dissipated with the departure of educated Poles. The dominance of Polish culture in Wilno, conventionally dated from the founding of the Commonwealth in 1569, came to an end with the deportations of 1944–46. The Lithuanian Poles who found themselves resettled west to communist Poland were unable to render the federal idea plausible in their new setting, the central Poland many of them had always considered a different country. Torn from their physical surroundings, they were unable to articulate local patriotism. Censored by communist Poland, they were unable to publish their proposals for or even memoirs about the lands taken by the Soviet Union. Caught in a new social reality, they raised children whose own national identity would be indistinguishable from the national identity of other young Poles raised in a self-consciously "homogeneous" communist Poland. The historical sense of "Lithuania" wore away. Wilno became, in a famous postwar poem, "The City Without a Name."[39]

Its name became, as we shall see, "Vilnius."

Chapter 5 Epilogue:

Soviet Lithuanian Vilnius
(1945–1991)

> When a lute is struck too heavy a blow,
> Its strings sound once ere rending.
> In the confusion of sounds, a song's beginning is found
> Though no one expects the ending.
> —Adam Mickiewicz, *Konrad Wallenrod* (St. Petersburg, 1828)

This part of the book was introduced by the opening lines of Mickiewicz's 1834 masterpiece, *Pan Tadeusz*. In the nineteenth and twentieth centuries, the meaning of its opening line—"Lithuania! My fatherland!"—underwent three transformations, which we can recapitulate in terms of those three very words. The first transformation had to do with how nineteenth-century activists defined themselves and their nations: with what the first word of the poem—"Lithuania"—was to mean. We observed the shift from nostalgic reverence for the political nationality of the old Grand Duchy of Lithuania to the anticipation of national states. The last third of the nineteenth century brought out the contradictions of Mickiewiczean Romanticism, revealing the economic, social, and linguistic tensions within the early modern Polish idea and the potential of exclusionary modern nationalism to resolve them. Divided after 1863 into competing national translations, the tropes of Romantic nostalgia also served modern nationalists, who anticipated the "rebirth" of national states. While Polish federalists and Belarusian patriots stayed close to Mickiewicz's meaning, by the end of the nineteenth century he had been crowned as national poet by modern Polish and Lithuanian nationalists. In the hard world of international politics, the ethnic nationalists had chosen the more effective rendering. The careless readers were the better prophets.

The second of these three transformations involves the cruel simplifications that state independence imposes on ideas of nationality. It has to do with what happens when anticipation becomes possession, with the poem's second word— "my." The collapse of empires at the end of the First World War opened political, military, and diplomatic competitions among bearers of various national ideas: modern nationalisms, early modern federalisms, and Bolshevik internationalism. The victors in the territories of the old Grand Duchy of Lithuania were Polish and Lithuanian nationalists, and in some measure the Bolsheviks. From these competitions arose independent Polish and Lithuanian states, which lasted for two decades, as well as a Belorussian Soviet Socialist Republic, which lasted for seven. As we have seen, the Second World War, the Final Solution, and Soviet deportations did incomparably more than the policies of interwar Poland and Lithuania to homogenize populations. Postwar Soviet policy dispersed the remnants of the early modern federalist tradition. The most important of Stalin's decisions was to grant historically multinational Vilnius to the Lithuanian Soviet Socialist Republic.

How did Wilno, a city with a tiny Lithuanian minority under Polish rule in 1939, became Vilnius, capital of a Lithuanian nation-state, in 1991? Destruction opened the way for this reconstruction. Nazi and Soviet policies opened the physical and political space for the recreation of Vilnius as a Lithuanian city. With the Soviet reoccupation of Lithuania and Vilnius begins this third transformation of Mickiewicz's opening line, the redefinition of his "fatherland." After the Second World War, Vilnius became Lithuanian in a modern national sense. Under Soviet rule, Lithuanian culture assimilated the city where Mickiewicz was educated, thereby fulfilling an old dream of Lithuanian nationalists. As we have seen, this can only be understood against the background of the liquidation of Jewish and Polish culture in Vilne/Wilno. About 90 percent of Vilne Jews had been killed in the Holocaust, and about 80 percent of Wilno Poles left for Poland after the war. Resettlement, a general Soviet policy, was directed locally by Lithuanian communists. On 30 May 1945, a few weeks after the German surrender, the Lithuanian politburo decided to throw the republic's resources behind the removal of Poles from Vilnius.[1]

A LITHUANIAN VILNIUS

Within the entire Lithuanian SSR, but excluding the city of Vilnius, only about one-third of the individuals who registered as Poles for "evacuation" were actually resettled. Tens of thousands of Poles from the Lithuanian countryside were not required to register for repatriation, and tens of thousands more who registered to leave for Poland were then prevented from doing so. This was rather clearly a policy of the Lithuanian repatriation commission, protested at every point by Polish communists in Warsaw. Poland had empty fields to be farmed in the spring of 1945, and its repatriation officials anxiously awaited Polish peasants from Lithuania. In some cases Lithuanian repatriation authorities demanded that individuals registered for evacuation have German documents demonstrating their Polish nationality. At a minimum, they demanded proof of Polish citizenship, in keeping with the letter of the repatriation agreement. In Vilnius, however, the situation was totally different. Here Lithuanian repatriation authorities exploited the general Soviet policy to create the space for a newly Lithuanian Vilnius. In Vilnius every Pole was forced to register for repatriation, and 80 percent of those who registered as Poles were actually resettled.[2] The result was the de-Polonization of Wilno, and a turning point in the history of Lithuanian nationality. Vilnius had been the object of desire of the Lithuanian national movement from its origins. Lithuanian national activists had preferred to operate in Vilnius in 1905 and in 1918. The Polish seizure of Vilnius in 1920 was the central preoccupation of interwar Lithuanian. Yet Vilnius had never been a Lithuanian city in the terms of modern nationalism, in terms of the national identity of its people.

Soviet censuses give us a preliminary idea of what happened next. Of 236,100 inhabitants of Vilnius in 1959, 79,400 (34 percent) identified themselves as Lithuanian to Soviet census-takers, 69,400 (29 percent) as Russian, 47,200 (20 percent) as Polish, 16,400 (7 percent) as Jews, and 14,700 (6 percent) as Belarusian. Lithuanians were a plurality in Vilnius for the first time in modern history, and the 34 percent of 1959 was a spectacular relative increase from the 1 to 2 percent of 1939. At the same time, Lithuanians barely outnumbered Russians, and were outnumbered by Slavs (Russians, Poles, and Belarusians) almost two to one. By 1989, the time of the last Soviet census, the population of Vilnius had more than doubled to 576,700 inhabitants, and its 291,500 Lithuanians constituted a majority of 50.5 percent. The Russian, Polish, and Belarusian percentages had fallen to 20 percent, 19 percent, and 5 percent. Even if taken together as Slavs, they were now outnumbered by Lithuanians.[3] Given the belief that Soviet rule was Russifying, and given the Russification of Minsk, Riga, and Tallinn over the same period, these numbers cry out for explanation.

NATIONAL COMMUNISM

The Lithuanization of Vilnius is partly explained by an apparent compromise between Soviet authorities and Lithuanian communists. In the second half of the 1940s, Lithuanian communists carried out the counterinsurgency, deportation, and collectivization policies required by Stalin. A Lithuanian, Antanas Sniečkus (1903–1974), served as secretary of the Lithuanian Communist Party from 1936 until his death in 1974. He weathered interwar conspiracies, wartime armed struggle, postwar purges; he survived Stalin and Khrushchev and lived well into the Brezhnev period. In communist history only Mao served longer as general secretary. As a veteran of interwar politics, he understood the centrality of Vilnius to Lithuanian nationalism.[4] Having been granted Vilnius over the objections of Belarusian communists, Sniečkus had every reason to make the most of this tremendous asset. Having deported Poles from Vilnius, he and Lithuanian comrades, we may surmise, had little desire to see them replaced by Russians. Of course, non-Lithuanian communists must have understood the importance of Vilnius to Lithuania. After all, in the early years of the Lithuanian SSR, the majority of the Lithuanian party were non-Lithuanians.[5] In the service of consolidating Soviet power in Lithuania by national means, cadres imported from other Soviet republics presided over their own marginalization from Lithuanian politics.

Like Soviet Latvia and Soviet Estonia, Soviet Lithuania was allowed to have a local-language university. The university in Vilnius, founded as a Jesuit academy in the sixteenth century, supported by Tsar Alexander during the first third of the nineteenth, Polish in the 1920s and 1930s, was reopened as a Lithuanian university after the Second World War. In Autumn 1945, 86.4 percent of entering students were recorded as Lithuanians, and only 1.6 percent as Poles. Before the war, in the 1937–38 academic year, the first language of 72.6 percent of students had been Polish, and only 2.7 percent spoke Lithuanian. A starker reversal is scarcely to be imagined. Indeed, in three ways the university's national character was more clearly defined within Soviet Lithuania than it had been in interwar Poland. First, if the 86.4 percent figure is accurate, it demonstrates a clear intention to bring Lithuanians from the countryside to Vilnius. Second, whereas interwar Wilno University assimilated Belarusians, postwar Vilnius University excluded them. Even though Vilnius was surrounded by Belarusian-speaking villages, and situated only forty kilometers from the Belorussian SSR, the proportion of Belarusians in its university was kept at around 1 percent.[6] Third, and most fundamentally, the Soviet Union and its institutions ascribed nationality. The above Polish statistics for 1937–38 are based upon interwar students' self-reported mother tongue. In postwar Vilnius University, all students had a "nationality" inscribed in their Soviet internal passports, and thus in university records.

These institutional changes provided a special local backdrop for the general Soviet policy of urbanization. Since Vilnius was virtually empty after the war, and since Lithuanian peasants were nearby, their numbers in the city had to increase. Yet Soviet urbanization was not designed to favor the main republican nationality in its capital—as the examples of Lithuania's Russified southern and northern neighbors show. It appears that Lithuania's slow industrialization in the 1950s favored local migration to the capital rather than the massive pan-Soviet influx experienced by Tallinn, Riga, and Minsk.[7] Meanwhile, and partly as a result of the Catholic prohibition on family planning and abortion, Lithuanians also had a very large number of children in the 1950s and 1960s. Yet identity cannot be reduced to fertility and demography. That migrants from the countryside and their children regarded themselves as Lithuanians is as a political fact revealing a new social setting. For about four hundred years, Polish culture had accompanied social advance in Wilno. After the destruction of the centers of Polish culture in historic Lithuania, this path was now closed. The Lithuanization of Vilnius must be seen not only in the physical removal of Poles from city, but also in the elimination of Polish civilization as the urban way of life.

Even after centuries of assimilating to an urban civilization, a rural folk can more or less suddenly assert the superiority of its own culture inside the city walls.[8] The conditions for the shift are the discrediting or the removal of the people who had previously set the tone: in Wilno, those people had been Poles. Before the resettlements of 1944–46, Poles had not only been the numerical majority in Wilno, but the bearers of urban or high culture as such. Quality was more important than quantity. In the late nineteenth century, Russian governors of Vil'na had feared Polish nobles for the assimilatory power of their culture. Early Lithuanian activists feared the attractions of Polishness, which they all knew from intimate personal experience, rather than actual Polish people. In the interwar period, Lithuanian statesmen who claimed Vilnius feared Polish civilization. In 1944–46, Soviet resettlements as implemented by Lithuanian communists broke the centuries-long hold of Polish culture on Wilno. The choice to remove Poles from Vilnius but keep Poles in the countryside was made by people who understood the history of nationality. As a result, Poles became in Lithuania what they had never been: a peasant nation. Not only were they fewer in number, they were lower in status.

A door was opened. In the 1950s, Lithuanians could become what they had never been: an urban nation. Their language became, for the first time in modern history, a badge of status in Vilnius. Social advancement in Vilnius no longer required the Polish language. Children born in Vilnius in the 1950s of rural or small-town Lithuanian parents could be educated in urban Lithuanian schools. The number of general secondary schools quadrupled in the first decade of Soviet rule, and Soviet Lithuanian schools actually included more instruction in Lithuanian language than their prewar Lithuanian counterparts.[9] In the 1960s, the majority of sixteen-year-olds in Vilnius with one Lithuanian and one non-Lithuanian parent regarded themselves as Lithuanians.[10] Though the presence of a Lithuanian university in Vilnius was a historical novelty, it could be taken for granted by the numerous generation then coming of age. About 10 percent of the Lithuanians counted by the 1989 census had at least one non-Lithuanian parent. Some of them had two.[11] Under Soviet rule, Lithuanian identity in Vilnius had assimilatory force.

There was a separate compromise: between Lithuanian communists and the Lithuanian intelligentsia. Some 20,000 Lithuanians had taken up arms against Soviet rule, of whom most were killed in action or sent to Siberia. Between 1945 and 1953 about 120,000 inhabitants of Soviet Lithuania, or 5 percent of the republic's population, were deported. Among the deported were many of Lithuania's leading writers and scholars and 1,000 of Lithuania's 1,300 Roman Catholic priests.[12] After 1953, many of the deported returned. They found a Soviet Lithuania with Vilnius as its capital, and a Vilnius on its way to becoming culturally Lithuanian. Immediately after Stalin's death the proportion of Lithuanians in the Lithuanian Communist Party began to increase. The arrangement accepted by much of the Lithuanian intelligentsia was party membership in exchange for some freedom to preserve Lithuanian culture. The achievements were formidable. Literary Lithuanian was corrected, standardized, and confirmed as a language of scholarship. Lithuanian poetry and prose enjoyed notable successes. Vilnius University became a haven of Baltic studies.[13]

DURABLE ROMANTICISM

This compromise lasted for decades. By 1970 the recorded membership of Lithuanians in the party was no longer hugely disproportionate to the number of Lithuanians in the republic (66 percent to 80 percent). That year Lithuania was recorded as having the third-highest per capita income in the Soviet Union, behind only Estonia and Latvia.[14] Within prescribed Soviet formulae, Lithuanian communists could boast not only of economic development, but of Lithuanian culture. Hence General Secretary Snieckus, in a book published in 1970, associated the nation's love for its capital Vilnius with Lenin's 1895 visit to the city.[15] The point was that Lithuania owed its capital to benevolent communist policies. Lenin's successor Stalin had indeed granted Vilnius to Lithuania. Stalin and his successors did have a measure of understanding of what mattered to Lithuanians. Even the Russian language was altered in the service of the Soviet compromise with Lithuanian nationality. The Russian word Lenin would have used during his visit of 1895 was "Vil'na." This was replaced by the Lithuanian word "Vilnius"—in Russian-language history books. We have observed the sudden and violent end of Jewish "Vilne" and Polish "Wilno," and paused to ponder the dashed hopes for a Belarusian "Vil'nia." The quiet surrender of Russian "Vil'na" under Soviet rule calls for some reflection.

As we have seen, interwar Lithuanian politicians feared Russian culture less than Polish, and Lithuanian leaders in 1939 expected that Soviet rule, if it came, would break the Polish connection and allow Vilnius to become Lithuanian. The correctness of this hardheaded prediction, made under enormous duress, should deter us from regarding Lithuanian nationalism as irrational. In postwar Lithuania, indubitably Romantic notions proved their political force. The postwar bow of the Russian to the Lithuanian language, in particular, invites us to revisit the linguistic emphasis of Lithuanian nationality. As we have seen, the distinctive Baltic Lithuanian language was important in the success of the Lithuanian national movement in the late nineteenth century. The interwar Lithuanian state spread literacy in this language. In Soviet Lithuania, the Lithuanian language again served as a mark of continuity with the ancient past. The difference between Slavic and Baltic languages is a brute fact; the idea that Lithuanian is purer than its Slavic rivals is a Romantic notion. The idea that the Lithuanian language is very closely related to Sanskrit, a view which is justified in qualified form in philology, remains in the popular mind as a powerful national idea to this day. This suggests the continuity of Romantic traditions, their successful propagation under various political regimes, and then their final success under Soviet rule.[16]

How did Soviet power support Romantic nationalism? As chapter 2 argued, the Lithuanian nationalism formed in the late nineteenth century involved Romantic tropes circulated by Germans after the French Revolution, modified by Mickiewicz in the 1820s and 1830s, subverted by Lithuanian national activists in the 1880s, and articulated as politics during the Revolution of 1905. Chapter 3 demonstrated that interwar Lithuanian nationalism, as propagated by an independent Lithuanian state, concentrated on Poland's seizure of an ostensibly Lithuanian Vilnius in 1920. After 1920, the early modern, historical idea of Lithuania all but vanished. Although there were exceptions, the predominance of the modern, ethnic idea of nationhood was fairly clear among both Poles in Wilno and Lithuanians in Kaunas by 1939. Lithuanian ethnic nationalism triumphed in Soviet Lithuanian Vilnius after the Second World War.

The old joke—"Vilnius is Lithuanian, but Lithuania is Russian"—was actually false. Lithuania was Soviet, which proved to be something else than Russian, especially in Vilnius. The dreams of Lithuanian Romantics in the nineteenth century, as interpreted by Lithuanian nationalists in the twentieth, were realized under Soviet rule. The synthesis of medieval and modern was achieved, as linguistic practice in Vilnius closed the yawning gap between dreams of dominance and medieval power. Language softened the blow of early modern "statelessness" in Vilnius, as it had elsewhere in Lithuania during the interwar period. To be sure, language was a mark of distinctiveness for Lithuanians under Soviet rule, as it was for all of the Balts. At the same time, Soviet power allowed Lithuanians to confirm in social practice Romantic beliefs that the age and beauty of the nation were preserved in its language. The first history of the Lithuanian language published in English, conveying to an international audience the relationship of modern Lithuanian to ancient proto-Indo-European, was written by a graduate of Soviet-era Vilnius University.[17]

Ethnic nationalism, in Lithuania and elsewhere, despises ambiguous early modern traditions and prizes fantasies of medieval purity and power. In Vilnius, Soviet power broke early modern legacies as no Lithuanian institution could have done. The Molotov-Ribbentrop pact undid the Lublin Union: 1939 undid 1569. In 1841, the Romantic historian Narbutt had figuratively broken his pen to protest the creation of the Polish-Lithuanian Commonwealth; in 1939 Molotov and Ribbentrop set their pens to the document which led to the end of the Polish connection with Lithuania. 1569 established the largest early modern nation in Europe; 1939 began the final division of Poles and Lithuanians into small, modern, ethnic nations. Meanwhile, Soviet rule also provided Lithuanians with the opportunity to minimize the old historical connection to Poland. In the grand compromise wherein Lithuanian communists mediated between Soviet power and Lithuanian society, Poland played the important role of common foe. Having granted territory to Soviet Lithuania at the expense of Poland, Stalin and his successors could present themselves as guarantors of the status quo.[18] Throughout the Soviet period the Lithuanian intelligentsia decried the Polish "occupation" of Vilnius in 1920, an interpretation consistent enough with the general Soviet line of Polish imperialism to be comfortably tolerated. Even in the 1980s, Lithuanian activists generally believed that Poles were obsessed with Vilnius, and would stop at nothing to get it back.[19]

As everywhere in the Soviet Union, the Molotov-Ribbentrop pact was taboo in the Lithuanian SSR. During the Gorbachev period, Lithuanians recalled it as a national tragedy in massive public demonstrations. This was courageous. Lithuanians portrayed themselves as innocent victims of its provisions. This was forgetful: their country gained Vilnius as a result. Lithuania's 1939 occupation of Vilnius, if it was mentioned at all, figured as the "return of Vilnius." Lithuanians took for granted that the Molotov-Ribbentrop pact was illegitimate, but that the incorporation of Vilnius that followed was legitimate. "The reversal of the Molotov-Ribbentrop pact" was a slogan of the Lithuanian national movement during the late 1980s.[20] A literal reversal of the Molotov-Ribbentrop pact would have returned Vilnius to Poland. As the Soviet Union disintegrated in the early 1990s, Soviet authorities in Moscow and Poles in Lithuania were quick to make this point.

NAMES AND THINGS

Over the course of a century, the Lithuanian national movement, independent Lithuania, and Soviet Lithuania undermined the connection to Poland implicit in the traditions of the Grand Duchy of Lithuania—all the while appealing to Mickiewicz. Lithuania was redefined as a modern national unit with a capital in Vilnius: in ideology by the national movement, in aspiration by the interwar state, and in fact by Soviet Lithuania. As we have seen, Soviet Lithuanian Vilnius achieved what interwar Polish Wilno never managed: a monument to Mickiewicz ("Mickievičius") as a national poet, unveiled in 1984. The Mickievičius statue was a rallying point for a Lithuanian national movement unleashed by General Secretary Mikhail Gorbachev's reforms within the Soviet Union in the second half of the 1980s.

A leader of this movement was Vytautas Landsbergis (1932–). His family history will serve us as a parting reminder of the fundamental difference between early modern and modern nationality in Lithuania. In the nineteenth century, the Landsberg family, like the rest of the Lithuanian gentry, partook in early modern Polish civilization. In the early nineteenth century, Kazimierz Landsberg studied in Polish at the Russian imperial university at Wilno. Like Mickiewicz, he took for granted the superiority of the Polish language and the ultimate return of the Polish-Lithuanian Commonwealth. Kazimierz Landsberg fought in Warsaw against Russian imperial rule in the uprising of 1830–31, the failure of which inspired Mickiewicz to write *Pan Tadeusz*. As we have seen, Wilno University and Polish schools in Lithuania were closed after this uprising. All the same, between 1831 and 1863 Polish cultural superiority remained unchallenged in historic Lithuania.

The next generation of Landsbergis's family history reminds us, however, that a Russian nationality policy emerged after the defeat of the next rising, of 1863–64. Gabriel Landsberg was also raised by a family that spoke Polish, but unlike his father studied Lithuanian in high school. Allowed to attend university in Russia, he returned from Moscow as an activist of the Lithuanian national movement. He married a Polish woman, with whom he spoke Polish. Although he never spoke Lithuanian well, he was proud that all five of his children did. His youngest children came of age in imperial Russia after the Revolution of 1905. As we have seen from the case of Mykolas Römer'is, it was after 1905 that many Lithuanian Polish gentry families began to take the idea of a modern Lithuanian nationality seriously.

In this next generation, the Landsbergis genealogy recalls the centrality of Vilnius to Lithuanian activists, and how the Polish seizure of the city in 1920 clouded their achievement of Lithuanian independence. The youngest of Gabriel's five children grew up to become the architect Vytautas Landsbergis-Žemkalnis (1893–1993). One of his interwar monuments concerned the Gediminas Castle in Vilnius. Vilnius was then part of Poland, and the castle was a site of Lithuanian nationalist longing. In a certain way, the Second World War allowed art to become life. When the Soviet Union granted Vilnius to Lithuania in 1939, Landsbergis-Žemkalnis was the first Lithuanian soldier to enter Gediminas Castle—or so, at any rate, went the story he told his son. During the brief Lithuanian interregnum in 1939–40, and then again in the Lithuanian SSR, Landsbergis-Žemkalnis worked to construct a Lithuanian Vilnius. ("Žemkalnis," incidentally, is simply a lithuanization of "Landsbergis.") Today, a street of Vilnius bears his name.

His son, Vytautas Landsbergis, cultivated a more private art within the constraints of the Lithuanian SSR. Vytautas Landsbergis *fils* exemplified the achievements of the Lithuanian intelligentsia within the Soviet system. He finished conservatory as a pianist in 1955, received his doctorate in musicology in 1969, taught for thirty years, wrote many books. He specialized in the music of the Lithuanian artist and composer Mikalojus Čiurlionis (1875–1911), a figure officially restored from Stalin-era disgrace to the Lithuanian national pantheon in 1961. Landsbergis's eight books on Čiurlionis represent a productive commitment to the continuation of Lithuanian national culture, which of course involved creating something new. Vytautas Landsbergis represented, after all, the first generation of the Landsbergis family whose mother tongue was Lithuanian rather than Polish. Incidentally, Mikalojus Čiurlionis, now known to all Lithuanians as the "artist of the nation," could not speak Lithuanian as a child. Čiurlionis's mother tongue was Polish. He learned Lithuanian from his wife Sofija Kymantaitė (1886–1958). Let us not imagine a return to the folk: she was a writer and translator, and spent her formative years among the Cracow art nouveau known as Young Poland. Čiurlionis defined himself as a Lithuanian only after the Revolution of 1905. In the cases of Landsbergis and the hero of his academic work, we must see nationality not as a kind of ethnic fate, but as a political choice within definable historical circumstances.[21]

The circumstances of such individual choices in the present join in a strange harmony with collective myths of a national past. In the Lithuanian case, modern national activism meant rejecting palpable continuities with the early modern Commonwealth in favor of historical myths about the medieval Grand Duchy of Lithuania. This meant choosing one version of Mickiewicz over another. Mickiewicz's political respect for the early modern Commonwealth was set aside; his Romantic myths of the medieval Grand Duchy were politicized. Landsbergis's patrimony (or rather patrinomy—his last name) reminds us how the early modern Polish nation was supplanted by a modern Lithuanian nation, how an elite idea of politics expressed in Polish was replaced by a folk conception expressed in Lithuanian. Lithuanian national politics involved an alliance of the modern and the medieval against the early modern. Early modern principles of legitimacy, the authority of gentry families, or the political institutions of the Commonwealth, were rejected. The age and beauty of medieval history legitimized the modern effort to seize power in the name of the people.

Vytautas Landsbergis's first name recalls the myth of medieval Lithuania that served as the national past. Vytautas the Great was a medieval grand duke of Lithuania who resisted union with Poland. In interwar Lithuania, Vytautas the Great was associated with the Lithuanian golden age before the Lublin Union 1569, and with Lithuanian revanchist designs upon Vilnius. In Soviet Lithuanian Vilnius, Vytautas continued to stand for hostility to the Polish connection.[22] As Lithuanians liberated themselves from Soviet rule, they elevated Vytautas the Great again to the first rank of national heroes. The form of national revival symbolized by Vytautas the Great, the restoration of an ancient Lithuania without a Polish connection, was substantiated in politics by Vytautas Landsbergis. In 1988, Landsbergis was elected leader of the Lithuanian national movement Sąjūdis. In 1990, he presided over the parliamentary session during which Lithuanian independence was declared. In 1991, he was elected to chair the parliament of an independent Lithuanian republic with a capital in Vilnius. In September of that year, Landsbergis's government began a diplomatic dispute with Poland, in which Landsbergis demanded that Poland accept the Lithuanian status of Vilnius—between 1920 and 1939.

This unusual diplomacy was the consequence of a particular view of the past, which neglected the early modern connection with Poland in favor of a romantic view of medieval Lithuania. This neglect was a hallmark of Lithuanian nationalism and a purposeful answer to Polish culture, the attractions of which were well known to every generation of Lithuanian activists. Even the Romantic view of medieval Lithuania, the Garden of Eden in the Lithuanian myth, was articulated most beautifully by Mickiewicz in Polish. Konrad Wallenrod, Mickiewiczean hero of the poem that opens this chapter, was a medieval Lithuanian knight. His heroism lay in his ability to conceal his own identity and bide his time in the service of the enemy until the proper moment for action arrived. The name Mickiewicz invented for his greatest medieval heroine, "Grażyna," entered the Lithuanian language, and was borne, for example, by Landsbergis's wife. The emphasis on the medieval and the rejection of the early modern was consistent with, and indeed motivated, the spread of the modern ethnic nation. The age of the Lithuanian language became the beauty of its culture, and then the beauty of its culture became the power of mass literacy and universal suffrage. These, of course, had a force of their own.

As after the First World War, after the collapse of the Soviet Union Lithuanian authorities conveyed historical myths to a mass public. The popular demand for historical truth was met with the republication of interwar history texts, especially those of the leading national historian and mythmaker, Adolfas Šapoka. Even Narbutt's (Polish-language and imposingly long) history of Lithuania was published in Lithuanian in the 1990s. As after the First World War, after the collapse of the Soviet Union the danger was that historical myth legitimized as political discourse would prevent Lithuanian governments from executing a rational foreign policy. The fear of Polish civilization so appropriate to national revival risked weakening the Lithuanian state in international relations. The first signs were not encouraging. Landsbergis's initial coldness to Poland fit a national consensus that emerged astonishingly quickly and showed remarkable intergenerational range. As Lithuanian-Polish relations stalled in the early 1990s, Lithuanian schoolchildren were asked to select the most shameful event in national history. More than any other, they chose the 1569 union with Poland.[23]

Part II The Embattled Ukrainian Borderland

Chapter 6 Early Modern
Ukraine (1569–1914)

You boast that, once, we brought Poland down.
Yet when Poland fell, you were crushed as well.
Then fathers spilt blood for Moscow and Warsaw,
Bequeathing to sons their chains, their renown!
—Taras Shevchenko, "To the Dead, the Living, and the Yet Unborn . . ."
  (Viunyshcha, 1845)

The Lublin Union of 1569 defined early modern Ukraine by transferring East Slavic lands from Lithuania to Poland. Most of the lands of
Kyivan Rus' had been acquired by Lithuania in the fourteenth century, Kyiv city coming under Lithuanian dominion in 1363. Polish
King Kazimierz (the Great) had seized Galicia and L'viv in 1349. For
about two hundred years, most of the patrimony of Kyivan Rus', including the lands we now call Ukraine, was divided between Lithuania and Poland.[1] Before 1569, Lithuania had the lion's share of the old
Kyivan principalities, but Poland's Galicia (the Rus' Palatinate) was
the most prosperous and advanced of these lands. The 1569 Lublin
Union was thus a repartition of old Rus', on terms favorable to
Poland. Lithuania retained its more northerly Slavic territories now

known as Belarus. Lithuania ceded to Poland its most southerly territories, the Bratslav, Kyiv, and Volyn' regions, most of what is now Ukraine. Orthodox nobles of Rus', who after two centuries thought of themselves as Lithuanians, found themselves within the Polish Kingdom. Bracław, Kijów and Wołyń joined Galicia as territories within the Polish Kingdom where the main religion was Orthodoxy, the vernacular was Ruthenian, the liturgical language was Church Slavonic, and the script was Cyrillic. Kyiv city, the capital of ancient Rus', was suddenly part of Poland.

The Union between the Grand Duchy of Lithuania and the Polish Kingdom was organic and negotiated, while the absorption of Ukraine by Poland was precipitous and decreed. The spread of Roman Catholicism within Lithuania had begun with baptism of the sovereign in 1386, and continued slowly for nearly two centuries before the constitutional union with Poland in 1569. Ukraine, on the other hand, was an Orthodox land suddenly brought into intense contact with Western Christendom at the height of the controversies over Reform. Reform marked a change in the balance between Western and Eastern Christianity. In the medieval period, Orthodox Rusian churchmen had provided Vilnius and Lithuania with East Slavic languages and culture. As Polish high culture came to dominate Vilnius, as Lithuania granted Ukraine to Poland, and as Western Christianity was subject to Reform, the tables were turned. A source of high culture in medieval Lithuania, Ukraine became the target of civilizers in early modern Poland. Ukraine had provided medieval Lithuania with Christianity and writing; Ukraine received from early modern Poland Reformed Christianity and the printed book. In these ways, the 1569 transfer marks the end of medieval Rus', as continued within Lithuania; and the beginning of early modern Ukraine, comprised of East Slavic lands included in Poland. The Ukrainian national poet Taras Shevchenko called Vilnius "the most glorious of cities"; the Ukraine of which he wrote begins with a connection to Warsaw.

Just as the history of medieval Rus' begins with the Orthodox baptism of Grand Duke Volodymyr in 988, so the history of early modern Ukraine begins with conversions of Ukrainian nobles to Western Christianity after 1569. In sixteenth-century Poland, Protestants first, and Catholics in response, brought to bear the printed word, the vernacular, and techniques of disputation revived by the Renaissance. After 1569, these intellectual fireworks were released in Ukraine, the main pyrotechnicians being the Jesuits. The effect was spectacular, especially against a darkening sky. As Reform raised religious disputation in Poland to a very high level, Orthodoxy in Ukraine continued its long intellectual decline. Its limitations inhered in the language created to spread eastern-rite

Christianity among the Slavs. Old Church Slavonic, the remarkable creation of Cyril/Constantine, had allowed the spread of the Gospel throughout East and South Slavic lands. Although Old Church Slavonic served the medieval purposes of conversion from paganism to Christianity very well, it was insufficient for the early modern challenge of Reform. It provided no link to classical models. As centuries passed, it was ever less able to provide Orthodox churchmen with a means of communication among themselves—or with their flock, when this idea arose. As the various Slavic languages emerged (or diverged), Church Slavonic lost both its original proximity to the vernacular and its universal appeal. By the early modern period it had declined into local recensions which neither matched local speech nor represented a general means of communication among Orthodox churchmen.[2]

In the sixteenth century, the humble literature of the Orthodox church was dwarfed by that of the Protestants and Catholics.[3] Both Protestants and Catholics initially tried to use Church Slavonic in their schools and publications in Ukraine, before deciding that what they had to say could only be conveyed in Polish. Unlike all of its competitors, Polish was at once a living language and a language of culture, amenable to propaganda and proselytism. Churchmen's use of Polish in Ukraine was not national prejudice, but a choice of weapons in a battle for souls. Proponents of Church Slavonic did rise to the challenge. Konstantyn Ostroz'kyi, the greatest of the Volhynian princes, sponsored the publication of the first complete bible in Church Slavonic. Pamvo Berynda published a lexicon. Petro Mohyla founded an Orthodox collegium, which later became the Kyiv Academy. It used Church Slavonic, although the textbooks were generally in Latin and the composition generally in Polish. Because they were forced to learn other languages and classical rhetoric and disputation, Ukrainian churchmen became the outstanding interpreters of Church Slavonic texts, which made them much desired in Moscow. All the same, they too found the Polish language best suited their needs. After 1605, the majority of polemical tracts written by Orthodox churchmen were in Polish (though the titles, pseudonyms, and terms of abuse were often of Byzantine origin); after 1620, Orthodox churchmen usually signed their names in Polish; after 1640, most official documents in Ukraine were written in Polish. Mohyla, who died in 1647, wrote his will in Polish.[4]

One important response of the local Orthodox hierarchy was a project for Union with Rome. To end the Eastern Schism was a matter of the greatest importance for Rome after 1054; in the absence of a total solution the Catholic Church had enacted several local Unions with churches of other rites. After

Fig. 13. The Ostroh Bible, published in 1581. Early modern Ostroh boasted an Orthodox academy, a yeshiva, a mosque, and a Unitarian Church. Ostroh is today a town in Rivne oblast, western Ukraine.

1569, the political conditions were in place for such a local Union in the new Polish-Lithuanian Commonwealth. The ecclesiastical separation of the metropolitan sees of Moscow and Kiev had been established in 1458, with the latter entirely within the boundaries of the Commonwealth. After the new territorial disposition of 1569, most of these Orthodox lands fell within Poland rather than Lithuania. Polish Jesuits such as Piotr Skarga (1536–1612) supported Union with the Orthodox; papal emissaries such as Antonio Possevino explained to Rome the possibility of a regional Union; King Zygmunt III was a keen advocate on security and religious grounds. Yet Union was by no means a plot of Rome or Warsaw. The 1596 Brest Union came from the bosom of Orthodoxy, as bishops sought to preserve their church. The Orthodox Patriarchy of Constantinople was discredited by its obvious dependency on Ottoman power; the new Patriarchy of Moscow was established by dubious methods. Jeremiah II, Patriarch of Constantinople and highest authority of the Orthodox Church, enjoyed the unpleasant distinction of having been imprisoned by both the Ottomans and the Muscovites. Having been forced to elevate the metropolitan see of Moscow to a patriarchy, Jeremiah tarried in Poland's Ukrainian lands in 1588 and 1589. Jeremiah ordered annual synods at Brest, which prepared the Union of Orthodox and Catholic Churches promulgated in the Commonwealth in 1596.[5]

Opponents saw the Brest Union as an attempt to eliminate the Orthodox Church in the Commonwealth, which it was. After all, the Orthodox bishops who proposed and established Union believed that they were joining the Catholic Church, retaining their eastern rite while gaining equal status within that larger body. The Vatican treated Union as part of a tradition of ending schisms by way of regional arrangements. King Zygmunt III therefore had a point when he claimed that the "Greek faith" he was bound to protect was the Uniate Church, as the full and legitimate successor of the Orthodox Church in the Commonwealth. The politics of Union forced cooperation between Protestants (now a smaller minority relative to an enlarged Catholic Church) and Orthodox (whose church had legally ceased to exist in the Commonwealth). During the crisis of the late fifteenth and early sixteenth centuries, Protestants found themselves in sympathy with the Orthodox for reasons of doctrine and practice as well as political survival. The most prominent opponent of the Brest Union was Konstantyn Ostroz'kyi, the Volhynian prince who published the Slavonic Bible. Armed with arguments drawn from Protestant sources (that the pope was the Antichrist, for instance), Ostroz'kyi used the institutions of the Commonwealth to protest against Union.[6]

Fig. 14. A sixteenth-century eastern-rite church. Niżankowice/Nizhankovitse straddles the Bug/Buh river, today the border between Poland and Ukraine.

Ostroz'kyi was able to mobilize some nobles from the Wołyń/Volyn' and Kijów/Kyiv regions in local diets to protest Brest. Religion, in this peculiar way, brought some Ukrainian nobles into politics. For Orthodox townsmen, the Brest Union represented a threat to their social position by Polish immigrants. Here religion stood for conservatism. In the parishes, the Uniate Church failed to unify the Orthodox clergy or elevate the eastern rite such that it could satisfy the majority of the Ukrainian gentry.[7] From controversy over Union arose a political lexicon. The traditional sacral designation "Rus'" had been used in a political sense for centuries; now the vague military term "Ukraina" took on something like a political meaning as the homeland of the Orthodox in Poland.[8] The Lublin Union of 1569 had separated East Slavs in Ukraine from their northern counterparts in the Grand Duchy; the Brest Union of 1596 provided the occasion to consider this new territorial settlement in political terms. Rather than creating a single church within the Commonwealth that could assimilate eastern traditions, the Brest Union created a confusing situation in which all Christian churches in Ukraine posed political problems. Most pregnant was the gap between reformers and peasants, for whom the motives of Reform and Union were totally obscure.

THE DEFINITION OF EARLY MODERN
UKRAINE, 1569–1648

Earlier, we noted an odd and important feature of the resolution of the Renaissance language question in Poland and Lithuania. Whereas nobles of both realms accepted Polish as the language of learning and politics after 1569, this had different long-term social consequences in the two realms. In Poland the educated classes shifted from an imported language of state and literature, Latin, to a codified version of the vernacular, Polish. In the Grand Duchy of Lithuania the educated classes shifted from a language of government similar to the vernacular of much of the country, Chancery Slavonic, to an imported language of state and literature, Polish. This sidelined the Belarusian vernacular, which joined the Lithuanian vernacular in political and cultural irrelevance. We then saw that the elite status of Polish weakened its case when national politics came to mean mass politics in the modern period. In Ukraine, the same can be said about the answer to the language question after 1569: rather than the Ukrainian vernacular being elevated or Church Slavonic being revived, Polish simply won the day. Whereas in Poland the answer to the language question brought letters closer to common speech, in Lithuania and Ukraine it distanced the literate elite, lay and church alike, from the commoners (chart 1, p. 48).

A further point can be made about the outcome of religious Reform in Ukraine. Like Polish nobles, many Ukrainian nobles were swept away by the Reformation. Much of the Ukrainian gentry converted from Orthodoxy to several varieties of Protestantism in the sixteenth century. As in Poland, the children and grandchildren of such nobles in Ukraine were drawn to Counter-Reformation, and converted to Roman Catholicism. Polish and great Ukrainian nobles thus ended by sharing a religion, Roman Catholicism. Yet whereas the Counter-Reformation removed a new religious difference between Polish lords and Polish peasants, it created a new religious difference between Roman Catholic Ukrainian lords and Orthodox Ukrainian peasants. When in the modern period popular religion and the common speech became platforms of national politics, the Polish language and Roman Catholic religion were bound to be presented as alien to Ukraine. There was, however, one institution which served both. The Uniate Church survived in Ukraine, as a minority religion among both gentry and peasants. When Orthodoxy regained legal status in the Commonwealth in the 1630s, Union ceased to be a universal aspiration and became a minority eastern-rite Church. As we shall see, in the right political conditions the Uniate Church became one platform for modern ideas of Ukraine nationality.[9]

In the religious and political life of the new Commonwealth, early modern Ukraine differed more from Poland than did Lithuania. In Lithuania, Roman Catholicism had taken root long before, and was a faith of peasants as well as nobles. Lithuania was a full partner in the politics of the new Commonwealth, Ukraine was not. Whereas the Lithuanian middle gentry could choose between Lithuanian and Commonwealth law to protect their freedoms, Ukrainian middle gentry found themselves at the mercy of their richer and more powerful brethren. In the political economy of the new Commonwealth, Ukrainian lands played a particular role. As the Commonwealth became the breadbasket of Western Europe, and as gentry succeeded in binding peasants to the land, property was ever more the way to wealth and power.[10] Property was for the taking in Ukraine.

In Lithuania, gentry were able to use the executive power they retained after 1569 to protect their landholdings, and in any case the Lithuanian Statutes remained the highest law. The 1588 Statute of the Grand Duchy of Lithuania was designed in part to protect native Lithuanian landholders. No such Ukrainian defenses existed. In the decades after 1569, a few Polish families gained enormous landholdings in Ukraine, and thousands of petty Polish nobles and Jews followed to work for the great lords. Fewer lords owned more land. By 1658, perhaps 2 percent of the population of Ukraine was noble, as opposed to about 10 percent of the population elsewhere in Poland.[11] Ukrainian nobles of local origin profited most from the new order. The richest ones recruited Polish and Jewish soldiers and assistants. Polish hirelings brought economic practices such as leasing, which allowed great tracts of land to become proper latifundia; Jewish administrators were drawn from the Polish crownlands by magnates keen to profit from their skills. As gentry took on Polish ways and Jews took up their leases, the Orthodox peasantry was reduced from poverty to penury. Nathan of Hanover, graduate of the Ostroh Yeshiva and famous chronicler if the bloodshed that followed, compared the suffering of the peasants to that of the Jews under Egyptian bondage. The Ukrainians, he wrote, "were looked upon as lowly and inferior beings, and became the slaves and handmaids of the Polish people and the Jews . . . "[12]

This intense stratification allowed impressive cultural attainments at the peak of society. Polish women brought court life to Ukraine, creating milieux that allowed cultural trends to be observed and to spread. Just as the Italian Renaissance had been rendered attractive in Poland by the person and entourage of the Italian princess Bona Sforza, wife of Zygmunt I and mother of Zygmunt II, so a generation later the Polish Renaissance was communicated to Ukraine in magnate courts organized by Polish women. Less than a century after 1569 we find enormously wealthy estates in Ukraine whose guardians were as Polish as the Poles, if not more so.[13] Ukraine provided new summits for Polish high culture; but in their shadow lurked rebels.

1648 AND ALL THAT

In the three crucial generations between the Lublin Union of 1569 and Bohdan Khmel'nyts'kyi's uprising of 1648, Polish nobles entered Ukraine and Ukrainian magnates became more Polish. Increasing social differences combined with new religious and cultural differences to create deep political divisions. These were compounded by the constitutional order of the new Commonwealth. It was a republic of Two Nations, not Three; and it was before all a republic of the nobility. The Commonwealth was thus ill designed to incorporate the free society of the Cossacks, armed men generally of peasant rather than noble origin. In 1569, the Polish Kingdom had inherited the Cossacks along with Ukraine from Lithuania. Lithuania had relied upon the Cossacks to defend its southern borderlands from the Crimean Khanate. Poland found that the Cossacks were a tremendous military asset, not only in defense but in attack. The Polish cavalry was the best in Europe at the time, but it was most effectively used to end battles, and the state had difficulty paying for the standing infantry needed to begin them.[14] For a time, the Cossacks filled this gap. Their value was demonstrated in the wars with Sweden in 1601–2, Muscovy in 1611–12, and the Ottoman empire in 1621. The Commonwealth attained its greatest glory when its Polish and Lithuanian knights and its Ukrainian Cossacks fought side by side. The compromise found for such militarily useful commoners was the legal category of "registered" Cossacks. Registered Cossacks had personal liberty, but were disenfranchised if they were not noblemen. Since Cossacks as an estate were not represented in the parliament, that body took an ungenerous view of the number of Cossacks who should be registered. The nobility, by contrast, was enfranchised. Since great nobles had an interest in keeping peasants bound to the land, and a peasant who became a registered Cossack gained rights, they had an economic interest in keeping the number of registered Cossacks low. The policy after 1632 was to maintain the Cossacks as a small border guard, increasing their numbers only when necessary for war. The Commonwealth neglected to pay the registered Cossacks after 1643, which was much resented.[15] They faced mobilization without representation.

The Cossacks impotently petitioned parliament for the restoration of their traditional status. Like the Lithuanian middle gentry before 1569, some Ukrainian Cossacks after 1569 also wished to win the rights that nobles had secured for themselves within the Polish Kingdom. Unlike Lithuanian nobles, Ukrainian Cossacks had not begun the association with Poland from a position of formal equality, and lacked the institutional platform from which to negotiate. The Lithuanian gentry had observed Polish norms over the course of centuries, and had negotiated what became the Lublin Union with Poland over decades. Ukrainian Cossacks were thrust into direct contact with Polish practices, while a very few very rich magnates and their administrators represented Poland and Polishness in Ukraine. Catholicism had been introduced by degrees into Lithuania, beginning in 1386; and was familiar when not acceptable to nobles throughout the Commonwealth. Orthodoxy was the only religion the non-noble majority of the Cossacks had ever known. Although the 1596 Brest Union was a matter of disputation among Ukrainian gentry, it appears to have been simply shocking to most of the Cossacks.[16] Although after the 1630s Orthodoxy was once again recognized in the Commonwealth, Cossacks generally wished to remove the Uniate Church (and Roman Catholics, and Protestants, and Jews) from Ukraine. This did not mean that the Cossacks cooperated with the reinstated Orthodox hierarchy in Kyiv, whose advances were rebuffed by Khmel'nyts'kyi.

This suggests a deeper issue: the lack of a corporate elite in early modern Ukraine. Orthodoxy was defended by lay soldiers; Polish customs were taken for granted by rebels against Polish rule. There was a Ukrainian nobility; there was also the Cossack officer corps; there was some overlap between these groups. Differences in social origins, however, led to painful political divisions. The richest Polish and Polonized nobles dominated local politics, and sought to deny minor gentry (such as Bohdan Khmel'nyts'kyi) their traditional rights. Bohdan Khmel'nyts'kyi (ca. 1595–1657), a registered Cossack, fled to the Cossack headquarters after a Polish official stole his property, took his lover, and murdered his son. Khmel'nyts'kyi became Cossack hetman, and began the massive Cossack uprising of 1648. He became the most important figure in seventeenth-century Ukraine, but his own special case also illustrates how the arrival of Polish institutions inflamed and divided the local nobility. Meanwhile, the same economic trends that allowed certain Ukrainian nobles to enjoy great power within the Commonwealth also strengthened the Cossacks as a fighting force. As magnates tamed the Ukrainian steppes for the grain trade, peasants moved ever farther south, into territories raided for slaves by the Crimean Tatars, and often into the ranks of the Cossacks. For the peasantry, the Cossack life was the available alternative to magnate serfdom and Tatar slavery. The combination of incorporation by Poland, Union with the Catholic Church, the frustration of registered Cossacks, and the enserfment of peasants, explains how Khmel'nyts'kyi could after 1648 mount attacks which threatened the Commonwealth.

After Khmel'nyts'kyi allied with Muscovy at Pereiaslav in 1654, his Cossacks helped Muscovy make war on the Commonwealth. This brought a series of calamities which killed perhaps a third of the Commonwealth's population of ten million, and began its fatal decline as a European power. The turning point at which Polish-Ukrainian history failed to turn was the Union of Hadiach of 1658–59. Proposed by Hetman Ivan Vyhovs'kyi (died 1664), the Hadiach Union would have made elite Ukrainian Cossacks the third nation in a Commonwealth of Three Nations (Poland, Lithuania, and Rus'). Ukraine would have enjoyed a status comparable to that which Lithuania had secured: its own administration, army, and judiciary. The status of the Orthodox Church in Ukraine and throughout the tripartite Commonwealth would have been equal to that of the Roman Catholic Church. The plan's author, the erudite polemicist Iurii Nemyrych (1612–59), had just reconverted from Unitarianism back to

Orthodoxy. A portion of the Cossacks would have been ennobled, and enjoyed political rights and the privilege of ruling Ukraine. Yet Hadiach was a republican rather than democratic resolution, and the Ukrainian rising was rather democratic than republican. Hetman Vyhovs'kyi, like Hetman Khmel'nyts'kyi before him, straddled the republican world of Commonwealth courts and the democratic world of the Cossack steppe. An educated man, he saw the benefits of compromise, but could not bring the majority of Cossacks to his point of view. A crucial point of disagreement was the Uniate Church, which the Cossacks wished to see liquidated, which the Catholic Church insisted was beyond the reach of secular powers, and about which Vyhovs'kyi proposed an unpopular compromise. Vyhovs'kyi lacked the authority to bind the masses of free Cossacks who would not have been ennobled under his proposal, and the charisma to persuade them in time. As Muscovy renewed its attacks on the Commonwealth and supported Vyhovskyi's rivals, he was overthrown as hetman and fled Ukraine. Nemyrych, the author of the compromise, was slain by the Cossacks under his command. The mass of the Cossacks were mainly concerned to protect their personal freedoms, an object they pursued by what they thought were temporary alliances with Muscovy, Poland, and the Crimean Khanate. Although the Polish-Lithuanian parliament accepted the Hadiach Union, the Polish gentry lost interest in Union when it became clear that the hetmans did not really control the Cossacks, and the Cossacks did not really control Ukraine.[17]

The failure of the Hadiach Union in 1659 ended the Commonwealth's golden age, the era of glory, prosperity, and toleration inaugurated by the Lublin Union of 1569.[18] The Commonwealth founded in 1569 was a unique solution to the problems of religious and national strife threatening Europe's great powers. The problem of early modern European sovereigns was the clash of religious and political loyalty, their own and that of their subjects. As Germany was divided among Lutheran and Catholic princes, as France massacred its Huguenots, as the Holy Roman Emperor paid tribute to the Ottoman Sultan, and as even Spain's formidable power was challenged in the Netherlands and undermined by the Inquisition, Poland-Lithuania alone combined religious toleration, institutional reform, and territorial expansion.[19] The Polish-Lithuanian solution of 1569 was one of republican institutions to protect the rights of a sizable and variegated gentry. In economic terms, the prosperity of the Commonwealth and its gentry depended upon the grain trade with Western Europe, suggesting both the increasing relative economic backwardness of Poland-Lithuania, and the declining relative position of its peasants. Over the very long term, the absence of a central authority, the marginalization of the cities, and the backwardness of the countryside perhaps doomed the Commonwealth. Yet one can never be too certain: had events of the seventeenth century taken a different turn, had the conflict in Ukraine been resolved in the middle of the seventeenth century, the Commonwealth might have addressed these questions. In the period under discussion, 1569–1659, the crucial test for the Commonwealth was its ability to create, attract, and gain the loyalty of the political elite in Poland, Lithuania, and Ukraine. The Lublin Union had created and formalized a state of noble warriors and gentry citizens in Poland and Lithuania. The failure of the Hadiach Union prevented the application of this solution to Ukraine, and undermined it in Poland and Lithuania as well.

The Cossack rising would importantly mark the future of the Polish national idea, and the role of Poland in the Ukrainian national idea. In seventeenth-century Ukraine, it was easy to equate Poles and Catholics with masters, and the association only became stronger in the eighteenth and nineteenth centuries. Yet the key to the seventeenth century is not the clash between the Polish and Ukrainian nations, but the failure of the Commonwealth and the Cossacks to find a compromise. In Lithuania, such a compromise was found in 1569, and political and religious institutions remained a bridge between local elites and Polish culture well after dissolution of the Commonwealth in 1795. In Ukraine, no such political institutions were maintained, and the range of the Uniate Church was limited by the Cossacks. This leads to the misleading impression, in retrospect, that "Poland" and "Ukraine" were distinct in an era when they were joined in a single kingdom, and that "Poles" and "Ukrainians" were doomed to be enemies. The hetmanate used Polish currency, and Polish as a language of administration and even command. The negotiations of the mid-seventeenth century failed both sides, but the two parties understood each other. When the Commonwealth and the Cossacks negotiated, they did not need translators. The Cossack officers and the Polish nobility (groups that overlapped) shared one, two, or even three languages: Latin, Polish, and the vernacular Ruthenian (Ukrainian). When the Cossacks negotiated with the Muscovites, they used translators. Khmel'nyts'kyi had letters in Muscovite dialect translated into Latin, so that he could read them.[20]

Bohdan Khmel'nyts'kyi, leader of the Cossack uprising, comes down in history as a Ukrainian hero. Yet he was also a member of the Polish nobility, and he learned his Latin from the Jesuits. Jarema Wiśniowiecki, Khmel'nyts'kyi's great foe, comes down in history as a Polish magnate. He was indeed a Roman Catholic who owned 230,000 serfs. Yet Prince Jarema was also heir of an Orthodox clan, and descendant of one of the greatest Cossacks of all time. Wiśniowiecki must be seen as part of the Ukrainian problem within Poland. After all, it was he who challenged the Polish tradition of the equality of nobles by demanding a prince's throne in parliament. His refusal to concede any of the lands he regarded as his own to Muscovy was a persistent diplomatic problem for Warsaw.[21] Although the period 1569–1659 established crucial foundations for the later emergence of modern nations, the moment was one of struggle for Ukraine among Ukrainians within the new legal, political, religious, cultural, and economic framework of the Commonwealth. Wiśniowiecki/Vyshnevets'kyi and Khmel'nyts'kyi/Chmielnicki are seen by modern people as leaders of nations because Ukraine failed the Commonwealth, and the Commonwealth failed Ukraine. This was a political failure: as the Ukrainian poet Taras Shevchenko would have it, "the Cossacks punished the nobles, for the nobles ruled poorly." The collapse of the early modern political order of the Commonwealth stands at the origins of modern Poland, Ukraine, and indeed Russia.

LITHUANIA, POLAND, UKRAINE:
RUSSIA, 1648–1772

Eight years after Hadiach, Ukraine was split along the Dnipro River between the Commonwealth and Muscovy by the Treaty of Andrusovo. Today, the years between 1648 and 1667 are seen from a Ukrainian point of view as the time of a great Ukrainian rebellion against Polish oppressors; or from a Russian point of view as the moment when the stray Ukrainian stream found its way into the great Russian river.[22] It is more fruitful to observe a point of contact between Muscovy and Western politics and religion. The Cossack rising was grounded in the realities of the Commonwealth: while rejecting the inequality that Polish institutions had created in Ukraine, it presumed the existence of rights that the Commonwealth protected. Under Poland, in the three generations between 1569 and 1648, the ancient notion of democratic Cossack freedoms was shot through by the republican notion of gentry rights within a state. Article 3 of the 1654 Pereiaslav agreement with Muscovy even specified that the Cossacks would retain the rights they had enjoyed "under the Polish king." Although the Muscovites appeared similar to the Cossacks as fellow Orthodox believers, they represented a very different political order. The Cossacks were, after all, fighting for toleration of Orthodox religion, and had a legitimate claim within a system that was supposed to guarantee the equal position of Christian faiths. In the end, however, the Cossacks allied with a power where Church was utterly subordinate to State. Muscovy's traditional practice of imprisoning (and sometimes executing) Orthodox authorities was incomparably more brutal than any practice within the Commonwealth.

Thus the transfer of part of Ukraine exposed Muscovy to new ideas. Muscovy inherited, along with Kyiv, Orthodox churchmen formed by the controversies of the Reformation, Counter-Reformation, and Union. Mohyla's Kyiv Academy was at once the largest educational institution in the tsar's domains. Like the Chernihiv and Kharkiv collegia, it provided classical education along Baroque lines, mainly in Latin and Polish, to tens of thousands of East Slavic students. Jan Kochanowski, the outstanding poet of the Polish Renaissance, was taken as a model for student compositions; Polish modes of versifying prevailed in East Slavic lands absorbed by Muscovy through the eighteenth century. These academies, founded to defend Orthodoxy against Catholicism, were in close contact with Protestant Europe. For the next hundred and fifty years, these Ukrainian schools provided Moscow and the St. Petersburg with doctors, journalists, and civil servants. In the second half of the seventeenth century, not before, books were translated in Moscow in large numbers. The source languages were Greek, Latin, and Polish, and the translators were churchmen from the Commonwealth.[23] The language question was posed in Russia as Muscovite dialect confronted East Slavic, West Slavic, and European rivals.[24] In these ways, the incorporation of Kyiv and left-bank Ukraine forced Muscovy into contact with Europe.

Having adapted to the cultural attraction of western Christianity in the age of Reform, Ukrainian churchmen confronted in Muscovy a state and a church with limited cultural connections to the Byzantium they claimed to embody. Although Kyivan churchmen had never before regarded Moscow as a center of Orthodoxy, they adapted quickly to the new political situation of the second half of the seventeenth century. They provided the manpower for Patriarch Nikon's modernization of the Orthodox Church, and then later for the reforms of Peter the Great. After Andrusovo, Ukrainian churchmen sought to draw the support of their new sovereign by recasting the history of Muscovy in a way that linked church and state, and dignified their own position. Their cooperation with the Muscovite dynasty involved the invention of Russian history. One Ukrainian churchman invented the idea of the "transfer" of the Kyivan princely seat to Moscow, an idea which came to organize Russian national myth and historiography. In the 1670s professors of the Kyiv Academy were ideologists of the new regime. In these ways, the absorption of eastern Ukraine put into practice a transition from a limited geographic and political notion of Russia as the territory of Muscovy to an imperial idea of Russia as Great Russia (Muscovy),

Little Russia (Ukraine), and White Russia (Belarus).[25] Such political concepts, developed in the early modern period, took on new meaning in the modern age of nationalism.

RUSSIA, POLAND: UKRAINE, 1772–1918

The Russian empire, as Muscovy was called after 1721, really included two very different Ukraines. As we have seen, left-bank Ukraine (east of the Dnipro) had fallen under Russian control by the Treaty of Andrusovo in 1667. Hetman Ivan Mazepa (1639–1709) and his successor in exile, Pylyp Orlyk (1672–1742), sought to preserve the autonomy of their left-bank hetmanate by the traditional gambit of alliance with foreign powers. In civilization and education, both were men of the old Commonwealth, and they represented an officer corps self-consciously modeled on the Polish-Lithuanian nobility. As Tsar Peter I failed to protect Ukraine during the Swedish war, Mazepa and some Cossack officers considered the terms of Pereaiaslav violated, and mulled over an old copy of the Hadiach Union with the Commonwealth.[26] The moment for an alliance with Poland-Lithuania had passed, however. Muscovy's victory over Mazepa's Swedish patrons at Poltava in 1709 marked the end of the autonomous hetmanate, and the beginning of the full integration of Cossack elites into the new Russian state. This absorption of left-bank Ukrainian institutions had been in progress for three generations when the Russian empire gained right-bank Ukraine.

Russia seized right-bank Ukraine (west of the Dnipro) when the Polish-Lithuanian Commonwealth was partitioned in 1772, 1793, and 1795. In right-bank Ukraine, in the tsar's new Volyn', Podolia, and Kiev provinces, about one-tenth of the population were Polish gentry, one-tenth were Jews, and most of the rest were Ukrainian-speaking peasants. After the 1830 uprising, Russian authorities deprived most Polish nobles of their privileges, transforming them (legally if not quite socially) from poor nobles into poor peasants. In two ways, this change tended to further collapse "Poles" into "landlords" in Ukraine. The gentry who escaped were the great landholders, who represented Polishness in Ukraine. Meanwhile, the petty nobles deprived of their status assimilated to Ukrainian language and culture.[27] The end of old landholding customs also allowed magnates to push their poorer (Polish!) brethren from the land; the arrival of Russian power allowed them to call upon the Russian army to quell Ukrainian peasant uprisings. The Uniate Church was largely absorbed by Russian Orthodoxy in 1839, thus dividing Ukraine into a majority of Orthodox believers and a very small minority of Roman Catholics. The Uniate Church survived in the Kholm Eparchate of Volhynia until 1875: here the situation was more complicated, but Uniate Ukrainian landlords tended to identify with Roman Catholic Polish nobles rather than Orthodox peasants and Russians.

The 1863 rising, a national turning point in the Russian empire's Lithuanian and Belarusian lands, left little trace in Russian Ukraine. Whereas tens of thousands of Polish and Lithuanian gentry fought in central Poland and Lithuania, in Ukraine Polish landlords collaborated with Russian rule.[28] In Lithuania, the gentry fought to revive the institutions and traditions of the Grand Duchy, a cause inapplicable in Ukraine, since there were no analogous Ukrainian inheritances. Whereas Lithuanian and Belarusian peasants took part in the old Grand Duchy, Ukrainian peasants were more likely to betray gentry conspirators to the tsar's police or even to fight with his armies. Russian generals sought to portray the rebels as Poles who wished to enserf the Ukrainian peasantry. It is nevertheless too soon to speak of a clear division among modern Polish and Ukrainian nations. The most successful Polish general of the 1863 uprising in Ukraine was Edmund Różycki, whose Volhynian troops called him "Bat'ko" (Ukrainian for father) and marched into battle singing Ukrainian songs.[29] Language was not yet a dividing line between nations, the goals of the uprising were political rather than ethnic, and some Volhynian gentry were willing to die for the idea of a restored Commonwealth.

Still, for solid social and economic reasons, the line of both noble and peasant participation in the 1863 rising was the northern border of Ukraine, as created in 1569.[30] In right-bank Ukraine, the political and social system that had sparked the massive revolts of the seventeenth century was consolidated in the Russian empire under continued local Polish rule in the eighteenth.[31] There were still peasant risings, memorably recorded by the Ukrainian poet Taras Shevchenko, although their scale is unknown. Russian rule in the nineteenth century, superimposed on the primitive agrarian economy inherited from the Commonwealth, brought about a staggering gulf between a tiny group of Polish lords and the mass of Ukrainian peasants. Serfs were given personal freedom in 1861, but could not easily secure enough land to survive. It was not hard to persuade them that the rebels of 1863 wished to enserf them again. By 1900, only about 3 percent of the population in the tsar's Volhynian, Podolian, and Kiev provinces reported Polish as their first language. At this time, about four thousand Polish families owned as much land as three million former serfs.[32]

These right-bank territories, where the gentry was Polish, were absent from Russian notions of "Ukraine" for much of the nineteenth century. For Russians, Ukraine was rather the left bank, absorbed by the empire in 1667. The earliest articulation of Ukrainian patriotism by Russian subjects came from the left bank, from the new university at Kharkiv, in the 1820s and 1830s. Later Ukrainians saw the Kharkiv revival as a bridge between the defunct hetmanate (whose officers were fully co-opted by the empire by 1785) and the modernizing Russian empire after the Crimean War (1853–56). It was seen as a bright beacon during the "dark time" of political impotence. This modern patriotic scheme requires an important qualification. The novelty of the Kharkiv revival was not its attention to Ukrainian culture, but rather its association of Ukrainian culture with the Ukrainian lands. Broadly conceived, Ukrainian culture was a bulwark of the Russian empire, providing many of its legitimating myths, its folksongs and folktales, and indeed its educated civil servants. For more than a century after the foundation of the Russian empire in 1721, Ukrainians had provided many of its outstanding architects, apologists, and adventurers. Only from the 1820s did cracks begin to appear in this Ukrainian tradition of imperial service, and dilemmas appear for people of Ukrainian culture. Stricter ideas of official nationality forced Ukrainians to choose between public service and private inclinations; meanwhile new ideas of folk patriotism from the West provided a basis for an identification with the people of Ukraine. In rough terms, elite Ukrainians served the tsars so long as they were welcome in the capital of an empire that admitted multiple variations of Russia; when narrow ideas of Russia were imposed on Ukraine, a corner was turned.[33] The Crimean War, then, marks not only a change in Russian attitudes toward Ukraine, but a change in Ukrainian attitudes toward Russia.

In the middle of the nineteenth century, defensive patriotism from the left bank combined with the Romantic guilt of certain landlords from the right bank, and met in Kyiv/Kiev/Kijów to form a populism with something like a national character. Many Kievans, often people of Polish descent, tried to take politics to the Ukrainian peasantry. Kyiv/Kiev/Kijów was Polish in culture, and remained a puzzle to Russians two centuries after its incorporation into Russia.[34] Tsarist officials disagreed about whether populism was helpful (since awakened Ukrainian peasants would realize that they were Russians), or harmful (since Ukrainian activists were sometimes of Polish origin.)[35] After the 1863 rising, Ukrainian activism was opposed as part of a general Polish plot. The Valuev Decree of July 1863, famous for supporting the view that the Ukrainian language "has not, does not, and cannot exist," blamed its propagation on the Poles.[36] The possibility that Ukraine might be a nation separate from both Poland and Russia came late to Russians, and once conceived was categorically denied. The 1876 Ems Decree, which banned the publication and import of all Ukrainian works, reflected a modern association of language to nationality and the novel realization that the Ukrainians might be a nation. In the final quarter of the nineteenth century, the idea that Russia was a single nation, and that all East Slavs were Russians, became hegemonic.[37]

During this same period, the Ukrainian idea developed by Russian subjects found an audience in another empire. The poetry of Taras Shevchenko (1814–61) was read in Austrian Galicia as well as in Russia. Shevchenko was an extraordinary figure, a peasant son who saw Vil'no and Warsaw, a serf painter redeemed from his bondage for the sake of his art by admirers in St. Petersburg, a poet of freedom who established the grammar and the grace of the modern Ukrainian literary language.[38] With the abolition of serfdom, which took place the year of Shevchenko's death, his achievement paved the way for a modern Ukrainian politics in which culture was connected, in theory and in practice, with the peasantry. After 1876, varieties of modern Ukrainian politics were borne to Austria by Russian subjects. Mykhailo Drahomanov (1841–95), the most influential of Ukrainian political activists, found his way to L'viv after he lost his university chair at Kyiv in 1876. Mykhailo Hrushevs'kyi (1866–1934), the greatest Ukrainian historian, was hired away from Kyiv by L'viv University in 1894. Vyacheslav Lypyns'kyi (1882–1931), the greatest Ukrainian political theorist, emigrated to Austrian Galicia in 1908. The list includes Dmytro Dontsov, the most famous Ukrainian nationalist: but his ideas found purchase in a twentieth-century Galicia that took the modern nation for granted, a Galicia that came into being in the final quarter of the nineteenth century.

AUSTRIA, POLAND: UKRAINE, 1772–1918

How did the Ukrainian idea become modern national politics, and why in Austria? It appears, at first, that Polish dominance was far more secure in Austrian Galicia than in Russian Ukraine. The lands of the Commonwealth seized by Austria in the partitions of 1772 and 1795, known as "Galicia and Lodomeria," were home to more than two million East Slavic peasants. Catholic Poles were the available ruling class, and Galicia was left under the control of Polish landholders. Although Poles were the majority in the western part of the province, where Cracow was the largest city after it was incorporated in 1846, and Ukrainians the majority in the eastern part, where Lwów/L'viv was the largest city, Galicia was a single province. By the final quarter of the nineteenth century, the population of the western half was perhaps 88 percent Polish and 7.5 percent

Jewish, with a handful of Germans and East Slavs. The population of the eastern half of Galicia, by contrast, was perhaps 65 percent Ukrainian, 22 percent Polish, and 12 percent Jewish. These figures held steady until the First World War.[39] To the position of Galician Jews we shall return. Here our purpose is to divine the origins of Ukrainian politics.

Although initial Austrian land reforms scarcely improved the lot of Ukrainian peasants, religious reforms were of great potential importance. In 1774 Empress Maria Theresa rechristened the Uniate Church the "Greek Catholic" Church, to be equal to the Roman and Armenian Catholic Churches. In 1775 she opened fourteen places for Greek Catholics at the Barbareum Academy in Vienna. Her successor Joseph II founded a General Seminary for Greek Catholics in Lemberg/Lwów/L'viv in 1783, and opened Lemberg University in 1784. Between 1787 and 1809 the university included a Studium Ruthenum for Greek Catholics who did not know Latin well enough to attend regular courses.[40]

There was no immediate connection between liberated Greek Catholic peasants and educated Greek Catholic churchmen. In the first half of the nineteenth century, Greek Catholic priests saw themselves as continuators of the Polish high culture and the religious variety of the recently defunct Commonwealth. They did what their brethren in the Russian empire could not: preserve the Church founded in 1596 under the Commonwealth after the Commonwealth's demise in 1795. When they celebrated the elevation of the Lemberg/Lwów/L'viv episcopate to the status of metropolis in 1808, they did so in the Polish language. A few students of the General Seminary did publish in the Galician Ukrainian dialect as early as the 1830s, but this was favored by neither the church nor the state. The most noted of these was Markiian Shashkevych, son of a noble family that had spoken Polish for generations. Other churchmen published grammars of Ukrainian in German and Polish.[41] Loyalty to early modern Polish traditions first failed these churchmen during the Revolution of 1848, when a sharp difference of interests appeared between those who spoke their language (Polish gentry) and the faithful of their parishes (Ukrainian peasants). Encouraged by Austrian officials, a few Ukrainian leaders emerging from the Greek Catholic clergy tabled their own proposals for the future of Galicia.

After the Revolution of 1848 was put down with the aid of Greek Catholic peasants, serfdom was abolished and peasants were briefly given limited representation in the Austrian parliament. An imperial patent of 1850 promised Ukrainians equal treatment. Yet Ukrainians did not displace Poles as the ruling class in Galicia, as Poles quickly adapted to the postrevolutionary situation. Between 1849 and 1859 the policy of reaction in Galicia was implemented by a Polish count, Agenor Gołuchowski, who placed local Polish nobles in key posts in the Austrian administration.[42] Because the revolution had set Polish gentry and Ukrainian peasants against each other, and because its aftermath revealed the limits of Austrian support, after 1848 leading Greek Catholics were drawn to Russia. The appeal of Russia peaked around 1867, when Vienna granted informal autonomy to Galicia on terms favorable to the Polish aristocracy. Of course, Greek Catholic Russophiles after 1848 were never simple "Russians," any more than their Polonophone predecessors before 1848 had been simple "Poles." Russophiles in Galicia argued that contemporary Russian had been created by scholars from Ukraine in the seventeenth and eighteenth centuries, and could therefore serve as the literary language of all East Slavs.[43] They regarded their eastern Galicia as a member of a larger family of East Slavic nations.

Since the Uniate (Greek Catholic) Church had been totally removed from the Russian empire in 1875, Galician priests who flirted with the Russian empire were of necessity flirting with Orthodoxy. Vienna supported the Greek Catholic Church as part of a Catholic bulwark of its power in its borderlands with Russia. In 1882, a leading Russophile persuaded a village of Greek Catholics to petition Austrian authorities for permission to convert to Orthodoxy. "Ukrainophiles," advocates of the use of the local vernacular and the distinctness of local people from Russians, gained more support from Vienna. The Vatican also treated Ukrainophilia as a lesser evil than Russophilia, and favored Ukrainophile over Russophile priests. A similar shift flowed from the secular politics of the 1880s. After the Ukrainian representation in the Austrian Reichsrat (parliament) dropped from seventeen to three after the 1879 elections, much of the Greek Catholic elite saw the sense of reaching out to the peasantry. Some of them drew the further conclusion that the local vernacular, the Ukrainian language, was the best means to this end. In 1889, electoral success demonstrated the political utility of the Ukrainian language.[44]

Within the shell of nineteenth-century Austria, Greek Catholic priests shifted from the use of Polish as the vehicle of high culture in Galicia (roughly 1795–1848), to an identification with Russia which allowed them to distance themselves from the Poles (roughly 1848–90), and then finally to modern appeals on behalf of a "Ukrainian nation" divided between Austria and Russia (after 1890). The center of their concerns shifted from the religious practice of local Greek Catholics, to the social condition of the peasant masses, to national justice for millions of "Ukrainians." By the time Andrei Sheptyts'kyi was

Fig. 15. Andrei Sheptyts'kyi (1865–
1944), Greek Catholic metropolitan.
Sheptyts'kyi did much to connect
Greek Catholic faith and Ukrainian
politics in Galicia. The label
"nationalist" still seems not to fit
a man who had Polish brothers
and sheltered Jews from the
Final Solution.

named metropolitan of Galicia in 1900, his idea of Greek Catholicism as a national church was plausible. Leo Sheptyts'kyi had proposed to Empress Maria
Theresa that Greek Catholicism be accorded equal status with Roman Catholicism in Austria; his illustrious descendant Andrei proposed that a Ukrainian
Greek Catholic Church would confer upon his flock of three million equal national status with Roman Catholic Poles. In the last quarter of the nineteenth
century, the Greek Catholic Church opened hundreds of schools, most of them
teaching in the vernacular (Ukrainian). These schools were increasingly national in their orientation.[45] As metropolitan, Sheptyts'kyi democratized the
Church itself.

GALICIA: UKRAINE (CIRCA 1900)

Galician Ukrainophilia was thus structurally similar to, if more modest than,
the Russophilia it supplanted. Both Russophilia and Ukrainophilia indulged in
linguistic dreams of unity. Russophiles used a bizarre mixture of Galician di-

Fig. 16. St. George's Cathedral, Lwów. Lwów was a seat of three separate Catholic rites: Greek, Roman, and Armenian. This cathedral was Sheptyts'kyi's seat as Greek Catholic metropolitan of Galicia.

alects, Church Slavonic, and elements of literary Russian; Ukrainophiles wished to treat Galician dialects as a Ukrainian language, with little knowledge of dialects further east. Both Ukrainophilia and Russophilia were territorially ambitious. Galician Ukrainophiles and Galician Russophiles alike used an unknown but massive group of Slavs to the east to bolster confidence and solidify claims. These similarities help us to see how many individuals could shift from Russophilia to Ukrainophilia without enduring a sense of contradiction.

The Ukrainophile orientation had an elective affinity to other ambitious and idealistic projects of Slavic nationalities under Austrian rule. The nineteenth-century shifts in national orientation in Galicia were, for example, no more striking than those of Bohemia.[46] Just as Czechs dreamed of enlisting the Russian empire and the rising Balkan nations as counterweights to German power, so Galician Ukrainians imagined their eastern neighbors as an answer to local Polish rule. Like the Czechoslovak (and Yugoslav) ideas, the Ukrainian idea was a tempered Pan-Slavism: a Pan-Slavism close enough to nationalism to win local support, and close enough to realism to nurture some hope of eventual success.

The Ukrainian idea bore a family resemblance to the contemporary aspirations of some Poles in Austria to turn Galicia into a "Polish Piedmont" which would eventually unify the rest of the partitioned Polish nation. The Italian kingdom of Piedmont, of course, began the unification of Italy (more or less complete in 1870), which preceded the unification of Germany (complete in 1871). A difference between Poles and Ukrainians in Galicia was that Poland was seen by everyone as a historical nation, like Germany and Italy, with a tradition of statehood.[47] Poles aspired to recreate the Commonwealth as it existed in the increasingly warped mirror of their increasingly modern nationalist imaginations; Ukrainians sought to break the looking glass, melt the fragments, shape something new.

Andrei Sheptyts'kyi's Polish origins are emblematic of the novelty of the Ukrainian idea; his continued presence in Polish life reminds us of the importance of the Poles in the Ukrainian idea's crystallization at the end of the nineteenth century. Poles were for Ukrainian activists models, rulers, and rivals. Poles were models in that the Polish nation seemed to have great autonomy within Austria. Poles were rulers in that this autonomy conferred real power upon Polish aristocrats: more than 90 percent of high administrative posts in Galicia were held by Poles. Poles were rivals in that Polish political forces keyed to modern nationalism, such as the National Democrats, sought to spread Polish culture as national culture throughout Galicia. This left Ukrainian activists confronting not only government by Poles, but a national movement determined to create a Polish civil society and (eventually) a Polish national state in Galicia. In fact, loyal Polish aristocrats and the Polish nationalists were themselves in opposing camps, and took different stances on a number of issues, including the Ukrainian question.

The early 1890s found Polish officials in Galicia executors of a general Austrian policy favoring the Ukrainophile over the Russophile orientation. A committee composed of Polish noblemen decided to standardize the Ukrainian language according to the Ukrainian vernacular orthography rather than the various systems favored by the Russophiles. Polish gentry also dominated the committee that filled the new chair of East European history in Lwów with Mykhailo Hrushevs'kyi (1866–1934), a Russian subject. Austrian imperial policies as executed by loyal Austrian Poles in Lwów/Lemberg/L'viv established a link to Kijów/Kiev/Kyiv. In Kyiv, the main problem for Ukrainians was the Russian censor, and many Ukrainophiles were Poles. Hrushevs'kyi, the student of a Ukrainian historian of Polish origins, Volodymyr Antonovych, was surprised to find that Poles in Galicia were hostile to the Ukrainian cause.[48] His appointment, the result of a brief political conjuncture in Galicia, had lasting national consequences for all Ukraine. Hrushevs'kyi's arrival in L'viv from Kyiv in 1894 provided intellectual support to the Ukrainophile orientation in Galicia. His lectures in the Ukrainian language lent it credibility as a means of scholarship and enlightenment.

The first volume of his *History of Ukraine-Rus'*, the most important text in the construction of a Ukrainian historical narrative, followed in 1898. Its most substantial innovation was the elaboration of a coherent history of Ukraine, beginning with Kyivan Rus'. The methodology that allowed this achievement drew from Kyivan populism: the people, along with the polities, were presented as actors in history. In this way a conjuncture of imperial politics brought to L'viv a historical vision that could resist all imperial claims. By refuting the Russian historiographical claim that Moscow had inherited ancient Kyivan traditions, Hrushevs'kyi provided the basis for a political challenge to the Russian claim to all Ukraine. By treating the common people as part of history, Hrushevs'kyi undermined the traditional distinction between "historical" and "unhistorical nations," the basis for the Polish claim to Galicia. In the nineteenth century, nations were thought to be "historical" if their elites could be associated with a state tradition. Once history was redefined to include the people, that fact that Galicia had been a Polish crownland, or that Ukrainian elites had accepted Polish civilization, was no longer dispositive.[49] Hrushevs'kyi was a novice in Galician politics, but implications of his work for the local Ukraino-

Fig. 17. Mykhailo Hrushevs'kyi
(1866–1934), historian. His scheme of
East European history, inspirational
in Ukraine, has not yet been generally
assimilated by scholars.

phile cause were immediately apparent. Galician Ukrainian activists already knew that if the people were treated as constitutive of the nation, eastern Galicia was a Ukrainian land. The Russian imperial census, published in 1897, allowed Galicians to imagine a far larger Ukraine to their east.

Although Austrian imperial concessions of the early 1890s directly and indirectly strengthened the Ukrainophile orientation, Ukrainian activists came to see them as inadequate. Especially after the scandalous electoral manipulations of 1895 and 1897, they were thinking increasingly in national terms, and national status demands equality with rivals. As we have seen, Ukrainian activists wished for what Polish officials exercised (power) as well as what Polish nationalists sought (a mass nation). In other words, Ukrainian activists matched their demands to what they saw as Polish successes in Galicia and their goals to those of Polish nationalists. Immediate Ukrainian demands to Vienna were a partition of Galicia and Ukrainian autonomy in the eastern part; proportional representation in the Galician and Austrian parliaments; and the Ukrainization of Lwów University. The long-term goals were the creation of a Ukrainian nation and the establishment of a Ukrainian state with "ethnic" borders.[50] These harder edges of the Ukrainian idea came from a new generation of secular activists, no longer only Greek Catholic priests but their sons or daughters, sometimes even the children of the Ukrainian peasantry educated in post-1848 Austria.

Whereas Sheptyts'kyi represents the transformations of old elites (Greek Catholic clergy and Polish gentry), the poet Ivan Franko (1856–1916) is taken to represent a new kind of secular intelligentsia arising from the Ukrainian soil. His pedigree reminds us, however, that the political idea of ethnic nationalism was conceived by elites before it was accepted by peasants: and that the elites often failed to meet "ethnic" definitions of nationhood themselves. Franko's father was a village blacksmith, and of German origin; his mother was of petty Polish noble origin. In 1864 he was sent to study in a German-language school of the Basilians, a Greek Catholic order concerned to preserve the connection of their church with the Latin West. More important than his childhood or "ethnic" origins were his confrontations with Polish culture, Russian politics, and European ideologies in the final quarter of the nineteenth century. In 1876 he met the historian Mykhailo Drahomanov (1841–95), an exile from Russian Ukraine who had just lost his professorship in Kyiv. Drahomanov persuaded young intellectuals such as Franko that their Russophilia should be sublimated into brotherhood with the Ukrainian people. In the 1880s, thanks to a public trial and writings in Polish, Franko became a famous socialist in L'viv/Lwów. In 1890 he co-founded a peasant Radical Party oriented toward the socialist transformation of Galicia, and its separation into eastern (Ukrainian) and western (Polish) districts. In 1897 he broke loudly with Polish politics (writing in German) and with Ukrainian politics (writing in Polish). Already a friend of Hrushevs'kyi, Franko now became his protégé. On Christmas Eve, 1899, the two men and the other leaders of a new National Democratic party published an appeal to all classes of Ukrainian society for the general endeavor of national sovereignty. While Franko continued to believe that an elite must organize politics, his views of the ideas that should guide elites had undergone an important change.[51]

By 1900, Franko was an advocate of Ukrainian independence within what he and others of his generation called "ethnographic" borders. Like Franko, many of the leading Galician Ukrainian national activists in 1900 had been socialists ten years before. This was exceedingly common in the Europe of the day, not least in Poland. (The founder of Polish National Democracy, Roman Dmowski; its youth organizer, Zygmunt Balicki; and its social theorist, Stanisław Grabski, had all been on the left in their youth.) The general connection between the seemingly contradictory ideas of socialism and nationalism is that of idealistic faith in the yet untried people; the particular impulse that pushed Ukrainian activists from socialism to nationalism was real competition with the Poles. Ukrainians influenced by Drahomanov believed that Ukrainian socialism would arise from the Ukrainian people, Polish socialism from the Polish people, and so on. This version of the socialist faith in the masses led inevitably to the question as to just who the masses were. In this way the invention of Ukrainian and Polish "ethnic groups" was no stranger than, and indeed flowed logically from, the prediction that the Ukrainian and Polish masses would lead a revolution. Since the Ukrainian people was constituted almost entirely of peasants, it was easy to conflate the revolutionary idea of the people with the new scientific idea of an "ethnic group." The 1897 Russian imperial census, which inquired about language, created the mental map of a great land of ethnic Ukrainians to Galicia's east. The idea of a Ukrainian "ethnic group" also provided a natural defense against Polish socialists who presumed that socialism would mean a revival of the old Commonwealth, and against Polish nationalists who based their claim to Galicia on culture rather than numbers.[52]

In Galicia, these conclusions of the secular intelligentsia were reached by 1900, just as Sheptyts'kyi began to transform the Greek Catholic Church into a democratic instrument of Ukrainian national revival. Social, religious, and linguistic differences of early modern origin were now recast in modern national terms by both radicals and churchmen. The peasantry was not part of the nation in the early modern Commonwealth; the definition of a modern Ukrainian peasant nation marked the Pole as exploiter and alien. The Greek Catholic Church was a survival of the early modern Commonwealth; it became a major instrument in the creation of a modern Ukrainian nation. Roman Catholicism, at the same time, came to signify Polish nationality as well as religious belief and practice. Much of the vocabulary of Ukrainian literature arose from Ukraine's early modern contact with Poland, but the codified vernacular was seen by all as a Ukrainian national language. It followed that Polish was no longer the language of cultural exchange, and it was demoted to the status of one national language among many.

To see the difference between the modern definitions triumphant in Galicia and the historical debates that continued in Lithuania, let us return for a moment to the legacy of the Romantic poet Mickiewicz. In 1900, Mickiewicz provided terms of reference common to Ukrainians and Poles, just as he did for Lithuanians, Belarusians, and Poles. For example, some Ukrainian nationalists unsure of Sheptyts'kyi's reliability and conviction called him a "Wallenrod." The reference is to the Mickiewiczean hero who claims to be of one nationality, then betrays his fellows in the name of another. Some Ukrainians feared that Sheptyts'kyi, having become the head of the local Greek Catholic Church, would turn out to be a Pole. In Lithuania, "Wallenrod" was a positive example for conspirators. In Ukraine, a "Wallenrod" was a traitor. Moreover, the Mickiewiczean idea of a "Wallenrod" most pertinent to Ukrainian-Polish relations in 1900 is importantly different from the Mickiewiczean "Fatherland" central to Polish-Lithuanian-Belarusian contests. The "Fatherland" presumes complex loyalties; "Wallenrod" (on this interpretation) presumes a national essence.[53]

Franko's personal attitude to Mickiewicz makes this point more starkly. Franko's turn away from Polish culture, and rejection of cooperation with Poles, was expressed in his denunciation of Mickiewicz as a "Poet of Treason." Rather than treating Mickiewicz as part of a shared canon from which exemplars could be drawn, Franko cast the poet as a source of Polish nationalism. This was to accept the terms of Polish integral nationalism, that the nation comes from below, by rejecting of one of its idols, the nationalized Mickiewicz of Polish National Democracy. It was also to reject historical conversations still ongoing in old Lithuania. In Lithuania, Mickiewicz stood for the vitality of ancient institutions, portrayed in *Konrad Wallenrod* and elsewhere. As we have seen, the emerging Lithuanian myth portrayed 1569 as the end of Lithuanian culture. Lithuanian statehood, however, survived until 1795, and important Lithuanian institutions lasted well into the nineteenth century. The 1569 Lublin Union did not create political institutions to secure Ukraine within the Commonwealth. By and large, Lithuanian activists in 1900 accepted the need to prove that theirs was a historical nation, that their modern peasant constituents inherited a historical polity. By intellectual demonstrations, they transformed Mickiewicz's "Lithuania! My Fatherland!" into Kudirka's folkish "Lithuania! Our Fatherland!" Ukrainian activists went a step further, and treated the people themselves as the object of history. This resolved tensions, and opened wide vistas. If Ukraine was its people, a Ukrainian state should extend wherever they were found.[54]

Chapter 7 Galicia and Volhynia at the Margin (1914–1939)

Before the First World War, it appeared that the Ukrainian cause in Austrian Galicia had greater hope for success than the Lithuanian cause in the Russian empire. Whereas there were fewer than two million speakers of Lithuanian, the Ukrainian "ethnic group" was counted in the tens of millions. Unlike Lithuanians in the Northwest Territory of the Russian empire, Ukrainians in Austrian Galicia voted in parliamentary elections, formed legal political associations, and published legally in their native language. Democratic politics crystallized modern national identifications within the Habsburg domains, and manhood suffrage placed a powerful tool in the hands of advocates of peasant nations such as Ukraine. The idea that "ethnicity" was a better argument than "tradition" was confirmed as democratic practice corroded the traditional position of the Galician Polish gentry. Secular elites had begun to propose Ukrainian national independence, as churchmen transformed the Greek Catholic Church into a national institution. During the First World War, in which Austria fought Russia, Vienna persecuted Galicians it regarded as pro-Russian, indirectly aiding the Ukrainian cause. Galician Ukrainian politicians in Vienna favored the establishment of an independent Ukraine in lands taken from the Russian empire, with close associations with a newly autonomous eastern Galicia. This was a breath away from open support of Ukrainian independence in all Ukrainian lands. Independence seemed like a real possibility after the February Revolution in Russia and the proclamation of a Ukrainian National Republic in Kyiv in early 1917. Galician Ukrainians took seriously the rhetoric of Wilsonian self-determination after the American entry into the war in April 1917. There was some cause for optimism, no matter who won the war: or so it seemed.[1]

The Achilles heel of peasant nations, and the weak point of ethnic politics, is the city. Any form of independent Ukraine would require a capital, and in western Ukraine that capital would have to be L'viv. Yet Poles dominated Lwów. The best estimate is that a bit more than 52 percent of the city's inhabitants would have called themselves Poles, since 51.9 percent declared themselves Roman Catholics in the Austrian census of 1900, and at this time there were probably more Greek Catholic Poles than Roman Catholic Ukrainians. 75.4 percent of Lwów's inhabitants claimed Polish as their mother tongue, but this is far too high, since Yiddish-speaking Jews were denied that choice in the census. Before the First World War, the Galician Diet in Lwów was the seat of the only Polish-speaking assembly on the lands of the old Commonwealth. The city itself was the site of a recent victory of Polish culture: in the previous two generations the language of its schools, university, and public life had shifted from German to Polish. At the end of the First World War, as Austria collapsed, Poles knew that they were outnumbered by Ukrainians in eastern Galicia. Two-thirds of the population was Greek Catholic in religion; in the forty-four administrative divisions of eastern Galicia, Poles were a majority in exactly one: the city of Lwów itself.[2] The Polish claim to eastern Galicia was based upon their predominance in Lwów and upon the civilization they believed they had brought.[3] Lwów stood both for an ancient Polish presence, and for a recent political triumph.

In Warsaw in 1918, the conviction that Lwów was a Polish city was stronger than, for example, the sense that Wilno was a Polish city. Wilno had been the capital of something called "Lithuania," whose historical relationship to "Poland" was at least worthy of discussion. "Ukraine," on the other hand, was not recalled as a political entity within the Commonwealth, and Lwów was seen as a historically Polish city. Though founded by Orthodox princes in 1264, the city was indeed between 1349 and 1772 part of the Polish Kingdom (in the Rus' Palatinate). Much, of course, had changed since 1772 under Austrian rule: the size of the city increased by a factor of about seven (from about 20,000 to about

Fig. 18. View of Lwów. It is today L'viv, Ukraine. The view is much the same now as it was then.

140,000), and Polish elites reestablished hegemony under a new set of political rules. If the city could become culturally Polish under Austrian rule, Poles thought, surely the same would happen to its hinterlands under Polish rule. Polish language and Roman Catholic religion, they believed, would bring civilization to eastern Galicia. Although National Democrats such as Stanisław Grabski imagined a compromise with Russia over eastern lands, while leading federalists such as Józef Piłsudski hoped for an alliance with Ukraine against Russia, no Polish politician of any stature imagined that Lwów would be anything but Polish. In April 1919 the Polish constituent assembly unanimously resolved that all of Galicia should be annexed.

Jews, not Ukrainians, were Lwów's most visible minority. Jews had been invited to the city by medieval princes of Galicia and kings of Poland. They prospered in Galician towns and cities in the sixteenth century, and became a considerable urban presence. Until the eighteenth century, Galician Jews preserved communal life according to their privileges within the Polish-Lithuanian Commonwealth; within Austria, they were subject to the assimilatory and Germanizing policies of the empire. Jews formed much of the middle class and professional elite of Lemberik (the Yiddish pronunciation of "Lemberg"), as well as much of the small working class. After Galicia gained autonomy in 1867 on terms favorable to the Poles, Jews learned Polish in Austrian schools. The decline of Austrian liberalism after the financial crash of 1873 undermined the political option of choice of secular Jews. After the 1879 parliamentary elections, cultural integration coincided with political cooperation, as Galician Jewish deputies joined the Polish Club in parliament and ran as its candidates. By the turn of the century, however, matters were quite different. The advent of modern Polish and Ukrainian nationalisms forced secular Jews toward more exclusionary ideas of politics. That Jewish nationalists (Zionists) sealed an electoral alliance with Ukrainians in 1907, after universal male suffrage was introduced, demonstrated their grasp of the new rules of national politics.[4] Throughout this period, Jewish cooperation with Poles (and then Ukrainians) must be understood within the framework of the multinational Austrian polity. What would happen if Austria ceased to exist was an unhappy question for all Jews.

The modern national duo of literary language-vernacular tongue was very difficult for most Jews to imagine. For most Jews, Hebrew remained the sacred language, and Yiddish the language of normal intercourse, while Polish or German was needed for commerce. After the Constitution of 1867, Galician Jews enjoyed equal rights, and could consider themselves Austrians par excellence, regardless of whether or not they mastered Polish or German. Moreover, languages learned in youth need not correspond to the work of maturity. Jewish supporters of assimilation to German culture of the 1820s made their point in Yiddish; Jewish advocates of integration to Polish life of the 1870s argued in German; then the Zionists of the 1890s wrote and spoke Polish. The second generation of Zionists, in the early twentieth century, gritted their teeth and used the vernacular Yiddish as a language of politics. Themselves fluent in some combination of Polish, German, and Yiddish, Zionists imagined a future in which all Jews would use Hebrew in daily life.

Even for Jewish nationalists, the modern national trio of language-territory-state was impossible to envision in Europe. The Jews were perhaps 13 percent of the population of eastern Galicia as a whole in 1900, and a majority in many towns. Yet here as elsewhere in Eastern Europe there was no region in which they were a majority and could contemplate a separate state. Even as the democratization of Austria encouraged Zionists to concentrate on political work within the Diaspora rather than on plans for the move to Palestine, the problem of territory remained even more intractable than the problem of language. Even for Jewish nationalists, the First World War presented more risks than opportunities. Zionists knew that the principal of territorial self-determination could not serve their needs: even with the destruction of Austria, there was no way to establish a Jewish state in Europe. During the First World War, the goal of most Jews in Lemberik was very conservative: to keep what they had until peacetime.

WARTIME DEFEAT AND UKRAINIAN
NATIONALISM (1918–1920)

In the light of Polish claims and Jewish presence we see the radical nature of the aim of Galician Ukrainian activists in 1918: to found in Galicia a Ukrainian national republic with a capital in L'viv. In some sense, this resembled the desire of Lithuanian activists to found an independent Lithuania with a capital in Vilnius. Yet in the aftermath of the First World War, between 1918 and 1920, little Lithuania was de facto protected by a German army stranded in the East; was saved from the Soviet Union by Poland; and survived as a neighbor of a defeated Germany, a defeated Soviet Union, and a Poland which had taken Wilno by force. Relatively few Lithuanians perished in any of these struggles, whereas more than a million inhabitants of Ukraine died in the state-to-state wars, internecine conflicts, partisan actions, bandit raids, and pogroms that prevailed in 1918–20.

Ukrainians expected more, and got less. Geopolitical fortune counted for more than national sacrifice, and organized mobilization for more than sheer numbers. Even though Austria-Hungary and imperial Russia were destroyed, there was not a square centimeter of Ukrainian territory that Poles, White Russians, and/or Bolsheviks did not regard as part of their natural inheritance. The victorious Entente powers disagreed among themselves as to the disposition of Galicia and Volhynia, but none of them at any material time took any Ukrainian claim very seriously. At the relevant moment, 1918–20, their concern was to defeat or at least restrain Bolshevik Russia. Entente support of General Anton Denikin's White Russian army precluded support for Ukraine, since Denikin was a Russian nationalist and considered Ukraine part of Russia. After Denikin's defeat, the Western powers supported Poland as a counterweight to Bolshevik Russia, which implied accepting Poland's claim to eastern Galicia and Lwów.[5] The two Ukrainian states founded after the war, with capitals in L'viv and Kyiv, had to meet Polish and Russian challenges without allies. In these circumstances, Ukrainian elites required an extraordinary effort of organization, which was lacking. The Kyiv state was riven by ideological disputes among its leaders, crippled by the weakness of crucial institutions such as the army, unable to make itself heard among the peasantry, and thus overwhelmed by an array of external (and internal) military forces.[6]

Galician Ukrainians were more successful in their attempt to found a West Ukrainian Republic in L'viv. The most dramatic moments were the Ukrainian seizure of key buildings in L'viv on the night of 31 October 1918: and the counterattack of Polish residents on 1 November. Unfortunately for Galician Ukrainians, Poles could call upon a regular army. In particular, the arrival of General Józef Haller's army from France in April 1919 was decisive. Its troops driven east beyond the Zbruch river, the West Ukrainian Republic was defeated by July 1919, and forced to establish a government-in-exile in Vienna. The war cost Galician Ukrainians fifteen thousand men, created a generation of frustrated veterans, and confirmed a prevailing belief that Poland was the main enemy of Ukraine. The war's end left L'viv/Lwów and eastern Galicia inside Poland, and made about three million Ukrainian speakers and just under one million east Galician Jews citizens of the Second Polish Republic. Unfortunately for Galician Jews, the national alternatives which arose from the ruins of Austria offered little room for the uncommitted. Local Poles and Polish soldiers saw Jewish neutrality and Jewish self-defense as support for Ukraine. Polish attacks on Jews killed at least seventy in Lwów in 1918–19.[7]

The First World War and the collapse of empires led to national state-building projects in Warsaw, Kyiv, and L'viv. But the Habsburg collapse motivated other speakers of Ukrainian to build states with very different goals. Of the three million or so speakers of Ukrainian in Galicia, perhaps 150,000 were Lemkos: East Slavic inhabitants of the hills and mountains of what was fast becoming the new Polish-Czechoslovak border. In November 1918, when Galician Ukrainians declared Ukrainian independence in L'viv, the Lemkos founded a separate administration. Here, in the Beskidy ranges of the Carpathian mountains, the Ukrainian idea was alien. Local Lemko elites were Russophiles, but their main concern was with the integrity of their lands, not with national loyalty. The Lemko administration first petitioned for the annexation of Lemko territories by Russia, then for their inclusion within Czechoslovakia. Lemkos considered incorporation by Poland the worst of all possible solutions, especially if this involved (as it did) the division of Lemko lands by a new state border. Polish troops confirmed just this outcome when they suppressed the Lemko "state" in spring 1920.[8] The Lemko case reminds us that the end of Habsburg rule was not accompanied by nationalism everywhere, that groups can organize for political goals other than national independence, and that the Ukrainian movement had by no means yet penetrated all of Galicia.

THE RIGA SETTLEMENT, 1921

Polish-Ukrainian strife delayed Polish leader Józef Piłsudski's plan for a Polish-Ukrainian alliance against Russia, since Poles and Ukrainians could not fight on the same side of a war until Poland's southeastern border was delineated to Polish satisfaction. In effect, Poland could only ally with one Ukrainian state after it had destroyed the other. When the time came, the alliance between Piłsudski's Poland and the crumbling Kyiv state of Symon Petliura was too little, too late. In April 1920 Petliura conceded western Ukraine to Poland, and allied with Piłsudski in an attack on Soviet Russia. From a Galician Ukrainian point of view, this was betrayal by Kyiv. From Petliura's perspective, this was the last chance to preserve statehood in the Ukrainian heartland. From Piłsudski's point of view, the alliance was an opportunity to defeat the Red Army, and the solidify Ukraine as a buffer state. It was a risky move for Piłsudski, since the Polish National Democrats opposed Ukrainian independence, now dominated an elected National Assembly, and would profit from any failure in the east. The National Democrat Stanisław Grabski resigned as chair of the parliamentary foreign affairs committee in protest at the alliance with Ukraine. Kyiv was quickly won in May 1920, then just as quickly lost. Bolshevik troops counterattacked, threw back Polish and Ukrainian forces, and advanced to the suburbs of Warsaw and Lwów in August 1920.

In the end Polish and Ukrainian troops were triumphant, but Polish resources were exhausted, Polish public opinion divided, and Polish authorities in disagreement about how much territory to take from defeated Bolshevik Russia. As we have seen, the Polish constituent assembly represented central Poland, and was heavily National Democratic. The Polish position in the Polish-Bolshevik pourparlers was determined by Stanisław Grabski, who favored adding only territories which (he believed) could be assimilated by a nationally Polish state. This meant in practice all lands the National Democrats considered to be "ethnically Polish," as well as "historically Polish" territories which were compact and featured cities of Polish culture. Adolf Joffe, the Bolshevik negotiator, was pleased to gain territories for Moscow that were occupied by Polish troops. At Riga in March 1921, Polish and Bolshevik negotiators partitioned what we now see as Belarusian and Ukrainian lands, Poland taking most of Volhynia and all of Galicia, and agreeing to recognize Soviet Ukraine and Soviet Belorussia.[9] Having violated the spirit if perhaps not the letter of article 4 of its alliance agreement with Petliura's Ukraine, Poland interned its Ukrainian allies.

As a result of its victory in two eastern wars, the first against the West Ukrainian Republic (1918–19) and the second against Bolshevik Russia (1919–20), Poland absorbed Galicia and most of Volhynia. This was part of the new territorial disposition in Europe following the end of the First World War, characterized in eastern Europe by the creation of smaller states from larger ones. This territorial settlement is usually considered under the rubric of "Versailles," but in the east borders were determined by forces beyond the control of the Entente powers. As always when maps are redrawn, one must pause and be clear about old names in new circumstances. "Volhynia" had named a medieval principality, a district of the Grand Duchy of Lithuania, a palatinate of Poland during the Commonwealth, and a *gubernia* of the Russian empire. Independent Poland took most, but not all, of that *gubernia* in 1921. The rest of historic Volhynia was divided, on the Soviet side, between the Kyiv and Vinnytsia oblasts of the Ukrainian Soviet Socialist Republic (SSR). That the Soviet Union established in 1922 included a Ukrainian SSR was the most important consequence of the attempts to establish an independent Ukrainian state in 1918–20.[10] There was no nominal recognition of "Ukraine" within Poland, but there was a palatinate of "Volhynia." By "Volhynia" we shall mean that province ("Województwo Wołynskie", or "Wołyń"), as well as the southern part of the Polish palatinate of Polesie.

This book has spoken of "Galicia" in the sense of the Ukrainian "Halychyna," the eastern half of the Austrian crownland known in English as "Galicia." Austrian Galicia had less historic coherence that the Russian *gubernia* of Volhynia: it simply embraced the territories Austria took from the Polish-Lithuanian Commonwealth in the last quarter of the eighteenth century. Austrian Galicia included Polish territories to the west, where the main city was Cracow; as well as eastern lands where (as a rule) the countryside spoke Ukrainian, the towns Yiddish and Polish, and the main city (Lwów) Polish. Having defeated the West Ukrainian Republic, independent Poland recovered the Galician territories the Commonwealth had lost to Austria, eastern and western alike, Lwów as well as Cracow. The term "Galicia" survived in the Polish language of culture, but not on maps of Poland. Poland divided the eastern half of Austrian Galicia into three palatinates, Lwów, Stanisławów, and Tarnopol, collectively known as "Eastern Little Poland" (*Małopolska wschodnia*). It is interesting to recall that the historical name of these provinces within the old Polish Kingdom was the "Rus' Palatinate." These three interwar palatinates of "Eastern Little Poland" (as well small parts of Cracow and Lublin palatinates inhabited by Ukrainians) are what we will mean by "Galicia." Ukrainians in interwar Poland continued to speak of "Eastern Little Poland" as "Halychyna," both of which we shall translate as "Galicia."[11]

Pressured by the Entente powers, Poland promised political autonomy to the formerly Austrian territories of Galicia, though not the formerly Russian territories of Volhynia. In the early 1920s, Polish policy was to treat its Ukrainian citizens well enough that the Entente powers would recognize the Polish claim to eastern Galicia, which they did in 1923. The situation of Ukrainians left in Soviet Ukraine by the Treaty of Riga was at first in some ways much better, and then in every way much worse. Whereas Polish democracy was alien, unrepresentative, and eventually curtailed, Soviet communism was brutal, totalitarian, and eventually genocidal. At first, while Poland fitfully pursued "national assimilation," Soviet policy helped to create a modern Ukrainian culture. The 1920s were a period of unequaled Ukrainian creativity in Soviet Ukraine, as Ukrainian intellectuals were co-opted by the Communist Party and encouraged to create in their native language. The great Ukrainian historian Mykhailo Hrushevs'kyi, who had been president of the briefly independent Kyiv Republic, was invited to return to Kyiv and work in Soviet Ukraine. Most books and newspapers were published, and most children educated, in the Ukrainian language. For a time, Soviet authorities even permitted a new Ukrainian Autocephalous Orthodox Church. This period of fruitful tranquility was cut short when Stalin ended the policy of Ukrainization, banned the new church, and destroyed the Ukrainian intelligentsia. Soviet Ukraine suffered more from Stalin's rule than any other European part of the USSR. Five million inhabitants of Soviet Ukraine died in the Great Famine of 1932–33.[12] Tens of thousands of educated Ukrainians, including the leading lights of the cultural revival of the 1920s, were killed in the purges of the late 1930s.[13]

The greatest disaster in Ukrainian history was in central and eastern Ukraine (in the Soviet Union), but it was in western Ukraine (in Poland) and in emigration that Ukrainian elites, most of them Galicians, had the time and the freedom to consider their national plight. Only in the 1930s did Galicia become the unrivaled center of the Ukrainian national idea, and only thereafter was Ukrainian culture something that was spread from west to east. Although the Galician version of the Ukrainian idea had universal aspirations, it was conditioned in the 1920s and 1930s by the particular position of Galician Ukrainians in Poland. The 1920s renaissance of Ukrainian culture in Soviet Ukraine was meant to be perceived abroad; news of the atrocities of the 1930s was suppressed. Recalling the domination of Polish elites before the war, disappointed by the failure of the alliance with Poland, betrayed at Riga, and frustrated by the quotidian experience of Polish authority, Ukrainian nationalists treated Poland as the greatest enemy of the Ukrainian cause. Although Poland quietly supported exiles from central Ukraine, its former allies in the march on Kijów/Kyiv, this was not appreciated by West Ukrainian nationalists.[14] At the same time, attention to Poland also circumvented widespread disagreement about the Soviet Union, which many Ukrainian activists saw as the creator of a Ukrainian state, the Ukrainian Soviet Socialist Republic.

Communism uses universalist language, but in practice communists often rule from a more or less national center. Nationalists, on the other hand, use particularist language, but nationalism has several universalist features: in principle it offers any group the right to self-determination; in social life nationalisms grow one from the other; and in international relations any group can copy any feature of nationalist ideology from any other. The minor nationalisms of interwar Europe, such as the Ukrainian, must therefore be understood partly by reference to the major ones, such as the Italian and the German. Europe after the First World War was divided between status quo and revanchist states, and revanchist nationalist movements naturally sought help from the latter. Especially after Mussolini came to power in Italy, Western ideologies seemed to offer a way to reverse Ukrainian national defeat. The Organization of Ukrainian Nationalists (Orhanizatsiia Ukrains'kykh Natsionalistiv, OUN) was founded by Galician Ukrainian veterans of the West Ukrainian–Polish war in Vienna in 1929. Although it included exiles from central and eastern Ukraine, its orientation was Galician.[15] Its hostility to Poland arose from political circumstance: Galicia had been incorporated by Poland, and Galician Ukrainians were Polish citizens. The impetus for the creation of the OUN was the participation of Galician Ukrainian political parties in the Polish elections of 1928, which to the disgust of Ukrainian nationalists had legitimized existing borders.[16] The OUN was an illegal, conspiratorial, and terrorist organization bound to destroy the status quo. Its goal was an independent Ukraine to include all Ukrainian territories (widely understood) but only Ukrainian people (narrowly understood). Its first congress, in 1929, resolved that "Only the complete removal of all occupiers from Ukrainian lands will allow for the general development of the Ukrainian Nation within its own state."[17] The last of the OUN's "Ten Commandments" is also clear: "Aspire to expand the strength, riches, and size of the Ukrainian State even by means of enslaving foreigners." Following the lead of Dmytro Dontsov, the young generation of the 1930s preferred ideology to history and dreamed of a violent revolution that would establish a Ukrainian state. The OUN's attention to matters of organization proved to be as important as its ideology.

Although in principle the OUN's enemies were all of the states that included territories inhabited by Ukrainians (the Soviet Union, Poland, Romania, Czechoslovakia), in practice it operated within and against Poland. By murdering respected Ukrainians willing to cooperate with the Polish state, and by murdering Polish officials intending to help Ukrainians, the OUN divided Ukrainians from Poles, and provoked Polish retaliations that seemed to justify its radical stance. Ukrainian nationalists assassinated or attempted to assassinate at least thirty-six Ukrainians, twenty-five Poles, one Jew, and one Russian. Among the Poles murdered were the conciliators Bronisław Pieracki and Tadeusz Hołówko.[18] The OUN considered itself to be at war with the Polish state, and its leaders recognized that victory required allies. The OUN counted on German help, since in the grand endeavor of building a Ukrainian state from Polish, Soviet, Czechoslovak, and Romanian territories, Germany was the only possible ally. Like the Italian and other European fascist movements, the OUN in the 1930s included leaders who sympathized with Nazi Germany and who believed that Adolf Hitler would aid them for ideological reasons. The late

1930s found the OUN collaborating with the *Abwehr,* the intelligence service of Nazi Germany.

GALICIANS AND VOLHYNIANS, 1921–1939

The ideology of the OUN is one matter, the position of Ukrainians in interwar Poland quite another. Interwar Poland counted among its citizens about five million individuals who spoke what we now call dialects of Ukrainian, and worshiped in Greek Catholic or Orthodox churches. Roughly three million of them were former Austrian subjects, usually Greek Catholics, in Galicia; roughly two million were former Russian subjects, usually Orthodox, in Volhynia. Polish officials and Ukrainian activists alike distinguished between Galician and Volhynian Ukrainians: from a Ukrainian nationalist point of view Galicians were reliable and Volhynians good candidates for national agitation; from a Polish etatist point of view Galicians were unreliable and Volhynians good candidates for political assimilation. Polish policy aimed to keep the "bad" Galicians from influencing the "good" Volhynians.

In Galicia, Polish policy was harsh enough to make new enemies, but far from the sort of tyranny which might have stifled Ukrainian civil society or crushed Ukrainian nationalist conspiracies. The most painful blow to Galician Ukrainians was the "Lex Grabski" of 1924, which replaced Ukrainian-language schools with bilingual (functionally Polish-language) schools. This was the work of the National Democrat Stanisław Grabski. Having taken on at Riga what he considered manageable populations of Ukrainians, Grabski intended that they be assimilated in the next generation. His law brought an explosion of private schools and alienated Ukrainian youth from Polish authority.[19] In 1925, while his brother Władysław Grabski was prime minister, Stanisław Grabski as interior minister blocked efforts to make land reform more equitable. Piłsudski's coup in 1926 might have marked a turning point. Henceforth "state assimilation" rather than "national assimilation" was Polish policy: citizens were to be judged by their loyalty to the state, and not by nationality. Sensing this turn of events as a threat, the OUN undertook a campaign of sabotage designed to force Piłsudski's hand. In response, but also to gain support for parties he favored in parliamentary elections, Piłsudski ordered hundreds of repressive countermeasures. These very often included public corporal punishment.[20] Such humiliation aroused lasting enmity.

Volhynia was a challenge of a different sort than Galicia. It was the second largest region of Poland, its fields, forests, and marshes scarcely marred by roads

Fig. 19. Ukrainian schoolgirls at the Institute of Basilian Sisters, L'viv, 22 June 1930.
Ukrainian culture survived outside the Polish state.

or rail links, its town innocent of sewers. The largest town was Równe (Rivne),
the majority of whose population of forty two thousand were Jews. Almost 90
percent of Volhynia's inhabitants, which is to say virtually everyone who was
not Jewish, worked the land (or owned it). By comparison with Volhynia, even
proverbially backward Galicia looked quite European, and quite national.
Whereas Galicia had just been mobilized by a great war between Ukrainians
and Poles, national movements were absent in the Volhynia of the early 1920s.
The Polish-Lithuanian uprising of 1863 had little resonance in Volhynia, where
Poles were fewer in number and Polish magnates had found an acceptable compromise with tsarist authorities. The Polish question, so fearful to Russian governors in Lithuania, was regarded as resolved by Russian governors in Ukraine.
68 percent of Polish Volhynia's population was classified as Ukrainians in 1921,
but neither they nor the 16 percent classified as Poles betrayed much inclination
to national action. Many if not most local Poles spoke Ukrainian, and some
were former Uniates, now Orthodox. Before 1914 there had been no national
Polish-Ukrainian disputes in Russian Volhynia comparable to those in Austrian Galicia.[21] On the other hand, the tradition of (Ukrainian) peasant rising
against (Polish) landlords was more than two centuries old. Between 1905 and

1907 alone, there had been 703 recorded cases of peasants violently asserting their claims to land.[22] Although the First World War and the Polish-West Ukrainian war had exposed young Volhynian men to the wider world of nationalism, as of 1921 the distribution of land had not yet been accepted by the peasants as part of a general national liberation. Landlords were not yet seen as an alien nation; the fatherland was still the property inherited from one's father; land reform was not yet connected to the homeland.

This would change. In the 1922 elections, Ukrainians in Volhynia voted for Ukrainians. Once in parliament, Ukrainian deputies were unable to prevent what they had been elected to stop: colonization by Polish settlers. Land hunger had been the most meaningful social question in Volhynia for three centuries. Poland did carry out land reform, and more or less ended feudal landholding practices.[23] In 1923 Wincenty Witos, the Polish agrarian leader, aligned his movement with the National Democrats. This ensured that agrarian politics in Poland was pro-Polish rather than pro-peasant, and that land reform would be designed to favor Poles. Thus older tensions about the possession of land began to overlap with newer national politics. The favorable treatment and special credits granted to Polish colonists made the connection between state power, language, and land clearer. Polish administrators appeared in Volhynia alongside the colonists. Since local Poles were seen as insufficiently educated to govern Volhynia, Poles from central Poland and Galicia were dispatched by the state. This influx of privileged Poles created a new stereotype that slowly, it seems, attached to Poles in general.[24]

Class and national tensions in Volhynia served Soviet propaganda. In the 1920s, the Soviet Union exported to Eastern Europe a version of communism that endorsed peasant ambitions and opposed existing national states. Two tactics of Lenin's, the alliance with the peasantry and the tactical use of national self-determination, were very appropriate in Volhynia; and indeed the Communist International's general exploitation of these questions was more fruitful in eastern Poland than anywhere else. The Polish Communist Party became so dominated by Ukrainians and Belarusians that Moscow had to call for a correction. Yet, as any true Marxist would have seen, plans for radical and uncompensated redistribution of land were popular for reasons of class structure. It was in Volhynia that economic and social conditions best matched those of Lenin's homeland: low productivity of the soil, high rates of natural population increase, a high proportion of the population engaged in agriculture, and extensive cultivation of the land. Soviet attention to the Polish state

Fig. 20. An inhabitant of Równo. The town is today Rivne, Ukraine. Towns in interwar Volhynia were largely Jewish and increasingly Polish, the countryside almost entirely Ukrainian. Now Volhynia is in Ukraine, and the towns resemble the countryside.

as the source of land hunger drew attention away from actual Soviet practice, and strengthened the national coloring of the land question in Volhynia. Propaganda was backed by demonstrations of force, as the Soviets organized and executed hundreds of armed raids on Polish settlers in Polish Volhynia in the early 1920s.[25]

The Polish state's positive achievements, in education for instance, proved to be of uncertain value in the larger political struggle. Polish policy created the first generation of educated Volhynian Ukrainians. But in backward Volhynia, where jobs were few and Poles ran the administration, there was little dignified work for Ukrainian elites. As the Great Depression stultified Poland's agriculture, there was little chance for a middle class to emerge from the land in Volhynia. The newly minted intellectual proletariat was thus good material for communists from Kyiv and nationalists from L'viv. Volhynian Ukrainians learned to read in Polish schools; they learned what to read from central Ukrainian communists and Galician Ukrainian nationalists. Galician Ukrainian nationalists passed easily into Volhynia despite the so-called "Sokalski line" dividing Galicia from Volhynia; Soviet agitators came and went with almost equal impunity across the Soviet-Polish frontier in eastern Volhynia. In this situation, democracy continued to bring results unnerving to Warsaw. In the provincial elections of 1927 Volhynian Ukrainians voted for the cryptocommunist Left. The Left also organized most of the public political demonstrations in Volhynia.[26] Given the sensitive geopolitical position of Volhynia, just west of Soviet Ukraine, this called for policy change. In 1928 Józef Piłsudski sent his old comrade-in-arms Henryk Józewski to govern Volhynia.

Incidentally, the riddle to be solved in Volhynia was the loyalty of the Ukrainian majority, not that of the Jewish minority. Ukrainian communism and Ukrainian nationalism were both revanchist: the one favored the expansion of Soviet Ukraine, the other the establishment of an independent Ukraine. Volhynia was also a hotbed of Zionism: but Zionism was not about destroying Poland, but about leaving it behind. Although 99 percent of Volhynian Jewish adults identified Yiddish or Hebrew as their mother tongue, and two-thirds of Jewish children were educated in Zionist private schools, this was seen in neutral or positive terms.[27]

Henryk Józewski (1892–1981), a son of Kijów and a sincere federalist, had been Piłsudski's agent within the Ukrainian government during the Polish-Ukrainian alliance of 1919–20. Józewski supported Piłsudski's policy of "state assimilation," and maintained that the legacy of the Polish-Lithuanian Commonwealth provided a foundation for Polish-Ukrainian cooperation. Józewski had a geopolitical vision; Volhynia would become an attractive Polish version of Ukraine, and thereby stem the flow of Bolshevism and nationalism. His failure reveals the contradictions of Polish statehood in Volhynia within the Riga frontiers. Józewski lacked support both from Polish society and from Ukrainian activists. The first did not understand why the Polish state was supporting Ukrainian society; the second wanted to support Ukrainian society without the interference of the Polish state. Although Józewski wished to create a Ukrainian civil society, he had no choice but to eliminate its instantiations. Correctly perceiving that Ukrainian cooperatives and educational societies provided cover for communists and nationalists, he eliminated such organizations and replaced them with surrogates supported by the state. This had little effect, since even the official organizations were often staffed by the same people. During the Great Depression, the limited resources of the Polish state did not allow for anything but local organizations, and local organizations had to be staffed by local people. Over the longer term Józewski's greatest hope was education, and it was he who was responsible for the introduction of Ukrainian language courses in all Volhynian state schools. Yet the proportion of teachers brought in from central Poland increased under this administration, and such people had no patience for his project and no knowledge of Ukrainian. Józewski worked to Ukrainize the Orthodox Church, one of the main goals of Ukrainian nationalists, but received no credit from them for doing so. In the end, Józewski succeeded where most Poles wished him to fail, and failed where most Poles wished him to succeed. He succeeded in fostering a Ukrainian patriotism in Volhynia, but failed to connect this new trend to Polish statehood.[28]

One person who thought that Józewski's labors could bear fruit was Stalin, who apparently feared that he would build a Ukrainian Piedmont that would draw Soviet Ukraine away from the USSR. These paranoid fears, not far from Józewski's and Piłsudski's intentions but far from the reality of Volhynia, may have provided part of Stalin's motivation to crush Soviet Ukraine by Famine in 1932–33. As usual, Polish federalists were seen as enemies by both communists in Moscow and National Democrats in Warsaw. The National Democrats despised Józewski, and after his patron Piłsudski's death in 1935 he lost control over Volhynia policy. The army took over, destroying Orthodox churches and confiscating property in an effort to strengthen the Polish presence. This antagonized Ukrainian society in Volhynia at what was, as we shall see, the worst possible moment.[29]

THE POLISH STATE AND UKRAINIAN POLITICS, 1921–1939

A comparison between interwar Ukrainian and Lithuanian civil society is instructive. We have seen that in 1918 the Ukrainian movement in Austria was more impressive than the Lithuanian movement in Russia. After 1918, the establishment of a Lithuanian state changed this balance by creating a Lithuanian national society. In the 1930s a new generation of educated Lithuanians was absorbed by a Lithuanian state apparatus and educational system; at the same moment Galician Ukrainians were left with social organizations from the nineteenth century, fewer educational opportunities than their grandparents had enjoyed under Austrian rule, and illegal or ineffectual political parties. For Galicians and Volhynians alike, careers in legal politics had limited appeal, careers in the backward local economy held little promise, and by the 1930s even careers in the Church were insecure. Although the OUN was not a mass movement while the Polish state lasted, the Polish state created conditions under which its attractiveness as an outlet for the frustration of young and educated Ukrainians grew and grew. Participation in OUN terrorism was a satisfying way for young Ukrainians to take part in what appeared to them to be national, revolutionary politics.

The marginalization of Ukrainians from legal politics was striking. Although one-third of Poland's citizens were classified as national minorities, no minority representative was ever a minister in any Polish government (nor a regional or local governor, for that matter). Few leading politicians took the national aspirations of Ukrainians or other minorities seriously, and rare were attempts to co-opt Ukrainian elites by offering them attractive alternatives to nationalism and communism. The Communist Party of West Ukraine was illegal from its origins in 1923, and the cryptocommunist Ukrainian Peasant-Worker Union (Sel-Rob) was banned in the early 1930s. These parties were criminalized because they opposed Polish statehood: but their illegality did not solve the problem of the loyalties of their adherents. The main current of Ukrainian political life was the UNDO (Ukrains'ke Natsional'ne Demokratychne Ob'iednannia, Ukrainian National-Democratic Alliance). Although UNDO activists generally regarded Soviet Ukraine as a stage in the creation of a Ukrainian state, their fascination with the Soviet Union was reduced by news of the purges and famine in Soviet Ukraine. From about 1935 the UNDO supported Polish statehood. Its new policy of engagement with legal authorities was always at risk of being undermined by Polish repression, and the OUN in-

Fig. 21. Jews and Christians buy and sell at the Lwów market.

tentionally provoked such repression by killing Polish officials. In the late 1930s, after Piłsudski's death, the Polish state returned with far greater aggression to a policy of "national assimilation." Army raids, public beatings, and burning churches helped the OUN spread the word of a coming war of nation upon nation.

Even in 1939, this was a political message, not a description of social reality. Ukrainian terrorism and Polish reprisals touched only part of the population, leaving vast regions unaffected. OUN activists assumed that all Ukrainian-speaking citizens of the Polish Republic were endowed with, or were becoming endowed with, exclusionary national identities. Later events incline both friends and foes of Ukrainian nationalism to imagine that Galicia and Volhynia were in the 1920s and 1930s home to a society of Ukrainians with clear nationalist views. As we have seen, far more Ukrainians were attracted to socialism, agrarianism, and national communism than to the integral nationalism of the OUN. There was no natural fit between the ideology of expatriate war veterans and frustrated intellectuals and the concerns of the 95 percent of Ukrainian-speakers in Poland who worked the land; there was no end in sight to traditions of Russophilia when even the Great Famine in Soviet Ukraine did not dim the hope of many local Ukrainian activists that Russia would one day bring social liberation. Lwów remained a center of Ukrainian nationalism, but Polish and Yiddish were the city's main languages. Even in the cities and towns, many of interwar Poland's Ukrainians were neither interested in national politics, nor possessed of a clear sense of national identity. Many others with a clear and sense of themselves as Ukrainians did not draw the conclusion that identification with a Ukrainian community must coincide with loyalty to a Ukrainian state. In the 1920s and 1930s a series of negative connections had been made: land hunger and religious persecution were newly linked to Polish rule. Yet the OUN's nationalist prescription, a Ukrainian state for ethnic Ukrainians alone, was far from popular. Its acceptance required a total war that destroyed the Polish state, warped the idea of law, wrecked local communities, and provided the worst sort of examples. This is the subject of chapters to come.

Fig. 22. Christians and Jews buy and sell at the Lwów market.

Here let us emphasize a simple fact: interwar Poland included hundreds of communities, barely touched by the state, whose residents knew who was Polish and who was Ukrainian, yet regarded their village or county as more important than some larger nation. A colorful example, to which we shall return, was the Galician village of Dobra Shl'iakhets'ka/Dobra Szlachecka. Here Ukrainian-speaking gentry owned the land and set the tone. Three Orthodox brothers ennobled by the king of Poland in the early fifteenth century established traditions in which loyalty to Polish authorities was combined with resistance to every attempt to restrict local autonomy. Their heirs were included in every Polish census of the nobility, and maintained their position in Austrian Galicia in the nineteenth century. In interwar Poland, the Ukrainophone gentry in Dobra still enjoyed wealth and status, protecting the forests they collectively owned, and offering their daughters as attractive prizes to Poles from beyond the village. Poles in the village attended Greek Catholic services and spoke Ukrainian in public. Jewish families were Dobra's innkeepers and traders. In 1939, Dobra was neither Ukrainian, nor Polish, nor Ukrainian-Polish. It was a local reality unto itself, Galician if you like, hovering perhaps on the edge of the national modernity the next chapters will describe: but bearing the traces of earlier ideas of nationality, ancient conceptions of political order that time alone did not efface.

Chapter 8 The Ethnic
Cleansing of Western Ukraine
(1939–1945)

Everything changed when the Polish state was destroyed by Nazi Germany and the Soviet Union in September 1939. For two years Poland's territory and citizens were divided between Hitler and Stalin. Between 1939 and 1941, while the terms of the Molotov-Ribbentrop pact held, most of Poland's Ukrainians fell under Soviet rule, while most Poles were ruled by the Nazis. In June 1941 Nazi Germany invaded the Soviet Union, occupying Galicia, Volhynia, and Soviet Ukraine along the way. For the next three years all of Poland's territory and citizens were at the mercy of Hitler. Nazi Germany established the *Reichskommissariat Ukraine* (which included Volhynia) but added Galicia to the *Generalgouvernement* (as its administration of the parts of Poland not absorbed into the Reich was known). In February 1943, after the largest battle in history, Paulus disobeyed Hitler and surrendered at Stalingrad. In spring 1943 the Red Army went on the offensive. In summer 1944 the Soviet Union forced the Germans from Ukraine, and redrew the Polish-Ukrainian border. By spring 1945 all of Poland's territory and citizens were at the mercy of Stalin. Galicia and Volhynia suffered a triple occupation: Soviet in 1939, Nazi in 1941, then Soviet again in 1944.

At every stage, the Second World War was far more brutal in Ukraine and Poland than on the Western Front. Between 1939 and 1941, Soviet and Nazi occupiers destroyed local societies and deported and murdered elites. After 1941, German soldiers on the Eastern Front were ordered to live off the land, and indoctrinated to believe that the Slavs were *Untermenschen*. Unlike the western campaign of 1940, the eastern campaign of 1941 was fought as a war against inferior races.[1] Between 1941 and 1944, organs of German power carried out the Holocaust of the Jews, often before the eyes of (and sometimes with the assistance of) locals. After 1944 Soviet power returned, this time with the new mission of creating homogenous national spaces. War, occupation, hunger, reprisals, deportations, and genocide defined the situation within which Poles and Ukrainians lived and died for six long years.

Ukraine and Poland both suffered enormously during the war, and the Soviet Union and Nazi Germany were enemies of both. Nevertheless, at every point, the war divided rather than united Ukrainians and Poles. The prewar disagreement about who had the right to rule Galicia and Volhynia was like a point which, in 1939, became the peak of a triangle: from which opinions divided, rolled downward with ever greater speed, ever further from each other, hitting bottom with a barrier between them. The previous chapter brought us to this initial point; the purpose of this one is to demonstrate how war gave national disagreement the new shape of national war. Before 1939, the disagreement about legitimate rule of territory was of limited practical importance. In wartime, it led to quarrels which were not only intractable in principle but which provoked each side to infuriate the other. It led important Ukrainian nationalist partisans to conclude, by 1943, that the future of Ukraine could best be secured by the ethnic cleansing of Poles. The implementation of this program brought about tens of thousands of civilian deaths, created the conditions for a Ukrainian-Polish civil war within the larger world war, and totally recast Ukrainian-Polish relations.

How a political dispute over the legitimate rule over territory of 1939 led to the ethnic cleansing of people from territory by 1943 is the main question of this chapter. It is one thing to wish for ethnic purity; it is quite another to create it. Although rhetoric about the removal of peoples was common in the Poland (and the Europe) of the 1930s, the experience of war rendered such a program plausible, and the attrition of war brought ethnic cleansers to the fore. The escalation from rhetoric to action can be explained by three consequences of war: (1) the reopening of the question of legitimate rule over Galicia and Volhynia; (2) the implementation of massive programs of ethnic cleansing and genocide designed by Stalin and Hitler; and (3) the decapitation of local societies, Polish and Ukrainian alike. Before we shift to a narrative account of the ethnic cleansing of Poles from what became Western Ukraine, let us consider these three factors.

LEGITIMATE RULE OVER TERRITORY

Once the Polish state was destroyed by Nazi Germany and the Soviet Union, the natural presumption in its favor disappeared, and differences of opinion about its legitimacy began to matter. As of September 1939, only sixteen years had passed since the Entente had approved Poland's eastern border. The foot soldiers of the 1918–19 West Ukrainian-Polish war were still men in their prime. For Ukrainian national activists, Galicia and Volhynia were still subject to a compelling Ukrainian claim, which now could be satisfied. People who saw Polish rule as an occupation now worked to establish a Ukrainian state in its place. People of Ukrainian culture who took less radical views still could see no particular reason, after 1939, why Poland should reestablish its power over them. Although the Organization of Ukrainian Nationalists (OUN) had been awaiting such a moment, it still faced a daunting task. The creation of states is inherently harder than their restoration: it gains fewer international allies; it fits poorly into international legal regimes; it seems to require revolutionary means. Precisely because it is so difficult, it gives rise to greater temptations. Ukrainian nationalists had a political motive to collaborate with the Nazis, since Ukrainians (unlike Poles) could see Germany as an ally in the struggle for independence.

Whereas politically active Ukrainians wished to create a new state to include the formerly Polish territories of Galicia and Volhynia, politically active Poles wished to restore Poland within its borders of 1939. For their part, Poles found it hard to forget that Ukrainian villagers had greeted the Wehrmacht with bread and salt in September 1939.[2] In the *Generalgouvernement,* the surplus of educated Ukrainians found visibly rewarding careers as journalists, teachers, professors, and bureaucrats.[3] The collaboration of Ukrainian elites with German authorities, arguably rational from the perspective of those who wished to found a Ukrainian state and build a Ukrainian nation, was treason in the eyes of the Polish resistance. It was easier for the Polish resistance to execute collaborating Ukrainians than Germans, as this was less likely to bring German reprisals against Polish civilians. It goes without saying that it was easier for a Polish resistance movement to target Ukrainian collaborators than fellow Poles.

Collaboration leaves a lasting stain. Ukrainians who welcomed Soviet rule in

1939 often changed their minds: but Poles could not forget initial joy at the destruction of the Polish state. Ukrainian nationalists who joined in the Nazi invasion of the Soviet Union in 1941 were quickly disillusioned: but that they had served in German uniforms was not easily forgotten. Yet one must not imagine that only Ukrainians collaborated with the Nazis, especially in what had been eastern Poland, in lands taken by the Soviet Union in 1939 and occupied by Germany only in 1941. After two years of Soviet rule, many had some reason to receive the German invasion of the Soviet Union as a liberation. (Although this seems impossible now, in summer 1941 some Jews imagined that German rule could be no worse than Soviet. It is possible that Soviet deportations had, proportionally, touched Jews more than anyone else; collectivization was especially hard on traders and small businessmen; the Final Solution had not yet begun. During the Soviet occupation, thousands of Jews had actually fled Soviet rule for German rule.) Among Poles in Galicia and Volhynia, subject to Soviet rule between 1939 and 1941, collaboration with the Germans never had the same stigma as in central and western Poland. Although Ukrainians were granted almost all positions of authority in Galicia, Poles played an important part in the German administration of Volhynia.[4]

Fig. 23. A failed attempt to cross the Bug/Buh River, from Soviet to Nazi occupation, probably in 1940. Tens of thousands of citizens of interwar Poland crossed the river in both directions, believing that the other occupation regime could not be worse.

Some of these tensions inhered in occupation, some were provoked by the occupiers. Both occupying powers divided in order to rule.[5] Soviet occupation provoked conflict between Poles and Ukrainians in 1939, to create the conditions of "revolution" which ostensibly justified extending the Ukrainian SSR west to include what had been Polish territories.[6] The Nazis allowed a Ukrainian Central Committee to operate in Cracow; nominally a relief organization, it was the quasi-official center of Ukrainian political life. Ukrainian members of the Central Committee wished to use German power to remove Poles and Jews from Ukrainian "ethnographic territory."[7] In Volhynia after 1941, the German occupier offered Ukrainians a chance to persecute Poles (1941–42), and then Poles a chance to do the reverse (1943–44). These were usually attempts to preserve order—division is a means to ruling, not an end in itself—although they had the effect of enlarging and arming national partisans. Attempts to implement Nazi ideology had similar nationalizing consequences. Unbelievably ambitious projects to create *Lebensraum* for Germans set Poles against Ukrainians. German attempts to colonize the Ukrainian-Polish borderlands near Zamość in 1942–43, in which the Ukrainian Central Committee played an organizational role, were designed such that they had to worsen Ukrainian-Polish conflicts.[8]

CLASSIFICATION AND ELIMINATION OF GROUPS

As this suggests, what Ukrainians did to Poles, and what Poles did to Ukrainians, cannot be reduced to an escalation of events concerning only those two groups, and so cannot be understood within narratives of national history. Most fundamentally, how Poles and Ukrainians treated each other was transformed by their contact with the practices of occupiers, both of whom classified individuals and deported or killed according to classification. Both the Soviets and the Nazis issued identity cards to everyone beginning in 1939, a seemingly banal policy with enormous consequences. The 1939 Lwów/L'viv joke had it that "a person is composed of body, soul, and passport"; as we shall see, identity documents issued in 1939 very often determined whether body and soul held together.[9] Before the implementation of the Final Solution in 1942, the Nazis moved hundreds of thousands of people in and out of occupied Poland according to bizarre schemes which were never completed. These provided a model: in December 1941 some Ukrainian activists in the *Generalgouvernement* assumed that mutual ethnic cleansing would resolve Ukrainian-Polish disputes. The leader of the Ukrainian Central Committee actually proposed future population exchanges "on the German model" to Poles.[10] The Soviets deported at least four hundred thousand Polish citizens, disproportionately Jews and Poles, between 1939 and 1941.[11] This represented about 3 percent of the population in these lands. These deportations ended only with the German invasion of June 1941. As German troops advanced into Ukrainian territory, the Soviet NKVD hastily executed thousands of political prisoners, most of them Ukrainians. This was presented by Ukrainian nationalists as an injury at the hands of Jews. At this moment of great vulnerability arrived the Nazis, who treated the NKVD murders as cause for Ukrainians to take revenge upon Jews. Characteristically, this propaganda was false, but effective.[12]

The years 1939–41 should be seen as the first stage in the general acceptance that individuals can be classified into groups and treated accordingly. From 1941, the Final Solution brought to public attention the idea that a group could be physically eliminated.[13] In late 1941 and throughout 1942 several thousand Ukrainians participated as policemen in the Final Solution in both Galicia and Volhynia.[14] The Final Solution was carried out before the eyes of Poles.[15] The central fact of the Holocaust in Galicia and Volhynia was the cold-blooded murder of local Jewry. In certain historiographical traditions, the Holocaust (or Shoah) put an end to the continuous history of Jews in Europe and created the conditions for a Jewish state elsewhere. It is easy to understand this point of view. Other historiographical traditions marginalize the Holocaust from a larger narrative of progress: of communist revolution, or of national development. These are harder to spot, but easier to criticize. To clear the way for a critical history of wartime and postwar Eastern Europe, one must gain some distance on both of these traditions, and imagine the Final Solution within a sequence of events, and its consequences on societies that watched or took part.

It bears repeating that the Nazi occupation of Volhynia in summer 1941 was the second imposition of totalitarian practices in three years. It was formative for many young Ukrainian men, but it was not their baptism into political power. Many of the young Ukrainians who joined the Nazi auxiliary police (*Hilfspolizei*) in 1941 had served as militiamen under Soviet rule since 1939. They were trained then to see Ukrainian-Polish differences as a class struggle with a national solution: the deportations of the professional classes, which were largely Polish. That said, from 1941 collaboration in the Final Solution changed the collaborators, transformed Ukrainian boys in Volhynia into the kind of men they could never have become otherwise. Ukrainians who joined the German administration and the German police in 1941 were acting on several motives: to continue a career they knew, to have influence over their own affairs, to steal property, to kill Jews, to gain personal status, to prepare later political actions. Because the Ukrainian state had to be created, while the Polish state only had to be restored, Ukrainian nationalists had a political motive to collaborate with the Germans and to encourage Ukrainian youth to join Nazi organs of power. Yet in daily practice cooperation with the Nazis had little to do with this political goal, which the Nazis opposed, and much to do with killing the Jews, a major Nazi policy. To repeat, the greatest change in Volhynian society was the murder of 98.5 percent of Volhynian Jews.[16] Yet our purposes require us to keep in view the consequences of the Holocaust for the collaborators. The Nazis trained Ukrainian policemen not only in the use of weapons, but in the hatred of Jews. From the SS young Ukrainian recruits received anti-Semitic indoctrination in their own language.[17] Understanding all this, Metropolitan Sheptyts'kyi wrote to Heinrich Himmler asking that Ukrainian policemen not be used to murder Jews. In November 1942 Sheptyts'kyi issued a pastoral letter, "Thou Shalt Not Kill."[18] The message Sheptyts'kyi had read from the pulpit of every Greek Catholic church was that no earthly end can justify murder.

By this time, a few thousand Ukrainian men had already committed political murder for a cause that was not even their own: the Thousand Year Reich of Adolf Hitler. The Final Solution had already taught them that the mass murder of civilian populations may be achieved by way of precise organization and the timely presence of men willing to shoot men, women, and children. Although extermination camps such as Sobibor were quite close, in Volhynia in late 1941 and throughout 1942 Jews were not transported by trains to camps but marched into open fields, and killed not by gas but by bullets. Village by village, town by town, an ancient civilization was removed from the face of the earth. Recall the Volhynian town of Ostróg, discussed earlier as a center of early modern controversies concerning Christian Reform. It was also a historical center of Jewish learning: the Khmel'nyts'kyi rebellion of 1648, which brought to an end the East Slavic renaissance in the old Commonwealth, was recorded by a graduate of the Ostróg yeshiva. Nathan Hanover's *Abyss of Despair* (*Yeven metsulah*) was, horribly, prophetic. Ostróg was one of the first Volhynian towns touched by the Final Solution. Two-thirds of its Jews had already been killed by the end of 1941, before ghettoes were established.[19]

Fig. 24. Inhabitants of interwar Ostróg. The town is today Ostroh, Ukraine. Though an early modern center of Christian study and disputation, the town was heavily Jewish before 1941.

Once the surviving Jewish population had been enclosed in ghettoes, the German SS carried out the major actions during the second half of 1942, with the assistance of the Ukrainian and German police. Urban Jews were led from their ghettos to pits a few kilometers away, stripped of the clothes and belongings, forced to lie down, and machine-gunned by SS men. The Ukrainian police's duties included the murder of Jews who sought to escape the ghetto as it was liquidated, the murder of Jews who sought to escape along the way, and the murder of Jews who survived the machine-gun salvos. The Final Solution in smaller towns and villages is less well documented, but here the Ukrainian police played a greater part. All in all, about twelve thousand Ukrainian policemen assisted about fourteen hundred German policemen in the murder of about two hundred thousand Volhynian Jews. Although their share in the actual killing was small, these Ukrainian policemen provided the labor that made the Holocaust possible in Volhynia.[20] They worked right through December 1942.

The next spring, in March–April 1943, virtually all of these Ukrainian policemen left the German service to join the Ukrainian partisans of the UPA (Ukrains'ka Povstans'ka Armiia, Ukrainian Insurgent Army).[21] One of their major tasks as UPA partisans was the cleansing of the Polish presence from Volhynia. Poles tend to credit the UPA's success in this operation to natural Ukrainian brutality; it was rather a result of recent experience. People learn to do what they are trained to do, and are good at doing what they have done many times. Ukrainian partisans who mass-murdered Poles in 1943 followed the tactics they learned as collaborators in the Holocaust in 1942: detailed advance planning and site selection; persuasive assurances to local populations prior to actions; sudden encirclements of settlements; and then physical elimination of human beings. Ukrainians learned the techniques of mass murder from Germans. This is why UPA ethnic cleansing was striking in its efficiency, and why Volhynian Poles in 1943 were nearly as helpless as Volhynian Jews in 1942. It is one reason why the campaign against Poles began in Volhynia rather than Galicia, since in Volhynia the Ukrainian police played a greater role in the Final Solution. This links the Holocaust of the Jews and the slaughter of the Poles, since it explains the presence of thousands of Ukrainians in Volhynia with experience in genocide. But why did Ukrainian nationalists decide to eliminate Poles from Volhynia? How did people with such plans come to be in a position to order the ethnic cleansing of Poles in 1943? In 1942 Ukrainian policemen took orders from Germans to kill Jews; from whom did UPA partisans, largely the same people, take orders in 1943 to kill Poles?

THE DECAPITATION OF CIVIL SOCIETY

The demoralization and decimation of Ukrainian and Polish elites was perhaps the most important cause of Ukrainian-Polish conflict. The first Soviet occupation (1939–41) decapitated Polish and Ukrainian society by deporting and murdering elites. Poles and Jews were more likely to be deported or killed than Ukrainians; but then there were few educated Ukrainians. At least four hundred thousand Polish citizens were arrested and deported from Poland's former eastern territories to Kazakhstan or Siberia. Priority in deportation was given to state officials and professionals, thus leaving many settlements with no authority figures and no moral compass. Stalin had the NKVD murder more than twenty thousand educated Polish citizens whom the Red army took prisoner in 1939, including almost half of the Polish officer corps. Seven to nine hundred of these were Jews, reflecting among other things the presence of Jewish Polish officers. These are the crimes associated with the Katyń Forest, but they took place at other sites as well. As the Soviet Union withdrew from Galicia and Volhynia after the German invasion of 1941, the NKVD shot thousands more local Poles, Ukrainians, and Jews.[22] After 1939, on the German side, in the *General-gouvernement,* the Nazis murdered the Polish intelligentsia and imprisoned suspect Ukrainians. German repression also created the conditions for unforgettable injuries: as when Polish *Kapos* killed the two brothers of Ukrainian nationalist leader Stepan Bandera in Auschwitz.[23] Poles in the Chełm region liquidated 394 leaders of Ukrainian society on grounds of collaboration. As Ukrainian nationalists reported, this nationalized the Ukrainian-speaking population of the region.[24] After Germany invaded the Soviet Union in 1941, it arrested Ukrainian elites, including Ukrainian nationalists, in Galicia and Volhynia. The OUN's proclamation of Ukrainian independence in June 1941 led to dozens of arrests. In at least one case, the Germans were provoked by Soviet partisans into murdering several hundred educated Volhynian Ukrainians.[25]

Especially after Germany invaded the Soviet Union in 1941, the destruction of elites coincided with the militarization of Ukrainian and Polish civil society. During the war, the bearers of authority on both sides were no longer political institutions such as parties or governments, but military organizations such as partisan armies or self-defense militias.[26] Although the Polish Home Army was an impressive organization in many respects, its command structure was vulnerable. The Gestapo arrested its commander, General Stefan Rowecki, in June 1943. Other Polish partisan armies were loosely subordinated to the Home Army but represented particular political currents (such as the Peasant Battalions); others resisted Home Army command (such as the extreme right National Armed Forces). Although the Polish government was legal and recognized by the Western allies, it had little authority in Volhynia. Its representatives were surprised by the participation of Volhynian Poles in the German administration, and unable to prevent Volhynian Poles from joining the German police.

The Ukrainian case was starker. There was no state to organize an official army, and only the far Right was represented in the field. The rapid and dramatic change in the political representation of Ukrainian civil society was crucial to the direction of events after 1943. As we have seen, in interwar Poland, the terrorist OUN was a smaller organization than the democratic UNDO. After the UNDO and other Ukrainian political parties dissolved themselves during the war, the OUN became the only Ukrainian political organization in western Ukraine. In spring 1941, the OUN split into two branches, the OUN-Bandera and the OUN-Mel'nyk. The Mel'nyk branch of the OUN grouped older and better educated men; Stepan Bandera led a younger generational cohort more eager to strike a decisive blow. Battles between the OUN-Mel'nyk and OUN-Bandera in 1940 and 1941 left the OUN-Bandera as the leading national organization. After the OUN-Bandera defeated the OUN-Mel'nyk in a fratricidal war, the Nazis decapitated the OUN-Bandera. Bandera was arrested by the Germans after his OUN declared Ukrainian independence in L'viv in June 1941; perhaps four-fifths of the OUN-Bandera leadership were killed by the Germans in 1941–42. By 1943, the most powerful representative of Ukrainian political aspirations was the extreme branch of a terrorist organization, organized as an armed conspiracy, and directed in the main by young and inexperienced men.[27]

It was this maimed OUN-Bandera, led by Mykola Lebed' and then Roman Shukhevych, that cleansed the Polish population from Volhynia in 1943. Yet even within Volhynia and even by 1943, the OUN-Bandera was not at first the only expression of Ukrainian politics. There were two other Ukrainian partisan armies, the original UPA of Taras Bul'ba-Borovets, and the soldiers of the OUN-Mel'nyk. Bul'ba-Borovets, the most experienced partisan commander, rejected mass ethnic cleansing as a solution to the Polish problem.[28] The OUN-Mel'nyk, as we have seen, was at war with the OUN-Bandera. Both of these rivals were destroyed in early 1943 by the OUN-Bandera, and their soldiers incorporated by the OUN-Bandera's UPA. Along the way partisans loyal to the OUN-Bandera killed tens of thousands of fellow Ukrainians for putative links to Borovets or Mel'nyk. Although no one has yet taken up the subject, it is likely that the UPA killed as many Ukrainians as Poles in 1943.[29] The OUN-Bandera's willingness to betray and ambush its Ukrainian rivals, its successful recruitment of former policemen, and the attractiveness of its radical goals to local youth made it the dominant force in Volhynia in 1943.

Only one group of Ukrainian partisans intended to cleanse Volhynia of Poles. It was a group which arose during world war, and which owed its success to the particular conditions of Polish military defeat, genocide, and wounded civil societies. When in April 1943 OUN-Bandera leader Mykola Lebed' proposed "to cleanse the entire revolutionary territory of the Polish population," an act which totally recast Ukrainian-Polish relations, he was thirty-three years old.[30] Lebed's immature national tactic, as carried out by young men whose defining experience was of genocide, determined the course of events in Volhynia and prepared the way for Ukrainian-Polish war. Although war favored certain groups and certain strategies, it must also be said that the fateful decisions of 1943 were taken by leaders of the OUN-Bandera and no one else. They flowed from a particular strategy devised by certain individuals for a particular moment.

UKRAINIAN NATIONAL TACTICS: OUN-MEL'NYK

Having described the circumstances and the individuals, let us try to see the moment. The OUN-Bandera's tactic of ethnic cleansing was part of a strategy meant to further the goal of national liberation after the German defeat at Stalingrad. To see ethnic cleansing as a tactic, it may help to contrast ethnic cleansing with the OUN-Mel'nyk's contemporaneous tactic of renewed collaboration with the Germans. The retreating Germans were now willing to arm Ukrainians on a large scale, and the OUN-Mel'nyk accepted this proposition. Encouraged by the OUN-Mel'nyk, and wishing to avoid labor in the Reich, about 80,000 Ukrainians volunteered for service in the new *Waffen SS Division Galizien.* Only about 11,600 were trained, and the Germans had a special problem finding officers. Even Metropolitan Sheptyts'kyi, who sheltered Jews, reasoned that a Galician SS division was desirable as the nucleus of a future Ukrainian army. Though a man of the cloth his entire adult life, Sheptyts'kyi understood the military requirements of statehood. As the brother of a general who helped create the Polish army which defeated the West Ukrainian republic in 1920, Sheptyts'kyi knew from hard experience that a Ukrainian state without an army was an impossibility. Sheptyts'kyi's support of an SS division forces us to confront the basic difficulty of Ukraine's strategic position, and the desperate means even tolerant men could justify to themselves.[31]

The *SS-Galizien* began its career with the destruction of several Polish communities in winter and spring 1944. Best known is the burning of Huta Pieniacka in February 1944 and the murder of about five hundred of its inhabitants.[32] The *SS-Galizien* was not used for any major actions against the Jews, because the Final Solution had already been carried out. During 1942, the tremendous majority of Jews in Galicia and Volhynia had been murdered: most Volhynian and some Galician Jews individually near their homes or in mass executions in nearby forests and fields; some Galician Jews in death camps at Borovetsec, Auschwitz, Treblinka, Sobibor, and Majdanek. This ended Jewish history in Galicia. Not only great cities such as L'viv, but towns such as Brody— once the largest Jewish settlement in Galicia—were now empty of Jews. The *SS-Galizien* was destroyed by the Red Army in July 1944 precisely at Brody. The division was then reconstituted from more volunteers and sent to Slovakia and Yugoslavia to suppress anti-German risings: Ukrainian nationalists hoping to build a Ukrainian state left their own country at the order of foreigners to suppress the analogous strivings of others. Many of its soldiers deserted, often for the OUN-Bandera and its UPA. As the Germans fell back, the OUN-Mel'nyk strategy of collaboration lost credibility, and its support melted away. Andrii Mel'nyk himself sought a new patron, and was arrested by the Gestapo.

The *SS-Galizien* receives a great deal of attention, since the SS was the most horrible organ of Hitler's power, and the major organizer of the Final Solution. From a certain Ukrainian nationalist point of view, the *SS-Galizien* is seen as an institutional embodiment of Ukrainian goals. In today's independent Ukraine, one can view *SS-Galizien* uniforms in museum exhibits on nation-building in L'viv. Thousands of the reconstituted division's veterans managed to surrender to the Americans or British in Germany. Veterans in Italy were spared repatriation to the Soviet Union by appeals to Polish General Władysław Anders and Pope Pius XII; these appeals were only possible because the people in question had been citizens of Poland.[33] Granted combatant status by the Western allies after the war, *SS-Galizien* veterans made their way to England and Canada, and defended their actions for decades. Controversies about collaboration and nation-building aside, the *SS-Galizien* was marginal to the outbreak of ethnic cleansing against Poles.

UKRAINIAN NATIONAL TACTICS:
OUN-BANDERA

The cleansing of Poles was the work of the OUN-Bandera, which drew a different lesson from the German defeat at Stalingrad than the OUN-Mel'nyk. While the OUN-Mel'nyk saw an opportunity for more productive collaboration with the Germans, the OUN-Bandera perceived an urgent need for independent action. For the OUN-Bandera, the crucial moment was perhaps the increased activity of Soviet partisans in Volhynia from February 1943.[34] Wishing to claim for itself everyone willing to fight against German rule, as well as to absorb the Ukrainian policemen likely to leave their posts after Stalingrad, the OUN-Bandera decided in February 1943 to begin its own partisan actions. In March 1943 it created the UPA, tasked to fight the Germans, defend Ukrainians from the Soviets, and cleanse all Poles from Ukraine.[35] As Volhynian policemen left their posts that spring, the OUN-Bandera sent commanders north from Galicia. The success of Galicians in forming an army from Volhynians was an early sign that Ukrainian nationalism was taking hold throughout what we now call West Ukraine. For four years Volhynia had been buffeted by politics. Polish actions against the local Orthodox church had ended only with the Soviet occupation in 1939. The Soviets had mobilized Ukrainians in local politics while forcing them to build collective farms. The Germans displaced the Soviets in 1941, but kept local coercive authority in the hands of Ukrainians. As we have seen, the Soviets and the Nazis schooled the young policemen who became the core of the UPA in Volhynia in spring 1943. Volhynian Ukrainians were politicized in three rapid waves: one Polish, one Soviet, and one Nazi.

Thus the OUN-Bandera, heretofore more significant in Galicia than Volhynia, began its major armed operations in Volhynia. Although the precipitant causes of the creation of the UPA were local and tactical, its purposes were global and strategic. The OUN-Bandera opposed both Nazi and Soviet occupation of Ukraine, and drew fateful conclusions about the impossibility of a Polish minority in a Ukrainian state. OUN-Bandera leaders apparently believed that the Second World War, like the First World War, would end with the exhaustion of both Germany and Russia, and that Ukraine's final enemy would be a resurrected Poland.[36] The OUN had been founded by veterans of the West Ukrainian–Polish war; the OUN-Bandera collected younger men who had been imprisoned at the Polish Bereza-Kartuska concentration camp in the 1930s. Both generations knew that Poland could be expected to send its armies to Galicia and Volhynia as soon as it had the chance. On their view, Ukrainians had to form an army and strike during the war, before a revived Poland could once again, as after 1918, direct forces and settlers from central Poland.[37] Volhynian Ukrainians could be persuaded to accept a similar logic. A Volhynian peasant could easily see the Pole as the most determined colonizer, and Polish property as the biggest prize.

The Polish government in exile and its underground Home Army considered the same denouement most likely, and had planned just such an offensive.[38] They prosecuted the war in order to restore the Polish Republic within its 1939 frontiers, an aim taken for granted by Polish soldiers and supported by promises from the Western Allies. The Polish government did not believe that Nazi or Soviet aggression justified a change in its eastern frontiers, and understood that any compromise would be read as a concession to Moscow.[39] An independent Ukraine was acceptable, but only on Soviet territory. From a Polish point of view, German and Soviet exhaustion would open the field in the east for Polish forces to restore the status quo ante bellum, the proper state of affairs. As early as 1941, Polish commanders explained to London that a future rising against German power would involve a war against Ukrainians for Galicia and probably Volhynia as well, to be prosecuted if possible as a quick "armed occupation."[40] The Polish Home Army's plans for an anti-German rising, as formulated in 1942, anticipated such a war.[41] By 1943, Ukrainian cooperation with Nazi Germany had discredited Ukrainian partisans as potential allies to Poles; as defenders of the prewar frontiers of Poland, Home Army leaders had little to offer Ukrainians.[42] In 1943, the Home Army began to establish itself in Galicia (though not in Volhynia, where Poles were few).

Both the Polish Home Army and the Ukrainian UPA planned rapid strikes for territorial gains in Galicia and Volhynia. Had there been another Polish-Ukrainian regular war, as in 1918–19, the issue of who began the conflict would be moot. But the preemptive strikes against Poles envisioned by the OUN-Bandera in early 1943 were not military operations but ethnic cleansing. As we have seen, even before the war the OUN accepted a totalistic form of integral nationalism, according to which Ukrainian statehood required ethnic homogeneity, and the Polish "occupier" could be defeated only by the removal of Poles from Ukrainian lands. Unlike the OUN-Mel'nyk, in principle committed to the same ideas, the leadership of the OUN-Bandera believed that such an operation was feasible and desirable in 1943. From the OUN-Bandera point of view, the Jewish population had already been destroyed by the Germans; Germans and Russians would come and go; but Poles had to be removed from "Ukrainian lands" by force. Polish partisans wished to restore an old order; Ukrainian partisans, a step ahead, prepared a new one.

SLAUGHTER

In spring 1943, the UPA gained control over the Volhynian countryside from the Germans,[43] and began the murder and expulsion of the Polish population.

Fig. 25. The Ukrainian Insurgent Army (UPA), probably 1943.

In Volhynia, Poles were far too weak to even consider striking first. Poles were at most 16 percent of the Volhynian population in 1939 (about four hundred thousand people), and had been reduced to perhaps 8 percent (two hundred thousand people) by 1943.[44] They were scattered about the countryside, deprived of their elites by deportations, with no state authority except the Germans to protect them, and no local partisan army of their own. The OUN-Bandera decision to use its UPA against these Poles can only be seen as the ethnic cleansing of civilians.[45] Throughout 1943 UPA units and special security forces killed individual Poles and collectively murdered Poles in Polish colonies and villages or within Ukrainian villages.[46] For attacks on larger Polish settlements, UPA partisans mobilized local populations.

According to numerous and mutually confirming reports, Ukrainian partisans and their allies burned homes, shot or forced back inside those who tried to flee, and used sickles and pitchforks to kill those they captured outside. Churches full of worshipers were burned to the ground. Partisans displayed beheaded, crucified, dismembered, or disemboweled bodies, to encourage remaining Poles to flee.[47] In mixed settlements the UPA's security forces warned Ukrainians to flee, then killed everyone remaining the next day.[48] Occasionally the UPA would claim to be Soviet partisans, and/or propose joint attacks on the Germans with Polish partisans. Under such pretexts town meetings would be called, and then the UPA would murder the assembled population.[49] The policy of ethnic cleansing proved popular within the UPA, and found support among some Ukrainian peasants in Volhynia.[50] The UPA offered Ukrainians in mixed villages and towns material inducements to join in the slaughter of their neighbors. Many Ukrainians risked (and lost) their own lives by warning or sheltering Poles instead.[51]

Most attacks by UPA partisans, UPA security forces, and Ukrainian peasants on Volhynian Poles took place during March–April, July–August and late December 1943. By July 1943 the UPA had assimilated other Ukrainian partisan groups in Volhynia, numbered about twenty thousand troops, and was capable of simultaneous actions across wide territories.[52] The first edition of its newspaper, dated that month, promised "shameful death" to all Poles who remained in Ukraine.[53] The UPA was in a position to make good on its threats. Within about twelve hours, from the night of 11 July 1943 to the morning of 12 July, the UPA attacked 167 localities. This attack, incidentally, fell on the day of Orthodox celebration of Sts. Peter and Paul; a previous attack was known as "Bloody Good Friday for the Polaks"; another fell on Christmas Day. Since Roman Catholics celebrate Christmas earlier than eastern-rite believers, Christmas usefully separated Poles from Ukrainians, and placed Poles in flammable wooden churches. These were burned to the ground, and people who sought to escape shot. All in all, the UPA killed forty to sixty thousand Polish civilians in Volhynia in 1943.[54] These 1943 attacks were also a minor stage of the Holocaust of Volhynian Jews. Some of the very few Volhynian Jews who survived the winter of 1942 had done so by hiding with Polish peasants in the Volhynian countryside. When the UPA destroyed Polish settlements in 1943, it killed such Jewish survivors.[55]

THE END OF A POLISH VILLAGE, 29 AUGUST 1943

One of the settlements destroyed in Volhynia must stand for the hundreds of others. Although events in a single village cannot suggest the scale of the killing, they can provide a fuller sense of the methods and the stages than any generalization. Until 1943, Głęboczyca was a village of perhaps seventy Polish households, in the Włodzimierz district of Volhynia. It was established in the late nineteenth century, and had been a Polish village under Russian rule before Poland became an independent state. Much like neighboring Ukrainian villages, it was neither especially prosperous nor especially poor. It depended on trade with nearby settlements, and its farmers took part in Ukrainian cooperatives. Between 1939 and 1941, Głęboczyca resisted collectivization and was punished by local Soviet authorities. From summer 1941, the village was under German rule. Ukrainians continued to hold power, as they had during the Soviet occupation, now as German policemen and administrators. Ukrainians drew up the lists of those to be taken as forced laborers to Germany, choosing Poles where possible. In this way about half of the Polish families in Głęboczyca lost their most able male. Poles were also assigned a disproportionate share of the contingent to be supplied to German authorities. In summer 1942, the German and Ukrainian police found and murdered most local Jews. Jews were taken as individuals or in small groups and shot, in the hearing (if not in the sight) of the Christian population. In spring 1943 the local Ukrainian police left the German service to join the UPA in the forest. These new Ukrainian partisans attacked a German garrison, and took its arms for themselves.

The UPA now controlled the area. Poles found little reason to distinguish UPA dominion from German rule, since locally the same people with the same guns were in control. At first, the UPA's exercise of authority in Głęboczyca was not so different, if more thorough. The UPA made sure that Poles were unarmed, kept lists of family members, and searched homes to make sure no Poles had fled. It assigned Polish families to provide it with supplies; the Polish men who delivered the goods to the UPA base were often murdered. Young Polish men, especially those with education and talent, were murdered individually, apparently tortured to death. Poles in Głęboczyca also began to hear rumors of the destruction of other settlements, and by night could see the glow of burning villages in the distance. The general sense was that the rumors were too horrible to be true, and that even if they were true no such thing could happen here.[56] In August 1943, the hope was that the harvest could be gathered before escape was necessary. Beyond the natural tendency of people not to believe the unbelievable, and beyond the usual inclination of farmers to get in the harvest, there were three sources of this wishful thinking. First, distances were great and means of communication primitive, so people made judgments based upon personal experience. Second, survivors of attacks elsewhere were few, and fled to settlements larger than Głęboczyca. Third, local Ukrainians assured them that "good Poles," such as themselves, would not (to use the parlance of the time and place) be "slaughtered."

Just before dawn on 29 August 1943, UPA partisans and Ukrainians from neighboring villages surrounded Głęboczyca and moved to murder all of its inhabitants. Farmers already in the fields were surrounded and killed by blows from sickles. This alerted their wives, who were killed with bullets or farm implements or both. This made enough noise to give warning, and a few individuals escaped. At least 185 Poles were murdered. Some were decapitated, some were hanged, some had their skin torn from their muscles, some had their hearts gouged from their bodies, some were set aflame. Many were hacked into pieces with farm implements. Some suffered many, most, or even all of these tortures. The village was destroyed, and of it today there is no sign.[57]

VENGEFUL COLLABORATION

Most Poles who survived the terror in Volhynia fled their homes. The memory of atrocities perpetrated on loved ones ensured that thousands of them took their first opportunity to avenge their dead. Sometimes helped by the Home Army, sometimes helped by the Germans, Poles established about one hundred self-defense outposts.[58] Polish self-defense defeated some Ukrainian attacks, and in larger settlements such as Huta Stepańska took on considerable proportions. In some documented cases, the self-defense posts served as bases for Polish pacifications of Ukrainian villages. A few Jews who had taken shelter with Poles in 1942 escaped with them in 1943, and took part in self-defense. For Poles and even for Jews, towns controlled by Germans were an oasis of relative calm in the desert of that Volhynian summer.[59] The German administration deported Poles as forced labor to the Reich: not at all a bad thing in the circumstances. Soviet partisans drew recruits from such towns, young Poles (and probably a few Jews) wanting to take the fight to the UPA but needing arms. Perhaps five to seven thousand local Poles fought in Soviet partisan units.[60]

By turning on the Nazis and the Poles at the same time, in early 1943, the UPA drove them into each others' arms. Poles took their revenge on Ukrainians as German policemen. When Volhynian Ukrainians had left the German police to join the UPA, the Germans sought Poles to replace them. During the general slaughter of Poles, this was an easy recruiting task. Refugees from Głęboczyca, for example, were offered work in the police as they were fleeing the UPA. A Pole from Zofijówka colony, in the same part of Volhynia, joined the German police with 110 others after the general slaughter of 11–12 July 1943. As he recalled, "it was about getting weapons."[61] About twelve hundred Poles joined the German police at this time, while the Germans confused the situation by calling in a Polish police battalion from the *Generalgouvernement*. Polish policemen, local and nonlocal, committed atrocities against Ukrainians.[62] Although these policemen were traitors from the perspective of the Polish government in distant London, revenge by Poles in German uniforms was a solid reason for Ukrainians in Volhynia to believe UPA propaganda about the Polish enemy.

Of course, the UPA killed Polish civilians before they had even had a chance to ask the Germans for help. Consider these UPA reports from April 1943: "In the village of Kuty, in the Szumski region, an entire Polish colony (86 farms) was burned, and the population was liquidated for cooperation with the Gestapo and the German authorities." "In the Werbski region the Polish colony Nowa Nowica (40 farms) was burned for cooperation with the German authorities. The population was liquidated."[63] Those who used Polish collaboration as a justification for killing every man, woman, and child in Polish settlements in April had just left the German police themselves. In so doing, they unleashed a Satanic logic they could not have anticipated. German policy was to kill the family of any Ukrainian police officer who deserted, and to destroy the village of any Ukrainian police officer who deserted with his arms. These retaliations were promptly carried out by the Germans wherever they could, using newly recruited Polish policemen. Many who joined the UPA from the German police thus instantly lost home and family, and found a new reason to hate the Poles. By summer 1943, Polish collaboration was used as a general rationale for the cleansing action begun that spring. As an OUN-Bandera leader summarized the situation in August 1943, German security "uses Polaks in its destructive actions. In response we destroy them unmercifully."[64]

For the Polish government in London, the Volhynian tragedy was an incomprehensible distraction from its own war planning. The slaughter was unexpected, the reactions of Volhynian Poles were undesired, and the need to concentrate on the interests of Poland as a whole paramount. Even without a Ukrainian front, the Polish command faced an unenviable dilemma. As the Red Army moved to the offensive in spring 1943, and broke the German tank force at Kursk that summer, the prospect of a Soviet victory became real. As one of the Allies, the Polish government was expected to deploy its Home Army to aid the Soviet advance. As a representative of Polish interests, the government wished to be seen as playing a part in the liberation of Poland. Nevertheless, the Polish government was forced to redirect its limited resources to the war with the UPA. The Home Army on 20 July 1943 called upon Polish self-defense units to place themselves under its command. On 30 July 1943 it called for an end to the murders of civilians, and pronounced itself in favor of Ukrainian independence on territories without Polish populations. This did not stop the killings: indeed it may have confirmed the belief of Ukrainian nationalists that ethnic cleansing was the only way to win territory from Poland. In January 1944 the

Home Army formed the 27th Infantry Division (Volhynia), 6,558 strong, tasked to engage the UPA and then the Wehrmacht.[65] The Volhynian Division, the Home Army's largest, drew its strength from the Polish self-defense units formed to defend civilians against the UPA, and from former Polish policemen who left the German service. Absent the UPA's ethnic cleansing, the division would never have arisen.[66] Although the Polish government ordered that civilians not be harmed, in the field Polish partisans burned Ukrainian villages and killed Ukrainians found on the roads in Volhynia.[67]

Even though Volhynian Polish participation in the German police, Soviet partisan armies, and the Home Army followed UPA atrocities, it nevertheless furnished the UPA with useful sources of propaganda. Not only Volhynian Poles but the Polish government could be linked—falsely but effectively—to the Soviet and Nazi occupation. Consider the judgment of the August 1943 congress of the OUN: "The Polish imperialist leadership is the lackey of foreign imperialisms and the enemy of the freedom of nations. It is trying to yoke Polish minorities on Ukrainian lands and the Polish national masses to a struggle with the Ukrainian nation, and is helping German and Soviet imperialism to eradicate the Ukrainian nation."[68] Polish self-defense units did cooperate during 1943 with both Soviet partisans and with German troops in attacks on the UPA.[69] Yet this is a local fact with a local explanation. In general terms, Polish authorities and Polish forces cannot be seen as cooperating with either Nazi or Soviet "imperialism." The Polish Home Army had been fighting the Germans since its formation. Although the policy of the Allies dictated that Polish forces cooperate with Soviet forces, nothing had yet come of this by 1943. Far from cooperating with the London Poles, in April 1943 Stalin had seized on the pretext of the discovery of the Soviet mass murder of Polish officers at Katyń to break off relations. The UPA accusation looks no better if one considers the policy of Ukrainian nationalists. As for "eradication," the UPA was eradicating the Polish presence in Volhynia in 1943, using thousands of partisans who had helped the Nazis eradicate the Jews in 1942. As for collaboration, a better example was surely the *SS-Galizien*. This is not speak of the total dominance of Ukrainians in local administrative posts in the Galician district of the *Generalgouvernement:* as of early 1944, they outnumbered Poles 346 to 3.[70] Yet the purpose of such pronouncements was political agitation, and one must separate historical judgment from the experience of people at a given time and place. Such propaganda worked insofar as it framed the recent experience of Ukrainians.

Propaganda exploits the power of language to generalize from the particular, and the tendency of people to believe general claims they find consistent with their own personal experiences. Part of the diabolical utility of ethnic cleansing is that it provides national labels for particular atrocities. By murdering individuals in the name of the nation, ethnic cleansers not only humiliate, infuriate, and nationalize the survivors, they make individuals of their own group the targets of national revenge. Once vengeance is taken, survivors on both sides will see the other as the aggressor, and propagandists can present both sides as nations. What began as an attack by a small number of people against certain localities becomes, thanks to predictable revenge, nationalist vocabulary, and the power of language, a battle of nation upon nation. This is not a postmodern trick known only to scholars: it is a simple political truth that ethnic cleansers have exploited throughout the twentieth century. The UPA also understood the productive relationship between intensity of personal suffering, which they provoked, and density of social communication, which their propaganda created.[71] After both Soviet and Nazi occupation, the requirements of propaganda could hardly be ignored. When fulfilled, they allowed ethnic cleansing to become civil war.

CIVIL WAR

Volhynia is where the Ukrainian-Polish civil war began. The events of Volhynia explain the ferocity of Polish retaliations, which then provided the UPA with the propaganda material it deployed as cleansing spread to the south, to Galicia. To the west, across the river Bug/Buh, Ukrainian and Polish partisans engaged in an incredibly brutal, and evenly matched, armed conflict. In the eastern half of the prewar Lublin region, village after village was destroyed by both sides in late 1943. Polish partisans of the Peasant Battalions matched the UPA atrocity for atrocity. The testimony of one Polish partisan is worth quoting at length: "We reacted to their attacks, which reached unspeakable levels of barbarity, with a ruthlessness of our own. When we overran a Ukrainian settlement, we systematically took out the men of fighting age and executed them, often by letting them run forty paces ahead of us and shooting them in the back. This was considered the most humane method. Others in the unit, whose actions I will describe, behaved differently and exacted a terrible revenge. No one raised a finger to stop them. While I never saw one of our men pick up a baby or a small child with the point of a bayonet and toss it onto a fire, I saw the charred corpses of Polish babies who had died that way. If none of our number did that, then it was the only atrocity that we did not commit."[72] The Peasant

Battalions were not the only Polish partisans in the field killing Ukrainians and battling the UPA. In spring 1944 Home Army units set out to secure the Chełm region, and burned about twenty Ukrainian villages in the process.[73] All told, in the Lublin and Rzeszów regions, Poles and Ukrainians killed about five thousand of the other's civilians in 1943–44.[74]

The UPA campaign to rid "Western Ukraine" of Poles began in earnest in Galicia in January 1944. In 1943 in Volhynia, UPA practice seems to have been to attack villages and murder populations without warning; in Galicia in 1944 the UPA seems to have sometimes presented Polish families with the choice of flight or death. Consider an order from the UPA high command to its soldiers, issued after the slaughter in Volhynia, and during the cleansing of Galicia: "Once more I remind you: first call upon Poles to abandon their land and only later liquidate them, not the other way around."[75] This apparent change, in combination with a demographic balance more favorable to Poles, with better Polish self-defense, and with the mobilization and diversion of Home Army units, limited the death toll of Polish civilians to about twenty-five thousand in Galicia. UPA attacks on civilians in Galicia were still organized, and still brutal. As in Volhynia, UPA units often killed every inhabitant of a village, not sparing women or children. The UPA's security forces roamed the countryside, killing Polish families and individuals.[76] With ethnic cleansing rampant on both sides, the UPA claimed that Poles had begun the mutual slaughter. With the fact of local Polish collaboration with the Germans established in Volhynia, with the Polish government having ordered its Home Army to cooperate with the Red Army, the UPA treated all Poles as "Stalin-Hitler agents." The Ukrainian nation, the UPA claimed, had received a "stab in the back" from the Polish government and Polish agents of Stalin and Hitler.[77]

In L'viv in March 1944, Ukrainian police checked the German-issued identity cards (*Kennkarten*) of young men who dared to walk the streets, and executed those identified as Poles. It is now believed that they wished to steal these identity cards for themselves, hoping to avoid being punished as Nazi collaborators when the Red Army took L'viv.[78] In other words, Ukrainians who had collaborated with the Nazis wished to use German identity documents to pose as Poles to avoid the revenge of the Soviets. Whatever the motivation, these murders were received as a new level of terror within the city walls, where Poles had been safest. Polish partisans murdered 130 Ukrainian civilians in the L'viv suburbs. In the nearby countryside the UPA continued its strategic cleansing, wishing to encircle the city with ethnically Ukrainian territory. The UPA also worked to control the roads to L'viv, so as to block Polish reinforcements from the west. By June 1944, the UPA was killing Polish civilians and battling Polish partisans in every district of Galicia. As the Red Army approached, Poles were evacuated from villages and towns. As the enormous Soviet-German front advanced westward across Ukraine, the Home Army and the UPA fought along a front of their own that stretched for hundreds of miles.[79] In summer 1944, as the Red Army advanced into Galicia, there raged a general and pitiless Ukrainian-Polish civil war.

WORLD WAR

For most people, military history is local, and we can understand Poles and Ukrainians who concentrated upon this local front rather than upon the advancing Red Army. Yet to see even the local consequences of the Ukrainian-Polish civil war, one must place local conflicts within the context of the World War. The local conflict weakened both sides as the larger war approached, leaving Poles and Ukrainians divided as the Red Army approached. UPA attacks on Polish civilians had prompted more than twenty thousand Poles to take up arms against Ukrainians. Poles fought Ukrainians as German policemen, as Soviet partisans, as self-defense militias, and as a division of the Home Army. The Polish government in London also diverted Home Army units from the war against Germany.

The aim of Poland's Operation Tempest of summer 1944 was to defeat the Germans with Polish arms, and await the Soviets as representatives of an independent Poland. In military terms, it was a rising against German rule; in political terms, it aimed to present the Soviets with a restored Polish state. In the east, Tempest meant the confirmation of the legality of the Polish presence in Volhynia and Galicia. It was here that the Polish anti-German rising first confronted Soviet methods. Having engaged the UPA, fought the retreating Wehrmacht, and cooperated with the Red Army, the 27th Volhynian division of the Home Army was dissolved by the Soviet NKVD in stages between March and July 1944. Throughout spring 1944, the 5th Infantry Division and 14th Regiment of Uhlans of the Home Army fought the UPA for Galicia, and its crown jewel Lwów/L'viv. Between 23 and 27 July 1944, the Red Army, aided by a few thousand Home Army troops, drove the Wehrmacht from the city. After 29 July the Home Army units were dissolved under Soviet pressure.[80]

Poles and Ukrainians were denied the fight to the finish they had planned. There was no sequel to the Polish-Ukrainian battle for Lwów/L'viv at the end of the First World War. The Polish Home Army was destroyed in the east; Ukrainian partisans fled to fight another day. Polish-Ukrainian conflict was not thereby extinguished: Home Army veterans escaped deportation by joining Zygmunt Berling's Soviet-controlled Polish Army; later Galician and Volhynian Poles from this army would fight Ukrainian partisans and deport Ukrainian civilians in communist Poland. Some Galician and Volhynian Poles took immediate revenge on Ukrainians by joining special Soviet NKVD battalions. The UPA, for its part, emerged from hiding and recommenced the ethnic cleansing of Poles once the front passed.[81] The Soviet NKVD, now the force to be reckoned with, treated both Polish and Ukrainian partisans as "bandits" to be destroyed.[82] How the Soviet police ended the Polish-Ukrainian civil war by institutionalizing the Polish-Ukrainian ethnic cleansing is a subject of the next chapter.

Metropolitan Andrei Sheptyts'kyi, who had lobbied abroad for recognition of West Ukraine after the First World War, had few hopes for Ukrainian statehood after the Second. His belief that the next Soviet occupation of western Ukraine would last for decades was well founded. When he died on 1 November 1944 in L'viv, with him died some of what little remained of the political traditions of the old Commonwealth. Neither communist Poland nor Soviet Ukraine would have much use for what he represented. The Greek Catholic Church was banned in the Soviet Union. Stalin allowed the Russian Orthodox Church to claim the West Ukrainian faithful, and had a puppet synod declare the 1596 Brest Union null and void. In communist Poland, the Greek Catholic Church was associated by the regime with modern Ukrainian nationalism, rather than with the Polish-Lithuanian Commonwealth which created it. For that matter, to this day neither L'viv nor Warsaw has named a street for Sheptyts'kyi.

Chapter 9 The Ethnic Cleansing of Southeastern Poland (1945–1947)

In interwar Poland, most nationalists treated Poland's Slavic minorities as assimilable ethnic raw material. After Józef Piłsudski's death in 1935, Roman Dmowski's integral nationalism triumphed in political and social discourse, and was shared by the collective dictatorship of Piłsudski's lieutenants. German and Soviet occupation brought extreme solutions of national problems to the center of attention. Even before the mass killings of Poles by Ukrainians began in 1943, some nationalists in the tradition of Dmowski's National Democrats dreamed of expelling every Ukrainian from Poland. After 1943, politicians of other orientations also concluded that expulsions were the only alternative to granting the Ukrainians Galicia and Volhynia. Such wartime schemes envisioned the deportation of five million Ukrainians east of Poland's prewar borders, and taking Poles in return from the Soviet Union or an independent Ukraine.[1] Similar visions of purity captivated occupied Eastern Europe, where leaders of nations who had suffered far less than the Poles planned a total expulsion of enemy populations. Democratic Czech politicians, for example, were soliciting Allied support for a total purge of Germans and Hungarians.

In Poland, as in Czechoslovakia, this trend encompassed the entire political spectrum, from far Right to far Left. Polish communists, previously internationalists to a fault, quietly dropped support of minority rights from their program in the middle of the Second World War.[2] In the drastic circumstances of the destruction of Poland, Left and Right met. In the drastic circumstances of Poland's occupation by the Red Army, they met in Moscow.

Stanisław Grabski, the old National Democrat, joined Prime Minister Stanisław Mikołajczyk (1901–66) and the Polish delegation (representing the government in exile in London) in its meetings with Stalin in Moscow of August and October 1944. Grabski, who helped determine Poland's borders at Riga in 1921 and helped design the policy of national assimilation in 1924, also wished to influence the shape Poland took in 1944.[3] It goes without saying that Stalin was using Grabski, a man of considerable authority on the Polish right. Grabski was also using Stalin. Recall that in 1921 at Riga Grabski's personal triumph resided in granting the Soviets more territory than they bargained for, rather than less. Operating within the National Democratic tradition, Grabski was in the habit of creating the nation within appropriately confining borders, and accustomed to seeing Germany as a greater enemy than Russia. He regarded his plans for a "national state" as realistic, and called Stalin "the greatest realist of all." Stalin called Grabski a "great agitator."[4] In summer 1944, with the Red Army already in Lwów, Grabski calculated that Stalin could be persuaded to draw a compact and homogenous Poland on the map of postwar Europe. This is in fact what Stalin did. One's opinion about who outwitted whom in the exchanges between Stalin and Grabski depends a great deal upon whether one examines the Poland of the late 1940s, when communists have come to power and have appropriated national goals, or the Poland of the late 1980s, as a national society with few minorities gains sovereignty.

The summer of 1944 revealed a defeat of a certain tradition of toleration in the Polish left, and the willingness of Polish communists to accept a view of nationality long advanced by Polish nationalists. The most important example is Wanda Wasilewska (1905–64), the Polish communist with Stalin's ear at this moment. As it happens, Wasilewska was the daughter of Leon Wasilewski: the very same Polish federalist and Piłsudski ally whom Grabski had outmaneuvered at Riga in 1921. Leon Wasilewski, the first foreign minister of independent Poland, had placed great stock in history as the basis for his support of national toleration; his daughter, Red Army colonel and wife to a Soviet deputy foreign minister, played a key role in the deportations designed by the Soviet Union to begin history anew in Poland and Ukraine. Stalin called this "the dialectic," although he saw the issue simply in terms of the father being "against us" and the daughter being "for us."[5] Of greater interest is the collapse of traditional patriotism and the rise of modern nationalism between 1921 and 1944. In 1921, the nationalist Grabski had outmaneuvered Wasilewska's federalist father at Riga; in 1944 the nationalist Grabski's views and those of the communist Wasilewska were functionally the same. If there was indeed a synthesis in the postwar Polish communism Wasilewska pioneered in 1944, it was that of traditional National Democratic ideas of nationality and traditional communist subservience to the Soviet Union.

By 1944, Polish communists and nationalists agreed that nationality resided in the people themselves, not in traditions preserved by the elite. All proposals for federation, autonomy, and toleration in Polish politics had originated from the assumption that national groups had elites who could be swayed by reason to form a republican political community. This vestige of the old Commonwealth, represented (at times) by Józef Piłsudski, Leon Wasilewski, and Henryk Józewski, proved untenable even during the tempered mass politics of the interwar period. As the Second World War came to an end, the National Democratic idea that nationality resided in people was hegemonic. Of course, in the conditions of 1944 this folkish nationalism was no means a democratic conception. Nationality can make people objects of the state, as well as its subjects. If nationality resides in people, and national problems arise from the mismatch between people and territory, the simplest way to solve problems is by moving people. This reasoning holds whether or not one is a communist planning to rule Poland, or a nationalist concerned with the creation of a national society. Although Wasilewska called Grabski "senile," they acted in remarkable concert in 1944 and 1945. Grabski proposed comprehensive Polish-Ukrainian resettlements to Stalin; Wasilewska signed the treaty that provided for them; Grabski designed an implementation program for the Polish government. Wasilewska worked from Moscow to help Poles "repatriate" to Poland; Grabski traveled to Lwów to urge Galician Poles to accept reality and leave.[6]

To be sure, Grabski and Wasilewska had very different plans for Poland. Grabski hoped that Poland would preserve some measure of sovereignty, and died there in 1949 after recognizing his failure. Wasilewska accepted that Poland would become a dependency of the Soviet Union, and never returned to her homeland. A history of postwar Polish politics would expand upon these important differences.[7] For our history of Polish nationality, the key point is that the idea of a Poland for the Poles was no longer at issue between the national Right, which would not gain power, and the communist Left, which would. In interwar Poland national minorities had meant different things to the Left and the Right, but both navigated a polity in which their presence was taken for granted. Now their absence was taken for granted. In 1944 we can see the consensus about national homogeneity as it emerges: before it attains the invisibility of all matters of profound agreement, and the legitimacy of policies that have already been implemented.

NATIONAL FRONTIERS IN SOVIET POLICY

Just what was Stalin's policy toward postwar Poland and Ukraine? Stalin's interwar, wartime, and postwar decisions and proclamations revealed knowledge of the importance nationalists and populations attached to particular territories. The Soviet Union was fighting a "Great Fatherland War." Stalin told Grabski that the First World War had pushed Poland to the fore among "Slavic nations," and that the Second World War would do the same for Ukraine. Soviet irredentism towards Poland in the 1920s and 1930s had been framed in the ethnic terms of "Western Belorussia" and "Western Ukraine." In 1939, when the Soviet Union occupied what became Western Ukraine, propaganda spoke shamelessly of the reunion of brothers of the same blood, the unification of ancient Ukrainian lands, the ancient Ukrainian city of L'viv, and so on. After the German invasion in 1941, Khrushchev told "the great Ukrainian people" that their choice was "a free Ukraine" or "the yoke of Hitler."[8] As the Red Army pushed the Wehrmacht out of Ukraine in 1944, and as its millions of casualties were replaced by Ukrainian conscripts, such national rhetoric appeared again in even stronger form.[9] Soviet nationality policy in Ukraine changed under the influence of three years of unspeakably bloody war with a Nazi regime bent on racial triumph, and months of reports of Ukrainian-Polish conflict in Galicia and Volhynia.[10] By 1944, Stalin seems to have concluded that ethnic homogeneity in combination with the Molotov-Ribbentrop borders of 1939 would make both Poland and Ukraine easier to rule. Informed by Khrushchev of the scale of OUN and UPA resistance, Stalin may have reasoned that returning Galicia and Volhynia to Soviet Ukraine would help co-opt Ukrainian nationalism.[11] Stalin perhaps saw a way to give both Ukrainians and Poles something they wanted, while binding them to the USSR. The Poles would get their "national state," the Ukrainians would get their "West Ukraine," and all would be beholden to Stalin. On his own account, Stalin wished to resolve any outstanding national questions among Poland, Ukraine, and Belorussia while he had the opportunity.[12]

Although the Polish government in London (and some Polish communists) pled for Lwów, there was never any chance they would get it. Stalin seemed to understand that he had more to gain by giving the city to Ukraine than to Poland.[13] Moreover, Volhynia and Galicia had been joined to Soviet Ukraine between 1939 and 1941, and the restoration of the 1939–41 borders was Stalin's most clearly defined war aim. Poland was to be established as a very compact state, and L'viv and Vilnius were to return to the Soviet Union.[14] In 1943 at Teheran Stalin gained the approval of the Allies to restore the borders created by Molotov-Ribbentrop pact. Shortly after the Red Army crossed the old Polish-Soviet frontier, in February 1944, British Prime Minister Winston Churchill publicly approved Soviet territorial ambitions in the west. In October 1944 Stalin told Mikołajczyk and Grabski, in Churchill's presence, about the Teheran arrangement to restore the 1941 borders.[15] Mikołajczyk refused to accept this state of affairs, but Stalin had already legalized the new border in his own way. A secret agreement of July 1944 between Stalin and his puppet Polish Committee of National Liberation shifted the Soviet-Polish border to the west, much as in 1939.[16] Mikołajczyk's government fell on the issue of Lwów in November 1944.

In terms of Soviet practice, the novelty of 1944 was not the transfer of territory from Poland to Soviet republics, a policy of 1939, but rather the exchange of populations defined by nationality. A Soviet Ukrainian-Polish "evacuation" agreement of September 1944 provided for the resettlement of Poles and Jews from what had become West Ukraine, and the resettlement of Ukrainians from communist Poland.[17] Similar agreements governed the exchange of populations between Poland and Soviet Lithuania and Soviet Belorussia. To be sure, these "repatriation" accords (as they were generally known) must be seen in the light of the general practice of the time. The Western Allies assumed that the end of the war would be accompanied by border changes and mass transfers of people. Stalin took for granted that the end of the war would bring mass expulsions of Germans, and assumed that their flight from Poland and Czechoslovakia would proceed without Soviet assistance. As he said to the Czechoslovak prime minister: "We won't get in your way. Drive them out."[18]

One must not overstate the case. There were limits to Stalin's interest in ethnic homogeneity. The deportation of Poles from the Soviet Union concerned only Poles from territories that had been part of Poland before 1939. Deportations to the Soviet Union were limited to Poland itself. Had Stalin been keenly interested in the ethnic purity of all of his new satellites, his postwar deportation policy would have been more comprehensive. There were, after all, unanswered national questions in 1944–46 in Romania (Hungarian minority), Czechoslovakia (Hungarian minority), and Hungary (which desired to keep those Hungarians from becoming minorities by keeping territories it gained from Romania and Czechoslovakia as a German ally after 1938). There were also democratic and communist politicians in these countries petitioning Stalin for help in resolving these questions. As matters stand, it appears that Stalin chose to "resolve" national questions exacerbated by ethnic cleansing, those of Poland and Ukraine, but not to create national homogeneity everywhere he might have. Molotov urged the Czechoslovaks and Hungarians to follow the model established by the Soviet Ukrainian-Polish, Soviet Belorussian-Polish, and Soviet Lithuanian-Polish resettlements, but at no point did the Soviet Union impose that model. Hungary resisted the transfer of Hungarian minorities, and that was left at that. The further south the national question, the less interest Stalin seemed to take in its final resolution. It appears that Stalin had a general preference for ethnic homogeneity in his new satellites, but only deployed Soviet resources in places where there had been ethnic cleansing during the war. It also appears that Stalin regarded another German attack in his lifetime to be very possible, and wished to resolve completely all questions that would stand in the way of harmony between Russia, Poland, and Ukraine.[19]

We may then divide national questions Stalin might have resolved in the period 1944–46 into four categories. (1) Stalin wished to resolve the German question, and expected that it would be solved for him. He was right. (2) Stalin used Soviet resources to resolve the Polish questions in Lithuania, Belorussia, and Ukraine; the Ukrainian question in Poland; and also the Ukrainian question in Czechoslovakia.[20] (3) Stalin wished for the Hungarian questions in Romania and Slovakia to be resolved by deportations, but declined to use Soviet units, and did not in the end force Hungary to go along. He likewise supported population exchanges of Poles and Czechs, but did not implement them. (4) With respect to Bulgaria and Yugoslavia, Stalin did not speak of ethnic homogeneity but of the brotherhood of nations, and even of a future federal Europe. In general, the closer the national question to the invasion route German armies took in 1941 into the Soviet Union, the more interested was Stalin in resolving it. The closer a given national question was to Russia, the more Stalin used historical references, national stereotypes, and nationalist reasoning.

This was evident enough to Polish communists that they used nationalist reasoning in their appeals to Stalin. Jakub Berman (1901–84), a Polish politburo member who had survived the war in Moscow, noted that the new borders and population exchanges had resolved Polish-Ukrainian national questions, and appealed to Stalin for more Poles to be sent from Lithuania and Belorussia to build a stronger Polish state.[21] As this suggests, in the cases of Poland and Ukraine, Stalin's nationalist reasoning went so far as to justify the use of deportations not to punish but to build nations. This was an important change. No Soviet deportations before 1944 could be construed as designed to consolidate nations.[22] In the 1930s, Stalin had deported huge numbers of Soviet citizens on national grounds, but this was designed to forcibly relocate rather than build nations within homelands.[23] In 1939–41 in the formerly Polish territories of Galicia and Volhynia, Stalin had deported elites. Yet this was a policy directed against independent political and civil society, or against the upper classes: there was no attempt to deport, for example, every Pole. After the Red Army returned to Galicia and Volhynia in 1944, Stalin "evacuated" or "repatriated" entire national populations to "their" national homelands. He sent individuals classified as Poles west, to communist Poland. That nationality was inscribed in individuals was the Soviet view from the 1920s. That nationality could trump class was evident in Soviet policy in the 1930s. That nationality could create a Soviet interest in matching individuals to national territory was new after 1944.

Another book would be required to describe the evolution of Soviet nationality policy. There is much dispute about whether the Soviet Union in the 1920s and 1930s can be grouped with other European states within a narrative of modernization, and in this dispute nationality policy is often treated as modernizing.[24] On our evidence, this is true, but in a nicely dialectical way. The theoretical approach to nationality developed by Lenin and Stalin before the Bolshevik Revolution was only halfheartedly modern. It grew from a rejection of the crypto-nostalgic approach favored by the Austro-Marxists, which presumed the value of a multinational Austria and treated nationality as a matter of individual preference and local culture. At the same time, Lenin and Stalin rejected the modern view of nationality as the legitimate wellspring of political sovereignty. The early Bolshevik approach to nationality accepted that nationality was inherently political and related to territory and language, but rejected the modern claim to its political monopoly. In this way nationalism could be exploited, according to Lenin's view of self-determination, to create a multinational state.[25] Thus a multinational state could be governed, as was the Soviet Union in the 1920s, by distinguishing local nationality from ultimate political loyalty. The 1920s policy of *korenizatsiia* presumed that elites created in the spirit of local nationality would serve the Soviet state.

Toutes proportions gardées, this was an early modern approach to nationality, in the sense we have discussed in earlier chapters. It took for granted that party and state officials could be of various national origins, and yet at the same time constitute one party and one political unit, the Soviet Union (established in 1922). Even as local languages were encouraged and codified, Russian was treated as the main language of high politics in the Soviet Union. However, this early modern approach to *political* nationality was combined with a modern approach to *social* nationality. Rather than accounting for the variety of cultures and proposing a higher political loyalty for elites, as had early modern states such as the Polish-Lithuanian Commonwealth and Habsburg Austria, the Soviet Union actively defined and created nationality for the entire mass population. The territory of the Soviet Union divided into national territorial units, and every citizen of the state was eventually assigned a nationality. Modern nationalism treats the common people as sovereign on their national territory, and treats politics as a matter of pushing this simple idea up into the realm of high politics, forcing elite rivals into ever more contorted defenses, crushing them against the ceiling. Communism was such an elite rival. Here was a contradiction.

Whether or not Soviet policy actually spread modern nationalism, Stalin enacted deportation policies in the 1930s, and brought about the Great Famine in Ukraine, on the belief that certain groups were betraying the Soviet polity on behalf of their own nation.[26] Yet so long as these deportations were to distant regions within the Soviet Union, as in the 1930s, they could at least be reconciled with the original approach to nationality. In principle at least, punishment was correction. Siberia and Kazakhstan did sometimes create or at least perpetuate a Soviet identity among the deported. To deport populations from the Soviet Union, as after 1944, was to admit defeat. To take away Soviet citizenship (as after 1944), rather than forcing people to accept it (as in 1939), was to resign from internationalism.[27] By 1944, Soviet policy assumed not only that the political loyalty of individuals is rooted in their nationality, but that Soviet policy could not change this state of affairs. This was to accept not only a very modern diagnosis of political instability (the presence of alien nationals), but also a very modern prescription (the matching of national population to national territory).

This important change in Soviet policy in 1944 allowed the proclamation of Poland as a homogeneous communist state that year. However one sees the origins of Stalin's policies, the combination of border shifts and population transfers reoriented Polish communism. Polish communists did not set the policy of border changes and deportations of 1944, but they took part in its formalization and execution. Deportation was their introduction to political power, and their first contact with Polish society. Communists agreed to form front organizations called the "Union of Polish Patriots" (1943) and then the "Polish Committee for National Liberation" (1944). After the latter group signed the accord on "evacuation" and was sent to rule Poland, the former remained in Moscow and helped "evacuate" Poles.[28] Polish communists who remained in the Soviet Union, such as Wasilewska, worked to match populations to borders. Polish communists in Poland quickly came to understand that they had been handed a source of support the likes of which they had never before enjoyed. They argued, for the first time, that the interwar state had failed because of its nationality structure, and proposed what the National Democrats had proposed in the interwar period: a "national state." As the war ended, they came to power in the baggage of the Red Army to build something very much like ethnic communism.

From a demographic standpoint, the Ukrainian question was of minor importance in the ethnic homogenization of Poland; in politics, it was of major importance to the nationalization of Polish communism. More than ninety percent of Jews on what was becoming Polish territory had been murdered during the Holocaust. As to the Germans resident on the new western territories Poland received from Germany at the end of the war, General Secretary Władysław Gomułka (1905–82) put the matter clearly in May 1945: "We have to throw them out, since all countries are built on the national principle, not the principle of nationalities."[29] The expulsion of the Germans of which Gomułka spoke was a far more massive operation than the deportations of Ukrainians, but it began a year later, and as part of a general European project approved by the Allies. We therefore mark the nationalization of the Polish party at the Polish-Ukrainian border in September 1944. This was the moment when the Polish party endorsed ethnic communism, took a direct role in the transfer of peoples, and presented itself as a representative of the interests of the Polish nation. Well before they joined with Mikołajczyk and a few other noncommunists to form a "Temporary Government of National Unity" in June 1945, Polish communists had taken responsibility for the creation of a homogeneous state. This brought them support they could otherwise never have enjoyed.

THE "REPATRIATIONS," 1944–1946

About 780,000 individuals were resettled as Poles or Jews from Soviet Ukraine to Poland between 1944 and 1946. Neither "Soviet" nor "Ukraine" had especially positive connotations for most of these people, after the Soviet occupations of 1939–41 and then the Ukrainian cleansings of 1943–44.[30] In summer 1944 many Poles in Ukraine could still believe that Poland would, in the end, regain or even extend its Ukrainian territories, and faith that Britain and the United States could dictate conditions to the Soviet Union was widespread. A few months of Soviet rule changed many minds.[31] NKVD pressure revived memories of 1939–41, while the UPA continued the attacks on Polish civilians begun in 1943–44. Well after the end of the war, the UPA in Soviet Ukraine ethnically cleansed Poles who had not registered for "repatriation." It is likely that the NKVD created false UPA units and used them to destroy Polish settlements; it is also quite possible that NKVD units "unofficially" attacked Poles.[32] However that may be, the "repatriation" of Poles from Soviet Ukraine is best seen as an unofficially cooperative effort of the NKVD and the UPA. Arrests of priests and bishops signaled that Polish society had little chance of survival in Soviet Ukraine. The idea that "whoever doesn't go to Poland goes to Siberia" spread.[33] Representatives of the Polish government, executing what they understood to be a policy in the national interest of their own country, encouraged Poles in Ukraine to depart.[34] In the end, Poles who wished to stay were deported by force. Even the most stubborn, illiterate Polish peasants who had somehow survived in western Volhynia, found themselves dispatched by force to the Baltic. Interestingly, Soviet deportation concluded the ethnic redefinition of western Volhynia as a place without Poles, a project begun by the UPA. Soviet policy was to deport all Poles from territories of prewar Poland, but passed over Poles who had lived on the Soviet side of the prewar border. What had been Polish Volhynia (and became Volyn and Rivne oblasts of Soviet Ukraine) was all but emptied of Poles; the largest concentration of Poles was in what had been Soviet Volhynia, to the east (in what became Zhytomyr oblast).

Transportation to Poland was extremely primitive. The experience of departure was humiliating, especially for women, and the weeks spent on the train risked disease and death.[35] The Polish Committee for National Liberation felt compelled to create a Special Commission on Epidemics in September 1944. Upon arrival in Poland, resettlers were to be doused in DDT.[36] Another part of the tragedy, as irony would have it, was that since resettlement was limited to the regions Soviet Ukraine incorporated from postwar Polish territories, not everyone who wished to go to Poland could go. Even in these territories, prewar Polish citizenship could not be sufficient grounds for resettlement to Poland. If it were, people other than Poles and Jews, the millions of East Slavs with interwar Polish citizenship, could have moved to Poland. This would have undermined the ethnic purpose of the policy. Decisive were Soviet passports issued in

1939–41, since all Soviet passports included a nationality category. Of course, some people who in 1944 wished to be seen as Poles had in 1939 wished to be seen as Ukrainians, and so had the "wrong" nationality recorded in their passports.[37] Other Poles chose to remain, somehow avoided deportation, and in some cases began to call themselves Ukrainians. (These people can still be found today, identifying each other by their mothers' Polish first names on long bus rides from Ivano-Frankivsk, murmuring to each other in Polish in the back of L'viv trams, or switching to Ukrainian in a Kyiv café when a curious head is turned by a Polish nasal vowel.)

The "repatriations" in the other direction, from Poland to Soviet Ukraine, faced greater problems. To be sure, the new, more westerly border meant that the huge majority of interwar Poland's Ukrainian citizens found themselves in Soviet Ukraine without physically moving at all.[38] Poland lost 47 percent of its prewar territory to the Soviet Union, including all of its Volhynian and almost all of its Galician territories. Yet even in its more westerly position, Poland still included in the extreme southeast and south considerable stretches of territory inhabited by people speaking dialects of Ukrainian and worshipping in Greek Catholic and Orthodox churches. Although several thousand Ukrainians had already been murdered by Poles in the Lublin and Rzeszów regions, much of the more southerly and mountainous portions of this belt of terrain were as yet untouched by civil war.[39] In places that state power took longer to reach, Lemkos and Ukrainians had little reason to think that a communist order would be detrimental to their interests. These populations usually voted for the Left in interwar Poland, and as late as early 1945 could still associate communism with internationalism, and even in some cases the Soviet Union with a positive idea of a Great Russia. The Lemkos of the Beskidy mountains inhabited the westernmost part of these lands. Relatively unscathed by the war, these Lemkos had generally seen no reason to commit to any modern nationality. After the change in borders, the Lemkos were about a third of Poland's Ukrainian-speaking population.

Some Lemkos who accepted "repatriation" from Poland to Soviet Ukraine in late 1944 seem to have done so because they regarded the Soviet Union as the homeland of Russian peoples.[40] They saw themselves as a member of the Russian family of nations, in the inclusive and pluralistic sense of the term. Some of them probably went as Ukrainians, as well. Many of them were horrified with the conditions they discovered in Soviet Ukraine, and promptly returned to Poland. The difference between herding goats in the Beskidy mountains and working the kolkhoz in, say, Dnipropetrovsk oblast was very stark, and many who now had experience in both found they strongly preferred the first. Such "re-repatriates" produced interwar Polish documents, or claimed to be Poles and got new documents in the Soviet Union. Since they could often speak better Polish than Poles deported from the Soviet Union, this very often worked. Interwar Polish documents lacked a nationality category, an imprecision that gave these individuals some freedom to choose their fates, and the opportunity upon their return to Poland to spread what Soviet officials called "slanderous rumors" about life in the Soviet Union.[41]

After the First World War the main Lemko aspiration had been to remain in the same state with other Carpathian Slavic peoples. After the Second World War, the Lemkos' main hope was simply to remain in the lands that their people had inhabited for centuries. With the discrediting of Soviet Ukraine in 1944, this wish was fairly general by early 1945. It was then that the Polish regime began to exert pressure throughout the belt of Ukrainian and Lemko settlement. Young men who had not registered for "repatriation" were arrested. Polish security forces and the Polish army began to attack Ukrainian and Lemko villages. Although Lemkos and Ukrainians could not be always sure who their attackers were, they knew that they were Poles. Since Lemkos were forcibly resettled as Ukrainians, the Polish policy was effectively one of Ukrainization. Local Polish officials, who distinguished between Lemkos and Ukrainians, realized that this was the case. They consistently reported Lemkos' loyalty to the Polish state.[42] Officials at the palatinate level, however, saw the matter more abstractly. The palatine of Cracow district, for instance, thought matters would be simplest if Lemkos were treated as Ukrainians and deported, in the interest of forming "a homogenous state from the national point of view."[43] The first secretary of the Polish communist party and minister for resettlement affairs, Władysław Gomułka, actually ordered a halt to the forcible resettlement of Lemkos.[44] Like local officials who made distinctions, Gomułka was from the Lemko territories. That the order of the Polish first secretary was disregarded suggests that the decision to forcibly resettle Lemkos along with Ukrainians came from Moscow, or at least that Moscow's directives could be so interpreted.

In actions taken after the German surrender ended the Second World War in Europe, Polish communist forces killed perhaps four thousand Lemko and Ukrainian civilians. The Home Army and other Polish partisans killed certainly hundreds and very probably thousands more.[45] The official Polish army and Polish partisans were themselves deadly enemies, and throughout 1945 and especially 1946 were engaged in major fighting throughout the country. From a

Lemko or Ukrainian point of view, however, contact with the official army and the partisans it fought gave a taste of what was to come in communist Poland. When a Ukrainian or Lemko village was burned, it mattered little to the villagers what ideal of Poland the attackers represented. The Soviet Union was not attractive, but Polish nationalists helped Polish communists to render Poland intolerable. Just as the UPA helped Soviet Ukrainian officials deport Poles, so the Polish partisans helped Polish communists deport Ukrainians and Lemkos. Like Poles in Soviet Ukraine, Ukrainians and Lemkos in communist Poland faced both the wrath of nationalists and the homogenizing policy of communists. 208,000 individuals recorded as Ukrainians left Poland during the first eight months of 1945.[46] People who wished to stay looked for someone to defend them.

THE UPA IN POLAND IN 1945

The UPA's policy of ethnic cleansing, inaugurated in Volhynia in 1943, had become general practice by 1945. How did the UPA fare in these conditions, which it had helped to create? After the informal border shift of 1944, the main body of the UPA fought Soviet power in Soviet West Ukraine, its commanders regarding Poland as a peripheral field of operations. In early 1945, Iaroslav Starukh organized a new UPA command for Poland within its new westerly frontiers. Reorganization was complete by August 1945, when the new Soviet-Polish border was publicized. In 1945 in Poland, UPA units probably never numbered more than twenty-four hundred troops.[47] These troops were not, with a few exceptions, the same people who had cleansed Volhynia and Galicia in 1943–44. The vast majority of UPA soldiers in what was becoming postwar Poland joined in 1944, 1945, or 1946, and fought in the regions where they lived.[48] The further south and west they were in Poland, the longer it took Ukrainian nationalists to activate the UPA. The UPA fought in the Lublin region in 1943. In the Bieszczady mountains, the UPA arose in 1944. As late as fall 1945, after the German surrender and the end of the Second World War, Beskid Niski had no UPA presence, and its Lemkos were scornful of the very idea.

Khrushchev was correct in writing to Stalin that Polish partisan attacks on Ukrainian civilians helped UPA recruitment.[49] The main factor, however, was the desire to avoid deportation to the Soviet Union.[50] The link between the homeland and Ukrainian nationalism, never before made in many of these territories, finally became salient when Ukrainian nationalists promised to prevent deportation. This was a passage to a new universe of ideology. The OUN-Bandera was still the dominant force within Ukrainian nationalism, but after the German surrender differences between the OUN-Mel'nyk and the OUN-Bandera became less important. Veterans of *SS-Galizien,* supported by the OUN-Mel'nyk but opposed by the OUN-Bandera, now played a crucial role in the local UPA.[51] This can be ascertained on the basis of UPA records. Mykola Kopdo deserted the *SS-Galizien* for the UPA in 1944, and died commanding a UPA brigade in Poland. Dmytro Karvans'kyi, a prominent OUN-Mel'nyk activist, deserted the *SS-Galizien* for the UPA in February 1944. He died commanding a UPA company in Poland. Mykhailo Hal'o, commander of one of the four UPA battalions in southeastern Poland, also left the *SS-Galizien* in 1944. Marian Lukashevich, commander of one of three UPA tactical regions in Poland, was also a veteran of *SS-Galizien.*[52] Whatever the motives of the local Ukrainians who joined the UPA, they received their training from such officers.[53] In other words, the ethnic cleansing policies of communist Poland drove its Ukrainian citizens into the arms of former Waffen-SS troops.

That said, the UPA was pursuing interests in Poland in 1945 that we can ascertain and describe. Most of its actions were designed to halt deportations, and its recruiting propaganda presented it as an organization that would defend Ukrainian homes.[54] Propaganda is propaganda, but it does suggest why people joined. The balance of civilian deaths in southeastern Poland tends to confirm that the goals of the UPA at this time and place were resistance and defense rather than ethnic cleansing. In September 1944, right after the front had passed, the UPA issued orders halting the "mass anti-Polish actions," at least within the borders of what was becoming communist Poland.[55] Even though the OUN-Bandera continued to regard southeastern Poland as ethnic Ukrainian territory, there was no strategic reason to cleanse Poles from what was going to remain Poland. Murders of civilians and liquidation of settlements continued, but were henceforth announced as retaliations for Polish attacks. The UPA command opposed the deportation of Ukrainians from southeastern Poland to Soviet Ukraine, treating "repatriation" as a device to exterminate Ukrainians in Soviet camps and destroy the Ukrainian nation.[56]

In this project the UPA's major problem was the ubiquity of "information" about nationality. In determining resettlement, Polish communist officials used German documents and their helpfully unambiguous "P" or "U." Since everyone respected German efficiency, it was assumed that anyone without a document showing Polish nationality was in fact Ukrainian. In doubtful situations, Polish officials would use church records, on the logic that anyone not Roman Catholic must be Ukrainian. UPA partisans burned such cadasters to destroy "information" about who was Ukrainian in a given locality. UPA soldiers also set to work blowing up train tracks and locomotives, bringing down hundreds of miles of telephone poles (and probably tapping the lines left standing), destroying bridges, and assassinating officials charged with "repatriation." The UPA burned depopulated Ukrainian villages, to prevent them from being resettled by Poles. When the Polish army was sent to assist resettlements in September 1945, the UPA attacked it directly.[57]

The UPA was more audacious than the contemporary Polish anticommunist resistance. The Home Army had been officially dissolved in August 1945, its commanders deciding that further struggle against a communist state called "Poland," within borders recognized by the Western allies, would not serve the Polish cause. Some units of the Home Army resisted the order to disband, and fought on in what became known as the AK-WiN (Armia Krajowa—Wolność i Niezawisłość, Home Army—Freedom and Independence). As we have seen, these same geopolitical facts had led the UPA to reorganize and to change its strategy. Ukrainian and Polish partisans were now desperate enough to see that continuing attacks on civilians were a waste of time and energy. The UPA and the AK-WiN reached a truce in spring 1945.[58] By this time, Ukrainian and Polish partisans had only one hope, and it was a hope they shared: that a Third World War would begin, and communism would be overthrown by the Americans and the British.

COMMUNISM, THE POLISH STATE, AND ITS
UKRAINIAN CITIZENS, 1945–1946

The resettlement policy which drove Ukrainians and some Lemkos into the arms of the UPA also drove local leaders to appeal to the new central authorities. In July 1945, a delegation of Ukrainians defended their rights in Warsaw at a meeting at the Ministry of Public Administration. The replies they received foretold what was to come. "Although the Citizens are unanimous in wishing to remain here, I think that this will be impossible," said the delegate from the Council of Ministers. "Having reached an understanding with the Soviet Union to establish an ethnographic frontier, we have a tendency to be a national state, and not a state of nationalities."[59] The "national state," or ethnically homogenous state, had been a code word of the interwar National Democrats. It was the title of one of Grabski's books.[60] The "state of nationalities," on the other hand, had been associated with Piłsudski's federalism and with Jewish autonomy. In the casual appropriation of "the national state" by representatives of a Polish government dominated by communists, we see a corner turned. The state's attitude to nationality was not shared by all of its citizens. Speakers of Ukrainian who did not yet accept this principle, including Russophile Lemkos, were surprised and disappointed by the harmony of Soviet policy and Polish nationalism. A delegation of Lemkos from several regions of Poland wrote to Soviet authorities in September 1945, asking not to be forcibly evacuated. These Lemkos expressed their regret that their lands were not incorporated into the Soviet Union. Their appeal concluded, "If the Soviet Union does not want our land, then it does not want us either, so leave us where we are, so long as we are not necessary to you."[61]

Soviet policy had just taken a turn in the opposite direction. At the request of Soviet plenipotentiary for repatriation affairs Nikolai Podgornyi, on 3 September 1945 Polish authorities ordered three infantry divisions to deport remaining Ukrainians to the Soviet Union.[62] The ranks of two of these three divisions included Poles from Volhynia, some of whom exacted personal revenge for the slaughter of 1943. Polish soldiers killed hundreds of Ukrainian civilians as they forced about twenty-three thousand of them to evacuate the country in late 1945. Polish units were often led by Red Army officers, responsible for several of the most horrible massacres of Ukrainian civilians. These officers had taken high positions in the Polish Army, and of course appeared in Polish uniforms. (Some of them, such as the notorious Colonel Stanislav Pluto, were of Polish origin. More often, Soviet officers and repatriation officials removing Ukrainians from Poland had Ukrainian surnames.) The modus operandi of the Polish Army in late 1945 and early 1946 was to halfheartedly attack an UPA unit, destroy a village and murder Ukrainian civilians after the UPA unit escaped, wait for the UPA to destroy a Polish village in retaliation, and then repeat the cycle. One example must stand for dozens of others. At Pluto's orders, Polish soldiers murdered the civilian inhabitants of Zawadka Morochowska on 25 January 1946. Soldiers killed fifty-six people, mostly women, children, and the aged. They burned people alive, mutilated faces with bayonets, disemboweled the living.[63]

In April 1946 Polish authorities organized Operation Group Rzeszów, tasked to complete the expulsion of Ukrainians from Poland. A quarter of a million people were classified as Ukrainians and forcibly resettled to Soviet Ukraine between April and June 1946. During the entire period of "repatriations," between October 1944 and June 1946, 482,661 people classified as Ukrainians departed for the Soviet Union. In rough terms, 300,000 were forced to do so, 100,000 were effectively coerced by nearby violence or homelessness, and the rest chose to leave. Operation Rzeszów killed about 910 Ukrainians, but did little damage to UPA structures.[64] At its conclusion, it was believed that the Ukrainian "problem" in Poland had been resolved.

OPERATION VISTULA IN PRINCIPLE, 1947

In early 1947, Polish authorities realized that this was not the case, and that a "final solution" of the Ukrainian "problem" would require a new policy. Soviet forces, which had organized the "repatriations" of 1944–46, were less available. The Soviet NKVD was leaving Poland, and the Soviet repatriation infrastructure had been dismantled. In 1946, Poland had resisted the end of repatriations in the hope of getting the maximum number of repatriates from the Soviet Union. Stalin's patience with this was exhausted.[65] This meant that any further resettlements would be internal, as a Polish general prominent in the "repatriations" promptly recommended. "Since the Soviet Union is no longer taking these people," Deputy Chief of Staff Stefan Mossor proposed in February 1947, "it is necessary to resettle them by individual family throughout the entire area of the Recovered Territories," the northern and western regions Poland received from Germany.[66] In 1946, far more Polish communist forces were deployed against the Polish than against the Ukrainian opposition. In winter 1946–47, the army was used to falsify the January 1947 parliamentary elections. These election results, and the amnesty of the same month, ended meaningful armed opposition by Poles to the Polish regime. As more units of the Polish army became available in 1947, the UPA continued to fight.

After Deputy Defense Minister Karol Świerczewski was assassinated by the UPA on 28 March, the Politburo decided at once to "resettle Ukrainians and mixed families in the regained territories (especially in northern Prussia), not forming any tight groups and no closer than 100 kilometers to the border."[67] In all probability, General Świerczewski's death provided a wonderful occasion for an action Polish authorities wished to carry out on political grounds. Of course, priorities matter, and we cannot say for sure what would have happened in April if not for that murder in March. Nor can we be entirely sure about the Soviet attitude to the operation. The Polish plan must have had Soviet approval, and it was perfectly consistent with Soviet practice. Soviet authorities on the other side of the border were prosecuting an incredibly brutal war against the UPA and deporting family members. Moreover, Soviet agents were deeply involved in the planning of what was christened "Operation Vistula."[68] It is the Soviet role in the initiation of the action that remains unclear. One high-ranking Polish official, trusted by Moscow, tried to warn Stalin that the policy of resettling Ukrainians within Poland was irresponsible and likely to fail. Alarmed by the Polish Politburo's sudden decision, the Polish vice minister for repatriation affairs went straight to his Soviet contact, late at night, and told him personally that the Polish Politburo had taken an important decision in haste without consulting Moscow.[69]

It is very possible, indeed probable, that he was mistaken. We cannot know for certain. It would be naive to imagine that the Polish policy could have been ordered without Moscow's approval; it is also naive to imagine that the Soviets initiated every policy. We can observe from the definition of policy in March and April 1947 that Soviet staffers cooperated with native Poles in Operation Vistula. For example, Lieutenant Colonel Wacław Kossowski, a Red Army officer and Soviet plant in the Polish general staff, recommended on 29 March "the complete extermination of the remnants of the Ukrainian population in the southeastern border region of Poland." On 12 April, the State Security Commission, the central organ charged with eliminating organized resistance to the communist regime, accepted the recommendation.[70] The commission approved a laconic report delivered by Stanisław Radkiewicz, minister for public security. Radkiewicz was an interwar Polish communist who had spent the war in the Soviet Union and served in the Red Army. He was charged with internal security the moment the Red Army crossed into Poland, and remained head of the secret police through 1954. Also present was Defense Minister and Marshall Michał Rola-Żymierski, another client of Stalin. Żymierski had served in Piłsudski's Legions and earned the rank of general in the interwar period, but had been dismissed from the army on a corruption charge. He joined the Soviet-sponsored Polish Army during the war, and was beholden to Stalin for his rapid promotion to its highest rank.

Even after their estimates were revised upward in early 1947, Polish military planners thought that the "remnants of the Ukrainian population" amounted to no more than seventy-four thousand individuals. In fact there were still some two hundred thousand speakers of Ukrainian in Poland (about 0.8 percent of the Polish population).[71] The absolute numbers are high enough to suggest the scale of suffering that forced relocation would bring; the relative proportions low enough to call into question the idea that Ukrainians (one-third of them Lemkos) threatened the Polish state. It is true that in 1947 some Ukrainians supported the UPA, and that this support had increased as Ukrainians were deported to the Soviet Union. It is also true that the main goal of the UPA was to establish an independent Ukrainian state, and some soldiers were willing to fight on against overwhelming odds. Although OUN and UPA leaders now concealed their final goal of Ukrainian statehood on all "ethnographically" Ukrainian territories, and limited their attacks on Polish troops, there can be no doubt about the basic conflict of interest between the UPA and the Polish state.[72]

It does not follow, however, that resettling the entire Ukrainian population was only considered in the context of the war with the UPA. In early 1947, the Polish Politburo and general staff considered the total resettlement of Ukrainians desirable in its own right, aside and apart from the expected destruction of the UPA. The army was assigned two tasks. The first was to "destroy the UPA bands." The second task was to carry out "an evacuation of all persons of Ukrainian nationality from the region to the northwestern territories, resettling them with the widest possible dispersion."[73] Polish commanders (including those reporting to Moscow) understood Operation Vistula as involving both combat and resettlement. Resettlement was to continue to the last Ukrainian, even if the UPA was quickly neutralized. In General Mossor's terms, the point of Operation Vistula was to "resolve the Ukrainian problem in Poland once and for all."[74] Resettlement was designed to ensure that Ukrainian communities could never arise again in Poland, that postwar Poland would be, in the terms postwar communists inherited from interwar nationalists, a "national state."[75]

The very name of the operation suggests the centrality of resettlement. The Vistula is a river: it flows from Cracow through Warsaw to reach the Baltic near Gdańsk, dividing contemporary Poland roughly in half. This is not incidental. Before and during the Second World War rivers had washed the boundaries of the homogenous national territories imagined by nationalists: Polish nationalists called for Ukrainians to be expelled east beyond the Zbruch River; Ukrainian nationalists warned Poles to flee west beyond the San. Soviet policy was, in effect, to compromise on the river and then carry out deportations in both directions: the River Bug/Buh became the Polish-Soviet Ukrainian border, and more than a million Poles and Ukrainians were "evacuated" across it in both directions. Operation Vistula fit squarely into this tradition, with a black irony. The river Vistula defined the northern and western borders of the Lublin, Rzeszów, and Cracow palatinates of postwar Poland, in which Ukrainians lived and from which Ukrainians were to be resettled. Whereas nationalists traditionally aimed to expel ethnic foes over a river and "back" into the enemy's national territory, and whereas Soviet and Polish communists had realized such plans after their own fashion in 1944–46, in 1947 the Polish regime dispersed its citizens of Ukrainian nationality in the "wrong" direction, to the north and west, to the side of the river Vistula where Ukrainians had never been present and could be expected to assimilate.

Operation Vistula was designed to match the ethnic geography to the political geography of the new Polish state. In 1947, with Jewish survivors emigrating and remaining Germans hastening to change their nationality, Polish authorities decided to resettle "every person of Ukrainian nationality." Even mixed families, even communities which had not supported the UPA, even Lemkos who did not identify with the Ukrainian nation, even decorated Red Army veterans, even party members trained in the Soviet Union, even communists who had helped "repatriate" fellow Ukrainians in 1944–46: all were to be forcibly resettled. Nationality, here as during the "evacuations," was decided by blood, religion, and in practice by the letter "U" in Nazi identity documents.[76] The aspirations of the policy (to be applied to "every person") confirm that the Polish "national state" was the starting point of Polish "people's democracy."

The Polish communist regime stood to gain in popularity by combating Ukrainian nationality, by "resolving" the last national problem on Polish soil. Hegemony over the idea of the nation had been a major goal of communist propaganda since the foundation of the Union of Polish Patriots in 1943; the genius of excluding the UPA from the national amnesty of January 1947, of prosecuting Ukrainian partisans under different laws than Polish ones, and finally of Operation Vistula in summer 1947, was that such actions defined that national community plainly in ethnic terms.

OPERATION VISTULA IN PRACTICE, 1947

Leadership of Operation Vistula was entrusted to General Mossor, who had joined the communist party only in 1945. Mossor had been a soldier in Piłsudski's legions during the First World War, and a military planner in interwar Poland. He had been involved in anti-Ukrainian actions before the war, and had taken part in Operation Rzeszów in 1946. The military operations against the UPA, and the army's role in resettlement, were apparently planned by two Soviet Poles: Colonel Michał Chiliński, chief of staff of the operation, and Lieutenant Colonel Wacław Kossowski, who was detailed to head the staff's operations section.[77] Operation Vistula joined infantry divisions with internal security forces into a force of 19,335 men. Most of these soldiers were veterans of the war against the Polish underground. Having spent a year shooting at fellow Poles, often former comrades in arms, these soldiers must be considered as appropriately demoralized. At the time Operation Vistula began, the Operation Group outnumbered the UPA something like twenty to one.[78]

Mossor, Kossowski, and Chiliński were concerned in the first instance with the destruction of the UPA. When operations began in late April 1947 in the Rzeszów area, Mossor was unimpressed by the performance of his soldiers in battle.[79] Realizing that encirclement tactics were failing against more committed and experienced enemy troops, Polish commanders decided to simply pursue every UPA unit until it was cornered and destroyed. This was an old Soviet antipartisan tactic. It never defeated an UPA unit in Poland, since UPA soldiers simply broke into small groups and regrouped later, but it did exhaust and frustrate the Ukrainians. As the war became a hunt, Polish communications were characterized by a thorough familiarity with Soviet protocols of antipartisan warfare. Polish commanders carefully explained how to use police dogs to trace retreating partisans through the forest, how to destroy the reinforced bunkers where UPA soldiers took shelter, and the like.[80] When trapped in their bunkers, UPA soldiers often committed suicide rather than surrender. In so doing they were following orders. They were also avoiding the torture that surely awaited them if they were taken alive.[81]

Meanwhile, the dispersion task proceeded, first in Rzeszów palatinate, then in Lublin and Cracow palatinates. In the four months which followed 28 April 1947, the Operation Group moved some 140,660 individuals identified as Ukrainians from southeastern to northern and western Poland. Just as the first round of evacuations and deportations had removed about 75 percent of the Ukrainians remaining in Poland in 1944–46, Operation Vistula resettled about three-quarters of those who remained in 1947.[82] Operation Vistula perfected tactics used in Operation Rzeszów. Soldiers would enclose a village and seal off the area to prevent UPA intervention, then a military or security services officer would read a list of names of those to be resettled. Those identified as Ukrainians were given a few hours to pack, and then relocated to intermediary sites. If men tried to escape when the army encircled the village, they were shot. In general men moving about during the operation were likely to be shot. In some cases Polish soldiers shot men in flight, only to find the "P" for "Pole" in the German identity documents in the dead men's pockets. Members of households where men were absent were tortured in order to locate UPA soldiers. Several villages were burned as their inhabitants watched.[83] Vistula was distinguished from Rzeszów by the more complicated role played by the security services, since Polish authorities were now charged not only with deportation but also with a complex resettlement inside Poland. The final destination and degree of dispersal of groups was determined by the judgment of intelligence officers, whose colleagues were waiting to receive their instructions in sealed envelopes at the end of the line.

Military and security officers relied on local informers, of both Polish and Ukrainian nationality, to denounce their neighbors as UPA partisans. Individuals singled out as Ukrainian partisans could be judicially murdered or sent to a concentration camp. Military courts, empowered to judge civilians, sentenced at the very least 175 Ukrainians to death for collaborating with the UPA.[84] Most of these sentences were carried out the same day. About 3,936 Ukrainians, including 823 women and children, were taken to the Jaworzno concentration camp, a wartime affiliate of the Auschwitz-Birkenau complex. There, routine torture was accompanied by typhus epidemics and shortages of food and clothing.[85] Several dozen Ukrainians died in Jaworzno, including two women by suicide. Twenty-seven more Ukrainians, mostly infants and the aged, died on trains during resettlement. In terms of the number of people repressed, imprisoned, sentenced to death, and actually killed, Operation Vistula was the most massive exercise of terror by the Polish communist regime during the entirety of its existence.

The 1947 resettlement defeated the UPA in Poland. Once most Ukrainians had been resettled, resistance was not only next to impossible, it was essentially pointless. Most soldiers had been fighting to protect their homes, and now they had lost. Those hundreds wishing to continue the fight against communism had little reason to do so in Poland. Chased unceasingly by Polish troops, UPA battalions broke ranks.[86] Some partisans allowed themselves to be resettled in northwestern Poland; others fought their way across the sealed borders to Czechoslovakia, whence several hundred reached the West. Incredibly, hundreds crossed the sealed Soviet border to fight on with the main body of the UPA. The flight of the UPA marked the final step in the consolidation of the new Soviet-Polish border, the homogenization of the Polish population, and the liquidation of armed resistance to the Polish regime.

Chapters 6 and 7 were devoted to an evocation of the historical durability and modern contestation of Galicia and Volhynia; chapters 8 and 9 have described the rapid transformation of several inheritances from the old Commonwealth (1569–1795), from the multinational empires (1795–1918), and from the brief period of Polish rule (1918–39). In eight years, between September 1939 and September 1947, German power advanced and withdrew, Soviet power was installed twice, East European Jewish civilization was destroyed, Poles and Ukrainians ethnically cleansed each other, and a new and durable frontier separated Poles from Ukrainians. Operation Vistula ended the history of Galicia and Volhynia, and began the history of Western Ukraine and southeastern Poland.

The conclusion of Operation Vistula coincided with the consolidation of communist power in Poland; the homogenization of Poland coincided with the establishment of a communist power in Eastern Europe. The rejection of the Marshall Plan in summer 1947 by East European states brought down Churchill's metaphorical Iron Curtain. As world war gave way to cold war, national questions were settled, forgotten, or transformed. Driven from Poland, the UPA fought on in the Soviet Union for nearly a decade; Mykola Lebed', the Ukrainian nationalist perhaps most responsible for the Volhynian terror that began the Polish-Ukrainian civil war, was employed by U.S. intelligence.[87] Romen Shukhevyeh, the UPA commander, died in battle in Soviet Ukraine. The new European order was built on the presumption that Poland, a national state ruled by communists, could align with the Soviet Union. As we shall see in the next two chapters, eastern questions played a special role in the consolidation of Polish communism and the Soviet-Polish alliance—and then in their disintegration.

Chapter 10 Epilogue:
Communism and Cleansed
Memories (1947–1981)

The Poland that emerged in 1945 covered a very different part of Europe than the Poland that was destroyed in 1939. Half of Poland's prewar territory was lost to the Soviet Union in 1939, and a third of its postwar territory was gained from Germany in 1945. Gone were Wilno and Lwów, gained were Gdańsk and Wrocław. Postwar Poland was crushingly Polish: perhaps 97 percent of its citizens would have self-identified as Poles. Yet if we impose Poland's postwar borders on prewar Europe, we find that its postwar territories were home to four groups in 1939: Poles, Germans, Jews, and East Slavs (Ukrainians and Lemkos). In 1939, only about three-fifths of the people on the territories that became Poland in 1945 were Poles.[1] In general outlines, we have seen how three-fifths become almost everyone: the Jews were murdered, the Germans were expelled, and the Ukrainians were deported, while Poles were "repatriated" west from the Soviet Union. In concentrating on the consequences of the resettlement of Poles and Ukrainians, this chapter will endeavor to reveal some of what was destroyed so that Poland could be reconstructed.

ETHNIC CLEANSING AND SOCIAL MEMORY

The cleansing of Poles from what became western Ukraine and the cleansing of Ukrainians from what became southeastern Poland ended hundreds of years of mixed settlement of borderlands. Since the early modern period, the three main languages of Galicia and Volhynia had been Ukrainian, Polish, and Yiddish, the four main religions Orthodoxy, Greek Catholicism, Roman Catholicism, and Judaism.[2] Galician and Volhynian Jews were all but annihilated in the Holocaust, and many of the survivors emigrated after the war. Poles and Ukrainians continued to inhabit these lands, but by 1947 were divided for the first time by a durable border between political units called "Polish" and "Ukrainian." Galicians were left to consider Russians as the major national minority, and Russian as a language of power and culture.[3] After six centuries of rule from Cracow, Warsaw, and Vienna, rule from Moscow was something new.

In what had been Polish Volhynia, perhaps 7,000 Poles remained in 1947, down from 350,000 in 1939. This was a reduction of 98 percent. In what became Soviet Ukrainian Galicia there were perhaps 150,000 people who called themselves Poles, compared to 1.8 million before the war. This was a reduction of 92 percent. On the far smaller Galician territories that remained in Poland after the border shift, there had been perhaps 600,000 speakers of Ukrainian in 1939; by 1947 there were only about 30,000: a reduction of 95 percent. In Volhynia and Galicia taken together, about 97 percent of the Jewish population was killed during the war. In Volhynia the figure reached 98.5 percent.[4] Even with every conceivable qualification, these changes bespeak a drastic alteration in the settlement of a considerable region of Europe. The Final Solution of 1941–44 was Nazi policy; the "evacuation" of national minorities in 1944–46 was Stalinist policy: but the former facilitated, and the latter continued, the Ukrainian-Polish ethnic war that began in 1943.

Ukrainians remember ethnic cleansing by a "Polish" regime, and recall the UPA as the organization that helped them. The memory of the UPA became an essential element of Ukrainian identity in postwar Poland. Most of the Ukrainians deported from Poland in 1944–46 settled in western Ukraine. For them as well, the UPA became the main institutional repository of national identity.[5] Ukrainians resettled to Soviet Ukraine sometimes complain that their fate is forgotten by Ukrainians in Poland, who attend only to 1947 and to Operation Vistula.[6] They have a point. The Ukrainian question was not "resolved" only in Poland, or indeed only in Poland and western Ukraine. Between 1944 and 1946, 159,241 individuals identified as Ukrainians were sent to central or eastern Ukraine. 323,858 were resettled to Western Ukraine.[7] Operation Vistula resettled 140,660 individuals within Poland. In quantitative terms, Operation Vistula concerned less than a quarter of the Polish citizens resettled as Ukrainians. More people were sent to central and eastern Ukraine than to western Poland: they too faced adjustments to a new situation, and in almost every respect their situation was worse.

Whereas Ukrainians who remained in Poland remember 1947, Poles resettled from Volhynia and Galicia remember the slaughter by Ukrainian partisans of 1943 and 1944. To be sure, the barbaric mass murder of Polish civilians by the UPA in Volhynia in 1943 and Galicia in 1944 was one of the most terrible episodes of the war. Polish survivors and their families almost always regard the UPA as a band of murderers. Survivors found themselves dispersed throughout postwar Poland, under a communist regime that did not acknowledge their memory, since discussions of lost prewar territories were taboo. Polish survivors also bore a tremendous share of the national humiliation flowing from the collapse of the civilizing mission in the east, an idea once as essential to Polish national identity as the frontier was to the American, or the empire was to the British.

These Ukrainian and Polish memories are different in substance: they contain contradictory accounts of events, and different heroes and villains. They are similar in form: both speak of the destruction of ways of life, and of the compulsion to begin anew. Consider, one after the other, a pair of Ukrainian and Polish recollections. "No one ever dreamed that such a great Ukrainian village, which shone with Ukrainian life, could be in such a short time, in such a brutal, barbaric way, torn from the surface of the earth." "Volhynia aflame, the glow of the flames, I see it still and I cannot rid myself of it, I cannot forget it. What happened in Volhynia will remain in my memory to the end of my days."[8] Historical disagreements regarding 1943–47, about who started the conflicts and who suffered most, flowed from different definitions of groups, borders, and periods. Ukrainians rightly think that Polish groups struck first in most areas of what became postwar Poland. Poles rightly think that the OUN-Bandera's decision to destroy the Polish element in what became western Ukraine began the entire cycle. Ukrainians rightly believe that more Ukrainians than Poles were killed on territories now in Poland: about eleven thousand Ukrainians to about seven thousand Poles. Poles rightly believe that, taking into account all contested territories, Poles were killed in greater numbers: about seventy thousand Poles to perhaps twenty thousand Ukrainians.[9]

SOCIAL MEMORY AND MODERN NATIONALITY

It does not deform the facts, today, to link these human recollections and body counts to opposing Polish and Ukrainian memories, which correspond to the two modern nationalisms that prevail in Poland and western Ukraine. At the same time, it is important to see that terrible events which are recalled today often clarified the national identity of the Poles and Ukrainians who retell them. The perspective of 1947 was tremendously different than the perspective of 1939. Teenagers and adults who cleansed each other during the 1940s were once children who (sometimes quite literally) played together in the 1930s. The recollection of the Volhynian Pole "Waldemar Lotnik," who took part in the ferocious mutual cleansings of late 1943 on the Polish side, is typical: "But it was with Ukrainians that I spent most of my childhood, learnt to read and write, skated on frozen lakes in winter and discovered shards of Russian and German ammunition, left over from the First World War, in the forests and fields . . ."[10] He does not say so, but he certainly spoke Ukrainian with these children.

The very way "Lotnik," and others like him, lived to tell the tale defies the presumption of inborn national traits, gives the lie to cultural definitions of national identity, and alerts us to difference between prewar and postwar accounts of nationality. Lotnik—a Pole telling a very Polish story, remember—would have been killed at several points had he not been a *native* speaker of Ukrainian and Russian. He owed the "nine lives" of his memoir's title to the fact that he spoke languages *other than* Polish. At one point, he almost perished because his eastern accent *in Polish* caught the ear of a savvy Red Army officer looking for deserters. Some Polish children escaped death in Volhynia in 1943 because they spoke Ukrainian with Ukrainian children they played with, and could say their prayers in Ukrainian when stopped on the road by strangers. Volhynian Ukrainian families who wished to save Polish children taught them the Lord's Prayer in Ukrainian. Although we have seen that religion served as a marker for putative nations, and that churches sometimes provided havens for national activists, this was the first moment in which religion mattered chiefly as a sign of nationality for societies in general. If one defines modernity as the period when nationality counts for more than religion, modernity begins in Volhynia and much of Galicia in the 1940s.

We know of these cases of survival from the memoirs of survivors. For obvious reasons, the circumstances of death are harder to specify than the circumstances of survival. There are nevertheless enough cases of mistaken identity leading to murder in 1943 and 1944 to confirm the general idea that nationality was by no means transparent—even to nationalists. In an atmosphere of mutual mass murder on national grounds, people made incorrect judgments that led to horribly absurd deaths. The Poles who surrounded the Galician village of Zubrza in summer 1944 wished to take revenge on the Ukrainian nation by killing Ukrainians. The village's five Poles were not convinced that these unknown attackers were really Poles: local Poles apparently thought the armed outsiders were an UPA brigade, masquerading as Poles to reveal the village's Poles. In accordance with this reading of the situation, these five Poles pretended to be Ukrainians. Their calculation was wrong; the attackers really were fellow Poles. The ruse was successful; their fellow Poles took them for Ukrainians, and killed them. In a matter of life or death, both killers and victims were unable to recognize members of their own nationality.[11]

Southeastern Poland in 1947 admitted similar ambiguities. The very way Operation Vistula was prosecuted and resisted reveals the falsity of simple accounts of clearly distinguishable "Poles" and "Ukrainians" in conflict. In May 1947, for example, the Polish regime created a false UPA brigade, composed of speakers of Ukrainian, in an attempt to draw the OUN leader from his bunker. A meeting was arranged. But the disguise worked all too well: on its way to the rendezvous, the Polish "UPA" unit was mistakenly attacked by Polish security forces. Incidentally, even the real UPA soldiers who arrived in time to watch this transpire could not tell that the false UPA brigade was not one of theirs. In a separate incident one month later, a real UPA unit escaped encirclement by the Polish army by striking up a popular Polish revolutionary song ("When the nation takes the field, weapon in hand . . .") and singing its way through Polish lines. Ironies such as these were a product of ethnic cleansing and a sign that it was incomplete; the success of ethnic cleansing meant the beginning of the end of such surprises.[12]

Ukrainians cleansed by Operation Vistula in 1947 sometimes spoke better Polish than the Poles cleansed from Volhynia by the UPA in 1943: but when these groups met in the Recovered Territories of northern and western Poland, people usually "knew" who was the Pole and who the Ukrainian.[13] Politics and memory trumped observable cultural traits such as language. This is not to say that Lemkos and Ukrainians could not pass as Poles: tens of thousands of them did. The point is that by 1947 everyone accepted that nationality was unitary and exclusive, that individuals were of exactly one nationality. Eastern Poles and Ukrainians resettled in western Poland often had a great deal in common, at least in contrast to the natives around them: but a new "eastern" culture conspicuously failed to emerge.[14] Only in the most extreme situations did such similarities tell. A Volhynian Pole recalled, as his single positive memory of having Ukrainian neighbors, a reciprocated invitation to Christmas dinner and the fresh fish UPA veterans somehow procured—in the Siberian gulag. Christmas dinners were important occasions to both Poles and Ukrainians before the war, and reciprocal invitations were not uncommon in the 1930s. It took Siberia to reproduce such cordiality in the 1940s.[15]

The Polish state reinforced felt divisions, and supported a modern conception of Polish nationality. The very chaos and mobility of the postwar period helped in this project. When a fifth of the prewar population has been killed, a quarter of all villages have been destroyed, a third of the population has been resettled or moved from somewhere else, and one half of the cultural centers (Lwów and Wilno) have been lost to foreign rule, local loyalties count for less than they would, and recent memories for more than they might. Detailed study of the years after 1945 demonstrates that the very process of creating a working class in Poland involved the making of a Polish working class nationalism.[16] But individual experiences during the war provided much of the material with which the state worked, and were often sufficient in and of themselves.[17] Both ends of the gun are transforming: there is perhaps no experience so nationalizing as to have been both cleansed and cleanser. Such people have something to remember and something to forget, something to grieve and something to justify.

SIMPLIFICATION AND NATIONALIZATION

We can see the triumph of modern nationality in communist Poland on the example of regional groups. "Volhynians" are now counted among the most forthright of Polish nationalists: not at all the case before 1939.[18] Lemkos (or their children and grandchildren) are now part of Ukrainian civil society in Poland: again, something unthinkable before the war. Nationalism is now the main current in Ukrainian political life in Poland, which had never previously been the case. Recall too the tens of thousands of Ukrainian peasants who profited from the slaughter of Poles in Volhynia, or the tens of thousands of Poles resettled to southeastern Poland after Operation Vistula. Volhynian Ukrainians who today refuse to speak of annihilated Polish villages, like Polish priests who today destroy Ukrainian cemeteries in southeastern Poland, smooth out the past.

What happened to villages full of wrinkles, such as Dobra Shl'iakhets'ka/
Dobra Szlachecka? After six centuries of existence as a distinct local reality, and
after decades of relative indifference to modern ideas of nationality, Dobra was
transformed almost beyond recognition between 1939 and 1947. In 1939–41 the
Soviets deported Ukrainians they accused of "collaborating" with the interwar
Polish state. In 1942–43 the Germans murdered most of the Jews. The Germans also sent Ukrainian national activists and communists to Auschwitz. In
1944–45 the UPA murdered Ukrainians it found uncooperative, and Poles it
suspected of "collaborating" with the new regime. On 6 January 1945 a Polish
army battalion found a UPA brigade in Dobra: the UPA escaped, and the army
killed twenty-six inhabitants of the village. The Soviets resettled half of the survivors in 1946, the Polish regime the other half during Operation Vistula in
1947. Eighty villagers were interned in the concentration camp at Jaworzno; a
Dobra woman gave birth there.

In Dobra, as elsewhere, the violent application of ascriptive definitions was
divisive. Those who found the body of the fourteen-year-old boy murdered by
the UPA for collaboration were, we may assume, never quite the same. This
must also hold for the twelve-year-old girl who watched Polish soldiers murder
her father on Christmas Day. It would be too much to say that Dobra was nationalized by the war: neither was it free of national activism before the war, nor
are its surviving former residents all committed Ukrainians or Poles. We can
safely maintain that experiences of war closed early modern possibilities of self-
identification, and activated more modern ones. Since modern nationality car-
ries with it a certain lexicon, one of the closed possibilities is easy description of
a lost reality in our postwar idiom. Today, the terms "Polish" and "Ukrainian"
impose themselves upon survivors' stories even as they hasten to add that these
terms meant something different before the war.[19]

The fate of Dobra Shl'iakhets'ka/Dobra Szlachecka, terrible as it was, seems
lyrical when compared to that of Polish settlements in Volhynia obliterated in
1943. Recall the fate of Głęboczyca, discussed in chapter 8. The UPA decision to
kill everyone in such places left even clearer images in the minds of the survivors. One Głęboczyca boy, having spent the night in the family stable, awoke
at dawn on 29 August 1943 to see his father surrounded in the field by Ukrainians. One of the Ukrainians struck his father (age fifty-six) in the back of the
head with a sickle; his father dropped to his knees, then, convulsing, fell forward and died face down in the soil. The boy watched as his mother (age forty-
three) ran, screaming, towards her dying husband. She was ordered to stop and
did, a Ukrainian took aim and shot her, and then another killed her with a blow

from a sickle as she lay on the ground. A Głęboczyca girl returned home that morning to see her neighbor's head rolling on the ground, a child killed by having its head beaten against a pillar, and other villagers murdered with pitchforks and sickles. She crept towards home in time to see her eleven-year-old sister beaten to death. The rest of her family were already dead.[20] Poles fled Galicia with similar memories. Hucisko, a Polish village south of L'viv, was destroyed by the UPA on 12 April 1944. A local woman returned to find men hanging from trees, their skin hanging from their muscles, their hearts torn from their chests. Other men, women, and children, dead on the ground, were burned and mutilated beyond recognition. She was able to identify her young son's ruined body only by the bread she had packed in his pocket earlier that day.[21]

In this light, it is striking that Polish survivors of the Volhynian and Galician terror sometimes make the sorts of distinctions in their memoirs that are worn away as their names become numbers and their stories become histories.[22] Indelible personal memories, with time, contributed to national forgetfulness.[23] To attend to individual memories is to see the false elements of national memories, but also the collective suffering which makes coherent myths inevitable. Even when victims of ethnic cleansing preserve a sense of ambiguous identity, as is sometimes the case, or have nuanced stories to tell, as is often the case, their accounts are invariably reduced to their most common and most terrifying elements as they circulate within a national society. Retellings and rewritings erode and refine. The transformation of places such as Dobra (which still exists in Poland), and even more the obliteration of Polish settlements such as Głęboczyca and Hucisko (which would now be in Ukraine if they existed), removed barriers to the creation of simplified national histories.

Deportation prepared the way for myth by privileging nation over locality. Individuals were deported on the basis of Nazi or Soviet identification documents with nationality categories issued after 1939, although these documents may not have reflected a modern national identity. Be that as it may, the experience of deportation confirms national identity not only by its ethnicizing implementation, but by its sociogeographical consequences. In 1944–46, Poles and Ukrainians alike were resettled into areas which were alien at the level of locality, but familiar at the level of nationality. A Lemkini who finds herself in L'viv after the Second World War will know little of urban life, but she will know to pray in some of the local churches and how to speak the Ukrainian language (after a fashion). A Volhynian Pole resettled from L'utsk to Gdańsk will have never seen the sea, but he will be a Roman Catholic and speak a Polish comprehensible to most of the people around him. In new surroundings, "national" characteristics such as religion and language come to the fore. Deportation creates lowest-common-denominator nationalism.

COMMUNIST AND NATIONALIST HISTORY

A few years after Operation Vistula had resettled Poland's Ukrainians, Polish archaeologists discovered the sarcophagus of Prince Danylo, ruler of Galicia and Volhynia in the thirteenth century.[24] Because the dig was on the Polish side of the border, near the contested city of Chełm/Kholm, it was not made public. Polish communist authorities needed to prevent the perception of "Ukrainian" settlement in "Poland"—seven centuries in the past. This Polish concern fit Soviet practice. After all, in schoolbook history, the Soviet Union was "descended" from medieval Kyivan Rus', whereas communist Poland was "descended" from the medieval Poland of the Piast dynasty. Poles and Russians were taught that their "ethnic groups" had stood in place for nine hundred years, awaiting the proper political and territorial realization of their "nationhood."

The "descent" of modern communism from medieval duchies and kingdoms allowed communists to sidestep the half-millenium of Polish cultural expansion to the east (from the beginning of the fourteenth century to the end of the nineteenth) and the political success of the Polish-Lithuanian Commonwealth (1569–1795). The Commonwealth was a troubling example of many things Soviet communism wished to abolish: constitutional traditions, representative institutions, cooperation among Poles and East Slavs, and intellectual flexibility and political toleration in the realm of nationality. Ukrainians who reject the substance of the Soviet reading of Ukrainian history often accepted its form. To believe that Ukraine rather than Russia "inherits" Kyivan Rus' also risks neglecting the heritage of the Commonwealth. Of course, Poles who thought of the Polish-Lithuanian Commonwealth as "Polish" in the modern sense were also wrong. The Commonwealth was Europe's largest early modern realm, governed by early modern Europe's largest citizenry, the noble nation. As early modern nationality was reconstructed in the nineteenth century, it begot a brood of modern nationalisms intent to discover separate origins in a more distant past. This trend in nationalism informed communists and their opponents in the twentieth.[25]

This communist idea that ethnic nations were stable entities with durable boundaries threw shrouds over interesting problems of modern history. For example, the complicated pattern of the assimilation of Polish-speaking peasants to Ukrainian culture (and vice versa) in interwar Galicia and Volhynia is now of only specialist academic interest. For most, these people were always (or at least always destined to be) what they eventually became. Now that Volhynia and eastern Galicia have become western Ukraine, both Ukrainians and Poles have forgotten just how different these regions were once considered to be. Separated by the Russian-Austrian border for more than a century before 1918, kept apart by Polish policy between 1918 and 1939, divided between Soviet and Nazi occupation regimes between 1939 and 1941, and then between the Nazi *Reichskommissariat Ukraine* and the Nazi *Generalgouvernement* between 1941 and 1944, these regions are today the heart of a rather unproblematic "Western Ukraine." Galician Ukrainians today sing "My Volhynia" under L'viv's Habsburg-era gaslights as if it were the most natural thing in the world.[26]

Most important for the emergence of modern from early modern nationality is the new significance of religion. Between the Brest Union of 1596 and the end of the First World War, Greek Catholicism and Orthodoxy were rivals. As a result of Russian and Austrian imperial policy, eastern Galicia was predominately Greek Catholic, and Volhynia predominately Orthodox at the beginning of the twentieth century. The union of Galicia with Volhynia within interwar Poland created the opportunity for Galician Ukrainians to propagate modern nationalism on Volhynian Orthodox territory. They had some success in the 1920s and 1930s, and great success during the Second World War. In the ethnic cleansing of Volhynia in 1943 we must see not only the removal of Poles, but an alliance of Greek Catholics and Orthodox against Roman Catholics. It was part of the creation of a western Ukraine in which differences of religion between Greek Catholicism and Orthodoxy mattered less than identification with the Ukrainian nation. It closed an early modern divide between religions by solidifying the modern divide between nations.

The same can be said of southeastern Poland. In the framework of the early modern Commonwealth, or early modern Polish civilization, Greek Catholicism was a partner of Roman Catholicism. As early modern nationality succumbed to modern, this association perished along with it. The ethnic cleansing of southeastern Poland was not only an action taken against Ukrainians by Poles, but an action taken by Roman Catholics against both Greek Catholics and Orthodox. Postwar Poles accept that the Greek Catholic and Orthodox Churches were both Ukrainian. In the 1990s, for example, the Polish mayor of Przemyśl, once largely Greek Catholic, claimed that Ukrainian culture was

more foreign to him than Eskimo culture. To anyone who knows Przemyśl/
Peremyshl or Poles and Ukrainians, nothing could be more absurd: except perhaps the behavior of some of the townspeople. They physically occupied a local
church that Pope John Paul II wished to return to Ukrainian Greek Catholics.
The beneficiaries of their action, Roman Catholic Carmelite monks, then proceeded to destroy the church's dome on the grounds that its "eastern" shape destroyed Przemyśl's "Polish" skyline. Here again religion is subordinated to
modern nationalism, and common early modern civilization is obscured rather
than revealed. The Habsburg-era dome was in fact modeled not upon an eastern basilica (or an igloo), but upon St. Peter's in Rome.[27]

NATIONAL HISTORY AS COMMUNIST
LEGITIMATION

We can see the progress of modern nationality on the example of individuals as
well as towns, regions, and religions. Wojciech Jaruzelski, for example, was of a
family loyal to Piłsudski's early modern, federalist conception of nationality. In
1947, young Captain Jaruzelski was ordered to resettle Ukrainians in Operation
Vistula. Captain Jaruzelski believed that Operation Vistula was about the Pol-
ish army protecting the Polish state. Jaruzelski was taught to see the UPA as
Nazis. Throughout the postwar period, the Polish regime justified its general
Ukrainian policy by this association. There was something to it, of course. The
UPA in Volhynia ordered former German policemen, collaborators in the Final
Solution, to murder Poles. The UPA in Poland incorporated Waffen-SS deserters as well as German policemen, and learned from the German occupation.
The UPA was part of an organization, the OUN-Bandera, which was ideologi-
cally committed to ethnic purity. Poles are right to remember all this: but they
forget that the UPA was successful in many of its endeavors because its causes
were specifically Ukrainian ones, and its organization equal if not superior to
that of any Polish institution operating on Polish territory. The Polish regime's
association of Ukraine with Germany allowed Poland to refight the Second
World War on better terms in 1947. It also shrouded the extent to which the
Polish regime's own rhetoric and policy were redolent of the German occupation. General Mossor, commander of Operation Vistula, spoke of a "final solution" to the Ukrainian problem. Operation Vistula exploited German identity
documents and a German concentration camp.[28]

Operation Vistula meant that the communist regime could and did speak of a Polish "national state." Although this could not quite be said, the creation of a Poland for the Poles was a great legitimating achievement of Polish communists.[29] Of the four major changes which made it possible to speak of Poland as a "national state," the Holocaust went largely unmentioned, the expulsion of Germans was treated as reason to be loyal to the Soviet Union, the "repatriations" were a Soviet operation, and only the final cleansing of Ukrainians remained as a local Polish achievement.[30] Even during the reforms of the Gomułka period (1956–70), the Polish regime directed attention to the two wartime enemies, the Germans and the Ukrainians, and to its success in keeping them at bay. In 1968, official anti-Semitism was deployed by those who challenged Gomułka, and by those who defended his position. In November and December 1968, the leading political weekly commemorated the fiftieth anniversary of Poland's independence by asking the country's leading intellectuals to comment on changes in the "typical Pole." None of the respondents questioned the essential identification of the "typical Pole" with the ethnic Pole. Only one suggested that in the creation of an ethnically homogenous polity something had been lost.[31]

After a generation of communism, by let us say 1970, only a modern conception of nationality functioned in Polish society. A Pole was at once a citizen of Poland, an ethnic Pole, and (in all likelihood) a Roman Catholic. Far better than interwar Poland, communist Poland spread the national idea by extending education and promoting social mobility. After a generation, and in conditions of political rapprochement, the sense of the German threat began to decline in about 1970. At the same time, the fear of Ukrainians in Poland remained steady. Indeed, the peak of official anti-Ukrainian ideology was during the Gierek era, the 1970s, as Poland was officially declared ethnically homogeneous.[32]

In 1980 and 1981, Gierek and then his successors were forced to contend with Solidarity, an independent labor union and then a mass social movement with as many as ten million members. While Solidarity was unquestionably a patriotic movement, its leaders evinced a very different attitude to Ukraine. During the months of relatively free speech, intellectuals spoke of the impossibility of Polish independence without Ukrainian independence. The Solidarity labor union sent its greetings to the nations of the Soviet Union, a gesture appreciated in Ukraine. As Polish communists sought to discredit Solidarity, they emphasized its support for equal rights for Ukrainians in Poland. Finally, in December 1981, Solidarity was crushed by martial law. General Wojciech Jaruzelski, now general secretary of the Polish party, head of the Polish state, and commander of the Polish army, ordered the operation. Thirty-four years after his participation in Operation Vistula, he was again convinced that Poland had to be saved by self-invasion.[33] Was this an ending or a beginning? Most modern Polish nationality include hostility to Ukraine? Or could one imagine, with Solidarity, a free Poland in accord with its eastern neighbors?

Part III The Reconstructed Polish Homeland

Chapter 11 Patriotic
Oppositions and State Interests
(1945–1989)

After the negotiated revolution of 1989, Solidarity formed a noncommunist government, which moved quickly to establish an eastern policy. After the disintegration of the Soviet Union in 1991, Poland's relations with independent Lithuania and Ukraine quickly improved. Lithuanian politicians came to see their western neighbor as the key to European integration, while Ukrainian presidents traveled to Warsaw to seek historical reconciliation. Disputes with Lithuanians about Vilnius, or with Ukrainians about Galicia and Volhynia, were so well managed as to be nearly invisible. As we have seen, the Second World War and its aftermath broke some of Poland's links with the east, and spread modern nationalism. Perhaps war in the 1940s had created the preconditions for peace in the 1990s? Perhaps ethnic cleansing set the stage for national reconciliation?

Such suppositions only make sense in retrospect, from the vantage point of a northeastern Europe without postcommunist conflict. The image of a peaceful region arose not from the order Polish policy inherited, but from the order it created.[1] The innovation of Polish policy was to understand nationalism, and channel it toward regional stability. Between 1989 and 1991, when the Soviet Union was still intact, Polish policy acted as if Lithuania, Belarus, and Ukraine were becoming nation-states. Polish diplomats added a proviso: that independence would mean accepting Soviet-era borders. This was at once a prediction of a future without the Soviet Union, and an effort to prepare the stable regional order that would then emerge. It reflected a new Polish grand strategy, prepared in emigration, and debated for fifteen years before 1989. Its authors were Jerzy Giedroyc and Juliusz Mieroszewski, who framed it within their understanding of Polish nationality. Since it arose from consideration of the conflicts discussed in parts 1 and 2, and since it brought the peace that is the subject of part 3, their variant on modern nationality deserves sustained attention.

THE EASTERN INTERESTS OF A POLISH STATE

Jerzy Giedroyc (1906–2000) was involved, by birth or by choice, in all of the eastern questions of interwar Poland. He was born in Minsk, then still the capital of a Russian imperial province, to an old Polish Lithuanian gentry family. Giedroyc's studies in Moscow were interrupted by the Bolshevik Revolution, and he returned home. As imperial Russia's Northwestern Territory, the lands of the old Grand Duchy of Lithuania, was contested by Polish and Bolshevik armies in 1919, Giedroyc and his family left Minsk for Warsaw. As we have seen, the federalist Piłsudski's armies won the war, but the nationalist Grabski determined the peace. Polish negotiators gave Giedroyc's native Minsk to Bolshevik Russia. Like many a Lithuanian Pole before him, Giedroyc found Warsaw poor and gray. Giedroyc studied Ukrainian history and literature at university, and made the acquaintance of leading Ukrainian activists.[2] His contacts spanned the spectrum of Ukrainian political life, from Dmytro Dontsov, the ideologist of integral Ukrainian nationalism, to Vasyl' Mudryi, the head of the left-leaning and democratic UNDO. Giedroyc was fascinated by Metropolitan Andrei Sheptyts'kyi, head of the Greek Catholic Church. As a journalist and civil servant, Giedroyc urged the Roman Catholic Church to improve relations with Sheptyts'kyi's Greek Catholic Church. On state business, and at his own initiative, he visited the Hutsuls, a poor Ukrainian-speaking people in southeastern Poland.

Giedroyc was repelled by the integral nationalism of the National Democrats, and attracted by Piłsudski and his nostalgic vision of a Poland of many nationalities. A generation younger than Piłsudski, Giedroyc too was a Lithuanian Pole who took an interest in Ukraine. Like Piłsudski, Giedroyc was a

Fig. 26. Jerzy Giedroyc (1906–2000),
Polish intellectual and grand
strategist. Giedroyc redirected Polish
political thought. Photograph taken
in Paris in the late 1940s.

pragmatist whose highest value was Polish statehood, and who did not conflate the nationalism of Polish society with the interests of the Polish state. For
Giedroyc, the historical attachments of Poles and other nationalities were important only in their relation to the Polish state. Because Giedroyc believed that
national minorities could destroy Poland, he concluded pragmatically that the
Polish state had to satisfy their aspirations so far as possible. In particular, this
would have involved keeping faith with earlier commitments by extending political autonomy to Ukrainians in Galicia. In general, it would have required
engagement with all minority populations, in order to determine how the Polish state could serve them, and how local nationalists could be deprived of
arguments to use against Polish statehood. Interwar Poland lacked a general
policy for its eastern minorities; yet there were Poles, such as Giedroyc and Volhynian governor Henryk Józewski, who devoted themselves to the problem.

   As we have seen, the Second World War sharpened national conflicts on the
territory of interwar Poland, allowing massive and bloody Ukrainian-Polish
cleansings. The war's aftermath brought massive deportations and took from
Poland two of its most important cities, Lwów and Wilno. During the war
Giedroyc maintained his interest in eastern questions, and kept up friendly
contacts with representatives of other nationalities, including Ukrainian na-

tionalists. Having served under General Władysław Anders in the Polish Army, he made his way to Paris, and founded a Literary Institute and the review *Kultura*. Between 1947 and 1989, *Kultura* was the most influential Polish émigré publication. It is quite possible that Giedroyc, over the course of these four decades, was the single most influential Polish intellectual. He enjoyed influence at home because he treated emigration in an unusual way. From France, Giedroyc intended to influence politics within communist Poland, rather than create a substitute Poland abroad. In this he differed from the main body of Polish émigrés, who sought to preserve the political institutions of interwar Poland in London exile. Having chosen nostalgia, many London Poles saw no reason to criticize the old order, or to resign from territories lost to the Soviet Union.[3] Giedroyc believed that a newly independent Poland would be something other than a revival of interwar Poland, and that preparations should begin immediately. Giedroyc understood that the Second World War had reposed without resolving Poland's eastern questions, and worked to create the platform upon which new solutions could be sought by a future sovereign Poland. Although Giedroyc rarely wrote, his editorial decisions marked out a *Kultura* line on eastern policy.[4]

Kultura treated Poland's postwar eastern border as the eastern frontier of a future sovereign Poland. This may seem like common sense, but it was very controversial among Poles, and unusual among East European émigrés in general. This border was first drawn by the Molotov-Ribbentrop pact in 1939 and confirmed by the Yalta accords of 1945, events that Poles regarded as the great diplomatic betrayals of the twentieth century. Giedroyc's innovation was to see these territories not as Polish lands lost to the Soviet Union, but as contested territories that could now serve nations comparable to the Polish nation. Although Lwów and Wilno had become L'viv/Lvov and Vilnius/Vil'nius as a result of the triumph of the Red Army and the choices of Stalin, *Kultura* treated them as part of Soviet Ukraine and Soviet Lithuania, and in the final analysis as Ukrainian and Lithuanian.[5]

REALISM AND ROMANTICISM

In 1973 and 1974 Giedroyc's closest collaborator, Juliusz Mieroszewski (1906–86), provided the theoretical justification for the eastern grand strategy of a future sovereign Poland. The supreme concern remained the interests of a future Polish state, and a guiding assumption remained that certain wartime changes should not be reversed. Giedroyc had long contended that Poland had no interest in challenging the territorial status quo; Mieroszewski sought to show that Poles had a positive interest in maintaining it. He proposed the strengthening of the Lithuanian, Belarusian, and Ukrainian nations within the respective Soviet Socialist Republics, including on territories taken from Poland in 1945. He contended that a future sovereign Poland should support the independence of Lithuanian, Belarusian, and Ukrainian nation-states. The recommendation for Polish foreign policy presumed a prediction: that such a sovereign state would soon arise, and have to deal with independent eastern neighbors. Mieroszewski was one of the few students of politics who made the correct prediction, writing of the springtime of nations to come in the twentieth century in both Eastern Europe and the Soviet Union.[6]

In the early 1970s, this seemed rather romantic. The Soviet Union was a nuclear superpower which appeared to be winning the Cold War. Poland was a Soviet satellite, its most recent upheavals of 1968 and 1970 easily quelled by its communist regime. Lithuania, Belarus, and Ukraine were constituent republics of the Soviet Union, whose dissidents were a harried few. Hugely formidable Soviet conventional military forces were concentrated in precisely the region in question. Yet, as the eventual fate of the Soviet Union makes clear enough, *the real* in international relations includes not only the state of affairs at a moment in time, but the direction of its change as time proceeds, the apprehension that multiple directions of change are possible, and the realization that individuals use states to force events onto one course rather than another on the basis of ideals. *Realism* as a mode of analysis must be pragmatic, but it must also (if it is to avoid paradox) include an awareness of the goals which call for pragmatism, the end toward which pragmatic measures are the means. These ends are not themselves realistic, they cannot be derived from the world as it is, but must arise from individuals' sense of how the world ought to be. Interests are incoherent without ideals.

It follows that what appears idealistic may be realistic. Mieroszewski was right about the fate of the Soviet Union, and about the need for an anticipatory Polish eastern policy. His own consideration of future Polish interests, precisely because it was clear about ends and means, escaped the confines of the old Polish dilemma of realism and idealism. He treated Lithuania, Belarus, and Ukraine not by reference to their traditional connection with the Polish nation, but in the context of the security of a future Polish state. Imagining the geopolitical position of such a Polish state, Mieroszewski anticipated threats from (1) an independent Russia and (2) imperialist Polish nationalism. Mieroszewski feared that conflict with Russia over Ukraine, Belarus, and Lithuania would entrench harmful versions of both Russian and Polish nationalism. Mieroszewski's program was not an expression of sympathy toward the Lithuanian, Belarusian, and Ukrainian peoples, but a plan to prevent conflict over territory and deflect Russian and Polish nationalism. Mieroszewski noticed that the creation of Lithuanian, Belarusian, and Ukrainian Soviet Socialist Republics within the Soviet Union had created an intellectual opening for such a strategy. Because Lithuania, Belarus, and Ukraine could be seen as political units, he thought it possible to convince Poles that these Soviet republics were but a step away from national statehood. The analogy between a satellite Poland and Soviet republics was strained, but it was made possible by the structure of the Soviet Union. Because the borders of the Lithuanian, Belarusian, and Ukrainian SSRs with each other, the Russian SFSR, and Poland were already visible on maps, it was possible to advocate the preservation of existing borders in a future order of nation-states.[7]

From his recognition of the centrality of Russia and his understanding of the organization of the Soviet Union followed the conclusion that the countries Mieroszewski called "ULB" were key to the security of a future sovereign Poland. If independent Ukrainian, Belarusian, and Lithuanian states could sustain themselves, they would moot the old Polish-Russian competition. It was thus in the Polish interest to make the survival of such states more likely. Hence Mieroszewski also argued that territorial adjustments by Poland in the east could not be in the Polish interest; and that advocacy thereof would alienate another generation of Ukrainian, Lithuanian, and Belarusian national elites. Beginning immediately, he argued in the early 1970s, Poles should not only renounce revanchism in the east, but support the aspirations of the Lithuanian, Belarusian, and Ukrainian nations to independent statehood. Although this conclusion flowed from realistic considerations, Mieroszewski understood that it could provide Polish foreign policy with a moral dimension. As a realist, he could see that this moral dimension might inspire Poles to act.

POLISH TRADITIONS AND THE *KULTURA* PROGRAM

Federalism. Giedroyc was born in Minsk, Mieroszewski spent his youth in Galicia, and it is easy to see the *Kultura* eastern program as continuing the elite early modern patriotism of Piłsudski and, more distantly, of Mickiewicz. Giedroyc was indeed an admirer of Piłsudski from childhood, and Mieroszewski believed that Mickiewicz understood freedom better than Poles of his day. Yet the unit of analysis in Giedroyc and Mieroszewski's theory of international relations was the nation-state, a modern form alien to early modern traditions. Mickiewicz was nostalgic for a Polish-Lithuanian Commonwealth in which nationality meant something entirely different than it does now, and Piłsudski wished to create a federation united by Polish high culture. Giedroyc and Mieroszewski were preparing Poles for the fully modern world of nation-states. Mieroszewski assumed that a sovereign Poland would be a nation-state, and that Ukraine, Lithuania, and Belarus could become nation-states as well. He disdained nostalgia for the old Commonwealth, not because he found it unsympathetic personally, but on the pragmatic grounds that it could only be seen as imperialism by Ukrainian, Lithuanian, and Belarusian patriots. As he realized, once one is committed to seeing Lithuania, Belarus, and Ukraine as equal nations rather than as colorful addenda to a Polish state tradition, the legacy of the Commonwealth becomes treacherous ground.

As we have seen, Lithuanian nationalism was based upon the particular view of the Commonwealth as poisonous to Lithuanian culture, while Ukrainian nationalism idealized rebellions against the Commonwealth. Poles themselves tended to see the early modern Commonwealth in modern nationalist terms, and therefore tended to regard its eastern territories as part of their own history.[8] All of these readings are so deeply false that no amount of scholarly compromise can reconcile them. They can all, however, be placed within a set of parallel national readings of history, if one accepts the political principle of multi-nationalism. This is what Mieroszewski proposed. In Mieroszewski's vision, the evident sympathy for Lithuanian, Ukrainian, and Belarusian *peoples* implicit in Mickiewicz's poetry and Piłsudski's federalism became normative respect for Lithuanian, Ukrainian, and Belarusian *nations*. While Polish federalists had assumed the superiority of Polish culture in the east, Mieroszewski welcomed distinct Lithuanian, Belarusian, and Ukrainian national elites. The understanding of Poland as an old nation and Lithuania, Belarus, and Ukraine as young nations, whatever its merits as history, was rejected in politics. It was replaced by propositions, asserted in the present tense, that all four peoples were nations deserving of states. The *Kultura* program can be seen as updated federalism: if one accepts the crucial qualifications that cooperation with eastern neighbors is a question of relations among friendly states, and that the recognition of these states requires that Poland abandon the territorial ambitions and civilizational claims of the old federal vision. Federalism assumed early modern nationality. The *Kultura* program was an accomodation with modernity.

Nationalism. There was nothing new about seeing Poland as one modern mass nation among others: this was the premise of the National Democrats. Likewise, there was no innovation in the proposal to resign from eastern territory. This was the course taken by the National Democrat Stanisław Grabski when he resigned from Minsk, Kamieniec Podolski, and Berdyczów in his negotiations with the Bolsheviks at Riga in 1921, and urged Poles to evacuate Lwów after his 1944 discussions with Stalin. National Democrats assumed that eastern territory could be given to Russia in exchange for the good graces of Russian elites. The National Democrats brought the category of modern nations into Polish political life, but counted Russians and Poles as the only nations between Warsaw and Moscow. Ukrainians, Lithuanians, and Belarusians were treated as demographic raw material or ignored entirely. On the National Democratic view, Polish elites should come to terms with their Russian counterparts, over the heads of the peoples in between. Although invariably framed as realism, this view depended upon national prejudice as well as national strategy. By assuming that Ukrainians, Belarusians, and Lithuanians could never create viable states, National Democrats constrained the framework of their realism. "Modern Poles" revealed the traditional limits of their vision of politics by associating modernity with Polishness.

The Polish communist regime assimilated this aspect of Polish nationalism, contending after 1945 that the present arrangement with the Soviet Union was in the interests of the Polish nation. Mieroszewski's grand strategy of the 1970s also accepted that present borders should be treated as permanent, and that Poland's eastern mission was obsolete. But by comparison with the interwar National Democrats and their postwar communist continuators, Mieroszewski's innovations were three. Most obviously, he presumed that Poland would regain sovereignty and the Soviet Union would collapse. Second, he proposed resigning from territory in favor of Ukrainians, Lithuanians, and Belarusians rather than in favor of Russians (in the National Democratic tradition) or Soviets (in the communist tradition). Third, he argued that the attitudes of elites in Moscow were not fixed, but could be influenced by Polish policy. The best way to influence these attitudes was not to grant the Russians what they desired. Leaders of an independent Poland would best ensure Poland's security by themselves resigning from territorial claims regardless of whether Russia did the same, and by supporting nation-states between Poland and Russia. This was presented as respect for the Russian nation.

Kultura synthesized the federalist tradition of Piłsudski and the nationalist tradition of Dmowski, presenting a realistic program for a future in which the nations of communist Eastern Europe would enter the contemporary international system as states. From Piłsudski it drew the romantic categories of Lithuania, Belarus, and Ukraine, although it put them to pragmatic uses. From Dmowski it drew the principle of realism, while rejecting as unrealistic his predisposition to compromise with Moscow at the expense of Lithuanians, Belarusians, and Ukrainians. From the postwar order created by Stalin and the Allies at Yalta and Potsdam it drew the durability and desirability of state borders drawn on national criteria. It was Giedroyc's and Mieroszewski's great intellectual achievement to unite this acceptance of state borders with the prediction that communist would collapse, and to imagine that such a situation would require a new Polish grand strategy. It was their great theoretical achievement to articulate the justification for such a strategy and to sketch its outline. It was their great political achievement to communicate their program in such a way that it was taken for granted before the revolution of 1989 by the Poles who would matter thereafter.

Fig. 27. The final number of *Kultura*, October 2000. As Jerzy Giedroyc promised, the monthly ceased publication upon his death.

POLISH POLITICS AND THE *KULTURA* PROGRAM

The Polish postwar emigration considered the *Kultura* program heretical. The huge majority of Polish émigrés in Western Europe believed that Lwów and Wilno must be returned to Poland. Until the very end of its existence in 1989, the Polish government in exile in London took the official position that Poland should renegotiate its eastern borders. This was grounded in the idealist conviction that since Poles had been wronged by the Molotov-Ribbentrop pact, decimated by the Second World War, sold out by the Allies at Yalta, and oppressed by communism for decades, Poland deserved justice in a future European settlement. The *Kultura* program had intellectual rivals as well, thinkers who called themselves realists and treated Russia as the only power in the east. While not (necessarily) interested in regaining territory for sentimental reasons, these realists argued that independent Poland would best protect its interests by striking a deal with Russia over the heads of Ukraine, Belarus, and Lithuania. Such views were represented by Stefan Kisielewski (1911–91), one of the most admired essayists of postwar Poland. Unlike the idealist revanchism of London, such realist accomodationism accounted for certain basic changes in the postwar order, and sought to communicate with Poles in Poland who were growing accustomed to them. Like realist accomodationism, the *Kultura* program spoke the language of interests, and thus could be rationally debated when platforms for debate arose.[9]

As indeed they did, even in communist Poland. A crucial peculiarity of the Polish communist experience was the extensive influence of organized political opposition upon society, especially in the 1970s and 1980s. Uniquely in Eastern Europe, the Polish opposition provided fora for discussion of matters beyond reform communism, economic downturn, and historical injustice. Polish opposition was extensive across four dimensions: in time, such that discussions and debates could actually progress; in breadth, such that it touched thousands or (during the Solidarity period) millions of individuals; in length, in that it involved a number of competing organizations; and in depth, in that numerous individuals lived lives of opposition, in which there was room to consider all aspects of life in a future sovereign Poland.[10] Figures such as Bogdan Borusewicz (1949–), Jacek Kuroń (1934–) and Adam Michnik (1947–), who were concerned with eastern policy in the 1970s, became famous within Solidarity in 1980–81, and then prominent in democratic Poland after 1989. They were not dissidents, as were their famous counterparts in the Soviet Union, but rather oppositionists, representatives of larger trends.

Mieroszewski's influence on the Polish opposition was clear in the 1970s. In 1976, the Polish Independence Compact (Polskie Porozumienie Niepodległościowe) published a program whose eastern policy followed *Kultura*. From 1977 the organ of the Committee for the Defense of Workers (Komitet Obrony Robotników, KOR) paid a great deal of attention to the eastern neighbors, and one of its information bulletins featured an open letter on reconciliation with Ukraine. By 1980 a consensus in favor of the *Kultura* program was apparent among the Polish opposition intelligentsia who would play important roles in Solidarity.[11] The *Kultura* program arose in Paris, but it could be reconciled with important trends in Polish politics, religion, and scholarship. The *Kultura* program began from the assumption, propagated by the Polish regime itself, that Poland's borders were where they belonged. Certain Roman Catholic bishops and priests with close ties to the secular intelligentsia, such as Bishop Karoł Wojtyła (from 1978 Pope John Paul II) were spreading the ideas of Polish coresponsibility for past eastern conflicts, and the need for reconciliation with eastern neighbors. In 1972, Father Jan Zieja addressed the words "we forgive and we ask for forgiveness" to Lithuanians, Belarusians, and Ukrainians.[12] Meanwhile, censored (legal) Polish historiography broke some of the limitations imposed by communism on the study of Ukraine, and uncensored (illegal) works of history questioned not only the justice of communist policies but the entire tradition of Polish eastern expansion.[13]

In 1980 and 1981, Solidarity as a mass movement of ten million members (a third of whom also were members of the communist party) provided the platform for the elite consensus in favor of the *Kultura* program to be shared within Polish society as part of a program of national liberation. The idea that the Polish opposition, and therefore Polish society, had much in common with the opposition movements of eastern neighbors became widespread. This was the first moment in modern Polish history when considerable numbers of Poles thought of their immediate eastern neighbors as equals, as nations in the same sense as Poland. These new habits of mind found expression in key articles in the Solidarity press, in statements of Solidarity leaders such as Kuroń, and finally in a resolution of the Solidarity congress of 1981. The Solidarity labor union's "Message to the Working Peoples of Eastern Europe" was addressed not to the Soviet proletariat but to the nations of the Soviet Union. At the time this was astonishingly, outrageously, foolishly, bold. Of course, the consequences of the general freedom of discussion allowed by the Solidarity period varied from eastern neighbor to eastern neighbor. Very little was said about Belarus. Poles found sympathizing with Lithuanians more palatable than sympathizing with

Ukrainians, although Ukrainian oppositionists were more attracted to the Solidarity model than the Lithuanians.[14] For many important Ukrainian thinkers and activists, *Kultura* had introduced a new model of Poland in the 1970s, one which they were prepared to see in Solidarity in 1980.[15]

After General Wojciech Jaruzelski crushed Solidarity by imposing martial law in December 1981, more opposition publications took up the question of relations with Lithuania, Belarus, and Ukraine. In some circles, the defeat of Solidarity was taken as evidence that Poles needed to make allies of eastern (and southern) neighbors. The most thoroughgoing of patriots, the Confederation for an Independent Poland (Konfederacja Polski Niepodległej, KPN), treated the eastern neighbors as enjoying a status equal to that of Poland. In 1987 the young radicals of Freedom and Peace (Wolność i Pokój) signed a declaration deploring Operation Vistula and asking Polish society to tolerate Ukrainians. Other underground organizations initiated dialogues with Lithuanian and Ukrainian opposition and émigré groups, on the basis of mutual recognition of existing borders. Throughout the 1980s, the arguments of Mieroszewski were considered at greater length and in greater depth. By 1989, the desirability of good relations with the eastern neighbors was the reflective view of much of the opposition, and had attained the status of political correctness among those who gave the matter less thought. Thanks to the *Kultura* program, historical revisionism, underground publications, and Solidarity, the consensus in Poland not only opposed revanchism, but supported the independence of eastern neighbors. A new political idea articulated in the 1970s had become a new political tradition by the 1980s.[16]

NATIONALISTS, SOCIALISTS, AND THE *KULTURA* PROGRAM

Giedroyc and Mieroszewski were men of the Left who believed that communism could be improved from within before Poland regained its full sovereignty. Their eastern program was attractive to post-Marxist intellectuals such as Adam Michnik, whom Giedroyc held in high regard. Michnik was a leading figure within Solidarity, and after 1989 edited Poland's most important newspaper. Yet the hegemony of the *Kultura* idea embraced not only post-Marxists such as Michnik, but also Polish oppositionists who considered themselves first and foremost patriots or nationalists. Much of the Polish Right passed through *Kultura* in the 1970s and Solidarity in the 1980s, and took for granted Poland's interest in the independence of its eastern neighbors. Grzegorz Kostrzewa-Zorbas (1958–), for example, was on the right of the Polish opposition, but did much to spread ideas associated with *Kultura*. From 1985 to 1989 he edited an illegal publication, the *New Coalition*, dedicated to the idea that the future of Eastern Europe would be a collection of freely cooperating nation-states. Kostrzewa-Zorbas worked for Solidarity's Minority Affairs Committee, and in 1989 wrote the memoranda that sketched the first stage of Poland's eastern policy. In the early 1990s Kostrzewa-Zorbas and Michnik, who agreed on very little else, were crucial in the implementation and popularization of a foreign policy friendly to Lithuania, Belarus, and Ukraine.

The most radical secular Polish patriots of the 1970s and 1980s were to be found within the Confederation for an Independent Poland. They placed the question of Polish independence squarely on the agenda of the Polish opposition in the 1970s, at a time when most oppositionists considered such directness unhelpful. Their leader Leszek Moczulski (1930–) considered the patriotism of Poland's eastern neighbors to be as praiseworthy as his own, and imagined that independent Lithuania, Belarus, and Ukraine would some day join independent Poland in a Baltic-to-Black Sea federation. This prediction was notable for the respect it paid to Poland's immediate eastern neighbors. Although Moczulski styled himself a federalist in the tradition of Piłsudski, Moczulski unlike Piłsudski spoke of Lithuania, Ukraine, and Belarus as nations in the same sense that Poland was a nation. Rather than using the early modern Commonwealth as a basis for Polish imperialism, Moczulski imagined it as the basis for an alliance of modern nation-states. Rather than believing that Polish culture could unify regional elites, as had Piłsudski, Moczulski was sensitive to the fears of the national elites of Poland's eastern neighbors. Although Moczulski's rhetoric as a parliamentarian after 1989 was notoriously unpredictable, his support for friendly policy to Ukraine, Belarus, and Lithuania was unequivocal.[17]

Much of the Roman Catholic press in the 1980s also contributed to the cause of a practical reconciliation with Poland's eastern neighbors, especially Ukraine.[18] As we shall see, some Roman Catholic activists would return to the issue of the ethnic cleansing of Poles by Ukrainians after 1989, and seek to link Polish minority policy to the minority policy of neighbors ("reciprocation"). They were a minority, even within the Polish Right; and their claims were not supported by the Roman Catholic hierarchy. In a general way, the Polish pope, John Paul II, was very solicitous of Poland's eastern neighbors. While Poles' attention to their pope is unreliable, this still set limits on acceptable Roman Catholic attitudes within Poland. There was no longer a political force on the Polish right that was programmatically hostile to Poland's eastern neighbors. By comparison to interwar Poland, when Roman Catholicism was strongly associated with National Democracy, this was an enormous change.

In Eastern Europe after the revolutions of 1989, destabilizing nationalism has usually been the work not of secular patriots or Christian nationalists, but of former communists seeking to preserve their position.[19] Most if not all violent conflict within Eastern Europe in the 1990s was initiated by political leaders who once exercised important responsibilities in a communist apparatus. This holds true not only of the wars in Croatia, Bosnia, Kosovo, Georgia, Moldova, and Chechnya, but also of the manipulation of national questions for electoral gain across the region.[20] Here as well, Poland was unusual. Polish communists had already consumed the last major national question in Poland by ethnically cleansing Ukrainians in 1947. This left any pretenders to postcommunist nationalism in Poland without a compact national minority to present as threat or use as scapegoat. In addition, the scale of Polish opposition in the 1970s and 1980s had created a special sort of communist party. The party allowed democratic elections within some of its affiliated organizations, and cultivated a young elite which was expected to replace Jaruzelski and his generation when the time was right for reform. In the meantime, many of these young communists were reading the same illegal publications as the opposition, *Kultura* in particular. Articles on Ukraine gave food for thought to the ambitious young communist Aleksander Kwaśniewski (1954–).[21]

After the elections of June 1989 brought to power a Solidarity-led government in August, the Polish communist party took up the challenge by reforming itself. Kwaśniewski, the former head of a communist youth organization, took over the party at its moment of transformation. In January 1990, the party changed not only its leadership, but its name and its program.[22] Led by Kwaśniewski, the socialists returned to power after the parliamentary elections of 1993. Kwaśniewski was elected president of Poland in 1995 and reelected in 2000. Poland's postcommunists did not rely upon nationalism in their electoral campaigns or programs. In this they differed not only from postcommunist parties throughout Eastern Europe (in Yugoslavia and Russia most notably) but also from the Polish communist party before 1989. Whereas Polish communism had been traditionally anti-Ukrainian, Polish postcommunism (as personified by Kwaśniewski) was pragmatically pro-Ukrainian. Indeed, after 1995 President Kwaśniewski directed a historical reconciliation with Ukraine.

The place of *Kultura* in this turn of events was obvious to all participants. Kwaśniewski corresponded with Giedroyc, and traveled to Paris to honor him.

That said, *Kultura*'s key connection was with Solidarity. Just as the transformation of the Polish communist party resulted from its competition with Solidarity in the 1980s, so Polish socialists continued the foreign policy of Solidarity governments in the 1990s. The socialists, when they came to power, also enjoyed the luxury of good relations with a peacefully unified Germany. In 1989, Solidarity governments confronted the less heartening spectacle of a unifying Germany that advanced an eastern policy far less reassuring than their own.

Chapter 12 The Normative
Nation-State (1989–1991)

The Second World War killed one in five citizens of Poland. Under the Potsdam Agreement, Poland received vast German territories and expelled millions of Germans. In the 1950s, fear of German revanchism generated support for the Polish communist regime and its alliance with the Soviet Union. In the 1960s, the Polish regime condemned as treason social initiatives such as the Polish bishops' message of reconciliation to the German bishops. Although public attitudes toward Germany improved after the West German-Polish treaty of 1970, Poles continued to believe that Germans would reclaim territory if given the opportunity. These fears were maintained by the legal position of West German governments that they could not act in the name of a future unified Germany, and also by the open revanchism of the West German expellee lobby. The expellees were the dominant force within the West German CSU (Christlich-Soziale Union), the sister party of the CDU (Christlich Demokratische Union) of Chancellor Helmut Kohl. For more than a year after Polish sovereignty was regained in August 1989, Polish leaders and the Polish public expressed greater fear of German reunification than of Soviet reaction.[1]

In 1989, political change within Poland moved forward step by step, many of the advances agreed with Polish communists, and some of them condoned by Soviet General Secretary Mikhail Gorbachev (1931–). Speaking in December 1988 at the United Nations, Gorbachev signaled that the Soviet Union's East European satellites could choose their own course in domestic politics. Poland's communists, motivated by the massive strikes of August 1988, had already discussed the possibility of roundtable talks with Solidarity leader Lech Wałęsa (1943–). In February 1989, they took Gorbachev at his word and agreed to begin negotiations with representatives of the then illegal trade union Solidarity. An agreement reached in April 1989 legalized Solidarity, and called parliamentary elections for June. These elections were rigged so that the communist party and its traditional allies were guaranteed a majority in the lower house of parliament, the Sejm. But Solidarity's overwhelming victory in the popular vote won it every seat it could contest in the Sejm (as well as ninety-nine of a hundred seats in the upper house, the Senate) and created a general sense that the communists lacked a mandate to govern. The decisive Solidarity victory was a surprise to both sides.

In August 1989, after the communists had failed to form a government, the Sejm approved a coalition headed by longtime Roman Catholic oppositionist Tadeusz Mazowiecki (1927–). This was the first noncommunist government in Eastern Europe since the installation of communist rule, and set a precedent that East Germans, Hungarians, Czechoslovaks, and Bulgarians would soon follow. Each step carried more or less unintended consequences: Gorbachev's UN address to the Polish roundtable, the roundtable to the rigged elections, the rigged elections to the Solidarity victory, the Solidarity victory to the formation of a noncommunist government, the end of communism in Poland to the end of communism in Eastern Europe generally. In 1989, it was not generally anticipated that revolution in East European satellites would raise the stakes of national movements in Soviet Lithuania and Soviet Ukraine, and thereby hasten the end of the Soviet Union itself. In fact, the end of communism in Eastern Europe made independence for Soviet republics seem like an attainable goal. 1989–91 was a strange twilight period, hard for us to fix in retrospect. For our purposes, it is important to keep in mind that sovereignty in Eastern Europe preceded the end of the Soviet Union by more than two years, and that newly sovereign Poland and the Soviet Union were subjects of each other's policy for a considerable length of time. In 1989, Gorbachev could have made his objections to Polish sovereignty known. Yet when the Berlin Wall fell in November 1989, Gorbachev told Mazowiecki: "it may sound strange, but I wish you success."[2]

GERMANY INTO EUROPE

West German reactions, unlike Gorbachev's pronouncements, were threatening. After the Solidarity victory in the June 1989 elections, West German Finance Minister Theo Waigel questioned the legality of the Polish western frontier. After the formation of Mazowiecki's noncommunist government in August 1989, Chancellor Kohl declared that the German question was back on the international agenda. Kohl traveled to Warsaw in November in 1989 to allay fears, but chose the wrong moment. Although Kohl gave his private assurances that he would affirm the German-Polish border in good time, he dared not repeat such statements in public for electoral reasons. At a dinner in the Radziwiłł Palace, Kohl learned that the Berlin Wall had fallen. Breaking off the day's conversations with Lech Wałęsa, Tadeusz Mazowiecki, and Bronisław Geremek, who were trying to explain why Poles feared German unification, Kohl flew to Berlin, and made rapid unification his policy.

Kohl's "Ten Point Program" for unification failed to mention borders. This raised two specters: that a unified Germany would seek to regain the territories it had lost to Poland after the Second World War; and that the new Europe, like interwar Europe, would be a governed by different diplomatic rules in the East than in the West. As Poles remember, the settlements that followed the First World War guaranteed Germany's western border with France, but not its eastern border with Poland. After the Second World War, there was no peace settlement as such, and West Germany reserved for itself the right to finally determine its eastern borders at the time of such a settlement. After the fall of the Berlin Wall, Poles had to be concerned not only that the present border be confirmed, but that it be confirmed with them. Poles feared that a German-Soviet agreement on borders would accompany a division of Eastern Europe into spheres of influence, and confirm the Soviet Union's domination of Poland.[3]

For the next year, from November 1989 through November 1990, West and East German politics centered around unification, while Polish foreign policy was concerned to contain the German question within Germany. Although Polish officials (unlike French President François Mitterrand or British Prime Minister Margaret Thatcher) did not seek to slow Germany unification, they tried to link it with a final settlement of the border question. They had few cards to play. Although Polish armies had fought with the Allies in the Second World War, Poland was occupied by the Soviet Union after 1944 and played no role in the postwar conferences at Yalta and Potsdam that decided Europe's future. Since the unification of Germany was treated as the final chapter of the unfinished postwar settlement, it was to be arranged by the two Germanys in agreement with the four wartime Allies (Britain, France, the Soviet Union, and the United States.) Despite Poland's protests, it was not included when the "2 + 4" negotiations began in February 1990.

The Polish position was that the Polish-German frontier should be reaffirmed before unification; the German position was that border treaty negotiations would begin after unification. Indeed, in March 1990 Chancellor Kohl suggested that Germany would not confirm the existing frontier unless Poland agreed to protect German minorities and to forgo future claims to war reparations. Since Poland had suffered titanic losses during the war, and since West Germany had excluded Poland from the peace settlement, this was seen as outrageous. This position was also rejected by West Germany's allies. In spring 1990 Prime Minister Mazowiecki made clear that he had no wish to see Soviet forces leave Poland until Poland's border with Germany was codified. Poland even proposed that Soviet troops remain in the eastern part of a future unified Germany. This was for a time the Soviet position, but Gorbachev was quickly persuaded otherwise. In any event, Poland's harmony of interests with the Soviet Union was limited. Even in February 1990 Polish Foreign Minister Krzysztof Skubiszewki had made clear to the Germans that Poland had no wish to see a united Germany become neutral, which was tantamount to accepting the membership of a united Germany in NATO. The Soviet Union opposed the future membership of a united Germany in NATO until Kohl's July 1990 meeting with Gorbachev in the Caucasus.

As it became clear in July 1990 that deutschmarks and U.S. engagement could produce not only German unification but the membership of a unified Germany in NATO, the Polish position was simplified. There was now little sense in courting the Soviets, whom West German Foreign Minister Hans-Dietrich Genscher was using to keep the Poles out of the process, and much sense in making sure that the Americans understood the border issue. The American "Nine Assurances," unlike Kohl's "Ten Points," did include the preservation of existing frontiers. The present East German-Polish frontier, on the American view, was to become the future German-Polish border. Polish Foreign Minister Skubiszewski took part in the third session of the "2 + 4" talks on 17 July 1990. Although Skubiszewski was operating from weakness and U.S. Secretary of State James Baker from strength, their positions were in broad outline the same: that German reunification was inevitable, but that its realization must resolve issues outstanding from the Second World War and bind the new Germany to European and Atlantic institutions. The first article of the

"2 + 4" treaty, signed in September 1990 in Moscow, confirmed the external frontiers of West and East Germany as the frontiers of unified Germany. Germany was unified on 3 October 1990. Skubiszewski and Genscher signed a Polish-German border treaty on 14 November 1990.[4] The battle for a border treaty before unification was lost, but for the war for unconditional recognition of existing frontiers was won.

EAST AND WEST

The very next day, 15 November 1990, Soviet and Polish delegations met for the first time to discuss the withdrawal of Soviet troops from Poland. In late 1990, a weight shifted from one side of the fulcrum to another, and a scale reversed its position. Relations with unified Germany quickly improved, and relations with the Soviet Union quickly deteriorated. Once a legal settlement of Poland's western border was reached, Germany could become "Europe"; as Polish and Soviet interests diverged and Gorbachev's position collapsed, the Soviet Union would become "Russia."[5] Poland feared Bonn less after it became the capital of a larger state, and Moscow more after it became the capital of a smaller state. This shift was obvious to Poles as soon as Poland's eastern neighbor became the major concern of its diplomacy.

The Polish officials who flew to Moscow in January 1991 to negotiate troop withdrawals were greeted by a lengthy oration from General Viktor Dubinin, commander of Soviet forces in Poland. "The unvanquished and proud Soviet Army," he told them, "which once defeated the Germans, will leave Poland at a time it regards as appropriate, with banners unfurled, in a way that it will decide for itself, and if anyone has a problem with this, the army cannot take responsibility for the population of Poland." The Polish approach was as legalistic as the general was bombastic: Polish diplomats pointed out to their surprised Soviet interlocutors that the Warsaw Treaty of 1955, which founded the Warsaw Treaty Organization or "Warsaw Pact," did not actually provide for the stationing of Soviet troops on Polish territory. After this exchange of views, or perhaps worldviews, the weary Polish negotiators were to return to Warsaw by way of Vilnius, where their plane was to refuel. As they neared the Lithuanian capital, they were told that they would continue straight on to Warsaw. They could see the reason from their windows: Vilnius was aflame, under attack from Soviet special forces.[6]

Even as Warsaw began troop negotiations with Moscow, it campaigned to improve relations with the individual republics of the Soviet Union and their anticommunist national movements. Whereas Bonn treated Moscow as the partner of choice in its *Ostpolitik* right to the end, Warsaw engaged its immediate eastern neighbors right from the beginning. This was the first sign that something besides traditional balance of power considerations guided Polish foreign policy in the east, and that Polish diplomacy was implementing the grand strategy described in the previous chapter. While maintaining good relations with Gorbachev, Polish officials took him at his word about the democratization of relations among the component parts of the Soviet Union, while drawing their own conclusions about where this might lead. Even as Poland sought to remove Soviet troops from Polish territory, it undertook a policy predicated on the possibility that the Soviet Union might soon cease to exist, and on the assumption that Poland could preemptively reframe historical disagreements with Russians, Lithuanians, Belarusians, and Ukrainians.

The German question remained in the background. As Poland turned its attention to its own eastern neighbors, the experience of regulating relations with Germany influenced Polish policy towards its eastern neighbors. Poland's position with respect to Lithuania, Belarus, and Ukraine was in certain ways similar to Germany's position with respect to Poland: like Germany, Poland had lost territory to its east after the Second World War, was home to millions of eastern expellees and their descendants, and felt obliged to protect eastern minorities. Of course, during the Second World War Poland was not aggressor but victim: but Lithuanians and Ukrainians of Poland's old eastern marches regarded Poland as an aggressor in Vilnius and L'viv. Since much of the Polish population continued to fear German revanchism in the early 1990s, the analogy with Germany could be presented as an argument in favor of a reassuringly pacific policy to Poland's own eastern neighbors. Poland should ask nothing more of its eastern neighbors, Polish diplomats explained to domestic critics, than Poland was prepared to give Germany. German revanchists helped Skubiszewski to make such arguments by taking an open interest in Poland's eastern policy. So did the German diplomats who used Poland's position towards its minority in Lithuania as a benchmark for German policy toward its minority in Poland. In at least one case, the Germans used a Polish position paper about the Polish minority in Lithuania as justification for greater rights for Germans in Poland.[7]

Krzysztof Skubiszewski (1926–), who negotiated first with Germany and then with the eastern neighbors, is the sort of figure history often passes over in silence. He succeeded in everything he undertook, and his successes brought peace. One would not wish to base such a claim on the peaceful course of German unification. Given the concern of West Europeans and the involvement of the United States, it is almost certain that German unification would have proceeded in a responsible manner regardless of Polish policy. The most that can be said is that Skubiszewski, a professor of international law and an author of a book on Poland's western border, patiently but forthrightly pursued a precise goal, and attained it. All the same, the encounter with West Germany illustrated some of the qualities Skubiszewski brought to relations with Poland's eastern neighbors, and added to the conventional wisdom within Solidarity and Poland's new democratic government. Since Skubiszewski was charged with foreign policy by Presidents Wojciech Jaruzelski and Lech Wałęsa, and supported by all the prime ministers with whom he served, his were the views that mattered. Unlike the situation that prevailed after the First World War, when Poland's early eastern policy was decided by parliamentary deputies negotiating with Bolshevik diplomats at Riga, after 1989 Polish eastern policy was firmly in the hands of professionals.

After the First World War, Polish elites were divided about eastern policy: some wished to create a federation, others to incorporate only those territories that could be assimilated by a national state. Skubiszewski faced no such divisions. The Solidarity opposition, now in power, had assimilated the *Kultura* eastern program: that Poland should not seek to change its eastern borders, that Poland had a positive interest in supporting the independence of Lithuania, Belarus, and Ukraine, and that Polish patriots should treat Lithuanian, Belarusian, and Ukrainian patriots as equals. Although he drew from other traditions, Skubiszewski partook in this consensus about grand strategy, and as a political thinker shared some of Giedroyc's and Mieroszewski's basic assumptions: that the supreme value was the Polish state rather than the Polish nation, and that the relevant frame of reference was not the past but the future.[8] He preferred the term "state interest" to "national interest," and spoke of history in order to clarify the interests of the state rather than the aspirations of the nation. "The national interest is identical with our raison d'état," was one his bywords. Another was: "History is not, and cannot be, the deciding factor in our view of today's reality, nor that which decides the manner of its formation. Europe is changing."[9]

The mention of Europe suggests one of the two major intellectual elements Skubiszewski added to the *Kultura* eastern program. Skubiszewski appreciated the power of the European idea and the attraction of European institutions, which (it must be said) totally escaped Giedroyc and Mieroszewski, despite the fact that one lived in Paris and the other in London for most of their lives. As relations with unified Germany rapidly improved, Skubiszewski's pragmatic argument for an eastern settlement shifted from expressed concern over German revanchism to the instrumental claim that Poland must resolve its eastern problems if it was to join Western institutions. Skubiszewski also grasped the practical importance of international law, both as a means to take usefully ambiguous action in the present, and as a first step towards resolving national problems inherited from the past. This, Skubiszewski's second intellectual contribution, was also absent from the *Kultura* line.

Three other contributions were more practical in nature. One was a style of principled patience, cultivated before 1989, which allowed Skubiszewski as foreign minister to keep his ultimate goals to himself even as he advanced toward them. This is of course an essential quality of a good diplomat, but in communist Eastern Europe the conditions for the development of such a temperament were not especially good.[10] Another practical quality was his capacity for independent hard work. Running a foreign ministry inherited from communists is a logistical challenge, and the relevant quotidian image of Skubiszewski's term is of him writing his own speeches while flying commercial airlines. A third was a wise choice of colleagues. Jerzy Makarczyk, charged with European and regional policy, accomplished much in a short time during a crucial period. Grzegorz Kostzrewa-Zorbas, the Solidarity activist who envisioned a "two-track" approach to Poland's eastern neighbors, was quickly engaged. Skubiszewski's ministry hired three hundred new personnel during his tenure.[11] This may seem like administrative trivia, but in the politics of postcommunist Eastern Europe the availability, recruitment, and placement of trained personnel were often of decisive importance. This is all the more true when the policy in question is as subtle as the Polish eastern policy of "two tracks."

TWO TRACKS

The two tracks of Polish eastern policy were (1) the Soviet central government in Moscow; and (2) the republican governments of the European Soviet republics, especially the Russian Federation, Lithuania, Belarus, and Ukraine. Skubiszewski believed that the Soviet Union would soon collapse; he explained that Polish policy simply reflected changes within the Soviet Union itself. Relations with Soviet authorities in Moscow concerned the support of Gorbachev and the withdrawal of Soviet troops. Polish policy paid more attention to the republics (the Russian Federation included) than to the center. Poland prepared for state-to-state relations by quasi-formally confirming borders, regularizing diplomatic contacts, and establishing the principle of good-neighborly relations in a series of declarations. Poland treated Soviet republics as full subjects of international law and as worthy of equal ethical as well as legal concern. Even before Skubiszewski traveled to the Soviet Union, he asserted that "in many areas our relations with the various republics are like relations with states which are completely independent and sovereign." His policy was the only one in the world to systematically engage Soviet republics.[12]

Lithuania was a special case. Lithuania was not regarded as having been de jure incorporated by the Soviet Union; it formally declared independence well before the end of the Soviet Union (in March 1990); and its independence demands triggered revanchist claims from the sizable Polish diaspora in Lithuania. Poland formally recognized Lithuanian independence in August 1991, as the second state (after Iceland) to do so. During the prior two years, Skubiszewski said that Lithuania's aspirations should be fulfilled in accordance with international law.[13] Between 1989 and 1991, representatives of the Polish minority within Lithuania seriously compromised the Polish state's efforts by demanding territorial autonomy. The Polish state distanced itself from such claims. Kostrzewa-Zorbas's October 1989 memorandum contended that the only partner for the Polish state was the Lithuanian opposition group Sąjūdis, and that Poland should do nothing to justify Lithuanian fears of Polish revanchism. Kostrzewa-Zorbas believed that Lithuanian fears of Poland were *more* justified than Polish fears of Germany—and put this judgment on paper a year *before* Poland and Germany signed a border treaty.[14] Skubiszewski consistently declared that Poland had no territorial claims upon Lithuania or any other eastern neighbor, and told advocates of border revisions that their preferred course would bring about bloody war and provoke German demands in the west.[15]

Despite its exceptional nature, the case of Lithuania emphasizes an important point: that the two-track policy treated the proper interlocutors of the Polish state as neighboring nation-states. At a time when Hungarian Prime Minister József Antall proclaimed himself the prime minister of the Hungarian diaspora, and Serbian President Slobodan Milošević used the plight of Serbs in Kosovo to gain power, Polish authorities treated the position of Polish minorities as a matter to be resolved between nation-states according to international legal and ethical standards. These comparisons of Poland to Hungary and Serbia comparisons are not far-fetched. True, Hungary lost two-thirds of its territory at Trianon in 1920, and two million Hungarians lived in neighboring countries in 1989. Although Poland was compensated in the west, it lost almost half of its territory in 1945, including two of the four important Polish cities.

More than a million Poles remained in the eastern neighbors in 1989, most of them in a compact strip of Lithuanian and Belarusian territory bordering upon northeastern Poland.[16] Half of the Poles in the Soviet Union lived within two hundred miles of the Lithuanian capital Vilnius. One could draw a rather large zone around and including the Lithuanian capital in which a plurality of the population would be self-identifying Poles. Poland, unlike Hungary and Yugoslavia, privileged neighboring states over such national diasporas. In 1990 and 1991 Poland was dealt with a Lithuanian nation-state which did not yet legally exist in preference to a Polish minority which was making clear demands. This is evidence of a grand strategy that apprehended the world as constituted of nation-states.

THE THIRD TRACK

There was an indisputable legal basis for "second track" contacts with the Soviet republics. These republics were legal entities created by the Soviet constitution, and their autonomy was encouraged by Gorbachev. There was even a sense in which Skubiszewski's treatment of the inhabitants of Soviet republics as "nations" was consistent with general Soviet practice. The Soviet Union was, after all, a state of nationalities, divided into territorial units named after nations, and populated by individuals required to enter a nationality on their passports. Yet from Lenin to Gorbachev, Soviet nationality policy did not envision the possibility of secession by the republics. There was thus less legal basis for the unofficial "third track" of Polish eastern policy: direct contacts between former Polish oppositionists (now in power in Warsaw), and Ukrainian and Lithuanian national activists (seeking to gain national independence and to destroy the Soviet Union). In 1989 and 1990 the informal third track of Polish eastern policy provided information about how to support national oppositions, and prepared Skubiszewski for his October 1990 visit to "the Soviet Union, Russia, Ukraine, and Belarus," in the terms of the official communiqué. In effect, the third track (oppositions) substituted for the second track (republics) during the year that Skubiszewski was preoccupied with Germany (fall 1989–fall 1990), and prepared the ground for the second track's success where it was most successful.

This was in Ukraine, rather than in Russia, Belarus, or Lithuania. Relations between Polish oppositionists and Russian dissidents were remote and sporadic, and in any case there was never anything like an organized Russian national opposition with the aspiration to "secede" from the Soviet Union. There was likewise, although for different reasons, no Belarusian interlocutor. The Belarusian national movement was tiny, and concerned with historical and symbolic issues about which Poles could say little and do less. Veterans of Solidarity were most enthusiastic about Lithuania's Sąjūdis, but Lithuanian oppositionists assumed that Poles wished to occupy their country and its capital Vilnius.[17] Lithuanian activists correctly took Polish Lithuanophilia as evidence that Poles saw Lithuanians as "younger brothers," but mistakenly connected Polish cultural confidence to revanchist designs. Lithuanian activists treated Polish culture as the greatest threat to their nation, and it took time after 1991 for this traditionally effective stance to admit the value of political cooperation.

In Ukraine's national movement, Rukh, Solidarity activists found a ready and willing interlocutor.[18] In Ukraine, the national movement was strong enough to contemplate independence, but weak enough to see that it needed allies. The success of Russifying policies in the Ukrainian Soviet Socialist Republic had consolidated a new view among the West Ukrainian patriots who organized Rukh: that Russia rather than Poland was the great threat to the Ukrainian nation.[19] Whereas Soviet rule consolidated the image of Poland as a national enemy among Lithuanian patriots, it forced reconsideration among Ukrainians who watched Ukrainian national culture wither in the 1970s. The Polish minority in Ukraine, although roughly as numerous as its counterpart in Lithuania, was in relative terms far smaller. While hostile Polish organizations proclaimed autonomy near the Lithuanian capital Vilnius, Poles in western Ukraine, far from the national capital of Kyiv, supported the Ukrainian national movement. Whereas Poles in Lithuania very rarely assimilated to Lithuanian culture, Poles in Ukraine spoke Ukrainian. For all these reasons, Ukrainian oppositionists were more receptive than Lithuanians to *Kultura* and Solidarity, and more willing to see Poland as a positive model.[20]

The third track of Polish diplomacy provided a timely confirmation. When Poland gained full sovereignty in August 1989, Ukrainian admiration for Ukraine's western neighbor peaked. A delegation from Solidarity attended the founding congress of Rukh in September 1989, Adam Michnik calling from the podium to a packed hall at two o'clock in the morning that "We are happy that at this moment of your national rebirth, which you have purchased in the heavy coin of trials, camps, suffering, and the death of the greatest sons of these lands, that Solidarity is with you, that Poland is with you. May fate smile upon you, may God give you strength. Long live a free, democratic, and just Ukraine!" His oration, the Solidarity banner, and the Polish flag were greeted with ovations.[21] They, in effect, inaugurated the third track of Polish eastern policy, opening the eyes of Ukrainian activists to the possibility of an ally in the West, and marginalizing anti-Polish trends in Ukrainian nationalism at its moment of political emergence. In 1989 and 1990 leading Ukrainian oppositionists met repeatedly with the Solidarity activists now directing Polish policy, broadly agreeing upon the official steps to be taken by independent Poland and Soviet Ukraine. This is why Skubiszewski's October 1990 visit to the Soviet Union, the centerpiece of the two-track policy, was most successful in Ukraine.[22]

KYIV, OCTOBER 1990

In Kyiv in October 1990 Skubiszewski signed a "state-to-state" declaration with Ukrainian Foreign Minister Anatolii Zlenko, including a pledge of nonaggression, acceptance of existing borders, and cultural rights for minorities on both sides. Skubiszewski and Zlenko emphasized that Poland and Ukraine acted "as sovereign states." The Polish delegation brought Ukrainian rather than Russian translators, a gesture which was well received. Henceforth Poland and Ukraine prepared to initiate formal relations as internationally recognized sovereign states, which is to say that they prepared for Ukrainian independence and the end of the Soviet Union.[23] After the failed coup in Moscow of August 1991, they exchanged permanent representatives, and Poland signed a declaration of intent to sign a state treaty with Ukraine. (On 1 August 1991, U.S. President George Bush urged Ukraine to remain within the Soviet Union.) When Ukrainian independence was confirmed by referendum in December 1991, Poland was the first state to formally recognize the Republic of Ukraine. From third-track contacts, Skubiszewski and the Polish government knew that this gesture was desired. Early recognition exceeded the expectations of Ukrainian patriots, earned the Polish ambassador in Moscow a summons from Soviet Foreign Minister Eduard Shevardnadze, and garnered disapproval from the United States. It also created the conditions for further development of unexpectedly good Polish-Ukrainian relations.[24]

Polish policy indirectly supported a civic idea of Ukraine that allowed for the peaceful achievement of independence, and the peaceful dissolution of the Soviet Union. Having considered Ukraine's multinational history, large Russian minority, and resonant Soviet history, certain West Ukrainian activists advanced a civic and territorial idea of the Ukrainian nation. This approach allowed national independence to spread across Ukraine during 1990 and 1991 as a political idea: one that could be supported by appeals to culture, economics, or local elite interests, as circumstances warranted. As the Ukrainian movement crystallized in 1989 and 1990, the consensus in favor of this civic approach was not yet clear. Much depended on Polish support of Ukrainian national activists, and Polish endorsement of existing borders. At a time when West German leaders would not publicly commit to the preservation of the existing border with sovereign Poland, Poland's first democratic government extended unconditional assurances to not yet sovereign Ukraine. Polish policy was more assertive in its dealings with the Soviet republics than that of the United States and other Western powers, and more generous on this fundamental question of borders than its own great western neighbor. Had Solidarity not taken power in August 1989, had Michnik and others not traveled to Ukraine in September 1989, anti-Polish sentiments would have enjoyed a wider hearing. Had Polish policy been hostile to Ukraine, some West Ukrainian activists would have been distracted from the civic project of nation-building, and they would have advanced a nationalism less appealing to Kyiv elites and the Russophone Ukrainian majority. Had Poland advocated peaceful changes in frontiers, as for example Hungary and Romania did at this time, much of the energy of West Ukrainian activists would have been diverted. In the event, a conciliatory Polish approach allowed Rukh to remain a centrist movement with the wide appeal to win a national debate and thereby contribute to the end of the Soviet Union. Rukh's civic approach to national issues contributed to the massive vote in favor of independence in December 1991.

The success of Rukh's campaign was mainly due to the political skills of West Ukrainians—including certain Ukrainian communists. In 1990 and 1991, Ukrainian national activists felt the winds of change, but Ukrainian communists tacked the sails. Without a measure of cooperation between Rukh and Supreme Soviet Chairman Leonid Kravchuk (1934–), it is unlikely that the boat would have reached shore. Kravchuk's tactful support of "sovereignty" assured West Ukrainians that their own views could be realized throughout Ukraine, while his political talent allowed other Ukrainians to regard independence as natural and advantageous. His awareness of Ukrainian nationalism, both as a former ideological secretary assigned to combat it in the 1980s, and as a native of Volhynia, allowed him to use patriotism without igniting national strife.[25] Had Polish policy been other than ostentatiously pro-Ukrainian, conservative communists would have had a strong argument to use against independence: the need for Moscow's support against Poland. In such a situation, Kravchuk's efforts to unite pro-independence elites and east and central Ukrainian voters behind independence and his candidacy for president (the referendum and the presidential elections were both held in December 1991) would likely have failed.[26]

The argument from foreign policy to domestic politics can be recast in broader terms. Thanks to Polish policy, for the first time in modern history Ukraine appeared to have only one national foe: the Soviet Union. Like Poles, and like Germans for that matter, Ukrainians have traditionally feared encirclement. From the partition at Andrusovo in 1667 to the partition at Riga in 1921, Poland and Russia always appeared prepared to cooperate at Ukraine's expense. The diplomatic miracle of autumn 1990 was that German unification was managed in such a way as to reduce Polish fears, while Polish independence was presented in such a way as to reduce Ukrainian fears. The daring of Polish policy, and the evidence that it was premeditated, was that the opening to Ukraine *preceded* reconciliation with Germany. Skubiszewski visited Kyiv and reassured Ukraine about borders *before* the German-Polish border treaty was signed. Polish policy removed the traditional Ukrainian predicament of encirclement, and thereby weakened the defenses of the extreme Ukrainian Left and channeled the energy of the Ukrainian national Right. This favored the political negotiation of Ukrainian independence, and contributed to the peaceful disintegration of the Soviet Union. This Ukrainian-Polish arrangement was, perhaps, as important to the course of events as contemporaneous, and far better-known, power struggles between Mikhail Gorbachev and Boris Yeltsin in Moscow.

MOSCOW, OCTOBER 1990

Skubiszewski's October 1990 visit to Moscow was a provisional success. Skubiszewski took pains to separate "Soviet Union day" from "Russian Federation day," paying as much attention to Russian as to Soviet authorities. The declaration Skubiszewski signed with Russian authorities was the first official document the Russian Federation signed with any outside state.[27] Polish-Soviet negotiations were underway on both a new state treaty and an agreement on the withdrawal of Soviet troops from Poland. In December 1990 Poland linked the withdrawal of Soviet troops to transit rights for Soviet troops returning from Germany. The main issues of dispute were the so-called "security clauses," which would have forbidden Poland to join alliances (except with the Soviet Union), cooperate with foreign intelligence services (except the Soviet one), or allow foreign armies (except the Red Army) to station troops on its territory. The dispute over transit was resolved and the security clauses withdrawn. On

10 December 1991, Poland and the Soviet Union initialed a treaty, and agreed upon dates for the removal of Soviet troops.[28] These agreements could not be implemented, as the Soviet Union ceased to exist that month.

The Russian Federation became the successor state of the Soviet Union. The goodwill Poland had gained by taking the Russian Federation seriously was of little consequence: after the dissolution of the USSR, everyone had to take the Russian Federation seriously. Since the Russian Federation lacked a separate republican communist party, there were no Russian "national communists" to provide willing partners for negotiations (as in Ukraine) or to lead national movements (as in Lithuania), or indeed to see Poland as a model for opposition-regime relations and democratic transitions. Since few if any Russian national activists regarded the end of the Soviet Union as a positive outcome for their nation, their orientation ill fit the preferences of their counterparts in Eastern Europe.[29] Since Russian dissidents thought they had little to learn from Poland, there was little tradition of friendly contacts between oppositions. Thus the second and third tracks of Polish eastern policy contributed little to relations with the new Russian state.

On the other hand, the first track (relations with the Moscow center) had succeeded, for a state treaty and an agreement on troop withdrawals had already been negotiated with Soviet central authorities. Poland was able to sign two new treaties with the Russian Federation very quickly, in May 1992. These negotiations repeated, at accelerated tempo, all of the steps of the previous round: bombast from the Russian military, "security clauses" from the Russian foreign ministry, and in the end a settlement which hewed close to the Polish negotiating position. The last Russian combat troops left Poland in October 1992.[30] Although there were few promising signs for the future of Russian-Polish relations, the two-track policy in 1990 and 1991 had created the legal foundation, political momentum, and negotiating precedents for the quick resolution of outstanding issues in 1992. Given that Russian-Polish relations only deteriorated thereafter, this rapidity was of great importance.

MINSK, OCTOBER 1990

The October 1990 visit to Minsk was a fiasco, as Skubiszewski found himself amidst the sort of multilateral historical issues his policy of crisp bilateral engagement with proto-nation-states was designed to avoid. At the time, Soviet General Secretary Mikhail Gorbachev was pressuring Lithuania to withdraw its declaration of independence, and using the Belorussian SSR as a cat's paw.

Knowing as we do that Vil'nia/Wilno/Vilnius was a historical object of desire of Belarusians as well as Poles and Lithuanians, we see the basis for such a tactic. Soviet Lithuania owed its capital Vilnius to Stalin's policy during the Second World War. When Lithuania declared independence on 10 March 1990, Gorbachev threatened to give Vilnius to someone else, and Lithuanians took him seriously. This manipulation from the Soviet center was supported by the Belarusian Communist Party. After a 29 March 1990 meeting with Gorbachev, the Belarusian Politburo announced that in the event of Lithuanian independence the Belorussian SSR would claim Vil'nia.[31]

While this official Belarusian revanchism supported a Soviet policy, it could appeal to a reading of history popular among the national intelligentsia: that Belarus had not been a party to any of the agreements which transferred formerly Polish territory to Lithuania, and thus in conditions of perestroika Belarus no longer need consider itself bound by them. Belarusian revanchism resonated with the Belarusian self-conception of a reborn Grand Duchy of Lithuania with a capital in Vil'nia. Leading Belarusian activists recalled nineteenth-century Vil'nia as the cradle of the Belarusian movement and interwar Vil'nia as home to their political predecessors. They imagined that Belarusian independence would signify the restoration of the Grand Duchy of Lithuania, and that Vil'nia would be thereby "returned" to Belarus. In 1989 the Belarusian Popular Front held its founding congress in Vil'nia at the invitation of Lithuania's Sąjūdis—but disappointed its hosts by claiming their capital city for Belarus. In the summer of 1990 important figures within the Belarusian opposition proposed a federation to Lithuanian national activists, who were not interested.[32]

The visit of a Polish foreign minister to Minsk in October 1990 set off a frenzy of historical arguments. Belarusian communist authorities told Skubiszewski that since Belarus had not been party to postwar agreements, it was not empowered to sign treaties that would confirm the frontiers of 1945. Even though Poland was the only sovereign state interested in supporting Belarusian independence, the Belarusian opposition was, for the time being, trapped by historical reasoning. Belarusian patriots complained of (nonexistent) Polish "terror" against the Belarusians in Poland, spoke of "ethnically" Belarusian territory within Poland, and proposed peaceful territorial adjustments to account for this "ethnic" reality. At the same time, they feared that Poland would reclaim the territories Stalin had stripped from Poland and granted the Belorussian SSR at the end of the Second World War. Although the Lithuanian SSR had received Vilnius, the Belorussian SSR had received more formerly Polish territory in 1945. Most Belarusian national activists also believed that Poles in

Lithuania were actually Belarusians to whom must be restored their true national identity—optimally within a restored Grand Duchy of Lithuania which
would include all Belarusian, all Lithuanian, and some Polish territories.[33]

The ideal of the Grand Duchy was of course a myth, but it was a myth of
long standing, containing fewer internal contradictions than the modern nationalism of Belarus's neighbors. Belarusian national activists partook in a continuing tradition, which began with the end of the Grand Duchy of Lithuania,
was continued by Mickiewicz's Romantic poetry, and ended—at different times
in different places—when early modern ideas of nationality embodied by federalism failed in practice. This tradition failed in Poland after 1921, when Piłsudski was unable to win the territory he needed for a federation, and when
democracy supported a simpler Polish nationalism. The tradition failed for Belarusians in Poland during the interwar period, as Belarusian activists in Vil'nia
were thwarted and disgusted by Polish policies. It failed in 1939 and 1945, as Belarusian communists could not join Vil'nia to the Belorussian SSR. It would fail
in Minsk after 1990, as neighbors rejected offers of federation, and as Belarusian
voters proved indifferent to the inherently elite federalist idea.

The weakening of Soviet power and discoveries of Soviet perfidy did not instantly create a modern Belarusian nation. The leader of the Belarusian National Front, Zenon Pazniak (1944–), discovered the mass graves at Kuropaty,
where the Soviet NKVD murdered at least one hundred thousand civilians between 1937 and 1941. The Kuropaty exhumations, which began in 1988, were a
founding moment of Belarusian nationalism. It would take time for Belarusian
national activists to move beyond such difficult and painful historical issues,
draw conclusions from the failures of attempts to resuscitate the Grand Duchy,
and to reorient upon the modern idea of a nation-state functioning within imperfect borders. Polish policy offered time—and a model. Skubiszewski held to
the line that borders were not under discussion, and that regulating the existing
territorial state of affairs must precede historical discussions. Polish policy supported a modern Belarusian nation-state, an idea with few Belarusian supporters. The Belorussian SSR, home to conservative party authorities and a nostalgic patriotic opposition, poorly resembled the proto-nation-states that the
Polish two-track policy was designed to engage. Although the policy of Belarusian communist authorities appealed to the views of an elite national opposition, this policy was executed at Gorbachev's prompting, and had nothing to
do with popular pressure. The Belarusian national movement was not in 1990
in any position to influence Belarusian or Soviet policy. In October 1990, Polish diplomats came away with the impression that the Belarusian party was

simply following instructions from Moscow, and using domestic national activists as a prop in its own puppet theater. Events to follow supported this view. After the failed coup in Moscow of August 1991, and after Lithuanian independence was universally recognized in September 1991, the Belorussian SSR shed its territorial and historical pretensions toward Poland and accepted the original Polish proposition of a joint declaration. Its signing in October 1991 was Belarus's first act of international politics.[34]

POLISH LITHUANIANS?

Unlike Belarus, in 1990 Lithuania was home to an organized and popular national opposition. The Lithuanian movement Sąjūdis enjoyed massive popular support, had seized the agenda of Lithuanian politics, taken control of the national assembly, and declared national independence. The attitude of the new Lithuanian leaders to the territory of the Lithuanian SSR was unambiguous: it was now the sovereign territory of an independent Lithuanian state. As we have seen, Vilnius and surrounding territories had not been part of interwar Lithuania. Stalin divided the northeastern segment of interwar Poland between Lithuanian and Belorussian SSRs, Lithuania getting the prize of Vilnius. Most Poles left Wilno in 1944–46; but Poles remained a solid majority in what became the Vilnius and Šalčininkai regions of the Lithuanian SSR (63.8 percent and 79.8 percent respectively, according to the 1989 Soviet census). Poles were also a majority on the other side of the Lithuanian-Belorussian border. Indeed, at least 50 percent of the Poles in the Soviet Union (an area of 22,272,000 square kilometers) inhabited an area of only 30,000 square kilometers along the edges of two small republics. Half of the Poles in the former Soviet Union inhabited one one-thousandth of its surface area, all of it territory which belonged to the Polish state before the Second World War, and all of it in sensitive border areas—doubly sensitive because the Lithuanian capital lines only forty kilometers from Belarus.

Soviet policy had formed two rather distinct Polish minorities in the Lithuanian and Belorussian SSRs. In the Belorussian SSR Poles were swamped by local Belarusians and migrant Russians, and not permitted to study in Polish schools.[35] Poles in Belarus therefore learned Russian, the language of social advancement, rather than master literary Polish or Belarusian. Perhaps one in ten Belarusian Poles spoke Polish at home in the 1990s. The situation was very different in the Lithuanian SSR. Whereas Polish schooling was liquidated in the Belorussian SSR, Poles in the Lithuanian SSR could choose to study in Polish, as well as Russian and Lithuanian. Since Lithuanian is much harder for Poles to learn than Russian, and since Russian was the language of power within the USSR, Poles avoided Lithuanian schools. Lithuanian schools and universities replicated and confirmed the Baltic/Slavic linguistic divide, created a clear social barrier between the two groups, and crated two potentially distinct political elites.[36] Even though Lithuanian was a language of politics in the Lithuanian SSR, fewer than one in six Poles in the Lithuanian SSR could speak Lithuanian in 1989.[37]

In the Belorussian SSR, local nationalism was weak, and a postwar policy of Russification was successful. Poles in the Belorussian SSR considered Russification rather than local nationalism the main threat, and were friendly to the Belarusian idea.[38] In the Belorussian SSR, Poles were less likely than the titular nationality to join the communist party. Poles were the least trustworthy nationality in Soviet Belarus from Moscow's point of view, and after the Second World War they were left to assimilate. Lithuania presented a different situation. Here local nationalism was quite strong, and Russification made little progress. Poles in Lithuania, unlike Poles in Belarus, feared local nationalism more than Russification. Poles in Lithuania recalled direct Lithuanian rule in 1939–40, associated Lithuanian officials with the German occupation of 1941–44, and after 1945 experienced the quasi-Lithuanization of their own lands within the limits allowed by Soviet rule. Poles in Lithuania still treated the Lithuanian presence in their lands as alien, and regarded Lithuanians with more far more antipathy than Russians.[39] Poles in the Lithuanian SSR were more likely than Lithuanians to join the Communist Party. Whereas Poles in the Belorussian SSR were seen as *less* reliable than the titular nationality, Poles in the Lithuanian SSR were seen as *more* reliable. The point is not that Poles came to terms with communism, while Lithuanians did not. The point is that Lithuanians and Poles made two different national compromises within the Lithuanian SSR, and that the Soviet regime could use one against the other.

This potential opposition between Lithuanians and Poles in the Lithuanian SSR was aroused in the late 1980s and 1990s, partly by the design of Lithuanian national activists and Soviet authorities, but also partly by accident. Having won a voice for themselves, Lithuanian national activists called Poles in Lithuania "Polonized Lithuanians," whose national essence would be restored to them by an independent Lithuanian state. The Lithuanian language law, which obliged nongovernmental institutions to function in Lithuanian, annoyed Poles who might otherwise have remained indifferent to Lithuanian independence. New difficulties in using the Polish forms of surnames convinced people

that Polishness itself had been criminalized. Poles had reason to expect land reform would discriminate against those whose property claims were based upon
interwar Polish documents. By 1990 local Poles thought that the goal of the
Lithuanian national movement was to force them to choose between assimilation and emigration, which was essentially correct.[40] As in 1940, so in 1990,
Lithuanian policy in the Vilnius region left little room for a political rather than
an ethnic identification with Lithuania.

After the March 1990 Lithuanian declaration of independence, Soviet central authorities mobilized local Poles. As the rest of Lithuania faced an economic embargo, regions with a Polish majority received shipments of goods
from the Soviet Union. As Moscow threatened to dismember Lithuania, Polish
organizations and Polish-majority regions declared their territorial autonomy.
Lithuanians were right to be suspicious of the leadership of the Polish minority,
many of whom were working with the Soviet KGB.[41] But autonomy was popular because local Poles were genuinely fearful of Lithuanian nationalism, and
because local elites could appeal to a vision of Polishness which was sincerely
and widely held. This was by now a simple Polish ethnic nationalism, associated with the Roman Catholic Church, and rooted in the idea that the best
Poles had stayed in their Lithuanian homeland. Federalist ideas were all but
dead by 1939. The Second World War, Soviet classifications and deportations,
and Lithuanian nationalism buried them for good.

In Warsaw, too, the traditions of the Grand Duchy of Lithuania were largely
forgotten, as a linguistic definition of the nation won the day. The Polish communist regime drew legitimacy from its supposed descent from medieval Piast
Poland, leaving the eastern territories of the early modern Commonwealth to
Soviet history. The political antidotes to communism exploited this error. The
efforts of *Kultura* and of the Polish opposition before 1989 were not directed toward returning the Commonwealth to Polish history, but rather toward creating parallel national readings of the history of Lithuania, Belarus, and Ukraine
on the Polish model. They advanced a historically dubious if politically generous multi-nationalism, recognizing the existence and legitimacy of other modern nations. They sought to turn the general belief about the historical inevitabil-
ity of the Polish nation-state into a presumption in favor of neighboring nations
becoming states. The modern nationalist idea that the Lithuanian nation-state
was a revived version of the old Grand Duchy triumphed not only in Vilnius,
but in Warsaw. Twentieth-century disputes over Wilno appeared to be nothing
more than a misunderstanding, and the territorial aspirations of Poles in Lithuania seemed incoherent and illegitimate. In the foregoing chapters, we have

distinguished between traditions and history, and have argued that forgetting of one's own traditions is required to construct one's own history.[42] Something similar could be said about national rapprochement: before nations can come to terms, each must see the other as a nation, as a formal equal. Nations must, at some minimal level, accept that other nations have national histories.

The acceptance of the mass nation as the source of political legitimacy and of the nation-state as the unit of history marginalizes people whose nations do not happen to match their states. Poles in Poland saw Poles in Lithuania as backward hicks and Soviet dupes. Kostrzewa-Zorbas, Polish patriot and contributor to Polish eastern policy, called Polish autonomists in Lithuania "Soviet people of Polish descent."[43] An exclusion from the national community could hardly be more explicit than that! Although Kostrzewa-Zorbas wrote this article before joining the Polish Foreign Ministry, it appeared just one month before his first memo to parliament proposing a two-track policy. Representatives of Rural Solidarity wrote an open letter to Polish peasants in Lithuania, saying that it was shameful to support Soviet power. The leading Polish daily newspaper mocked the Polish minority's declarations of territorial autonomy by asking if Russia's Pacific coast was also Polish.[44] Foreign Minister Skubiszewski and President Wałęsa opposed these territorial demands, proposing instead that Poles in Lithuania regard themselves as citizens of a future Lithuanian nation-state.[45]

Despite these disagreements of the moment, Poles and Lithuanians shared a historical paradigm. Both claimed descent from earlier states whose history they had adapted to contemporary conditions. Poland and Lithuania had intellectually partitioned the old Commonwealth, Lithuanian claiming the Grand Duchy and its medieval history, Poland claiming the medieval Piast kingdom. To be sure, Poles also thought of the early Commonwealth as a Polish state, but Lithuanians partook in this error by regarding the Commonwealth period as the end of Lithuanian civilization. Polish eastern policy was predicated on the existence of potential nation-states to the east, and in fact Lithuanians more than any other neighbor regarded the nation-state as their destiny. This does much to explain why Polish-Lithuanian relations, after an inauspicious start, were excellent by the end of the 1990s.

JANUARY 1991

At the beginning of the 1990s, however, there was still a great deal of modern history to be cleared away. For Lithuanian national activists, in charge of an embattled Lithuanian state, the association of a "Polish" minority with the

"Polish" state was too strong to be overcome quickly. Lacking experience with Solidarity and the new Polish elite, Lithuanians treated Lithuanian Poles as exemplary of Poles in general, and the newly sovereign Polish state as by nature an ally of the Polish minority in Lithuania and a partner of Russian imperialists in Moscow.

In January 1991, when Soviet special forces seized the Lithuanian television building in Vilnius, killing thirteen and wounding hundreds, the divergence among these four positions—Soviet authorities, Lithuanian patriots, the Polish minority, and the Polish state—came into sharp focus. Soviet officials spoke of partitioning Lithuania, treating the Belorussian SSR and the Polish minority as the proper recipients of Vilnius and surrounding lands.[46] Lithuanian patriots stood by their declaration of independence and urged national minorities to support their common cause. The parliament called a referendum on independence, which was supported by 90 percent of Lithuanian voters (with 86 percent of those eligible casting a ballot). The parliament also promised to create an administrative unit for the Polish minority. This promise, which in any case was never fulfilled, did not satisfy the Polish minority in Lithuania. As the crisis in Lithuania continued, the elected leadership of Polish-majority regions, as well as the leaders of the Union of Poles in Lithuania, pressed territorial demands. In May 1991 a congress of local Polish officials passed the most ambitious plan thus far for territorial autonomy: a "Wilno-Polish National-Territorial Authority." Its highest authority was to be a local parliament, its territory was to be governed by that parliament alone, it was to boast a flag and an army, and its residents were to be offered triple citizenship: Lithuanian, Vilnian, and Polish or Soviet. This was to all intents and purposes a declaration of independence.[47]

The Polish state condemned the use of force, distanced itself from the Polish minority, and endorsed Lithuanian independence in the strongest terms possible short of formal recognition. A joint declaration of the Polish Sejm and Senate made explicit the historical comparison between Poland and Lithuania.[48] The Polish government recalled its ambassador from Moscow, requested a meeting of the Conference on Security and Cooperation in Europe to discuss Moscow's attack, and then invited Lithuanians to join its delegation when the meeting was held.[49] 90 percent of Polish citizens surveyed in February 1991 favored the independence of Lithuania: exactly the same proportion of Lithuanian citizens voted for independence in the referendum of that very month.[50] At least fifteen thousand Poles demonstrated to protest Moscow's use of force: the Lithuanian flag was seen everywhere in Warsaw, especially around the Soviet embassy and at its gates. Throughout the country Poles filled trucks with medical supplies and food, and drove them to Vilnius.[51] In Vilnius, Lithuanian deputies besieged in the parliament building welcomed Solidarity activists, now Polish parliamentarians, who declared Polish sympathy and support. In Vilnius, Adam Michnik, editor of Poland's main newspaper, called out "Long live a free Lithuania!" In Vilnius, Jacek Kuroń, the most popular politician in Poland, said that he would remain in the Lithuanian parliament as long as was necessary, and that he was prepared to die there.[52] These were not empty words: in January 1991, no one knew what would happen next, and the Lithuanian government had already made plans for a government in exile in Warsaw. Foreign Minister Algirdas Saudargas (1948–), charged with this daunting task, was applauded to the echo in the Polish parliament for his cause and his courage.[53]

Polish relations with Lithuania in 1990 and 1991 were far more intimate than relations with the Russian Federation, Belarus, or Ukraine. At the same time, Poland did not sign any sort of state declaration with Lithuania, and disagreements about the Polish minority remained unresolved. These failures to build a legal infrastructure for political relations would later prove important. As in other cases, however, the policy of two tracks allowed Polish officials to recognize the historical fears of Poland's neighbors, to understand how the modern Polish state could be seen as the inheritor of an imperialist past.[54] Once Poland's eastern neighbors won independence in late 1991, disagreements with Lithuania would take pride of place. After the Soviet Union collapsed, the historical contest for Vilnius became the main focus of Lithuanian diplomacy. As it turned out, Polish support for Lithuania during the crisis had been the minimum Lithuanian activists expected, and was far from sufficient to resolve fears of Poland. Since the fear of Poland was basically a fear of Polish culture, no political initiative of Warsaw could suffice. Despite Polish political support, leading Lithuanian officials spoke of Polish nationalism and imperialism, and of the possibility of a Polish invasion of Lithuania and a Russian-Polish condominium. Lithuanian policy required that Poland correct the past as well as act in good faith in the present. In 1992 and 1993 Lithuanian demands for an apology for the "occupation" of Vilnius in 1920 met Polish refusals to negotiate history; Polish demands on behalf of the political rights of the Polish minority in Lithuania met with Lithuanian cries of interference in internal affairs.

This demonstrated the limits of the Polish eastern policy of two tracks, of recognizing eastern neighbors as equal nation-states. Once Poland's eastern neighbors were in fact nation-states, the policy was obsolete. Equal nation-states must have equal national histories, worthy of equal respect; and all nation-states must be allowed to decide their own internal policies, regardless of the objections of neighbors. Disputes over history and minorities thus require a different standard of adjudication than the right of nations to sovereign existence as states, the silent basis of Polish eastern policy in 1990 and 1991. From early 1992, Skubiszewski articulated a policy of "European standards" as a resolution to this dilemma. The policy of two tracks had exaggerated the strength of the nations to Poland's east, and thereby contributed to their independence. The policy of European standards exaggerated the clarity of European legal norms, thereby contributing to their transmission to the former Soviet Union. In other words, when Poland was dealing with Soviet republics, it treated them as nation-states; and when it was dealing with post-Soviet nation-states, it treated them as partners in European integration. Such a policy could work only when Poland itself was perceived not as the inheritor of national traditions, but as an integral part of Europe.

Chapter 13 European
Standards and Polish Interests
(1992–1993)

Opening a chapter of *Pan Tadeusz* entitled "Hunting and Diplomacy," Mickiewicz hailed the great Lithuanian forest of Białowieża, ancient hunting ground of the grand dukes. On 8 December 1991, in a hunting lodge in the Belarusian forest of Belovezha, Stanislau Shushkevich, Boris Yeltsin, and Leonid Kravchuk put an end to the sixty-nine-year history of the Soviet Union. The three republican leaders, representing founding members of the Soviet Union, announced that it was no longer a subject of international law. The dissolution of the Soviet Union established nation-states across the entire territory of the old Polish-Lithuanian Commonwealth. The Russian Federation, the Republic of Ukraine, the Republic of Belarus, and the Republic of Lithuania joined the Polish Republic in a new Eastern Europe. What would become of places like Białowieża/Belovezha, associated with all five countries? How would Poland, champion of border conservatism before the end of the Soviet Union, react to the final disintegration of its eastern neighbor?

Poland's two-track policy of 1989–91 had seemed utopian (and was practical) because it engaged the republics of a Soviet Union at a time when few thought the empire would disintegrate. A new policy of European standards in 1992–93 seemed utopian (and was practical) because it exploited the attractions of Western institutions at a time when there were few signs that these institutions would enlarge. Until 1993 the European Union (EU) refused to countenance an eastward enlargement. The position of NATO was less categorical, but during this period no eastward extension of the alliance was proposed. Nevertheless, Poland's normative anticipation of the enlargement of Western institutions proved an effective successor to the normative anticipation of the end of the Soviet Union. After the two-track policy contributed to the creation of nation-states in Eastern Europe, the policy of European standards improved relations among them.

IN EUROPE'S NAME

To understand what motivated the policy of European standards, one must begin with Polish interests. Poland's first eastern interest was that problems with eastern neighbors not hinder Poland's integration with the West. The first priority of Poland's post-Solidarity governments in 1992 and 1993 was to join the EU and NATO.[1] Foreign Minister Skubiszewski understood that perceived problems with eastern neighbors would be used as arguments against Poland's inclusion in these institutions, and sought to prevent such difficulties by arranging relations as quickly as possible. Poland's second interest in the east was the preservation of Lithuanian, Belarusian, and Ukrainian nation-states. This was understood as the best hedge against future Russian imperialism. Poland's third interest in the east was the protection of the Polish minority in the former Soviet Union, most of which was to be found in Lithuania, Belarus, and Ukraine. Although for brief moments the treatment of Poles in the east seized center stage in Polish domestic politics, it was consistently a lower priority in foreign policy than the return to Europe or the independence of the eastern neighbors. These three interests—Western integration, eastern consolidation, and minority protection—were to be furthered by state treaties with Lithuania, Belarus, and Ukraine. These treaties were to be based upon the declarations signed with Soviet republics in 1990 and 1991, during the two-track period, and included what Polish diplomats called "European standards."

"European standards" meant the territorial integrity of nation-states and the protection of the cultural rights of minorities. Poland had no territorial claims upon any of its eastern neighbors, and expected its eastern neighbors to resign from any such pretensions towards Poland. Poland would seek to protect the rights of Poles residing abroad as citizens of other nation-states, but oppose efforts by Polish minorities as collectivities to seek territorial autonomy. Likewise, it would offer the same kind of rights to national minorities resident in Poland, but oppose any territorial aspirations on their part. These principles applied to the negotiation of treaties. Recognition of Poland's eastern neighbors and confirmation of existing borders were not to be used as leverage in negotiating minority rights. Unlike West Germany, Poland immediately and unconditionally confirmed existing frontiers.

Three implications of this approach were quickly apparent. First, this was a policy whose crucial categories were the state and its citizens, not the nation and its members. As Skubiszewski put it: "Minority rights are not special rights, but rather human rights and fundamental liberties, which members of national minorities enjoy. The state has the obligation to assure national minorities full equality with other citizens by taking advantage of these rights and liberties. This is equality within the state—the same standard for all people, without regard for which group they belong to."[2] Second, this was a policy based upon international law rather than upon national readings of history. Skubiszewski was categorical: "History is not and cannot be the factor which determines one's view of today's reality, or which determines how today's reality is formed."[3] The policy of European standards set aside special pleading on behalf of this or that abused minority or this or that poorly designed frontier in favor of an immediate and comprehensive legal settlement between states within their present borders. Third, this was a policy of voluntary Europeanization. Rather than waiting for Europe to intervene, this policy sought to dampen conflicts before Europe realized they existed, and to introduce European norms in Eastern Europe before alternatives could crystallize.[4] The point was "to encourage all of our eastern neighbors that certain European models or standards, which we for several years have been treating as guiding, should be realized in their new states as well." Central were "European standards of minority rights."[5]

Poland was defining as well as introducing norms. Strictly speaking, there were no European standards for minority rights at the time. Especially after the Yugoslav wars began in summer 1991, European institutions presented progressively clearer targets to states which wished to join the EU. Yet these normative targets were by no means a simple reflection of standards already prevailing within the EU. The notion of minority rights was highly contested: major EU member states were governed by constitutions unfriendly to the very idea that national minorities exist. Skubiszewski appealed to the 1990 Copenhagen document of the Conference on Security and Cooperation in Europe, which was cited as a source of "standards" in the minority rights clauses of the 1991 German-Polish treaty. This was an attempt to extract a clear position from the furious debates over minority rights in the Europe of the early 1990s. As a matter of policy, the definition of national minorities as a group of people that so defined themselves, and the sharp distinction between cultural and territorial rights for minorities, were Polish conceptions. Forged during negotiations with Germany, when Poland was in the weaker position, they were applied in negotiations with Poland's immediate eastern neighbors, when Poland was in the stronger position. While claiming to appeal to a set of generally understood "European standards," Poland was in fact consolidating them. This approach was bound to meet the approval of Poland's western neighbors. The same point can be made about territorial integrity. True, European states and institutions would look askance at changes to state borders, but the contemporary cases of German unification, West German statements about the Polish border prior to unification, the revanchist constitution of Ireland, the ambitious territorial programs of pro-European parties in Spain, the United Kingdom, and Ireland and indeed British-Spanish disputes over Gibraltar, made it somewhat difficult to speak of an unambiguous "standard" in this field. Nevertheless, general postwar practice was clear enough, and the desire for stability in Eastern Europe still clearer—especially after the Yugoslav wars began in June 1991. Skubiszewski was right to think that the best way for an East European country to be seen as European was to avoid disputes about territory.

"European standards" marked Poland's most important agreements with Europe's most important state: the German-Polish treaties on borders (November 1990) and good-neighborly relations (June 1991).[6] Skubiszewski made sure that Poland asked nothing of its eastern neighbors that it did not want Germany to ask of Poland. In reaffirming Poland's border with Germany, Skubiszewski made clear that Poland would make no territorial claims on its own eastern neighbors. In treating the German minority in Poland as before all citizens of the Polish state, Polish policy created a situation in which it would be very awkward to demand more than that for its own minorities in the east. As the Polish ambassador to Lithuania recalled his procedure for dealing with the complaints of the local Polish minority: "Before I do anything, I always ask myself what I would do as a Polish official reacting to the complaint of German representatives in Poland."[7] There was also a positive side of the German example. In a general way, the use of "Europe" within Polish eastern policy was similar to the contemporary use of "Europe" in German Polish policy. In both cases, the promise of a European future was set against the national conflict of the twentieth century, and "Europe" provided the ideals and the rhetoric that motivated reconciliation among states.[8]

WERE EUROPEAN STANDARDS STANDARD?

The idea of "European standards" presupposed that the road to Europe is sign-posted, that there are certain routes which must be taken and others that must be avoided, and that Poland had a map and was a reliable guide. If you choose to follow European standards as we do, went the Polish argument to its eastern neighbors, you can join Europe just as we will. This argument was effective within the domestic politics of Poland's neighbors insofar as domestic political actors desired the return to Europe, and insofar as they perceived Poland as being further along the way. Of course, the Polish offer to confirm existing borders and to ask for reciprocal protection of cultural rights of minorities was attractive in itself, and as a practical matter the quick presentation of draft treaties accelerated negotiations. All of this may seem like nothing more than a normal and reasonable reaction to international circumstances. To see what was special about this approach, it may help to compare Polish *Ostpolitik* to contemporaneous foreign policies in Eastern Europe.

1. The policy of European standards treated minority rights as the cultural rights of citizens of another country, which could be listed in international treaties. This creation of an external arbiter—"European standards" codified in treaties—generally avoided the trap of tit-for-tat reciprocity present almost everywhere else in the region.

2. The policy of European standards emphasized that the fate of minorities is a domestic matter for the sovereign states of which they are citizens, while other approaches challenged the sovereignty of neighbors. Hungary rhetorically extended its political community to Hungarian populations in Slovakia, Romania, Yugoslavia, and Ukraine in 1990. Russian bombast on behalf of Russian-speakers in the "near-abroad" frightened neighbors. Yugoslav activism on behalf of ethnic Serbs caused four wars, two interventions by NATO, over a million refugees, and tens of thousands of deaths.

3. Similarly, the policy of European standards excluded territorial resolutions to minority problems. This differed from the initial Hungarian, Romanian, and Belarusian positions that peaceful border revisions were possible; from the Russian support of the armed occupation of part of Moldova; from Yeltsin's early suggestions that the border with Ukraine was not fixed; and from the at-

titude of the Russian parliament in the mid-1990s that Crimea must be returned to Russia by Ukraine. It differed most obviously from the Yugoslav policy of correcting borders by force.

4. The policy of European standards sought to introduce European norms *before* European institutions became aware of potential problems. This was in striking contrast to Hungary and Romania, which waited for European pressure (the OSCE Paris meeting of 1995) to resolve their differences in the mid-1990s; to Yugoslavia, which brought down NATO intervention against itself in the mid- and late 1990s; and to Russia, which ignored the preferences of Western institutions as it prosecuted two fantastically brutal wars in Chechnya, intervened regularly in the Caucasus, and occupied part of Moldova.

5. The policy of European standards sought to keep history out of diplomacy. Although many outsiders learned in the 1990s of the 1389 battle of Kosovo, very few needed to know of the 1386 dynastic union of Poland and Lithuania. Whereas the ethnic cleansing of Serbs by Croats in the 1940s was brought to public attention by the Yugoslav wars of the 1990s, the Polish-Ukrainian cleansings of the 1940s, equally savage and widespread, remained a subject for specialists.

In philosophy, the Polish approach was strikingly different from the Russian presumption that Ukraine and Belarus are stray "Russian" lands because all three "descend" from Kyivan Rus'. By now we know that there is no historical basis for such a view: the lands of contemporary Belarus and Ukraine were part of the Grand Duchy of Lithuania (1289–1795) and the Polish-Lithuanian Commonwealth (1569–1795) after the disintegration of Kyivan Rus'. For hundreds of years, the territories of today's Ukraine and Belarus were known as Rus' within the Grand Duchy or the Commonwealth. Muscovy (after 1721 the Russian empire, after 1922 the Soviet Union) did slowly advance across the lands of Rus': but Kyiv was not governed from Moscow until 1667, more than four centuries after the fall of Kyivan Rus'; and L'viv was not governed from Moscow 1939, seven centuries after the fall of Kyivan Rus'. Vilnius and Volodomyr Volyns'kyi, important sources of the chancery language attributed to medieval Rus', were cities in interwar Poland. They are today the capital of independent Lithuania, and a town in western Ukraine. If one imagines, then, that "descent" is relevant to diplomacy, Polish diplomats would have as much right to speak of "family ties" as Russian. In fact, Poland avoided this sort of metahistory, treating its eastern neighbors as equal nation-states.

These are five pitfalls the policy of European standards avoided. To appreciate the value of staying on level ground, we should keep in mind what we learned in chapters 1 through 10: that Poles, no less than Russians, Hungarians, or Serbs, have a complicated historical relationship to their neighbors; that this includes, in the twentieth century, open revanchism, official states of war, and massive ethnic cleansing; and that memories of war and injustice were prominent within the elites of Poland's eastern neighbors and among the Polish population. Indeed, when Poland's eastern neighbors won their independence in 1991, leaders, diplomats, and citizens on both sides of what had been the Soviet-Polish border raised just these historical issues. After the end of the Soviet Union, the policy of European standards functioned in the teeth of suddenly renewed national claims about the contested Lithuanian fatherland and about the embattled Ukrainian hinterland. The success of the policy should not blind us to the fact that the challenges were real.

UKRAINE, 1992–1993

No one in Poland or western Ukraine had forgotten the massive ethnic cleansing of the 1940s. Memories of the terror wrought upon Polish civilians by Ukrainian partisans, as well as memories of forced resettlements of Ukrainians by the Polish communist regime, created the suspicious atmosphere within which Polish eastern policy had to operate. Poles from Ukraine and Ukrainians in Poland could now freely tell their stories (and deny the stories of the other). Provocateurs could sell ghastly accounts of ethnic cleansing, complete with photographs, in which one side was innocent and the other guilty. Within Poland, surveys showed that Poles feared Ukrainians more than they feared Russians or Germans. In Przemyśl, an area which had seen horrifying Polish-Ukrainian civil war in the 1940s, a group of Poles laid claim to a formerly Ukrainian church, successfully defying the expressed wishes of a Polish pope. In 1991, as UPA brotherhoods began to form in western Ukraine, the Polish minister of justice proposed including the UPA's cleansing of Volhynia as a crime against humanity, to be subject to the same kind of law that would try Stalinist criminals.[9] This could only be rejected by Ukrainian national activists, who took pride in the UPA, and knew a good deal more about Stalinism than did Poles. Meanwhile, Ukrainians within Poland campaigned for legal reparations for their forced migration in 1947. Among their demands was that the present democratic Polish state apologize for Operation Vistula, the resettlement operation carried out by the communist regime in 1947. Ukrainian national activists in Ukraine supported this demand.

The Polish Senate had actually apologized in June 1990. Polish deputies were disappointed when the Ukrainian parliament offered no parallel apology for the Volhynian terror of 1943 in its reply of October 1990.[10] There was a logical problem here: a newly sovereign Polish state could apologize for actions of its communist predecessor more easily than a newly independent Ukrainian state could apologize for the actions of a partisan army. That said, the Ukrainian parliament's reply read as though Stalinism was to blame for all the ills that befell both societies, a characterization Poles who remembered the UPA could not accept. Ukrainians wondered why the Sejm, the lower house of the Polish parliament, did not join in the apology: but in 1990 the Sejm was not fully democratic, and was dominated by former communists unwilling to criticize policies of the 1940s. Indeed, Polish President Wojciech Jaruzelski was a veteran of Operation Vistula! In 1992 Ukrainian diplomacy took up the issue of a Polish apology for Operation Vistula.[11]

The Polish policy of European standards worked in precisely these circumstances. It was effective not because it sought to resolve these historical disagreements, but because it presumed that a legal settlement would precede attempts to address history. How did the law find political traction in the slippery field of historical disagreements? Ukrainian national activists were usually people who hailed from territories of interwar Poland, had seen or heard about Ukrainian-Polish conflict during the Second World War, and were in some cases children of OUN members or UPA soldiers. As argued in the last chapter, the premise of "law before history" was acceptable to Ukrainian national activists because of contact with Solidarity in the 1980s and with the new Poland since 1989. The West Ukrainians who remembered the bloody events of the 1940s were the very same people who regarded Poland as the road to the European future.[12] Among the Ukrainian participants in the informal third-track contacts of 1989–91 were the future head of the Ukrainian parliament's foreign affairs committee; a future ambassador to Poland; future advisors to the first presidential administration of independent Ukraine; the future mayor of L'viv; and the first two leaders of the Ukrainian national movement Rukh. Ivan Drach, for example, was the leader of Rukh before independence, and later charged with policy toward Ukrainians abroad. Just before independence, he explained that "We want to travel the Polish path. We know that the path to Europe (and perhaps this makes us different from Lithuania) really does lead through Poland." Dmytro Pavlychko, a Galician, later chaired the Ukrainian parliamentary committee on foreign affairs. Just after independence, he assured his fellow national activists that Poland had changed: "A completely new era has begun."[13]

The Polish-Ukrainian treaty of May 1992 did not require, nor did it bring, agreement about the 1940s. It was ratified by the Ukrainian parliament on 17 September 1992—on the anniversary of the Soviet invasion of Poland in 1939—after a stormy debate about Operation Vistula. Pavlychko had the last word, arguing that it would demonstrate "low political culture" to allow historical disagreements to prevent the commencement of good relations between states.[14] The issue of who should apologize for the ethnic cleansing of the 1940s continued to arise: during the visit of Polish Prime Minister Hanna Suchocka (1946–) to Kyiv in January 1993 ("I did not say, Mr. Prime Minister, that the Polish government will condemn Operation Vistula. I said that the Polish government will objectively explain the matter of Operation Vistula, and I demand the same of you, Mr. Prime Minister, with respect to the treatment of Poles in Volhynia, in western Ukraine"); that of the Ukrainian parliamentary foreign affairs chairman to Cracow in February ("We will never believe the lies and calumnies spread by Soviet historians about the UPA"); or that of the Ukrainian ambassador during a visit to Przemyśl ("You cannot place Operation Vistula and what happened in Volhynia on the same level").[15] This last was a good example of how historical debates reveal totally different views. It was a sentiment with which Poles could agree, believing that "what happened in Volhynia" was incomparably more terrible than Operation Vistula. West Ukrainians, and the Rukh movement, voiced their concerns about the Ukrainian minority in Poland, their desire for an official apology for the forcible resettlement of Ukrainians in 1947, and in some important cases their fears of a Polish resurgence in L'viv. Appreciating Polish support for Ukrainian independence, and hoping that a treaty with Poland could help Ukraine rejoin Europe, Ukrainian activists treated historical issues as less important than the present security of their state.[16] Ukrainian President Leonid Kravchuk accepted that Poland was Ukraine's road to Europe. On his account, the May 1992 treaty made Poland a more important partner for Ukraine than Russia. President Wałęsa noted, in more subtle language than President Kravchuk, that the treaty was important for third parties.[17]

Something fundamental had indeed taken place along the axis of Warsaw-Kyiv-Moscow. In recognizing Ukraine and confirming Ukraine's western frontier, Warsaw communicated that Poland would be a status quo power in Eastern Europe, and that minority concerns would not serve as a pretext for intervention in Ukrainian affairs. Russian policy was quite the opposite: Yeltsin had indicated that the Ukrainian border might have to be redrawn, and concern about Russians in the "near abroad" of former Soviet republics was resonant in Russian elite politics. Russians in Ukraine's Crimean Peninsula were demanding union with Russia, and the Russian parliament would soon declare the Crimean port of Sevastopol a Russian city. The tenor of official Russian pronouncements to Ukraine changed over the course of 1992, the first year of both countries' independent existence. Unaccustomed to seeing Ukraine as a distinct entity, puzzled Russian politicians declined to take Ukrainian independence seriously.[18]

By late 1992 Kravchuk was determined to press forward towards an alliance with Poland directed against Russian predominance in Eastern Europe, perhaps one in which Ukraine would provide a nuclear umbrella with the weapons it had inherited from the Soviet Union. Ukraine was, at the time, in possession of more nuclear weapons than any country except the United States and the Russian Federation. In spring 1993 Ukraine proposed a "Baltic-to-Black Sea Pact" of which the Ukrainian-Polish partnership would be the nucleus. This idea, long favored by Ukrainian national activists, was not just an attempt to balance Russian power. It was also meant to stabilize the middle ground between Russian dominance (seen as undesirable) and European integration (understood to be a matter of decades). It referred to the common Polish-Ukrainian experience within the Polish-Lithuanian Commonwealth, which was after all a great power between Western Europe and Russia.[19]

As we have seen, Polish diplomacy was keyed to the nation-state, and appeals to the Commonwealth were not persuasive. Provocations of Russia were seen as undesirable threats to Poland's statehood, and institutional links to Ukraine as hindrances to Western integration. Polish policy was friendly to Ukraine, but far from the level of support Kravchuk desired. Poland did explain to Western states why Ukrainian independence was important to European stability, and why Ukraine hesitated to give its nuclear weapons to Russia. These subjects were raised by President Wałęsa and Foreign Minister Skubiszewski with U.S. President Bill Clinton in April 1993. Yet while supporting Ukrainian independence and explaining Ukrainian interests, Poland also favored Ukrainian nuclear disarmament. Poland was agreeable to military cooperation with Ukraine, provided that it was not directed against Russia. Poland's policy toward Russian-Ukrainian disputes was one of equal distance, although Skubiszewski did unequivocally condemn the territorial claims of the Russian parliament.[20]

In the early 1990s, Poland and Ukraine were both constrained by dependence upon Russian energy supplies. The Polish finance minister pronounced himself "horrified" by the possibility that a Russian-Ukrainian conflict could limit gas supplies to Poland. In August 1993 Poland also agreed to help Russia build a gas pipeline to Western Europe that bypassed Ukraine. At about the same time, Polish authorities arrested a Ukrainian security services major on espionage charges, Yeltsin (temporarily) approved NATO enlargement, and Ukrainians began fear a Russian-Polish axis.[21] By late 1993 the Polish-Ukrainian relationship found its limits not in national disagreements about Ukrainian-Polish borderlands but in differences of interests regarding Russia. This was a sea change. The precedent of Ukrainian-Polish war at turning points of Ukrainian history was broken, and a new precedent for fundamental agreement about the geopolitics of Eastern Europe was set.

BELARUS, 1992–1993

Just as post-1989 Polish policy toward Ukraine succeeded in the teeth of historical disputes about the 1940s in Galicia and Volhynia, so post-1989 Polish policy towards Belarus succeeded despite renewed disputes over the city of Vilnius/Vil'nia/Wilno. In 1991 and 1992, Belarusian foreign policy was fragmented, with the foreign minister advancing territorial claims on Lithuania, and the speaker of the parliament retracting them. Foreign Minister Petr Krauchanka had the qualified endorsement of the small Belarusian nationalist movement, which concurred that Poles in Lithuania were Belarusians, and that the exclusion of Vil'nia from the Belorussian SSR in 1945 was a mistake to be rectified by independent Belarus as soon as possible.[22] Belarusian nationalists were giddy in 1992 with the success of national independence, but enjoyed little support in society and had little experience in politics. Parliamentary Speaker Stanislau Shushkevich was a rare figure: a Belarusian patriot who believed that the interests of Belarus would be best served by the integration of a Belarusian nation-state within its present borders into European institutions. He thus reassured Lithuanians about territorial claims, and treated Poland as the best available road to Europe.[23]

Shushkevich's main complaint was the Polonization of Belarusian peasants the Roman Catholic Church. Polish priests delivered sermons in Polish and decorated their churches with Polish national symbols.[24] One-fifth of the Belarusian population of ten million was Roman Catholic. Roman Catholicism in Belarus was traditionally the "Polish faith," but Roman Catholic families have also produced most of history's outstanding Belarusian activists. Their problem has been to convince the Roman Catholic population that it too was Belarusian, rather than Polish or "from here." Roman Catholic priests have enjoyed great influence in Belarus since the Counter-Reformation. In the special conditions of independent Belarus, the issue was whether Roman Catholics would choose to identify themselves as Belarusians or as Poles. In early 1992 Pope John Paul II reined in the Polish priests.[25] That this was a question for the Vatican suggests that the Belarusian anxieties did not really concern national minorities as such. Although there were perhaps 215,000 Belarusians in Poland and 417,000 Poles in Belarus, the problem was not that these individuals formed political communities or made controversial demands. The issue was how Roman Catholics, at some future point, would define themselves. As Shushkevich understood, Belarus and speakers of Belarusian were still experiencing the shift from early modern to modern politics that we encountered in parts 1 and 2.[26]

Other anxieties of patriotic Belarusians could be eased by secular actors. The Polish-Belarusian state declaration, signed in October 1991, reduced fears that Poland would claim Belarusian lands, and marked the end of Belarusian claims on Polish territory. Meanwhile, Lithuanian efforts helped soften Belarusian revanchism. Lithuanian historians entered into a dialogue with their Belarusian colleagues over the succession of the old Grand Duchy of Lithuania. From these contacts emerged the idea that the Grand Duchy had two distinct successors, the modern Belarusian and Lithuanian states. In other words, Lithuanians helped Belarusians shift from an understanding of the Grand Duchy which was more historically accurate (large, multinational, territorially vague), to one which was more consistent with a world of modern states (small, mononational, territorially modest). To become less dangerous in the modern international system, the Belarusian national myth had to became less true to the early modern world. Although the Grand Duchy of Lithuania remained the universal retrospect of Belarusian national activists, Belarusian nationalists ceased to believe that Belarus had to expand to include Vil'nia.[27]

In 1992, in the wake of Belarusian independence, Polish eastern policy offered Belarus a treaty with an important neighbor, confirming existing borders and establishing clear principles of minority rights. These proposals were acceptable to all major parties: the revisionist Foreign Minister Krauchenka, the steady Speaker Shushkevich, and the communist Prime Minister Viacheslau Kiebich. When the treaty was initialed in April 1992, Polish Prime Minister Jan Olszewski (1930–) made the seemingly innocuous remark that "relations between our countries can serve as a model for relations among other countries in our region."[28] The simple fact that Poland and Belarus confirmed their frontier shortly after the disintegration of the Soviet Union was very important to the region. It conveyed to Minsk the norm that nation-states are to be built and secured within inherited borders, and signified that any Belarusian revanchism toward Lithuania would have no Polish partner. It told Lithuanians that Poland had no claims to the better part of the northeastern territories Poland had lost in 1939. Most important of all, it communicated to Russians that revanchist tendencies would have no western collaborator. By legally confirming 93 percent of its eastern border by mid-1992 (206 kilometers with Russia in May, 428 kilometers with Ukraine in May, and 605 kilometers with Belarus in June, with only the 91 kilometers with Lithuania remaining), Warsaw sent a clear signal that it had no interest in eastward expansion. In these ways, the quick signing of treaties with Ukraine and Belarus realized the eastern program of *Kultura*.

Skubiszewski's main contribution to the *Kultura* grand strategy was the use of "European standards" as a way to transfer Polish norms to the east. When Shushkevich signed the Belarusian-Polish treaty in Warsaw in June 1992, he connected relations with Poland to Belarus's European destiny, and accepted European standards as the best resolution to the problem of minorities. Belarus then opened its first embassy not in Moscow, but in Warsaw.[29] For the next eighteen months Poland offered Shushkevich and like-minded Belarusians a window on the West, helping Belarus to join regional institutions and initiating military cooperation. Polish officials were aware of the tenuous appeal of their twin attractions, support of national statehood and access to Europe, and were alarmed as Shushkevich's position weakened and Belarus's orientation shifted eastward. In November 1992, Prime Minister Suchocka put the matter quite directly during a visit to Minsk: "Poland is interested in the independence of Belarus and wishes to be one of the elements connecting Belarus to Europe."[30] This was impolitic, but it was the issue. Belarusian nationalists enjoyed some visible influence after the failed coup in Moscow of August 1991, when the conservative Belarusian Communist Party allowed the republic to declare independence as a way to protect its own position from reformers in Moscow. Belarusian activists imparted a national form to the new state: but they were unable to control the state apparatus, let alone win over the population. They only had about thirty months to achieve these daunting tasks. Democracy in Belarus put nationality on hold. The direct election of Aleksandr Lukashenka as president of Belarus in 1994 ended fruitful cooperation with Poland and began a dictatorship of Soviet nostalgia. The lasting success of the Polish policy of European standards toward Belarus was that it created a legal framework for good relations between the two states, before it was too late.

LITHUANIA, 1992–1993

Historical disputes concerning Vilnius were sharpest with Lithuania. In chapters 3, 4, and 5 we considered the state of war which prevailed between Lithuania and Poland between 1920 and 1938, after Poland seized Wilno; the Polish government's outrage when Stalin gave the city to Lithuania in 1939; the end of Polish Wilno in 1944–46; and the Lithuanization of Vilnius under Soviet rule. We have just seen that the Vilnius region was contested in the late 1980s and early 1990s by the Lithuanian national movement, the Polish minority in Lithuania, Soviet central authorities, and the Belorussian SSR. The Polish state (successor to the entity which had actually lost these territories in 1939) was the only party to renounce all claims. The Moscow putsch of 19 August 1991 removed two of these five contestants, as Moscow's manipulations ceased and Minsk's position changed. At the same time, the coup brought tensions among the Polish minority, the Polish state, and the Lithuanian national movement to their highest point.

Several leaders of the Polish minority greeted the August 1991 coup as the renaissance of the Soviet Union, and planned their revenge upon Lithuania.[31] They were not supported by the Polish state. On 26 August 1991 the Polish government formally recognized Lithuanian independence. On 4 September the Lithuanian government dissolved the regional governments where Poles constituted a majority. On 14 September Lithuanian and Polish negotiators failed once again to agree upon a common declaration. The Polish state insisted that Poles in Lithuania be allowed to elect new local authorities to replace pro-Soviet elites; Lithuanian authorities reserved the right to rule Vilnius and Šalčininkai regions indefinitely through ethnic Lithuanian bureaucrats. While regions with a Lithuanian majority were allowed to elect their own regional governments, Vilnius and Šalčininkai regions were singled out for administrative rule. Landsbergis, now speaker of the Lithuanian parliament and the most powerful politician in Lithuania, spoke of Polish "nationalism and expansionism."[32]

Skubiszewski only agreed to come to Vilnius and sign a declaration on good relations after a Lithuanian promise to hold elections in the Vilnius and Šalčininkai regions. The signing of the declaration in Vilnius revealed the difficulties of Skubiszewski's position. For his pains he was attacked from both sides, by the Lithuanian Right and by the Polish minority in Lithuania. A petition of Lithuanian parliamentarians protested that the declaration "legalized the results of aggression," since it did not condemn the occupation of Vilnius by Polish forces in 1920.[33] This is an excellent example of how a historical claim made by one national party, once it enters politics, will bring an unanticipated reaction from another. Poles recall that Poland lost Wilno as the result of the Molotov-Ribbentrop pact of 1939, which everyone, including Lithuanians, regards as aggression. Thus if one were truly concerned not to "legalize the results of aggression," one would be forced to challenge all of the borders created by the Molotov-Ribbentrop pact. So doing would, of course, imply that Vilnius was legally part of Poland. By releasing "1920" from the Pandora's box of history, the Lithuanian Right unwittingly set free "1939." Polish activists claimed that Skubiszewski had disarmed himself by avoiding the Second World War, and had come to Wilno "walking on his knees."[34] The Polish government, another wrote, "was willing to barter away the rights of Poles in Lithuania."[35]

Rather than allow historical debate to spread to Poland itself, Skubiszewski urged Lithuanian deputies to think of the future instead of the past, repeated his assurances that Poland had no territorial claims, and promised that there would be no second General Żeligowski.[36] His direct reference to the Polish general who seized Wilno in 1920 was meant to demonstrate an awareness of Lithuanian historical anxiety, as well as the desire to calm it. Nevertheless, Lithuania demanded an official Polish apology for 1920. This was unacceptable to Poland, in part because of the general objection to regulating history by way of diplomacy; in part because that particular interpretation of events was regarded as biased; and in part because the property rights of Poles in Lithuania depended upon the legality of interwar documents. More fundamentally, any state which accepts that its previous borders were illegal opens the possibility of all sorts of territorial claims from the outside, creating a dangerous precedent for itself—and for its neighbors. Had Poland renounced the legality of its interwar claim to Wilno, for example, Russians and Belarusians would have had further arguments to use against the contemporary Lithuanian state. It was obvious to Lithuanians that a retrospective Polish renunciation of Vilnius would have automatically confirmed Lithuania's claim. Belarusians and Russians would have seen the matter differently.

It is not especially interesting to show that the Lithuanian presentation of the events of 1920 was historically false. Vilnius was anything but an ethnically Lithuanian city in 1920, and its exclusion from Lithuania allowed the interwar state to function as a national state with small minorities. Independent Lithuania in 1939, and Soviet Lithuania in 1945, owed the city to Stalin. After the destruction of the city's main communities, the Jews and the Poles, Vilnius became Lithuanian in population under Soviet rule, by about 1980. (The Ponary forest, recalled by Mickiewicz as the mythical source of the city of Vilnius, was the final resting place of the Vilnius Jews murdered in 1941.) Treating these deep transformations as the "return" of Vilnius, Lithuanian nationalists could claim that Vilnius had always been a Lithuanian city. Nations construct histories as they come into being, destroying traditions that scholars interested in the actual course of events will have to reconstruct. This suggests the more interesting point. Any apology Poland offered for 1920 would have been deeply incoherent, since by the 1990s no one on either side remembered what had happened. Back in 1920 Lithuanian national activists knew perfectly well that there were almost no Lithuanians in Vilnius. Their claim to the city was historical and political. It took the education policies of interwar and Soviet Lithuania for people to "learn" that Vilnius was an ethnically Lithuanian city when it was seized by Poland in 1920. Likewise, in 1920 Piłsudski and Żeligowski annexed Wilno not as nationalist Poles, nor as enemies of Lithuania, but as Polish Lithuanians. They were operating not within the paradigm of "ethnic" nation-states, but imagining that the Grand Duchy of Lithuania could be resurrected as a federation. Seven decades later, these motives and identifications were forgotten, blurred into the larger Polish narrative of national victories and defeats. Between 1920 and 1992 the ethnic idea of nationhood won a rather complete victory in both Lithuania and Poland.

By the time independent Lithuanian and Polish states were free to revisit the Vilnius question in the 1990s, everyone reasoned from the modern assumption of one nation, one state. However, it was possible to draw at least two different conclusions from this understanding. On the one hand, it could be made to fit a Westphalian understanding of the international system, tempered by late twentieth-century notions of international law and European cooperation. This was Skubiszewski's approach. On the other hand, for those who accept the modern principle of one nation, one state can attempt to force others to accept their account of their past. The introduction of one national history into the world of politics is bound to summon its doppelgänger in the form of a neighbor's national history. Lithuanian foreign policy was to get Poles to reject their own (wrong) reading of 1920 and accept the Lithuanian one (even more wrong). Skubiszewski refused this approach, continuing to treat nation-states in terms of their future as states rather than their past as nations, and to offer a European future to Poland's eastern neighbors. This eventually worked, but this time Skubiszewski needed a push from Europe itself.

NATO

On the night of 24 August 1993, in Warsaw, an intoxicated Boris Yeltsin declared in writing that Polish membership in NATO would not harm the interests of the Russian Federation. Although Yeltsin looked a bit regretful the next day, and later recanted in Moscow, this began the international debate over NATO enlargement. As some Lithuanian politicians were very quick to notice, Polish membership in NATO would leave Lithuania as a tiny buffer state between NATO and Russia. Since Russian troops withdrew from Lithuania at this time, Lithuania found itself with somewhat more room for maneuver in its alliance policy. The NATO option realigned Lithuanian elite opinion, allowing the abandonment of historical claims on Poland. Lithuanian (ex-communist) socialists, in government since November 1992, opposed NATO enlargement but favored rapprochement with Poland. Their leader, President Algirdas Brazauskas (1932–), advocated equal distance between Russia and the West. Lithuanian national parties, now in opposition, favored NATO enlargement, but opposed rapprochement with Poland. In October 1993 the Right pressed NATO upon the socialist president, while demanding that the socialist government reimpose direct rule on the Polish minority and force Poland to apologize for 1920. As the debate progressed in November 1993, some nationalist politicians saw that it would be very hard to get both of these things. On 13 December 1993, the performance of nationalist Vladimir Zhirinovskii in Russian parliamentary elections provided a timely reminder that international politics is about survival as well as prestige. On 29 December, the Lithuanian parliament recommended that the government apply for NATO membership. On 4 January 1994 President Brazauskas did so.[37]

Even in a world where Russia seemed more threatening and NATO more welcoming, Lithuanian nationalists remained divided about Poland. The threshold Ukrainian national activists had crossed before 1991, that Poland should be treated as a friendly state rather than an unfriendly nation, was still to be crossed by Lithuanian national activists in late 1993. Former activists of Sąjūdis were divided. Only at the end of 1993 did Landsbergis change his mind about the desirability of a treaty with Poland without a condemnation of Żeligowski. The second most important activist of Sąjūdis, Romualdas Ozolas (1939–), like Landsbergis the head of a conservative party in 1993, opposed the treaty even in the new situation. A humanist intellectual, in 1990 he edited the Sąjūdis newspaper while sitting on the central committee of the Lithuanian Communist Party. After Lithuanian independence he took a special interest in the

Polish minority, using the issue to become one of the most popular politicians in Lithuania. When Lithuania signed a treaty with Poland that did not mention Żeligowski, Ozolas proclaimed that Poland regarded Lithuania as a "half-sovereign state." The treaty, he declared, was a "a strategic defeat."[38]

The decisive group were Lithuanian nationalists who had come to think in strategic terms and had some experience with Poland. These were people who, while yielding to no one in their suspicions of Poland in 1991, had changed their minds before 1993, and could make a case for cooperation when the time came. A key example is Audrius Butkevičius. He had been thinking in terms of preserving the Lithuanian state for some time: as the coordinator of nonviolent resistance within the Lithuanian national movement; then as director general of national defense of the unrecognized Lithuanian state; then as minister of defense of independent Lithuania. He regarded the events of 1920 in typical Lithuanian terms, and in his official capacity initially treated Poland as a threat. In November 1991, while there were still thirty-five thousand Soviet troops in his country, Butkevičius had called Poland "the greatest security threat to Lithuania." Experience with Polish policy and NATO changed his mind. By July 1993, having accepted a gift of Polish arms, Butkevičius called the gesture "the greatest sign of trust that can be shown."[39] When the NATO question opened in late August 1993, Butkevičius proposed that Lithuania join Poland in applying to NATO. His position, both pro-Poland and pro-NATO, conquered the field at a time when public opinion and most of the Right (in opposition) was anti-Poland but pro-NATO, and most of the Left (in government) was pro-Poland but anti-NATO.

Once this position became a consensus, all difficulties in treaty negotiations were quickly resolved. Leaders of the Left, President Brazauskas in particular, mollified Landsbergis and the Right by recalling the Lithuanian version of prewar history at ceremonial occasions surrounding the signing of the treaty in April 1994. While accepting historical argumentation, they sought to subtly shift its meaning. They spoke of the point of view of future historians, of the historical reconciliations achieved in Europe after the Second World War, and of the tragic history of small nations whose quarrels invited the attention of outside powers.[40] This rhetoric signaled and effected a transition in the policy of the new Lithuanian state. This was the moment in the history of independent Lithuania when state interests in the future first took priority over national interests in the past. It was hastened by a Polish policy which was patient in dealing with Lithuanian nationalism, and fortunate in its support by European institutions. In October 1994, the Lithuanian parliament ratified the treaty 91–19–8, having watched the Polish parliament ratify the treaty earlier the same day by a vote of 295–0.

POLAND, 1992–1993

The unanimity of the Polish vote is striking. Lithuania had pursued an unusual foreign policy toward Poland; the fate of the Polish minority in Lithuania had aroused parliamentary interest on both the right and the left; Poland was renouncing all claims about the special status of Poles in Lithuania; Poland was finalizing an eastern frontier that was a Soviet creation; Poland was renouncing all claims to Wilno. The 295–0 vote and the standing ovation that followed bear witness to the prevalence of political calculation over patriotic nostalgia in the Polish parliament, and to the channeling of Polish nostalgia toward the support of modern Lithuania. This was part of the *Kultura* grand strategy, as implemented by Skubiszewski.

Between 1989 and 1993, during Skubiszewski's four years as foreign minister in center-right governments, he lost only one parliamentary vote, and that on a question of no practical significance. To say that Skubiszewski served during three national electoral campaigns and in four coalition governments is to understate the extreme fluidity of the environment within which he worked. In this light, the general insulation of foreign policy from domestic politics is striking.[41] Given the controversies in the Ukrainian, Lithuanian, and Belarusian parliaments over these countries' rapprochements with Poland, it is extraordinary that Poland itself pursued the policies of two tracks and European standards with no meaningful parliamentary opposition. History was no more forgotten by Polish than by Ukrainian, Lithuanian, or Belarusian public opinion: Ukrainians remained the most feared of Poland's neighbors, and Polish schoolchildren still learned the first line of *Pan Tadeusz,* "Lithuania! My fatherland!" by heart.[42]

The apparent separation of eastern policy from domestic politics was in fact a conscious recognition of the difference between state interests and national memories. Even as the Solidarity movement of the 1990s fragmented into rival parties, the 1980s traditions of solidarity with eastern neighbors held.[43] This consensus embraced all of the center-right post-Solidarity parties that governed between 1989 and 1993, with the exception of the Christian-National Union (which gained 8.7 percent of the vote in 1991, and which participated in governments until 1993). Deputies and ministers from this party were the only ones to challenge Skubiszewski's eastern policy. Christian-National Union politicians advocated "reciprocity" in relations with eastern neighbors: that Poland demand concessions on the basis of Polish perceptions that Polish minorities abroad were treated worse than minorities within Poland, that Poland suspend relations with Ukraine until the Ukrainian state apologized for the actions of the UPA in the 1940s.[44] These would have been obvious contraventions of the policy of European standards.[45]

The notions that Ukraine, Belarus, and Lithuania were equal nation-states, that the existence of these states was in Poland's interests, that future interests should be placed above historical disagreements, that Poland should apologize as well as seek apologies, dominated parliamentary debates. The number of times a deputy with roots in Poland's lost eastern territories made special claims based upon personal experience can be numbered on the fingers of one hand. The Polish Right generally supported the independence of Poland's eastern neighbors.[46] Although the parliament's lower house, the Sejm, was slow to produce legislation on minorities, Jacek Kuroń (then the most popular politician in Poland) acted as informal representative of their interests.[47] When necessary, Foreign Minister Skubiszewski could treat eastern and minority policy as flowing naturally from western policy. When Polish parliamentarians pressed for more aggressive protection of Polish minorities abroad, Skubiszewski scolded them for not knowing European standards. Since the goal of joining European institutions was shared across most of the political spectrum, and among most (if not quite all) ministers of the Solidarity governments of 1992 and 1993, this argument was very effective.[48]

Skubiszewski enjoyed the support of five prime ministers and two presidents: Wojciech Jaruzelski and Lech Wałęsa. Jaruzelski, president until December 1990, was not only the communist general who had implemented martial law in 1981, he was also an old soldier who had helped forcibly resettle Ukrainians in 1947. In office, his neutrality in questions of Polish foreign policy was part of his impressive contribution to Polish democracy after 1989. Solidarity's leader, Lech Wałęsa, was president for the rest of Skubiszewski's tenure. Although Wałęsa threw a wrench in the works with his proposals for a "second NATO" and his untoward contacts with Moscow, he exploited none of the national issues which might have undermined the Skubiszewski's policy. Wałęsa worked to keep the Ukrainian issue out of domestic elections, and in the critical parliamentary elections of 1989 supported a Ukrainian candidate as local communists played the national card. In visits to Lithuania, Belarus, and Ukraine, President Wałęsa stressed that Poland had no territorial claims, and told Polish minorities to regard themselves as citizens of the countries where they resided.⁴⁹ Since presidents elsewhere in postcommunist Europe—Yugoslavia and Russia most notably—used the issues of borders and diasporas to consolidate their power, this is worthy of note.

Although Skubiszewski was not a charismatic figure, none of the major media treated him as a target. To some extent, one can even say that his eastern policy was supported by the press. *Gazeta Wyborcza,* which began as an electoral newsletter for Solidarity in 1989, became the most popular newspaper in Poland. Its editor, Adam Michnik, was an ally of Jerzy Giedroyc, a student of the *Kultura* program, and a friend of Ukrainian and Lithuanian national movements. As the leading figure in the Polish media, he favored compromise and forgiveness. Although Michnik's approach was often rejected, his newspaper set the parameters of debate. As with the press, so with the Roman Catholic Church. While (for example) the Serbian Orthodox Church was calling upon its believers to fight for territory, the Polish Church followed a more peaceable course. True, throughout the 1990s Roman Catholic parishes destroyed the remnants of Ukrainian settlement in southeastern Poland, and popular clerics spread anti-Semitism and xenophobia from the pulpit and over the radio. Yet the ultimate head of the Polish Church, both in the formal hierarchy and the hearts of believers, was the Polish Pope, Karol Wojtyła, John Paul II. Wojtyła, like Michnik, had been engaged in eastern reconciliation since the 1970s. His papal message of love and toleration, although not always heeded, was patiently expressed. As the first Slavic pope, as the first pope to pronounce sermons in Lithuanian, Belarusian, Russian, and Ukrainian (as well as Polish), John Paul II set an example which was difficult to follow but impossible to misunderstand.

By the end of Skubiszewski's term in late 1993, the elite consensus for an eastern grand strategy was the popular wisdom as well, as Poles distinguished between lost national territories and present state interests.⁵⁰ With the right policy in place, it proved entirely possible for large elements of Polish society to be nostalgic for the Lithuanian fatherland, fearful of the Ukrainian borderland, while concerned most of all for the security of a Polish homeland. The consolidation of such attitudes was tantamount to the success of a particular variety of modern Polish nationality, concerned not with extending Polish power, spreading Polish culture, or restoring Polish statehood, but with preserving a Polish nation-state within its present frontiers.

Chapter 14 Envoi: Returns to Europe

Along with Poland's geographical position, reconciliation with Germany, and domestic reforms, its eastern policy prepared the way for integration with European and Atlantic institutions. The first clear signal that NATO would admit new members was provided by U.S. President Bill Clinton's visit to Prague in January 1994. The Clinton Administration began to campaign for enlargement in autumn 1994. The European Union openly considered an eastward enlargement at the Essen Summit of the European Council in December 1994. In both cases it was understood that Poland would be among the first states considered for accession. This redefinition of Poland's international position by the West altered its image in the East. Between 1989 and 1991, when Poland offered its eastern neighbors recognition, all of them were interested. In 1992 and 1993, when Poland offered European standards, some were more interested than others. When, after 1994, what Poland had to offer its neighbors was Europe itself, the split widened. Those among Poland's eastern neighbors which had become more or less clearly defined nation-states with European aspirations reacted positively (Lithuania and Ukraine), and those that had not reacted negatively (Belarus and Russia). These orientations were due to the domestic politics of these four countries, over which Poland and other outside actors exerted decreasing influence.[1]

The late 1980s and early 1990s were a special moment in European history, when Polish diplomats and intellectuals could believe that their model of liberation and development could serve their neighbors. When the issue was national sovereignty, Poland did provide such an example. Once the issue became success in particular political, economic, and cultural transformations, the analogy with Poland weakened.[2] Poland's postcommunist governments of 1994–97 failed to respond to these changes, which also limited the reach of more ambitious Solidarity governments after 1997.[3] After 1994, Poland's eastern policy became an extension of its western policy. The problems of this approach were most evident in relations with Russia.

RUSSIA AND BELARUS

Events of 1993 had transformed the image of Russia in Poland. President Yeltsin, having condoned Poland's NATO's candidacy in August, changed his mind in September. In October, his troops stormed the Russian parliament. This caught the attention of Poland's postcommunist socialists, who had just won a democratic election and were about to form a parliamentary majority. In December, Vladimir Zhirinovskii's nationalist Liberal Democratic party won more votes in the Russian parliamentary elections than any other. Zhirinovskii was known for his anti-Polish rhetoric ("whore of NATO," which had a heady career, may have been his coinage). This caught the attention of Polish society as a whole. In January 1994, 70 percent of Poles surveyed believed that Russia posed a military threat to Poland, the highest number since 1989, and significantly higher (for the first time) than the comparable figure for Ukraine.[4]

Yeltsin's Russia, which had never developed a policy toward Poland, treated Poland within the rhetorical categories of the NATO propaganda war. Until it became clear that NATO would enlarge despite Russian opposition, Moscow essentially ignored Warsaw. This attitude changed only after the U.S. Senate gave its advice and consent to NATO enlargement on 30 April 1998. At that point, Russian-Polish relations returned to life. Foreign Minister Bronisław Geremek (1932–) and President Aleksander Kwaśniewski were both greeted with considerable decorum in Moscow in 1998.[5] A Russian foreign minister visited Warsaw for the first time in 2000. Yeltsin's successor, Vladimir Putin, travelled to Poland in 2002. Opposition to NATO enlargement had been a matter of elite rather than public opinion in Russia, so such a volte-face was easy for Russian authorities. NATO enlargement did not even change the basically favorable attitude of the Russian populace to the United States.[6] There was no great hostility toward Poland or its membership in NATO among Russian voters. In the late 1990s, Russians ranked Poland as the most stable state in Eastern Europe, and a stunning 56 percent believed that Poland should be invited to mediate in ethnic conflicts within the Russian Federation.[7] Poland's eastern policy and domestic successes had changed the perceptions of the Russian people.

Like official Moscow, official Minsk resisted Polish overtures after 1994. Stanislau Shushkevich, the compromising Belarusian patriot, was pushed from power. Even during his period as speaker of parliament, most policy was set by the communist Prime Minister Kiebich, the country's leading newspaper was called "Soviet Belorussia," and the local KGB not only still acted like the KGB, it was still called the KGB.[8] Both Shushkevich and Kiebich, along with the national activist Zyanon Pazniak, were crushed in Belarus's July 1994 presidential elections by a young and inexperienced anticorruption activist, Aleksandr Lukashenka. This was the work of democracy: Lukashenka was not the candidate of the communist establishment, and his decisive defeat of Kiebich, Shushkevich, and Paznyak demonstrated that Belarusians wanted someone new.

President Lukashenka destroyed the democratic institutions and the national symbols of the young Belarusian state. In April 1995, he expelled nationalist deputies from the parliament, encouraged the others to ratify a treaty with Russia, and invited Russia to protect Belarus's border with Poland. In May 1995 he won a national referendum, making Russian an official language of the Belarusian state and removing Belarusian national symbols from state insignia. His bodyguard removed the Belarusian colors from the presidential compound, tore the flag into pieces, and gave them away as souvenirs. In November 1996 Lukashenka won another referendum, thereby extending his own rule and disempowering the legislature and judiciary. This plebiscite was carried out in farcical conditions, and provoked a joint appeal from Poland, Lithuania, and Ukraine. Nevertheless, its results reflected the preferences of most Belarusians for a neo-Soviet order. Lukashenka's domestic policy of Russification did not make him a Russian, but it did create immense problems for aspiring Belarusian patriots. When he was elected, 80 percent of first-graders studied in Belarusian; three years later, the figure had fallen to 7 percent.[9] By the end of the decade, there was only one Belarusian school in Minsk, the Belarusian capital.

This was a president who whitewashed Stalinist terror, banned the use of schoolbooks printed after the Soviet period, tore up contracts between Belarusian firms and Western investors, and "spit on the International Monetary Fund." As he said himself, "I will not be leading my people to the civilized world," since "Belarusian values have nothing in common with Western values." He called Belarusian patriots "fascists," the sort of people "who will break into your homes and rape your wives and daughters." He imprisoned his opponents, and then began to make them disappear.[10] He appealed to religious themes as an "Orthodox atheist," and opposed foreign "Western influences" such as Roman Catholicism, the religion of two million Belarusians or a fifth of the population. Lukashenka portrayed Poland as both a traditional Catholic threat, and as the vanguard of NATO. He claimed that Solidarity and the CIA were planning a coup in Minsk. He promised not to let western Belarus, where the Polish minority was concentrated, become a second Yugoslavia, and claimed that Polish aggression necessitated a Slavic union with Russia.[11] Lukashenka's foreign policy was pro-Russian, in the sense that he wished to gain as much as possible from the idea of a union with Russia.

Polish policy engaged the society more than the state. The beleaguered Belarusian national movement, anti-Polish at the beginning of the 1990s, was pro-Polish by the end of the decade. The Polish example taught oppositionists to think in terms of the rescue of a nation-state, rather than a revival of historic entities. After Solidarity's return to government in 1997, Warsaw engaged the Belarusian opposition, while trying to avoid the isolation of official Belarus from Europe. This was a return to the two-track policy of 1989–91, this time on the scale of Belarus rather than the entire Soviet Union. It included the quiet third track of informal contacts, which included aging Solidarity activists and dozens of new Polish nongovernmental organizations. While Belarusian activists had regarded this approach with suspicion the first time around, by the late 1990s such initiatives were welcome.[12] Whether they made any difference in the consolidation of Belarusian nationality is another question.

POLAND AND BELARUS

Although most Belarusians do not accept a modern form of the national idea, its future political success is certainly possible. The Belarusian population is not Russian, even if Russian is the language of power and culture. According to the 1989 Soviet census, 78 percent of the adult inhabitants of the Belorussian SSR called themselves Belarusian, 13 percent Russian, and 4 percent Polish. The 1999 census carried out by the Lukashenka regime found the proportion of Belaru-

sians had increased to 81 percent, while the proportion of Russians had fallen to
11 percent. The share of Poles remained about the same.[13] It is not Belarusian
self-identification, but the modern unions of "literary language-folk language"
and "language-nation-state" that Belarusian citizens find alien. We have attended to some of the limitations of Belarusian national politics. Since the
nineteenth century, Belarusian national activists have seen themselves as the in-
heritors of the territorial center, the language, and the traditions of the Grand
Duchy of Lithuania. As we have seen, the traditions of the Grand Duchy were
altered beyond recognition by Lithuanian and Polish national movements, as
well as Russian imperial and Soviet states. They have changed least perhaps in
the lands we now call Belarus. This loyalty to tradition is the problem.

Nationalism claims to be about continuity. In fact it must involve a reconstruction of early modern political traditions sufficiently radical to allow the
masses to understand and wish to enter a redefined political community. Nationalists maintain that old ethnic groups become modern nations, but the Belarusian case proves that political action must rework political tradition for either notion to make sense. If we believe in "ethnic groups," we must accept that
Belarusians were the "dominant ethnic group" of the old Grand Duchy of Lithuania. In 1795 a majority of individuals within the Grand Duchy spoke what we
would call Belarusian dialects. In 1895 the same can be said of the five Belarusian provinces of the Russian empire, and in 1995 for the Republic of Belarus.
Nevertheless, this "group" never became the vehicle for modern national politics. Modern Lithuanian and Polish nationalists have shown us that national
ideologies succeeded insofar as they transformed the Grand Duchy's legacies.
They took Lithuania's name in vain, a sure sign of the mixture of reverence and
forgetfulness characteristic of modern nationalism. The reorientation of Belarusian national activists toward the nation-state in the late 1990s therefore
bodes ill for the generational continuity of early modern Lithuanian traditions,
but well for the arrival of a third modern nationalism on early modern Lithuanian territories. Where modern Lithuanian and Polish nationalism have succeeded, modern Belarusian nationalism might eventually succeed as well.

Political action requires the right institutional, social, and cultural circumstances. Belarusian activists of the 1990s said, anachronistically, that the Belarusian nation "lost" assets such as the independence of the Grand Duchy in
the sixteenth century; the Chancery Slavonic language in the eighteenth; the
Uniate Church and poetry of Mickiewicz in the nineteenth; the city of Vil'nia
and the very name "Lithuania" in the twentieth. If we drop the teleology and
keep the contingency—drop the word "bad" but keep the word "luck"—we

see the importance of events beyond the control of national activists and local populations. These "losses" were junctures where circumstances did not favor the consolidation of a modern Belarusian national idea, movement, or state. Yet the most paradoxical "loss" is one that no national activist will mention: that Belarus did not enjoy the advantages of partition.

National histories present partition as a dismemberment of the national body. In fact, national activists divided by a state boundary enjoy certain advantages. Partition creates the possibility that one empire will use a national movement against another with the unintended consequence that the national movement prospers. Partition allows activists of the same nation but different empires to share ideas. A national movement within one empire may copy the tactics of other national movements within that same empire, then transfer them to conationals across the border. As we have seen, the division of Lithuanians and Ukrainians among nineteenth-century empires allowed for conversations with immigrants, visions of unification, and smuggling of books. During the nineteenth century, all of what is now Belarus was part of the Russian empire. Only for two decades in the twentieth century was Belarus divided: between Poland and the Soviet Union, between the world wars. Even though Stalin exterminated the Belarusian intelligentsia, and Poland closed every Belarusian school, this time of partition was a moment of national achievement.

Modern nationality involves the unity of the literary with the vernacular language, which in Eastern Europe means the education of the peasantry and the reorientation of the intelligentsia. The site for this convergence is the city, ideally a growing national capital. Belarusians' desired capital Vil'nia became a Polish Wilno in 1920 when Poland won a war with Bolshevik Russia; it became a Lithuanian Vilnius after Stalin granted the city to Soviet Lithuania in 1945. Belarusians' eventual capital Minsk, historically less important to the national cause than Vil'nia, became Soviet after Poland declined to incorporate it in 1921. Under Soviet rule Minsk became the one Belarusian city of any size, and after the Second World War a locus of Russification. Belarusian activists sorely missed medium-sized cities, the usual testing grounds for national revivals not yet ready to play in "deracinated" capitals. Modern nationality also presupposes a world of nations, each with a distinct high culture and a distinct name. As part 1 demonstrated, the early modern politonym "Lithuanian" became a modern ethnonym, and the Romantic poet Mickiewicz became a bard of modern Polish and (to a lesser extent) Lithuanian nationalisms. The Lukashenka regime of the 1990s was pleased to celebrate Mickiewicz as a vaguely Belarusian figure, just as the Soviet regime once endorsed him as a friend of Pushkin and the toiling masses. Only when Mickiewicz is (falsely) presented in Minsk as a modern Belarusian, as he is today portrayed (falsely) in Warsaw or Vilnius as a modern Pole or Lithuanian, will we have a sign that Belarusian nationalism has arrived.

The historical maneuvers that build modern nations are carried out by elites created in definable institutional circumstances. Here we recognize the most serious barrier to a Belarusian national revival: the scale of destruction in Belarus during Stalin's purges of the 1930s and during the Second World War. Stalin murdered most of the Belarusian intelligentsia in the late 1930s. One in four inhabitants of the territory of the Belorussian SSR in 1941 was dead by 1945. The Germans destroyed Minsk, its university, and its academy of sciences. Minsk was rebuilt in an era of Russification, its astonishing postwar growth creating a massive Russophone capital. There was one telling move in the opposite direction: the incorporation of formerly Polish territories in 1945.[14] The western expansion of the Belorussian SSR encompassed millions of people with different political experiences, and thousands of people with distinct connections to traditional institutions. The Uniate Church, for example, was established under the old Commonwealth in 1596. Although there was no Uniate Church in Soviet Belarus, it had been reestablished in interwar Poland. Thousands of Neo-Uniates from western Belarus became Soviet citizens after 1945. Just as many Belarusian activists in the 1880s and 1890s were of Roman Catholic background, so in the 1980s and 1990s many had some connection to these formerly Polish territories. Pazniak, the leader of the Belarusian National Front, was the grandson of a Belarusian politician active in interwar Polish Wilno. Pazniak's grandfather was among the hundreds of thousands of Belarusians murdered at Kuropaty and similar sites. Pazniak's ideas of Belarusian nationalism were consistent with an elite tradition, but alien to the Belarusian population educated in Soviet schools.[15]

Here a comparison between Soviet Belarus and Soviet Lithuania is instructive. Postwar Soviet policies allowed for an ethnic Lithuanian nation, while pushing rival Belarusian conceptions toward oblivion. Right after the war, an interwar Lithuanian communist took the reins in the Lithuanian SSR, and a Lithuanian-language university was established in Vilnius. The Belarusian Communist Party was meanwhile Russified, and wartime suffering became the basis of standard Soviet Belorussian history. By 1970, when a modern narrative of Lithuanian history was thoroughly institutionalized, national history had all but disappeared from Belarusian curricula. By 1980, when most schools in Vilnius taught in Lithuanian, not a single school in Minsk taught in Belarusian.

During the Gorbachev period of the late 1980s, the Belarusian national movement began with the discovery of basic facts, literally unearthing of the remains of Belarusians killed by the NKVD. The basic facts of Lithuanian history had long before been absorbed by Lithuanian society as a whole. The Belarusian narrative of descent from the Grand Duchy of Lithuania was by then the province of a very small number of educated elites. The Lithuanian version was known to most Lithuanians.[16]

Modern Belarusian nationalism, if it arrives, will probably involve a mythical notion of the Grand Duchy of Lithuania. This old idea will have to be reconstructed to account for the Orthodox religion and Soviet historical memory of the majority of the Belarusian population. Such a synthesis, like the appearance of Mickiewicz as a Belarusian nationalist, would be a sign of the modern turn of the Belarusian national idea. Some long-term trends speak in favor of such a possibility. If contingent historical facts can hinder national movements, they can also help them. Soviet Belarus, a small sliver of territory in 1922, was enlarged in 1923, 1924, 1926, and 1939. As a result, independent Belarus has generous and coherent frontiers. After the collapse of the Soviet Union in 1991, independent Belarus had most of the attributes of a sovereign state. In many respects the Belarusian state of the 1990s functioned better than its Ukrainian or Russian counterparts. Although Lukashenka was a bizarre dictator who hated Belarusian patriotism and promised to unite his country with Russia, his term in fact preserved a sovereign Belarusian state. For the first time, young people came of age in an independent Belarus, and travelers carried a Belarusian passport. For the first time, Belarusian national activists could envision capturing a state for an emerging nation. Independent Lithuania, Poland, and Ukraine all favored Belarusian statehood, also a historical novelty. Absent decisive Russian intervention, the emergence of a Belarusian nation is not to be excluded.

LITHUANIA, POLAND, AND EUROPE

Over the course of the 1990s, Lithuanians came to see Poland as a modern state, rather than as the source of the fatally attractive civilization of the era of national rebirth. This was the price of Polish political success: the realization that Polish culture, the height of achievement in much of early modern Eastern Europe, and a mark of distinction in Eastern Europe through the nineteenth century, was no longer terribly attractive. This was, incidentally, a dilemma inherent in modern Polish nationalism. The historical appeal of Polish civilization was its elite character; in making of Polishness a folk nationalism, nationalists destroyed its appeal. Polish culture could be attractive horizontally—to neighboring elites—or vertically—to the peasants and workers—but it could not be both at the same time. By averting crises in the early 1990s, Polish eastern policy allowed this long-term trend to take hold.

Once Lithuania and Poland ratified their treaty in 1994, political relations improved dramatically. Once the issue of an apology for the Polish seizure of Vilnius in 1920 was forced from the agenda, it became apparent that Poland and Lithuania had no strategic differences. Poland was seen as the road to Europe by the Lithuanian Right and the Lithuanian Left, and all Lithuanian governments and presidents treated it as such. Lithuanian and Polish parliaments, governments, and presidents institutionalized joint committees. Incidents involving the Polish minority in Lithuania were resolved institutionally, the Polish side invariably invoking European standards and the value of Polish help in European integration. In these ways, Lithuania and Poland approximated the preemptive dispute resolution characteristic of the EU, which both had applied to join. Poland but not Lithuania was included in the first wave of negotiating countries. As it became clearer in 1995–97 that Poland (but not Lithuania) would join NATO in the first wave of enlargement, Poland's "European" form of leverage only became stronger. One 1998 newspaper headline captured the issue well: "What the wife has to do with NATO and visas."[17] The answer: the Lithuanian and Polish languages have different suffixes to indicate female sex; Poles in Lithuania wished for the Polish suffix to appear in official documents such as passports; the Lithuanian government refused; then the Polish state applied the "European" leverage conferred by its closer association with NATO and the EU.

Poland's demands stayed within the realm of cultural rights enumerated in the 1994 treaty. Polish officials stressed that they regarded Poles in Lithuania as citizens of Lithuania. Because EU and NATO membership were so highly valued in Lithuania, and Polish support of Lithuanian membership so vocal in international forums, limited Polish advocacy of the minority led to little resentment.[18] President Algirdas Brazauskas said as early as 1996 that relations with Poland were the best they had been in the history of modern statehood. The Lithuanian Right, having returned to power, treated Poland very differently than it had in the early 1990s. The very foreign minister who had presided over the policy of demanding apologies called Poland Lithuania's "most important strategic partner."[19] By the end of the decade, Vytautas Landsbergis himself was treating the Lublin Union of 1569 between Poland and Lithuania as a positive event, an instance of "Lithuanian-Polish pragmatism."[20] As we have seen, the 1569 Lublin Union was portrayed as the tombstone of the Lithuanian nation by Lithuanian national activists from the 1880s through the 1990s. This new interpretation, by the most important Lithuanian nationalist of his time, suggests a more secure Lithuanian identity. Poland was no longer a hostile nation, to be understood in historical terms, but a neighboring state, to be understood in the categories of interests. The task of modernizing nationalists, the subversion of the traditional elite culture, yielded to the task of modern statesmen, the protection of existing national institutions.

UKRAINE, POLAND, AND EUROPE

Poland's reconciliation with Ukraine was spectacular. By the mid-1990s, anti-Polish opinions in Ukrainian society were almost entirely absent. Of course, whereas most Poles have some strong view about Ukraine drawn from contact with western Ukraine, most central, eastern and southern Ukrainians never had strong feelings toward Poland. Ukraine is a country as big as France, with fifty million inhabitants, and a disorientingly thorough history of suffering in the twentieth century. The horrible national conflicts discussed in chapters 8 through 10, although very important to West Ukrainians, made no impression on perhaps 80 percent of the population. After all, the cleansings of the 1940s are events of a lesser order than the famine of 1933 or the terrible civilian and military losses of the Second World War. Yet the positive image of Poland which developed among Kyiv elites was a new development, easily traced to Polish policy. Also impressive was the reversal among West Ukrainian patriots, too few to consistently determine policy, but numerous enough to sabotage a policy which concerned them directly. The Right, and even much of the extreme Right, was quickly convinced that Poland was an ally of Ukrainian independence.[21]

1993 and 1994 had been disappointing years for Ukrainian president Leonid Kravchuk and his patriotic advisors, as it became clear that Poland would not be an ally in the literal sense, and that postcommunist Polish governments (1993–97) were divided over whether priority was to be accorded to Ukraine or Russia. Kravchuk was replaced by Leonid Kuchma in 1994, to the general expectation that Ukraine would then reorient its foreign policy to Russia. In the event, Kuchma continued during his first term (1994–99) a foreign policy of integration with Western institutions. Integration with the EU was very popular in Ukraine, integration with NATO very unpopular; the Kuchma regime first loudly pursued the one, and then, more quietly, the other.[22] As it happened, the transfer of power from Kravchuk to Kuchma coincided with an important shift of U.S. policy toward Ukraine. The U.S.-Ukrainian-Russian Trilateral Statement of January 1994 had provided for the transfer of all nuclear weapons from Ukraine to Russia, thereby removing the main impediment to U.S. support for Ukraine. Support for Ukrainian statehood became a goal of American foreign policy.

That same month, January 1994, NATO announced its Partnership for Peace. Designed to appease East European candidates for NATO membership and mollify opponents of enlargement in Moscow, the Partnership failed to slow the enlargement debate. In 1994, however, it allowed Poland to draw favorable attention from the West for an eastern policy already in place. Poland offered Ukraine military cooperation within the framework of the Partnership, as the only one of Ukraine's neighbors to do so. The most radical plan was for a Ukrainian-Polish peacekeeping battalion, proposed in 1995, created in 1997, and dispatched by NATO to Kosovo in 2000. Ukrainian President Kuchma's first major overture to Poland was qualified support for Polish membership in NATO in June 1996. In Warsaw, he declared that "We regard NATO not as a defensive alliance, but as a mechanism of collective security, which unites democratic countries," emphasizing that he saw "no threat to Ukraine in connection with the enlargement of NATO."[23] Poland then supported a special NATO charter for Ukraine, along the same lines as the one that Russia was to receive. The NATO-Ukrainian charter was signed on 9 July 1997.[24] The next day U.S. President Bill Clinton congratulated cheering crowds in Warsaw on Poland's forthcoming membership in NATO.

From 1995, Polish President Kwaśniewski and Ukrainian President Kuchma presided over a formal Ukrainian-Polish historical reconciliation. Their great achievement was the reconciliation declaration signed in Kyiv in May 1997. It listed wrongs done by each nation to the other, including Operation Vistula and the terror in Volhynia, and expressed the need for mutual forgiveness.[25] Kwaśniewski and Kuchma also met regularly at historically significant sites, seeking to symbolically unravel tangled threads of memory. They laid wreaths at a cemetery in L'viv where Polish soldiers who fought against the West Ukrainian Republic in 1918–19 are buried; they unveiled a monument to the Ukrainians imprisoned in the Polish concentration camp at Jaworzno in the 1940s; they laid the foundation stone at an ecumenical cemetery at Kharkiv where Polish officers murdered at Stalin's orders rest; and they dedicated a memorial to the Ukrainian soldiers of the Ukrainian National Republic who died defending Ukrainian and Polish independence during the 1919–20 war with Bolshevik Russia.

Critics in Kyiv contended that such a reconciliation was unnecessary, since Poland and Ukraine enjoyed good relations as states. This overlooked the controversies between West Ukrainians and Poles which might have prevented political rapprochement. Critics in Warsaw made the point that one cannot decree historical reconciliation, and that meetings of presidents do little to change public opinion.[26] There is something to this, of course. Yet it disregards the fact that the more direct approaches to history tried in the early 1990s ended in fiasco. Had Ukraine or Poland chosen to emphasize the 1940s in the way that Lithuania emphasized the 1920s, political accord would have been delayed for years, at a time crucial to the sovereignty and security of both states. 1991 and 1992 showed that disagreements about the mutual ethnic cleansing of the 1940s would not be resolved quickly, but also that interstate relations could be established without prior agreement on historical issues. Precisely because Operation Vistula and the Volhynian terror were marginalized from state-to-state relations in the early 1990s, the two presidents could address them in the late 1990s on a firm foundation of legal agreements and political concord. During the first half of the decade, Poles and Ukrainians had agreed to "leave history to the historians" in the mutual interest of securing the state. In the second half of the decade, after issues of recognition, borders, and minorities were resolved, discussions of history could demonstrate the depth of Polish-Ukrainian rapprochement.

From 1996, the exceptional frequency, seriousness, and ceremoniousness of presidential meetings sent a clear signal to domestic political actors that they had little to be gained by exploiting history.[27] The lightest gestures were resonant. When Kwaśniewski mentioned that he met with Kuchma so often that his wife was jealous, he was reminding Poles that his wife's family had been cleansed from Volhynia by the UPA, and that the enterprise of reconciliation was mindful of such memories. When he remarked that his Ukrainian policy was approved by his father-in-law, he was turning a generation's memory of suffering to the service of future security.[28] (By the same token, the fact that Kwaśniewski was visibly drunk in Kharkiv undermined his personal attempt to communicate a historical vision of reconciliation.) There was a long way to go when this initiative of historical reconciliation was undertaken. Opinion polls of 1995 indicated that while levels of Polish sympathy to Germans had increased from 23 percent of respondents in 1993 to 43 percent in 1996, levels of sympathy towards Ukrainians increased from 12 percent to only 16 percent during the same period.[29] As Jacek Kuroń described elite opinion in 1997: "If you put an average Polish intellectual and an average German intellectual at a table and ask them to agree upon a version of Polish-German history, they will do so. There will of course arise certain differences, but it will prove possible to agree upon a common position. But if you sit down an average Polish intellectual with an average Ukrainian intellectual, they will tell each other exactly contradictory and irreconcilable different versions of history."[30] Contradictory, to be sure. But irreconcilable? By 1999 there was some reason to believe that historical reconciliation, in both the figurative and literal senses, was possible.

The central disagreements concerned the ethnic cleansings of the 1940s. As we have seen, these events did much to spread modern conceptions of nationality in Poland and western Ukraine. After all, the Polish Home Army founded its Volhynian division in 1943 as a result of ethnic cleansing by Ukrainian nationalists. Ukrainians in Poland were forcibly resettled by the Polish communist regime in 1947. We have discussed Volhynian Poles, and Polish Ukrainians, as the groups most clearly nationalized by war and ethnic cleansing. In the Poland of the 1990s, veterans of this Volhynian Home Army division were one of the nongovernmental organizations most concerned with preserving the memory of the Volhynian massacres of 1943, while the Union of Ukrainians in Poland regarded its main task as gaining reparations for Ukrainians who lost their homes in 1947. These were special interest groups of (collectively) the cleansed and (in individual cases) the cleansers. It is a polite understatement to say that these groups had opposing views of history, demands for justice, and political agendas.[31]

One might think that these two groups would be unlikely to gather together the historians who populate the cliché of Polish eastern policy: "leave history to the historians." In fact, the World Union of Home Army Soldiers and the Union of Ukrainians in Poland did just that: they found historians to write the hardest sort of history, the history of mutual ethnic cleansing. The historians recruited hailed from institutions not known for their soft line: the Polish Military Historical Institute in Warsaw (the Polish military carried out ethnic cleansings in 1945–47), and the Volhynian State University in L'utsk (in the heart of the territories cleansed by Ukrainian insurgents in 1943). The site of confrontation was the scholarly conference. These two nongovernmental organizations, and these two state institutions of higher learning, organized a series of seminars on Ukrainian-Polish relations. The seminars' format required comparative work: on each subject a Polish and a Ukrainian scholar delivered consecutive papers and published juxtaposed chapters. At the end of each session, all historians from both sides endorsed a joint statement, in both languages, of points of agreement and disagreement.[32] Although agreement was hard to reach, and the cooperative format frustrated all concerned, the output was greater in quantity and higher in quality than what scholars from either side would have published if left to their own devices. Ukrainian historians came to see 1943–44, and Polish historians 1945–47, in a different light.

NATIONS IN EUROPE

History, an enterprise which requires human effort, is often written from national motivations. History, in order to be scholarly, must in some way be freed from the limits this imposes. The emergence of this cooperative Polish-Ukrainian history is a sign that Minerva's owl is about to take wing, that a certain historical epoch is passing, at least in a certain part of Europe. It may be useful to frame the European future toward which Poles and others believed they were moving after 1989, and to make some modest predictions about the meaning of Europe to Poland's eastern neighbors in the twenty-first century.

Polish eastern policy between 1989 and 1991 had little to do with Western Europe. It was a policy of a newly sovereign nation-state whose diplomats and policymakers wished, for reasons of state interest, to aid in the construction of nation-states on the territory of the Soviet Union. Polish eastern policy in 1992 and 1993 bore on Western Europe only obliquely. Polish diplomats proposed "European standards" to their eastern neighbors. This was meant to prevent problems that could harm Poland's image in the West, to improve the Poland's position in the east, and to justify support of eastern neighbors to domestic constituencies concerned about Polish minorities. After 1994, Polish eastern policy was essentially the more or less clever redirection of the leverage conferred by the European institutions Poland was seen to be joining. Since Poland was seen to be ahead of Lithuania and Ukraine in its integration with Western institutions after 1994, Lithuanian and Ukrainian elites interested in the same success paid some attention to Poland. Poland joined NATO in March 1999. Despite the rancorous debate surrounding this event and expected further enlargements, the more important accession for both Poland and its eastern neighbors will be to the European Union.

The "return to Europe," the great slogan of opponents of communism and reformers of postcommunist states, was always an oxymoron. The Europe which preceded the imposition of communism in Eastern Europe was dead by 1989. To all but the most stubborn of nostalgics, the idea of a return to the interwar period does not bear much examination. What East Europeans meant by the "return to Europe" after 1989 was not a return to the past, but a leap forward to the achievements of postwar Western Europe, a leap for which common European culture provided the faith. Yet the institutional project of European integration had made great strides between the 1957 Treaty of Rome and the East European revolutions of 1989. East European countries expected to partake at once in norms and practices that had taken decades to accumulate. The European Union also changed a great deal between 1989 and 1999. As Poland and other East European candidates strove to demonstrate their fitness for membership, the EU became a political and economic union with a common external frontier and a common currency. Nevertheless, Poland expects to be included in the next EU enlargement, in 2004. Lithuania should accede to the EU at the same time. But there is essentially no chance that any of their three eastern neighbors, Belarus, Ukraine, and the Russian Federation, will be included in the EU before 2040. This compels us to imagine decades during which Poland and Lithuania will be the eastern marches of the European Union.[33]

In the early 1990s, the European Union appeared to face a choice between a rapid enlargement and continuation of its plans for a common currency. In the event, enlargement took so long that the common currency became a fait accompli. Meanwhile, another fundamental change in the structure of the EU was underway. While Poland and other East European states reformed themselves during the 1990s, the EU was removing the last impediments to internal movement among its member states, and creating a correspondingly tough external border. Designed to allow free movement within the European Union, the Schengen regime naturally concentrates police power on the EU's external borders. The terrorist attacks of 11 September 2001 consolidated this regime. This is cause for concern. The first two parts of this book illustrated the importance of contacts among educated elites in the reconstruction and the reconciliation of nations. As we saw in part 3, similar contacts were crucial to the elaboration of the *Kultura* grand strategy, to national reconciliation among Poland, Lithuania, Belarus and Ukraine, and to the peaceful dissolution of the Soviet Union. Since EU enlargement endangers the access of eastern elites to Poland, this lesson is worth considering. When Poland joins the EU, Russian, Belarusian, and Ukrainian citizens will find themselves materially and symbolically separated from "Europe."[34] The eight million Russian citizens who visited Poland each year during the 1990s, legally and illegally, will find their way blocked. Regardless of whether they regard Poland as a model, the experience will be frustrating and perhaps humiliating. A thick line between Poland and Belarus would also serve the dictatorial Lukashenka regime, or others like it.

Belarusian traders, the only group to have wrung concessions from Lukashenka, will find themselves separated from their markets. A majority of Belarusian traders in the 1990s had some connection to Poland, and thus to a wider world of free trade and democratic institutions.[35] To keep Belarusians from Poland is to close one democratic possibility in Belarus.

In 1997, Ukraine and Poland initiated a visa-free regime. The experience of Ukrainians in a large Slavic state where public institutions work and the free market functions is certainly of value in building social support for reform in Ukraine.[36] The Ukrainian state-building project is the keystone of European security in the twenty-first century; structural flaws include the absence of administrative and economic reform, and the weakness of the rule of law. This Polish-Ukrainian connection is thus of great importance for Europe as a whole. Polish Foreign Minister Geremek made this explicit in his 1997 official visit to Kyiv, which preceded his first trip to Brussels.[37] In the late 1990s, 2000, and 2001, Poland resisted EU pressure to annul its visa-free regime with Ukraine, arguing that Poland would meet its obligations when it formally acceded into the EU. This was the continuation by the post-Solidarity governments and President Kwaśniewski of an eastern policy which remained more pro-Ukrainian than EU partners (and Polish public opinion) would have preferred.[38] Yet once Poland actually joins the EU, its special arrangements with Ukraine will come to an end. Lublin and Brest, the sites of Poland's great political and religious unions with eastern neighbors in the early modern period, today lie just to the one and just to the other side of Poland's eastern border. When the Polish border matches the EU border, what will the EU offer its new eastern neighbors?

Ukrainian President Kuchma dreamed that the guardposts Poland built in the 1990s on its Ukrainian border would become as obsolete as those marking the French-German border.[39] Someday, perhaps, they will. For the time being, they symbolize Poland's commitment to joining the EU, to shifting the EU's external border from the Oder to the Bug River, between itself and Ukraine and Belarus. Although Poland can delay its implementation of EU recommendations, it must prove the fitness of its institutions before it joins the EU. Just as borders must be drawn, demarcated and guarded before they become obsolete, so Poland had to prove itself to be a successful state before it could join the European Union. In "returning to Europe," Poland will reach the logical conclusion not only of its western policy, but of its eastern policy. In supporting the sovereignty of eastern neighbors, in spreading European norms, and then transmitting European influence, the Poland of the 1990s was behaving as a sovereign nation-state with defined interests and goals. By accepting and propounding a particular model of the nation-state in northeastern Europe, Poland created conditions under which it could join the European Union. In joining the European Union, Poland will become one of a group of nation-states which have pooled sovereignty in traditional areas of state power.

This book began with a similar moment in European history: the 1569 Lublin Union. Warsaw and Vilnius, as we might say today, pooled their sovereignty at Lublin to establish the Polish-Lithuanian Commonwealth. The early modern Polish-Lithuanian Commonwealth was far greater in territory, ambitions, and European significance than the two small nation-states that today bear its names. Its citizens believed that they had created the best political order in the world. Their republic embodied practices of democracy, civil rights, religious toleration, and constitutional rule now regarded as European par excellence; but also created or sustained languages, religions, and myths now seen as Ukrainian, Belarusian, and Russian. The appeal of the early modern Commonwealth had more to do with a political ideal than with specific institutions, which is why its attraction outlived its polity by more than a century. Something similar can be said about the postmodern European Union: it is attractive not for its *acquis communautaire,* its body of law and practices, but for its savoir-faire, its reputation and civilization. It too is an elite project that embodies an attractive political ideal in complex institutions. As Poland and Lithuania join the European Union, Belarusians, Ukrainians, Russians and others will be drawn to the ideal of nations in Europe. The eastern enlargement of the European Union, a wise and noble policy, asks rather than answers the question of the eastern border of Europe.

Abbreviations

AK	Armia Krajowa
	(Polish) Home Army
EU	European Union
OUN	Orhanizatsiia Ukrains'kykh Natsionalistiv
	Organization of Ukrainian Nationalists
NATO	North Atlantic Treaty Organization
SSR	Soviet Socialist Republic
NKVD	Narodnyi Komissariat Vnutrennikh Del
	People's Commissariat for Internal Affairs
UNDO	Ukrains'ke Natsional'ne Demokratychne Ob'iednannia
	Ukrainian National-Democratic Alliance
UPA	Ukrains'ka Povstans'ka Armiia
	Ukrainian Insurgent Army
YIVO	Yidisher Visnshaftlekher Institut
	Institute for Jewish Research

Archives

AMPN   Archiwum Muzeum Polskiego, Dział Narodowościowy
            Archive of the Polish Museum, Nationalities Section
            (London)

AWKW   Archiwum Wschodnie, Ośrodek Karta, Wspomnienia
            Eastern Archive, Karta, Memoirs (Warsaw)

BUWR   Biblioteka Uniwersytetu Warszawskiego, Dział Rękopisów
            Warsaw University Library, Manuscripts Department
            (Warsaw)

CAWR   Centralne Archiwum Wojskowe
            Central Military Archive (Rembertów, Poland)

GARF   Gosudarstvennyi Arkhiv Rossiiskoi Federatsii
            State Archive of the Russian Federation (Moscow)

LCVA   Lietuvos Centrinis Valstybes Archyvas
            Lithuanian Central State Archives (Vilnius)

SPPL   Studium Polskiej Podziemnej
            Archive of the Polish Underground (London)

VUBR   Vilniaus Universiteto Biblioteka, Rankrašciu Skyrius Vilnius
            University Library, Manuscripts Department (Vilnius)

Document Collections

1947: Propam'iatna Knyha	Bohdan Huk, ed., *1947: Propam'iatna Knyha*, Warsaw: Tyrsa, 1997
Akcja 'Wisła'	Eugeniusz Misiło, ed., *Akcja 'Wisła,'* Warsaw: Archiwum Ukraińskie, 1993
Armia Krajowa w Dokumentach	*Armia Krajowa w Dokumentach,* 3 vols., London: Studium Polski Podziemnej, 1970–1978
Deportatsii	Iurii Slivka, ed., *Deportatsii,* 2 vols., Lviv: Natsional'na Akademiia Nauk Ukrainy, 1996–1998
Deportatsiia poliakiv z Ukrainy	Volodymyr Serhiichuk, ed., *Deportatsiia poliakiv z Ukrainy,* Kyiv: Ukrains'ka vydavnycha spilka, 1999
Desiat' buremnykh lit	Volodymyr Serhiichuk, ed., *Desiat' buremnykh lit,* Kyiv: Dnipro, 1998
Dzieje Konfliktów	Mikołaj Siwicki, ed., *Dzieje Konfliktów Polsko-Ukraińskich,* 3 vols., Warsaw: privately published, 1990–1994

Eksterminacja ludności | Władysław Filar, ed., *Eksterminacja ludności pol-*
polskiej na Wołyniu | *skiej na Wołyniu*, Warsaw: Zakład Poligrafii, 1999

Etnichni mezhi i derzhavnyi | Volodymyr Serhiichuk, ed., *Etnichni mezhi i*
kordon Ukrainy | *derzhavnyi kordon Ukrainy*, Ternopil': Ternopil', 1996

Litopys UPA | *Litopys UPA*, multiple editors, multiple volumes, ser. 1 and 2, Toronto 1978–

OUN-UPA v roky viiny | Volodomyr Serhiichuk, ed., *OUN-UPA v roky viiny*, Kyiv: Dnipro, 1996

OUN v svitli postanov | *OUN v svitli postanov Velykykh Zboriv*, Munich:
Velykykh Zboriv | OUN, 1955

NKWD o Polsce i Polakach | Wojciech Materski and Andrzej Paczkowski, eds., *NKWD o Polsce i Polakach*, Warsaw: ISP PAN, 1996

Pereselennia poliakiv ta | *Pereselennia poliakiv ta ukraintsiv/Przedsiedlenia*
ukraintsiv | *Polaków i Ukrainców, 1944–1946*, Warsaw: Rytm, 2000

Povstans'ki mohyly | Evhen Misylo, ed., *Povstans'ki mohyly*, Warsaw: Ukrains'kyi Arkhiv, 1995

Przesiedlenie ludności | Stanisław Cieselski, ed., *Przesiedlenie ludności*
polskiej | *polskiej z kresów wschodnich*, Warsaw: Neriton, 1999

Repatriacja | Eugeniusz Misiło, eds., *Repatriacja czy deportacja?* 2 vols. Warsaw: Archiwum Ukraińskie 1996–1999

Represyvno-karal'na systema | Ivan Bilas, ed., *Represyvno-karal'na systema v Ukraini*, Kyiv: Lybid, 1994

Śladami ludobojstwa | Leon Karłowicz and Leon Popek, eds., *Śladami ludobojstwa na Wołyniu*, vol. 2, Lublin: Polihymnia, 1998

Sovetskii faktor | T. V. Volokitina, ed., *Sovetskii faktor v Vostochnoi Evrope 1944–1953*, vol. 1, Moscow: Sibirskii khronograf, 1997

Teczka specjalna J. W. | Tatiana Cariewskaja, Andrzej Chmielarz,
Stalina | Andrzej Paczkowski, Ewa Rosowska, Szymon Rudnicki, eds., *Teczka specjalna J. W. Stalina*, Warsaw: Rytm, 1988

Trahedia Ukraintsiv Pol'shchi	Volodymyr Serhiichuk, ed., *Trahedia Ukraintsiv Pol'shchi,* Ternopil': Ternopil', 1997
UPA v svitli pol'skykh dokumentiv	Evhen Misylo, ed., *UPA v svitli pol'skykh dokumentiv,* Toronto: Litopys UPA, 1992
Vostochnaia Evropa	T. V. Volokitina, ed., *Vostochnaia Evropa v dokumentakh rossiiskikh arkhivov, 1944–1953,* vol. 1, Moscow: Sibirskii khronograf, 1997

Notes

CHAPTER 1. THE GRAND DUCHY OF LITHUANIA (1569–1863)

1. Juliusz Bardach, *Studia z ustroju i prawa Wielkiego Księstwa Litewskiego*, Warsaw: PWN, 1970, 18–21; S.C. Rowell, *Lithuania Ascending*, Cambridge: Cambridge University Press, 1994, 296–299; Zigmas Zinkevičius, *The History of the Lithuanian Language*, Vilnius: Mokslo ir enciklopediju leidykla, 1996, 71–76. On Poles and Germans, Paul Knoll, *The Rise of the Polish Monarchy*, Chicago: University of Chicago Press, 1971.

2. Reprinted as *Bibliia: Faksimil'nae uznaulenne Biblii, vydadzenai Frantsyskam Skarynaiu u 1517–1519 gadakh*, Minsk: Belaruskaia savetskaia entsyklapedyia, 1990–91. His Church Slavonic was colored by the vernacular of the Slavic gentry of the Grand Duchy, and influenced by the Czech of the Bible from which he worked in Prague. J. Sadouski, "A Linguistic Analysis of the Four Books of Kings Printed by Skaryna in 1518," Doctoral dissertation, University of London, 1967, 224–226. For Skaryna's vernacular prose, *Pradmovy i pasliasloui pasliadounikau Frantsyska Skaryny*, Minsk: Navuka i tekhnika, 1991; see also Arnold McMillin, *Die Literatur der Weissrussen*, Giessen: Wilhelm Schmitz, 1977, 40–47.

3. Moshe Altbauer, *The Five Biblical Scrolls in a Sixteenth-Century Jewish Translation into Belarusian (Vilnius Codex 626)*, Jerusalem: Dorot, 1992, 13–37. See also Paul Wexler, "The Reconstruction of Pre-Ashkenazic Jewish Settlements

in the Slavic Lands in the Light of the Linguistic Sources," in Antony Polonsky, ed., *From Shtetl to Socialism*, London: Littman Library, 1993, 3–18.

4. *Zbiór praw litewskich od roku 1389 do roku 1529 tudzież Rozprawy sejmowe o tychże prawach od roku 1544 do roku 1563*, Poznań: Drukarnia na Garbarach 45, 1841, 112. Privileges authorized Jews to maintain their law and religion, to use their own language and customs in community matters, and to trade without municipal citizenship. Consult Jacob Goldberg, *Jewish Privileges in the Polish Commonwealth*, Jerusalem: Israel Academy of Sciences and Humanities, 1985, 1–40.

5. A feat repeated in modern times, when the 1529 Statute was translated into Russian in Minsk in 1960 so that Soviet scholars could study it. Then the claim was made that the language, patently not Russian, was in fact Belarusian: K.I. Iablonskis, ed., *Statut Velikogo Kniazhestva Litovskogo 1529 goda*, Minsk: Akademiia nauk BSSR, 1960, 3–12. It is most reasonable to see Chancery Slavonic as a separate entity. Consult Jonas Žmuidzinas, *Commonwealth polono-lithuanien ou l'Union de Lublin*, Paris: Mouton, 1978, 79–82; Juliusz Bardach, "Od aktu w Krewie do Zaręczenia Wzajemnego Obojga Narodów," in Jerzy Kłoczowski, et al., eds., *Unia Lubelska i tradycje integracyjne w Europie środkowo-wschodniej*, Lublin: IESW, 1999, 14–18; Stanislovas Lazutka, "Język Statutów Litewskich i Metryki Litewskiej," *Lithuania*, 1–2 (22–23), 1997, 26–33.

6. Introduction to the 1566 Statute, written in about 1576 by Augustinus Rotundus Mieleski, in *Archiwum Komisji Prawniczej*, Vol. 7, Cracow: Polska Akademia Umiejetnósci, 1900, xx; see also Jürate Kiapene, "The Grand Duchy and the Grand Dukes in the Sixteenth Century," in Richard Butterworth, ed., *The Polish-Lithuanian Monarchy in European Context*, Houndmills: Palgrave, 2001, 86–87.

7. Halina Dzerbina, *Prava i siamia u Belarusi epokhi Renesansu*, Minsk: Tekhnalohiia, 1997.

8. Harvey Goldblatt, "The Emergence of Slavic National Languages," in Aldo Scaglione, *The Emergence of National Languages*, Ravenna: Loggo Editore, 1984, 125, 165.

9. Karin Friedrich, *The Other Prussia*, Cambridge: Cambridge University Press, 2000.

10. On the political system, Andrzej Kamiński, "The Szlachta of the Polish-Lithuanian Commonwealth," in Ivo Banac and Paul Bushkovitch, eds., *The Nobility in Russia and Eastern Europe*, New Haven, Conn.: Yale Russian and East European Publications, 1983, 17–46; and Mariusz Markiewicz, "The Functioning of the Monarchy During the Reign of the Electors of Saxony," in Butterwick, *Polish-Lithuanian Monarchy*, 172–192. See also Daniel Stone, *The Polish-Lithuanian State, 1386–1795*, Seattle: University of Washington Press, 2001.

11. Concise reviews of the historiography of the Lublin Union are Bardach, *Studia z ustroju i prawa*, 11–18, and Žmuidzinas, *Commonwealth polono-lithuanien*, 143–151. Important Russian interpretations of 1569 are presented by M.K. Liubavskii and I.I. Lappo. Foundational Polish, Ukrainian, Belarusian, and Lithuanian views are presented by Joachim Lelewel, Mykhailo Hrushevs'kyi, M.V. Dovnar-Zapolskii, and Adolfas Šapoka. The leading interwar Polish students of the Union were Oskar Halecki and Stanisław Kutrzeba; an important Soviet Belorussian contribution was that of V.I. Picheta; a Moravian Pan-Slav perspective is to be found in Francis Dvornik. An introduction in

English is Harry Dembkowski, *The Union of Lublin,* Boulder, Colo.: East European Monographs, 1982.

12. Pagan Lithuanian families had converted to Catholicism en masse in 1387, but most Lithuanian boyars were Orthodox and remained so for two more centuries. There were considerably more Orthodox than Catholic churches in Vilnius when the Reformation began.

13. Jerzy Ochmański, "The National Idea in Lithuania," in Ivo Banac and Frank Sysyn, eds., *Concepts of Nationhood in Early Modern Europe,* Cambridge, Mass.: Ukrainian Research Institute, 1986, 312–313.

14. Piotr Skarga's numerous publications concerning both Protestantism and Orthodoxy after 1577 are the best evidence. *Pisma wszystkie,* 5 vols. Warsaw: Ultima Thule, 1923–1930.

15. The defense of Lithuania is *Rozmowa Polaka z Litwinem,* Brest: Drukarnia Radziwiłłowska, 1565. Its author was already "rotund" when his yearly subsidy from the Polish crown was arranged in 1549, two years before he moved to Lithuania. Maurycy Krupwicz, ed., *Sobranie gosudarstvennykh i chastnykh aktov, kasaiushchikhsia istorii Litvy i soedinennykh s nei vladienii,* Vilnius: Zavadzkago, 1858, 38–39; Marja Baryczowa, "Augustyn Rotundus Mieleski, wójt wileński, pierwszy historyk i apologeta Litwy," *Ateneum Wileńskie,* 11 (1936), 144. It is remotely possible that Rotundus considered himself a scholar who could produce well-rounded sentences, *phrases bien arrondies.* In Classical Latin, it was possible to use "rotundus" to mean "well-rounded," as in prose; the first occurrence of this sense was perhaps in Cicero's *Orator,* which Rotundus knew. Yet this possibility was as remote in the sixteenth century as it is now: our Rotundus was probably just fat. To understand the difference between early modern and modern nationality requires a sense of when the meaning of words change and when they do not: to be "rotund" in the sixteenth century is the same as to be "rotund" today; to be "Polish" or "Lithuanian" is certainly not.

16. Paul Bushkovitch, "National Consciousness in Early Modern Russia," in Banac and Sysyn, *Concepts of Nationhood,* 356–357; Jaroslaw Pelenski, "The Origins of the Official Muscovite Claim to the 'Kievan Inheritance,'" *Harvard Ukrainian Studies,* 1, 1 (1977), 48–50.

17. Andrzej Kamiński, *Republic vs. Autocracy,* Cambridge, Mass.: Harvard University Press, 1993.

18. See chart 1, p. 48. This is also clear from a chronological review of the collections published by the Vilenskaia arkheograficheskaia kommissia in the series "Akty, izdavaemye Vilenskoiu arkheograficheskoiu kommissieiu," "Akty, izdavaemye Arkheograficheskoiu kommissieiu, vysochaishe uchrezhdennoiu v Vil'nie," and "Akty, izdavaemye Vilenskoiu kommissieiu dlia razbora drevnikh aktov."

19. Artūras Tereškinas, "Reconsidering the Third of May Constitution and the Rhetoric of Polish-Lithuanian Reforms," *Journal of Baltic Studies,* 27, 4 (1996), 300. See also Andrzej Walicki, *The Enlightenment and the Birth of Modern Nationhood,* Notre Dame, Ind.: University of Notre Dame Press, 1989. On Enlightment debates about Polish reform, Larry Wolff, *Inventing Eastern Europe,* Stanford: Stanford University Press, 195–283.

20. For an introduction to this issue, see Gershon David Hundert, "Some Basic Character-istics of the Jewish Experience in Poland," in Polonsky, *From Shtetl to Socialism*, 19–25; M.J. Rosman, *The Lords' Jews*, Cambridge, Mass.: Ukrainian Research Institute, 1990, 1–22. The locus classicus is Salo Wittmayer Baron, *A Social and Religious History of the Jews*, vol. 16, New York: Columbia University Press, 1976.

21. Jacob Goldberg, "Privileges Granted to Jewish Communities As a Stabilizing Factor in Jewish Support," in Chimen Abramsky, Maciej Jachimczyk, and Antony Polonsky, eds., *The Jews in Poland*, Oxford: Blackwell, 1986, 31–54; Daniel Beauvois, "Polish-Jewish re-lations in Russian territory," ibid., 81; Artur Eisenbach, *The Emancipation of the Jews in Poland, 1780–1870*, Oxford: Basil Blackwell, 1991, 126–127, 158–160.

22. Mickiewicz himself would later marry a woman of Jewish descent. Mickiewicz's compli-cated origins are simply a variation on a theme: the historian Joachim Lelewel (1786–1861), the outstanding teacher at Wilno when Mickiewicz studied and the greatest Pol-ish historian of his day, was the son of a German nobleman. For Mickiewicz ethnic no-tions of nationality were meaningless, so one cannot establish what he "really" was by "unmasking" his parents or grandparents. Introductions to the debate over Mickiewicz's origins are Anne Applebaum, *Between East and West*, London: Macmillan, 1995, 114–122; Irena Grudzińska-Gross, "How Polish is Polishness?" *East European Politics and So-cieties*, 14, 1 (2000), 5ff.; Neal Ascherson, *Black Sea*, New York: Hill and Wang, 1996, 144ff. For the Tatar Mosque, see Jan Tyszkiewicz, *Tatarzy na Litwie i w Polsce*, Warsaw: PWN, 1989, 287. The fundamental work is Wiktor Weintraub, *The Poetry of Adam Mickiewicz*, The Hague: Mouton, 1954, at 14–15 for these questions.

23. The expansion of Polish schooling in the Russian empire did not involve the Jews. In Vilnius, Russian rather than Polish provided Jews a window upon the wider world.

24. A. Bendzhius et al., *Istoriia Vil'niusskogo universiteta*, Vilnius: Mokslas, 1979, 64–66; Daniel Beauvois, *Szkolnictwo polskie na ziemiach litewsko-ruskich 1803–1832*, vol. 1, Lublin: KUL, 1991, 37–39, 273–275. The case of a Lithuanian Pole whose career was al-lowed by a Russian tsar creating durable emblems of Polish patriotism is hardly unique. Another such is Michał Kleofas Ogiński (1765–1833), whose Polonaise "Farewell to the Fatherland" in A minor is the most resonant of Polish Baroque compositions.

25. Compare Mickiewicz's lines about a lost Lithuania to Pushkin's about a discovered St. Petersburg: "Here we are destined by nature / To cut a window into Europe / To stand firmly by the sea." *Eugene Onegin* was finished in 1832, *Pan Tadeusz* in 1834. Pushkin and Mickiewicz were friends. See Jerzy Tomaszewski, "Kresy wschodnie w polskiej myśli politycznej," in Wojciech Wrzeziński, ed., *Między Polską etniczną i historyczną*, Wro-cław: Ossolineum, 1988; 97ff.; also I.I. Svirida, *Mezhdu Peterburgom, Varshavoi i Vil'no*, Moscow: OGI, 1999.

26. Jacques Barzun, *Classic, Romantic, and Modern*, Garden City, N.Y.: Doubleday, 1961, 14.

27. Nina Taylor, "Adam Mickiewicz et la Lithuanie," in Daniel Beauvois, ed., *Les confins de l'ancienne Pologne*, Lille: Presses Universitaires, 1988, 70.

28. N.N. Ulashchik, *Predposylki krest'ianskoi reformy 1861 g. v Litve i Zapadnoi Belorussii*, Moscow: Nauka, 1965, 5–6.

29. Jakób Gieysztor, *Pamiętniki*, Vol. 1, Vilnius: Bibljoteka Pamiętników, 1913, 36, 61, 136.

30. For his newspaper in the original and in Russian, K. Kalinovskii, *Iz pechatnogo i*

rukopisnogo naslediia, Minsk: Belarus, 1988. See also Piotr Łossowski and Zygmunt Mły-
narski, *Rosjanie, Białorusini, i Ukraińcy w Powstaniu Styczniowym,* Wrocław: Ossolineum, 1959, 166–186; John Stanley, "The Birth of a Nation," in Béla Király, ed., *The
Crucial Decade,* New York: Brooklyn College Press, 110–119.

31. Egidijus Aleksandravičius, "Political Goals of Lithuanians, 1883–1918," *Journal of Baltic
Studies,* 23, 3 (1992), 230–231; Nerijus Udrenas, "Book, Bread, Cross, and Whip: The
Construction of Lithuanian Identity within Imperial Russia," Doctoral dissertation,
Brandeis University, 2000.

CHAPTER 2. LITHUANIA! MY FATHERLAND!

1. Andreas Moritsch, "The January Insurrection and the Emancipation of Peasants in the
Polish—Russian Provinces," in Béla Király, eds., *The Crucial Decade,* New York: Brooklyn College Press, 180–182.

2. Algis Kasperovičius, "Kształtowanie się narodu litewskiego," in Krzysztof Jasiewicz, ed.,
Europa nie prowincjonalna, Warsaw: Rytm, 1999, 218–223; Miroslav Hroch, *Social Pre-
conditions of National Revival in Europe,* Cambridge: Cambridge University Press, 1985,
89; Vytautas Merkys, "Biskup Motiejus Valanczius a polityka narodowościowa rządu
Rosji," in Jerzy Kłoczowski et al., eds., *Belarus, Lithuania, Poland, Ukraine,* Lublin:
IESW, 1994, 317–318.

3. On Polish positivism, Jerzy Jedlicki, *A Suburb of Europe,* Budapest: Central European
Press, 1999; Stanislaus Blejwas, *Realism in Polish Politics,* New Haven, Conn.: Yale Con-
cilium on International and Area Studies, 1984.

4. Teodor Narbutt, *Dzieje narodu litewskiego,* vol. 2, Vilnius: Marcinkowskiego, 1841, 492.

5. Virgil Krapauskas, *Nationalism and Historiography,* Boulder, Colo.: East European Monographs, 2000, 31, 108.

6. Tomas Venclova, "Native Realm Revisited: Mickiewicz's Lithuania and Mickiewicz in
Lithuania," cited after the manuscript, 1–5, published in Polish in *Zeszyty Literackie,* 70
(2000). A similar role was played by the poetry of Józef Ignacy Kraszewski. On Daukantas see also Jonas Žmuidzinas, *Commonwealth polono-lithuanien ou l'Union de Lublin,*
Paris: Mouton, 1978, 148.

7. Jean Pelissier, *Les principaux artisans de la Renaissance Nationale Lituanienne,* Lausanne:
Léman, 1918, 25–45. Compare also the last two lines of Mickiewicz's popular "Ode to
Youth" (1820): "Hail, hail, the dawn of freedom / and salvation's sun to come."

8. Jerzy Ochmański, *Litewski ruch narodowo-kulturalny w XIX wieku,* Białystok: PAN,
1965, 137ff.; Krapauskas, *Nationalism and Historiography,* 15.

9. Jiří Rak, *Bývalí Čechové,* Prague: H&H, 1994, 127–140. Consult also Vladimír Macura,
Český sen, Prague: Lidové noviny, 1998, 14–53.

10. David Diringer, *The Alphabet,* Vol. 1, New York: Funk and Wagnall, 1968, 157–164.

11. Francis Dvornik, *The Slavs in European History and Civilization,* New Brunswick, N.J.:
Rutgers University Press, 1962, 301–303; Norman Davies, *God's Playground,* vol. 1, New
York: Columbia University Press, 1982, 69.

12. This argument about nationalism's spread draws from Liah Greenfeld, *Nationalism,*
Cambridge: Harvard University Press, 1992.

13. Narbutt, *Dzieje narodu litewskiego,* Vol. 1, 454–464; Krapauskas, *Nationalism and Historiography,* 74.

14. Wiktor Weintraub, *The Poetry of Adam Mickiewicz,* The Hague: Mouton, 1954, 115. The work in question is *Preussens ältere Geschichte,* 4 vols., Riga: Hartmann, 1808.

15. On Mickiewicz in France, Andrzej Walicki, *Philosophy and Romantic Nationalism,* Notre Dame, Ind.: University of Notre Dame Press, 1997, 265–267.

16. See Vladimír Macura, *Znamení zrodu,* Prague: H&H, 1995, 61–79, for a model argument about language and national revival. Lithuanian activists also wished to show that Mickiewicz was a Lithuanian in an ethnic and not only a political sense, seeking evidence that he knew the Lithuanian language. In general, history as compensation for impotence is as old as, well, history. See Anthony Grafton, *The Footnote,* Cambridge, Mass.: Harvard University Press, 2000, 155.

17. Cited after Czesław Miłosz, "Rodziewiczówna," *Kultura,* 522 (1991), 21.

18. Pelissier, *Les principaux artisans,* 45–59; Venclova, "Native Realm Revisited," 22.

19. Bardach, "Polacy Litewscy i inne narody Litwy historycznej," in Kłoczowski, *Belarus, Lithuania, Poland, Ukraine,* 366.

20. Ryszard Radzik, "Samookreślenie jako element świadomości etnicznej ludu białoruskiego w XIX wieku," *Przegląd Wschodni,* 4, 3 (1997), 616.

21. Valerius Czekmonas, "O etapach socjolingwistycznej historii Wileńszczyzny i rozwoju polskiej świadomości narodowej na Litwie," in Kłoczowski, *Belarus, Lithuania, Poland, Ukraine,* 457–463.

22. Wacław Jędrzejewicz, *Kronika Życia Józefa Piłsudskiego,* vol. 1, London: Polska Fundacja Kulturalna, 1997, 15–16.

23. Another response was a more internationalist socialism. Kazimierz Kelles-Krauz, the outstanding Marxist theorist of Piłsudski's party, was by family origin a Lithuanian Pole. See my *Nationalism, Socialism, and Modern Central Europe,* Cambridge, Mass.: Harvard University Press for Ukrainian Research Institute, 1997. The young Feliks Dzierżyński (1876–1926) was expelled from his Wilno school for speaking Polish. He turned to internationalist socialism, joined the Luxemburgian wing of Polish socialism which rejected the idea of a reborn Polish state, and ended his career in communist Russia as head of the Cheka. Robert Blobaum, *Feliks Dzierzynski and the SDKPiL,* Boulder, Colo.: East European Monographs, 1983. See also Bohdan Cywiński, *Rodowody niepokornych,* Paris: Spotkania, 1985; Norman Naimark, *The History of the "Proletariat,"* Boulder, Colo.: East European Monographs, 1979.

24. Piotr Wróbel, *Kształtowanie się białoruskiej świadomości narodowej a Polska,* Warsaw: Wydawnictwo Uniwersytetu Warszawskiego, 1990, 16.

25. Numbers cited after Steven Guthier, "The Belorussians: National Identification and Assimilation," *Soviet Studies,* 29, 1 (1977), 40–47. On "ethnic groups" and national history see Jeremy King, "Loyalty and Polity, Nation and State," Doctoral dissertation, Columbia University, 1998, 29–33. For the defense, Anthony Smith, *The Ethnic Origins of Nations,* Oxford: Blackwell, 1986.

26. M.V. Dounar-Zapolski, *Historiia Belarusi,* Minsk: Belaruskaia Ents'iklapedia, 1994, 360; Celina Gajkowska, "Wincenty Marcinkiewicz," *Polski Słownik Biograficzny,* vol. 19, Wrocław: Ossolineum, 1974, 588–590.

27. Mickiewicz cited after A.A. Loika and V.P. Rahoisha, eds., *Belarusskaia litaratura XIX stahoddzia,* Minsk: Vyhsheishaia shkola, 1988, 32; Dunin cited after his *Zbor tvorau,* Minsk: Dziarzhaunae Vydavetstva BSSR, 1958, 370.

28. Jan Czeczot, *Piosnki wieśniacze znad Niemna i Dźwiny,* Vilnius: Zawadzkiego, 1839. See also T.V. Valodzina, "Ian Chachot i brat'i T'ishkevich," in *Falklor,* Minsk: Belaruskaiia Navuka, 1997, 6; Marceli Kosman, *Historia Białorusi,* Wrocław: Ossolineum, 1979, 219; Weintraub, *Poetry,* 13; Arnold McMillin, *Die Literatur der Weissrussen,* Giessen: Wilhelm Schmitz, 1977, 82–83.

29. Walicki, *Philosophy and Romantic Nationalism,* 73.

30. Jan Zaprudnik, *Belarus,* Boulder, Colo.: Westview, 1993, 54–55; Kosman, *Historia Białorusi,* 220.

31. Edward Thaden, *Russia's Western Borderlands, 1710–1870,* Princeton, N.J.: Princeton University Press, 1984, especially 54, 68–69, 79, 121, 126; Patricia Grimsted, *The Foreign Ministers of Alexander I,* Berkeley: University of California Press, 1969, 104–150.

32. Dounar-Zapolski, *Historiia Belarusi,* 250.

33. Sofia Kuz'niaeva, "Nats'iial'nae adradzhen'ne i nats'iianal'naia s'viadomas'ts' belarusau u pershai palove XIX ct.," *Belaruski Histar'ichn'i Ahliad,* 1, 1 (1994), 57.

34. This is the function the same church served for Ukrainians in Austrian Galicia in the nineteenth century. State policy mattered because the Uniate Church was in dire straits in both places in 1795. Uladzimir Sosna, "Uniiatskae pi'tanne u belarusakau viosts'i," in M.V. Bich and P.A. Loika, *Z histor'ii Uniiatstva u Belarusi,* Minsk: Ekaperspekt'iva, 1996, 90–92.

35. L.K. Tarasiuk, "Adliustranne uniatskaii temat'iki u tvorchasts' Frantsishka Bahushevicha," in Ryszard Łużny, Franciszek Ziejka, and Andrzej Kępiński, eds., *Unia brzeska,* Cracow: Universitas, 1994, 526–531.

36. A sense of the church's institutional range in the 1830s is conveyed by G.I. Shavel'skii, *Posliednee vozsoedinenie s pravoslavnoiu tserkoviiu uniatov Bielorusskoi eparkhii,* Petersburg, Sel'skago Viestnika, 1910.

37. Jan Zaprudnik, "National Consciousness of the Byelarussians and the Road to Statehood," in Vitaut Kipel and Zora Kipel, eds., *Byelorussian Statehood,* New York: Byelorussian Institute of Arts and Sciences, 1988, 13; Jan Jurkiewicz, "Nasze widzenie Białorusinów w XX w.," *Dzieje Najnowsze,* 27, 2 (1995), 68.

38. Nicholas Vakar, *Belorussia,* Cambridge, Mass.: Harvard University Press, 1956, 82–83. The censor's recommendation in Frantsishak Bahushevich, *Tvory,* Minsk: Belarus, 1967, 202–205.

39. In fairness, Ernest Gellner at some points confronts the problem that modernizing states sometimes create one, and sometimes create more than one, nation. *Nations and Nationalism,* Ithaca: Cornell University Press, 1983.

40. On Russian elite opinion and the 1863 rising, Henryk Głębocki, *Fatalna sprawa,* Cracow: Arcana, 2000; M. Prudnikov, *Chego zhe khochet Pol'sha?* St. Petersburg: Glavnoie upravleniie voenno-uchebnykh zavedenii, 1863. On peasant self-definition, Radzik, "Samookreślenie," 612–614; M. Koszelew, "Polacy w oczach Białorusinów," *Dzieje Najnowsze,* 27, 2 (1995), 83–85.

41. On the shift, Theodore Weeks, *Nation and State in Late Imperial Russia,* Dekalb: North-

ern Illinois University Press, 1996, 45–73; Theodore Weeks, "Russification and the Lithuanians," *Slavic Review*, 60, 1, (2001), 109; Dominic Lieven, *Nicholas II*, New York: St.
Martin's 1993, 134–135; Witold Rodkiewicz, *Russian Nationality Policy*, Lublin: Scientific
Society of Lublin, 1998, 226–231; Pelissier, *Les principaux artisans*, 158–159; *O russkoi
pravdie i polskoi krivdie*, Moscow: Universitetskaia tipografiia, 1863, 28–29.

42. Łukasz Chimiak, *Gubernatorzy Rosyjscy w Królestwie Polskim*, Wrocław: FNP, 1999,
70–79; Andrzej Chwalba, *Polacy w służbie Moskali*, Warsaw: PWN, 1999, 66; Paul
Bushkovitch, "The Ukraine in Russian Culture," *Jahrbücher für Geschichte Osteuropas*,
39, 3 (1991), 347–350. See also L.E. Gorizontov, *Paradoksy imperskoi politiki*, Moscow:
Indrik, 1999; Vakar, *Belorussia*, 73. Josif Hurko, governor general of Warsaw and the
most famous Russifier in Polish history, was also of Polish-Lithuanian descent.

CHAPTER 3. THE FIRST WORLD WAR AND THE WILNO QUESTION (1914–1939)

1. M.V. Dovnar-Zapol'skii, *Narodnoe khoziaistvo Belorussii, 1861–1914 g.g.*, Gosplana BSSR,
1926, 8–28.

2. A 1909 official count of the city found 205,250 inhabitants, of whom 1.2 percent were
Lithuanian, 20.7 percent Russian, 37.8 percent Polish, and 36.8 percent Jewish. P. Gaučas
and A. Vidugiris, "Etnolingvisticheskaia situatsiia litovsko-belorusskogo pogranich'ia,"
Geografiia, 19 (1983), 62–63. The 1897 Russian census counted 40 percent Jews, 31 per-
cent Poles, and 2 percent Lithuanians. Nicholas Vakar, *Belorussia*, Cambridge, Mass.:
Harvard University Press, 1956, 12. See also Zinkevičius, *History of the Lithuanian Lan-
guage*, 288; Piotr Eberhardt, "Przemiany narodowościowe na Litwie w XX wieku,"
Przegląd Wschodni, 1, 3 (1991), 456–457.

3. Quotation from 1902, Egidijus Aleksandravičius, "Political Goals of Lithuanians, 1883–
1918," *Journal of Baltic Studies*, 23, 3 (1992), 234; from 1905, Jean Pelissier, *Les principaux
artisans de la Renaissance Nationale Lituanienne*, Lausanne: Léman, 1918, 177; consult
also Alfonsas Eidintas and Vytautas Žalys, *Lithuania in European Politics*, New York: St.
Martin's, 1999, 39; Piotr Łossowski, *Stosunki polsko-litewskie 1918–1920*, Warsaw: Książka
i Wiedza, 1966, 35–40.

4. Vitaut Kipel and Zora Kipel, eds., *Byelorussian Statehood*, New York: Byelorussian Institute of Arts and Sciences, 1988, 32–36, 37–52, 125–129.

5. Adam Maldzis, "Belaruska staulenne da Liublinskai unii," in Jerzy Kłoczowski et al.,
eds., *Unia lubelska i tradycje integracyjne w Europie środkowo-wschodniej*, Lublin: IESW,
1999, 154–155.

6. Mikhal Bich, "Ad idei adnaulennia Rech'i Paspalitay da barats'b'i za stvarenne nezalezh-
nay belaruskay dziarzhav'i," in Kłoczowski et al., eds., *Unia lubelska*, 173.

7. Aliaksandr Ts'vikevich, *"Zapadno-russizm,"* Minsk: Navuka i tekhnika, 1993 [1928], 314.

8. Guthier, "The Belorussians: National Identification and Assimilation," *Soviet Studies*,
29, 1 (1997), 40–47; Piotr Eberhardt, *Przemiany narodowóściowe na Litwie*, Warsaw:
Przegląd wschodni, 1997, 46; Piotr Eberhardt, *Przemiany narodowóściowe na Białorusi*,
Warsaw: Editions Spotkania, 1994, 14. These proportions are based on the 1897 census,
which collected data on native language.

9. On land, Witold Rodkiewicz, *Russian Nationality Policy*, Lublin: Scientific Society of

Lublin, 1998, 79; on language, Zofia Kurzowa, *Język polski Wileńszczyzny i kresów północno-wschodnich,* Warsaw: PWN, 1993, 221–311.

10. In this respect, the Polishness of these Poles resembled the Germanness of Austrian liberals, before the turn to mass national politics in Austria. Pieter Judson, *Exclusive Revolutionaries,* Ann Arbor: University of Michigan Press, 1996.

11. Juliusz Bardach, "O świadomości narodowej Polaków na Litwie i Białorusi," in Wojciech Wreziński, ed., *Między Polską etniczną i historyczną,* Wrocław: Ossolineum, 1988, 246–247; Aliaksandar Smalianchuk, "Histar'ichnaia s'viadomas'ts'i idealiohiia paliakau Belarusi i Litv'i na pachatku XX stahodz'dzia," *Belaruski Histar'ichn'i Ahliad,* 1,2 (1995), 32–40.

12. For example, Michał Römer, *Litwa,* L'viv: Polskie towarzystwo nakladowe, 1908. For other such works, Bardach, "Polacy Litewscy," in Jerzy Kłoczowski, et al., eds., *Belarus, Lithuania, Poland, Ukraine,* Lublin: IESW, 1994, 372–373.

13. Figures from the 1897 Russia census.

14. Eidintas and Žalys, *Lithuania in European Politics,* 18; Egidijus Motieka, "Początki nowożytnego państwa litewskiego," in Krzysztof Jasiewicz, eds., *Europa nie prowincjonalna,* Warsaw: Rytm, 1999, 224–231; Rimantas Miknys, "Wilno i Wileńszczyzna w koncepcjach Michała Römera i krajowców," ibid., 70; Vytautas Berenis, "Problem dziedzictwa kulturowego Wielkiego Księstwa Litewskiego w ideologii litewskiego ruchu narodowego," ibid., 467–473.

15. There were attempts to use the Polish language as a means to re-Lithuanize the reading public. Tadeusz Bujnicki, "Polskojęzyczne pisarstwo Litwinów w Wilnie," in Greta Lemanaitė and Paweł Bukowiec, eds., *Litwa,* Cracow: WUJ, 1998, 117–122.

16. The 1909 count, cited above, found 37.7 percent Polish and 36.8 percent Jewish. According to the 1897 Russian census, the city was 40.4 percent Jewish and 30.9 percent Polish. On commerce, Nancy and Stuart Schoenburg, *Lithuanian Jewish Communities,* New York: Garland, 1991, 354.

17. For the comparison of the Besht and the Gaon, see Moshe Rosman, *Founder of Hasidism,* Berkeley: University of California Press, 1996, 36–37. On the social origins of Zionists in Poland, Ezra Mendelsohn, *Zionism in Poland,* New Haven, Conn.: Yale University Press, 1981. On assimiliationism and nationalism in Vienna, Marsha Rozenblit, *The Jews of Vienna 1867–1914,* Albany, N.Y.: SUNY Press, 1983, 175–195. See also Joshua Levisohn, "The Early Vilna Haskalah," Doctoral dissertation, Harvard University, 1999.

18. Harry Tobias, *The Jewish Bund in Russia,* Stanford, Calif.: Stanford University Press, 1972, 46, 52–53; Henri Minczeles, *Vilna, Wilno, Vilnius,* Paris: Éditions de la Découverte, 1993.

19. Stefan Kawym, *Ideologia stronnictw politycznych w Polsce wobec Mickiewicza 1890–1898,* L'viv: Filomat, 1937; Józef Kozłowski, "*My z niego wszyscy . . .*" Warsaw: Czytelnik, 1978.

20. Assessment based on electoral data assembled in 2000 by Jeffrey Kopstein and Jason Wittenberg for their project "Rethinking the Social Bases of Dictatorship and Democracy in Interwar East Central Europe."

21. In 1939 Ksawery Pruszyński linked Dmowski's social origins to a new sort of Polish nationalism. *Niezadowoleni i entuzjaści,* Warsaw: Państwowy Instytut Wydawniczy, 1990, 637–644. A sober introduction is Andrzej Walicki, "The Troubling Legacy of Roman

Dmowski," *East European Politics and Societies*, 14, 1 (2000), 12–30. Brian Porter treats modern Polish nationalism as an abandonment of historical time: *When Nationalism Began to Hate*, Oxford: Oxford University Press, 2000. See also Patrice Dabrowski, "Folk, Faith, and Fatherland," *Nationalities Papers*, 28, 3 (2000), 397–416. Consult generally Piotr Wandycz, *The Lands of Partitioned Poland*, Seattle: University of Washington Press, 1993; Stefan Kieniewicz, *Historia Polska 1795–1918*, Warsaw: PWN, 1997; Antony Polonsky, *Politics in Independent Poland*, Oxford: Clarendon Press, 1972.

22. Vejas Liulevicius, *War Land on the Eastern Front*, Cambridge: Cambridge University Press, 2000.

23. Bich, "Ad idei adnaulennia Rech'i Paspalitay," 174–175; quotation from Vasil Zacharka, in Kipel and Kipel, *Byelorussian Statehood*, 97.

24. Ivan Lubachko, *Belorussia under Soviet Rule*, Lexington: University of Kentucky Press, 1972, 24–25.

25. Antanas Smetona, *Die litauische Frage*, Berlin: Das neue Litauen, 1917, 29.

26. Stanley Page, *The Formation of the Baltic States*, Cambridge: Mass.: Harvard University Press, 1959, 30–97; Wiktor Sukiennicki, *East Central Europe During World War I*, vol. 2, Boulder, Colo.: East European Monographs, 1984, 668–705.

27. Andrzej Garlicki, "Wilna żądają wszyscy," in Robert Traba, ed., *Tematy polsko-litewskie*, Olsztyn: Borussia, 1999, 72.

28. Piotr Łossowski, *Po tej i tamtej stronie Niemna*, Warsaw: Czytelnik, 1985, 105. For a sense of Lithuanian frustration, Juozas Gabrys, *L'Etat Lithuanien et Mitteleuropa*, 1917; Lituanus, *La vérité polonaise sur les Lithuaniens*, Lausanne: Bureau d'Information de Lithuanie, 1917.

29. Piotr Eberhardt, "Wizje i projekty Polskiej Granicy Wschodniej w latach 1914–1921," *Przegląd Wschodni*, 5, 2 (1998), 348–351.

30. Piotr Wandycz, *Soviet-Polish Relations, 1917–1921*, Cambridge, Mass.: Harvard University Press, 1969, 110.

31. Alfred Erich Senn, *The Great Powers, Lithuania, and the Vilna Question*, Leiden: Brill, 1966, 55.

32. Norman Davies, *White Eagle, Red Star*, London: Macdonald and Co., 1972; Lucjan Żeligowski, *Wojna w roku 1920*, Warsaw: Polska zjednoczona, 1930.

33. Wandycz, *Soviet-Polish Relations*, 209; Eidintas and Žalys, *Lithuania in European Politics*, 70, 77; Andrzej Ajnenkial, "Od aktu 5'ego listopadu do traktatu ryskiego," in Mieczysław Wojciechowski, ed., *Traktat Ryski 1921 roku po 75 latach*, Toruń: Wydawnictwo Uniwersytetu Mikołaja Kopernika, 1998, 27. This is the chain of events that followed in 1939: Polish defeat, Soviet cession of Vilnius to Lithuania, then Soviet occupation of Lithuania itself.

34. Lucjan Żeligowski, *Zapomniane prawdy*, London: Mildner and Sons, 1943, 32–43; Piłsudski quotation from Bohdan Skaradziński, "Fenomen litewsko-białoruskich formacji Wojska Polskiego," in Jasiewicz, *Europa nie prowincjonalna*, 902. See also Andrzej Nowak, *Polska i trzy Rosje*, Cracow: Arcana, 2001, 326–332.

35. Jan Dąbski, *Pokój ryski*, Warsaw: Kulerskiego, 1931, 78; Witold Wojdyło, "Traktat w Rydze w koncepcjach politycznych obozu narodowego," in Wojciechowski, *Traktat Ryski 1921*, 53–55. Grabski's secondary motivations are treated in Krzysztof Kawalec, "Naro-

dowa Demokracja wobec traktatu ryskiego," ibid., 31–45. On Wasilewski see Barbara Stoczewska, *Litwa, Białoruś, Ukraina w myśli politycznej Leona Wasilewskiego,* Cracow: Księgarnia Naukowa, 1998. On Piłsudski and Wasilewski, see Wasilewski, *Józef Piłsudski: Jakim go znałem,* Warsaw: Rój, 1935.

36. "Belorussia" signifies the Russian concept of the area as part of a Great Russian nation; "Belarus" signifies the patriotic view of the country as the inheritor of the Grand Duchy of Lithuania and Rus'.

37. I have in mind M.V. Dounar-Zapolski, *Historyia Belarusi,* Minsk: Belaruskaia entsyklopedia, 1994. The manuscript was complete in 1926. On Soviet exploitation of peasant and national questions in Poland, see George Jackson, *Comintern and Peasant in East Europe, 1919–1930,* New York: Columbia University Press, 1966, 22, 182, and passim.

38. It was published in communist Poland: Adam Mickiewicz, *Pan Tadeusz,* trans. Bronisław Taraszkiewicz, Olsztyn: Pojezierze, 1984.

39. A tradition in Belarusian historiography asks what would have happened had Riga brought all of the "ethnically Belarusian lands" into Soviet Belorussia; another that asks what might have happened had a Belarusian independent state somehow been created. These were not in fact possibilities. This study will pose a more limited counterfactual, having to do with propositions made and refused in the course of the pertractations. See Uladzimir Lad'iseu and Petr Br'ihadzin, "Rada BNR paslia R'izhkaha dahavora 1921 r.," *Belaruski histarychny chasopis,* 1 (1997), 48–50.

40. Michał Römer in Kaunas to Józef Piłsudski in Warsaw, 15 May 1922, in Anna and Andrzej Rosner, eds., *Pasmo czynności ciągiem lat idące,* Warsaw: Krąg, 1992, 158–162; on the pogrom, Ezra Mendelsohn, *The Jews of East Central Europe,* Bloomington: Indiana University Press, 1983, 52; on 1918–1920, Łossowski, *Stosunki polsko-litewskie;* on the 1920s, Alfred Senn, *The Emergence of Modern Lithuania,* Westport, Conn.: Greenwood Press, 1975.

41. There was a small memorial to Mickiewicz inside the Kościół Akademicki in Wilno.

42. *Słowo* (Wilno), 1 November 1924, 1.

43. Piotr Myślakowski, "Losy wileńskich pomników Mickiewicza," *Biuletyn Stowarzyszenia Wspólnota Polska,* October 1998.

CHAPTER 4. THE SECOND WORLD WAR AND THE VILNIUS QUESTION (1939–1945)

1. On Wilno in this period: Ezra Mendelsohn, *The Jews of East Central Europe,* Bloomington: Indiana University Press, 1983, 11–84; Jerzy Tomaszewski, ed., *Najnowsze dzieje Żydów w Polsce,* Warsaw: PWN, 1939, 179–198. See also Czesław Miłosz, *Rodzinna Europa,* Paris: Instytut Literacki, 1980, 78–89.

2. The Polish census of the city in 1931 found that of 195,100 residents 65.9 percent were Polish, 28.0 percent Jewish, 0.9 percent Belarusian, and 0.8 percent Lithuanian. Lithuanian demographers conceded that there were few Lithuanians in the city. Leonas Sabaliunas accepted a figure of 5.8 percent for the city and surrounding lands absorbed by Lithuania in 1940. Piotr Eberhardt "Przemiany narodowościowe na Litwie," *Przegląd Wschodni,* 1, 3 (1991), 468–469.

3. On Belarusian culture, Nicholas Vakar, *Belorussia,* Cambridge, Mass.: Harvard Univer-

sity Press, 1956, 121–135; Aleksander Wabiszczewicz, "Sytuacja szkolnictwa białoruskiego na Białorusi zachodniej," in Małgorzata Giżejewska and Tomasz Strzembosz, eds., *Społeczeństwa białoruskie, litewskie i polskie na ziemiach północno-wschodnich II Rzeczypospolitej,* Warsaw: ISP PAN, 1995, 190, 198; Aleksiej Litwin, "Problem Białorusi w oficjalnej polityce polskiej," ibid., 17–21.

4. Miłosz, *Rodzinna Europa,* 58.

5. Algis Kasperovičius, "Relituanizacja i powrót do macierzy," in Robert Traba, ed., *Tematy polsko-litewskie,* Olsztyn: Borussia, 1999, 103; Nerijus Udrenas, "History Textbooks and the Making of the Nation State," Masters thesis, Brandeis University, 1995, 14.

6. Tomas Venclova, "Native Realm Revisited," cited after the manuscript, 23, published in Polish in *Zeszyty Literackie,* 70 (2000).

7. Cited after Iver Neumann, "Poland as a Regional Great Power," in Iver Neumann, ed., *Regional Great Powers and International Politics,* New York: St. Martin's, 1992, 134–135. See M. Anysas, *Der litauische-polnische Streit um das Wilnagebiet,* Wurzburg: K. Triltsch, 1934, 1–2, 10; Augustin Voldemaras, *La Lithuanie et ses problèmes,* Paris: Mercure Universel, 1933, 15–18.

8. Alfonsas Eidintas and Vytautas Žalys, *Lithuania in European Politics,* New York: St. Martin's, 1999, 140–141.

9. Ibid., 122.

10. David Crowe, *The Baltic States and the Great Powers,* Boulder, Colo.: Westview Press, 1993, 83.

11. Eidintas and Žalys, *Lithuania in European Politics,* 180–181.

12. On the region: Marek Wierzbicki, *Polacy i Białorusini w zaborze sowieckim,* Warsaw: Volumen, 2000, 155–156; on the city: Iwanow, "Sprawa przynależności Wilna i problemy narodowościowe na Białorusj," in Giżejewska and Strzembosz, *Społeczeństwa,* 85–89.

13. *Polski Słównik Biograficzny,* vol. 18, Wrocław: Ossolineum, 1973, 1, 514; Anton Lutskevich, *Uspaminy ab pratsy pershykh belaruskikh palitychnykh arhanizatsyi,* Minsk: Belaruskaia savetskaia entsyklapedyia, 1991; Arnold McMillin, *Die Literatur der Weissrussen,* Giessen: Wilhelm Schmitz, 1997, 122.

14. Regina Žepkajte, "Okupacja Wilna przez Armię Czerwoną," in Giżejewska and Strzembosz, *Społeczeństwa,* 305.

15. Crowe, *The Baltic States,* 99–106, Alan Bullock, *Hitler and Stalin,* New York: Knopf, 1992, 645; Žepkajte, "Okupacja Wilna przez Armię Czerwoną," 302; Algis Kasperovičius, "Stosunek władz i społeczeństwa Litwy do Polaków ne Wileńszczyźnie," in Giżejewska and Strzembosz, *Społeczeństwa,* 307; Krzysztof Tarka, "Spór o Wilno," *Zeszyty Historyczne,* 114 (1995), 60; Sabaliunas, *Lithuania in Crisis,* 151–153. During the Second World War, the administrative center of Lithuania remained Kaunas, although according to the constitution the capital was Vilnius. It was in Kaunas that Japanese vice consul Chiune Sugihara issued ten thousand visas to Jews and saved five thousand lives. Hillel Levine, *In Search of Sugihara,* New York: Free Press, 1996.

16. Leonas Sabaliunas, *Lithuania in Crisis,* Bloomington: Indiana University Press, 1972, 153; Kasperovičius, "Relituanizacja i powrót do macierzy," 108.

17. Entry for 9 July 1941, his diary (Dziennik) in the manuscripts department (Rankrašču Skyrius) of the Vilnius University Library, F75–13. Herector VUBR.

18. The ostensible legal basis for this claim was the agreement with Bolshevik Russia of 12 July 1920.
19. S. Kairys, "Iš Vilniaus sugrizus?" *Mintis,* 10, 1939, 330, cited after Kasperavičius, "Relituanizacja," 109.
20. Sabaliunas, *Lithuania in Crisis,* 162. See also Crowe, *The Baltic States,* 143.
21. Diary entries for 4 February 1940 and 21 March 1940, VUBR F75–13. See also Longin Tomaszewski, "Społeczeństwo Wileńszczyzny wobec władzy Litewskiej i sowieckiej," in Giżejewska and Strzembosz, *Społeczeństwa,* 329; Eberhardt, *Przemiany narodowościowe na Litwie,* 1997, 151.
22. Kasperovičius, "Stosunek władz i społeczeństwa Litwy do Polaków na Wileńszczyźnie," 313; Žepkajte, "Okupacja Wilna przez Armię Czerwoną," 310–314.
23. Eberhardt, *Przemiany narodowościowe na Litwie,* 153–154.
24. This book will not address the issue of the comparability of the Nazi and Soviet regimes. In the 1970s and 1980s comparability was part of a West German debate, where it was related to the legacies of the Third Reich in contemporary West German society. A guide to the *Historikerstreit* is Charles Maier, *The Unmasterable Past,* Cambridge, Mass.: Harvard University Press, 1988; see also Hans-Ulrich Wehler, *Entsorgung der deutschen Vergangenheit?* Munich: Beck, 1988. A useful collection in English is Peter Baldwin, ed., *Reworking the Past,* Boston: Beacon Press, 1990. In the 1990s, the debate over comparability became French, as previous loyalties to communism were questioned after the collapse of the Soviet Union. See especially François Furet, *Le passé d'une illusion,* Paris: Calmann-Levy, 1995; see also my review "Coming to Terms with the Charm and Power of Soviet Communism," *Contemporary European History,* 6, 1 (1997), 133–144. Stéphane Courtois, ed., *Le livre noir du communisme,* Paris: Robert Laffont, 1997, was an international effort whose case for the murderousness of communism made the most waves in France and Italy. French and German debates met in *Le Débat,* 89 (1996).
25. Under cover of German rule, extreme Lithuanian nationalists called for the Germans to cleanse Vilnius of Poles, and were disappointed to learn that the Germans had other plans. Kasperavičius, "Relituanizacja," 114–115.
26. Statistical Report for March 1943 (34/67), F. R1399, A1, B. 9; "Lagebericht. Wilna, IV A 1 (Gestapo)," F. R1399, A1, B. 100; "An den Herrn Höheren SS-und Polizeiführer Ostland und Russland Nord in Riga. Verhalten litauischer Sonderkampfverbände," 11 May 1944; "Lagebericht. Bandentätigkeit," 24 April 1944, F. R1399, A1, B. 100, L. 1; Report of SS Commander Titel to Jeckeln in Riga, 15 May 1944, F. R1399, A1, B. 106; all in the Lithuanian Central State Archives, Vilnius.
27. Dina Porat, "The Holocaust in Lithuania," in David Cesarini, ed., *The Final Solution,* Routledge: New York, 1994, 160.
28. Yitzhak Arad, "The 'Final Solution' in Lithuania," *Yad Vashem Studies,* 11 (1976), 241; Yitzhak Arad, *Ghetto in Flames,* Jerusalem: Hava, 1980, 43–48.
29. Konrad Kweit, "Rehearsing for Murder," *Holocaust and Genocide Studies,* 12, 1 (1998), 3–26). On the role of Lithuanian Jews during the Soviet occupation, Dov Levin, *Baltic Jews under the Soviets,* Jerusalem: Hebrew University 30, 43. The author was a parliamentary deputy during the Soviet interregnum.
30. Arad, *Ghetto in Flames,* 429–432; Marc Dvorjetski *Le Ghetto de Vil'na,* Geneva: Union

O.S.E., 1946; diary of Icchak Rudaszewski, *Lithuania*, 3 (1991), 35–49; Michael Mac-
Queen, "The Context of Mass Destruction," *Holocaust and Genocide Studies*, 12, 1 (1998)
27–48. See also Knut Stang, *Kollaboration und Massenmord*, Frankfurt am Main: Peter
Lang, 1996, 73–112.

31. The death toll is higher than this suggests, as perhaps fifteen thousand Jews from Warsaw and central Poland fled to Vilne between 1939 and 1941. Most of them met their
death somewhere in Lithuania.

32. Abraham Novershtern, "Yung Vilne," in Yisrael Gutman, Ezra Mendelsohn, Jehuda
Reinharz, and Chone Shmeruk, eds., *The Jews of Poland Between the Two World Wars*,
Hanover, Mass.: Brandeis University Press, 1989, 386.

33. Tarka, "Spór o Wilno," 83.

34. Kasperavičius, "Relituanizacja," 117.

35. *Sovetskii faktor*, 73.

36. *Teczka specjalna J. W. Stalina*, 48.

37. This subject is treated at length in chapter 9.

38. Diary entry for 6 November 1944, VUBR, f75–13.

39. "Who will honor the city without a name?" asks the first line of Czesław Miłosz's "Mi-
asto bez imienia," published in 1969. On the predicament of Lithuanian Poles, see the
recollections in Jerzy Surwillo, *Rachunki nie zamknięte*, Vilnius: Magazyn Wileński,
1992, for example at 318.

CHAPTER 5. EPILOGUE: SOVIET LITHUANIAN VILNIUS (1945–1991)

1. Włodzimierz Borodziej, Stanisław Ciesielski, Jerzy Kochanowski, "Wstęp," in *Przesiedlenie ludności polskiej* 23–25; Valentinas Brandišauskas, "Migracje i przemiany de-
mograficzne na Litwie," in Krzysztof Jasiewicz, ed., *Europa nie prowincjonalna*, Warsaw:
Rytm, 1999, 1123.

2. On Poles in Vilnius, *Przesiedlenie ludności polskiej*, 111; on Polish authorities awaiting
Polish peasants, 109ff; on German documents, 159; on Kaunas Lithuania, 361–364.

3. Piotr Eberhardt, *Przemiany narodowościowe na Litwie*, Warsaw: Przegląd Wschodni,
1997, 167; Piotr Eberhardt, *Polska ludność kresowa*, Warsaw: PWN, 1998, 114–123. Cau-
tionary tales about census data are provided by Benedict Anderson, *The Spectre of Comparison*, London: Verso, 1998, 36–45.

4. An official quasi-memoir treats this period as a struggle to save the "Lithuanian nation."
M. Bordonaite, *Tovaryshch Matas*, Vilnius: Mintis, 1986, 89 and passim.

5. Barbara Christophe, *Staat versus Identität*, Cologne: Wissenschaft und Politik, 1997, 41.

6. A. Bendzhius et al., *Istoriia Vil'niusskogo universiteta*, Vilnius: Mokslas, 1979, 154, 194;
Marceli Kosman, *Uniwersytet Wileński 1579–1979*, Wrocław: Ossolineum, 1981, 57. The
figure for Jews fell from 13 percent in 1937–38 to 6.5 percent in 1945–46 to 1.6 percent in
1976–88. The first drop is a result of the fact that over 90 percent of Lithuania's Jews had
been murdered in the Holocaust. The second most likely reflects a preference of Soviet
Jews to study in Russian-language universities.

7. N.A. Aitov, V.G. Mordkovich, and M.Kh. Titma, *Sovetskii gorod*, Moscow: Mysl: 1988,

212–222; Romuald Misiunas and Rein Taagepera, *The Baltic States,* London: Hurst, 1983, 106, 125.

8. A.J.P. Taylor, *The Habsburg Monarchy, 1809–1918,* London: Hamilton, 1948.

9. Vytautas Vaitiekūnas, "Sovietized Education in Occupied Lithuania," in V. Stanley Vardys, ed. *Lithuania under the Soviets,* New York: Praeger, 1965, 186–187, 194.

10. V. Stanley Vardys, "Modernization and Baltic Nationalism," *Problems of Communism,* September–October 1975, 43.

11. Marek Śliwiński and Valerijus Čekmonas, "Świadomość narodowa mieszkańców Litwy i Białorusi," *Przegląd Wschodni,* 4, 3 (1997), 585; Vesna Popovska, *National Minorities and Citizenship Rights in Lithuania,* Houndmills: Palgrave, 2000, 45–49.

12. Eberhardt, *Przemiany narodowościowe na Litwie,* 176–179; Nicolas Werth, "Apogée et crise du goulag," in Stéphane Courtois, ed., *Le livre noir du communisme,* Paris: Robert Lafont, 1997, 262.

13. Zigmas Zinkevičius, *The History of the Lithuanian Language,* Vilnius: Mokslo ir enciklopediju leidykla, 1996, 322–324; Misiunas and Taagepera, *The Baltic States,* 159–165.

14. Vardys, "Modernization and Baltic Nationalism," 38–40; Eberhardt, *Przemiany narodowościowe na Litwie,* 203.

15. Antanas Snechkus, *Sovetskaia Litva na puti rastsveta,* Vilnius, 1970.

16. Compare Leonidas Donskis, "Lithuania at the End of the Twentieth Century," in Aleksandr Dobrynin and Bronius Kuzmickas, eds., *Personal Freedom and National Resurgence,* Washington, D.C. Paideia, 1994, 59–74. A radical version of this idea comes from contemporary Hindi nationalists, who claim that medieval Lithuania was a "Hindu-Buddhist" state. Douglas Spitz and William Urban, "A Hindu Nationalist View of Baltic History," *Journal of Baltic Studies,* 24 3 (1993), 297.

17. I have in mind Zinkevičius's *History of the Lithuanian Language.*

18. Virgil Krapauskas, "Marxism and Nationalism in Soviet Lithuanian Historiography," *Journal of Baltic Studies,* 23, 3 (1993), 255; Tomas Venclova, "Litwo, ojczyzno nasza," *Lithuania,* 26–27 (1998), 78; Jacek Borkowicz, "Polska—Litwa," *Polska w Europie,* 12 (1993), 34–35; Alicja Nagórska, "Języki—narody—kultury," *Lithuania,* 5 (1991), 194; Stephen Burant and Voytek Zubek, "Eastern Europe's Old Memories and New Realities," *East European Politics and Societies,* 7, 2 (1993), 375.

19. Greta Lemanaitė, "Stereotyp Polaka w oczach Litwina," in Teresa Walas, ed., *Narody i stereotypy,* Cracow: Międzynarodowe Centrum Kultury, 1995, 90–94. See also Marek Śliwiński, "Conscience nationale et la perception géopolitique des habitants de la Lithuanie," in Pierre Allan and Jan Škaloud, eds., *The Making of Democracy,* Prague: Economics University Press, 1997, 134–140; *Kultura,* 442–443 (1984), 133–135. These beliefs did not positively correlate with contact with Poles: Lithuanians who lived among Poles expressed the least antipathy, while Lithuanians in places where there were few or no Poles expressed the most. Śliwiński and Čekmonas, "Świadomość narodowa mieszkańców Litwy i Białorusi," 538–585. Their survey was taken in the early 1990s.

20. The number: Alfred Erich Senn, *Gorbachev's Failure in Lithuania,* New York: St. Martin's, 1995, 31. For documents concerning the protests, Izidors Vizulis, *The Molotov-Ribbentrop Pact of 1939,* New York: Praeger, 1990. On the debates of the late 1980s,

Christophe, *Staat versus Identität,* 104–122. See also V. Stanley Vardys, "Lithuanian National Politics," *Problems of Communism,* July–August 1989, 54, 62; Aleksandra Niemczykowa, "Litwa na drodze do suwerenności," *Lithuania,* 17 (1995), 105.

21. Vytautas Landsbergis, *Lithuania: Independent Again,* Seattle: University of Washington Press, 2000; on Čiurlionis see A.E. Senn, "The Lithuanian Intelligentsia of the Nineteenth Century," in Aleksander Loit, ed., *National Movements in the Baltic Countries,* Stockholm: Center for Baltic Studies, 1985, 314; Misiunas and Taagepera, *The Baltic States,* 148. See also Popovska, *National Minorities,* 57 and passim; and Vytautas Landsbergis, "Pieśń o tym, kim jesteśmy," *Lithuania,* 1 (1990), 16–21. Čiurlionis's rehabilitation was in part the result of efforts by Antanas Venclova.

22. As a victor over the Teutonic Knights in the Battle of Grünwald Vytautas was also conveniently, "anti-German." Alvydas Nikžentaitis, "Der Vytautaskult in Litauen und seine Widerspiegelung im Denkmal," *Nordost Archiv,* 6, 1 (1997), 131, 138–141. Compare Antanas Čaplinskas, *Vilnius Streets,* Vilnius: Charibde, 2000.

23. Vytautas Toleikis, "Historia w szkole litewskiej w perspektywie stosunków polsko-litewskich," in Robert Traba, ed., *Tematy polsko-litewskie,* Olsztyn: Borussia, 1999, 210–212; see also Birute Vareikiene, "Od konfrontacji do zrozumienia," ibid., 216–225; Christophe, *Staat versus Identität,* 141–165; Adolfas Šapoka, *Vilnius in the Life of Lithuania,* Toronto: Lithuanian Association, 1962.

CHAPTER 6. EARLY MODERN UKRAINE (1569–1914)

1. Other parts belonged to the Ottoman Empire and its vassals Moldova and the Crimean khanate, as well as to Hungary.

2. For the medieval origins of this difference, Dimitri Obolensky, *The Byzantine Commonwealth,* London: Phoenix Press, 2000, 322–343; Francis Thomson, "The Corpus of Slavonic Translations Available in Muscovy," in Boris Gasparov and Olga Raevsky-Hughes, eds., *Christianity and the Eastern Slavs,* Berkeley: University of California Press, 1993, 179–214; Nataliia Iakovenko, *Narys istorii Ukrainy z naidavnishykh chasiv do kintsia XVIII stolittia,* Kyiv: Heneza, 1997.

3. Lucien Febvre and Henri-Jean Martin, *The Coming of the Book,* London: Verso, 1976 [1958], 201–203, 248–332; Iaroslav Isaievych, *Preemniki pervopechatnika,* Moscow: Kniga, 1981. For a sense of how sharp disputation in Poland had become before 1596, David Frick, *Polish Sacred Philology in the Reformation and Counter-Reformation,* Berkeley: University of California Press, 1989. In one Protestant case the Church Slavonic was used in biblical translation: David Frick, "Szymon Budny and the Church Slavonic Bible," in Michael Flier and Simon Karlinsky, eds., *Language, Literature, Linguistics,* Berkeley, Calif.: Slavic Specialties, 1987, 62–66.

4. André Martel, *La langue polonaise dans les pays ruthènes,* Lille: Travaux et Mémoires de l'Université de Lille, 1938, 58–66, 142, and worthy of consultation in its entirety; also Ihor Ševcenko, *Byzantium and the Slavs,* Cambridge, Mass.: Ukrainian Research Institute, 1991, 170 and 670. The Uniate Church was actually slower to embrace Polish than Orthodox churchmen. Polish gains predominance in documents preserved in the Uni-

ate Church's archives in about 1650, and maintains that dominance until about 1800. More detailed data are presented in chart 1, p. 48.

5. Borys Gudziak, *Crisis and Reform,* Cambridge, Mass.: Harvard University Press, 1998, 209–238 and passim; Oskar Halecki, *From Florence to Brest,* New York: Archon Books, 223–286, 423–433; M.O. Koialovich, *Litovskaia tserkovnaia uniia,* vol. 1, St. Petersburg, 1859, 166–168.

6. On disputes: David Frick, *Meletij Smotryc'kyj,* Cambridge, Mass.: Harvard University Press, 1995, 181–192; Francis Thompson, "Meletius Smotritsky and the Union with Rome," in Bert Groen and Wil van den Bercken, eds., *Four Hundred Years,* Leuven: Peeters, 1998, 55–126; Teresa Hynczewska-Hennel, "The National Consciousness of Ukrainian Nobles and Cossacks," in Ivo Banac and Frank Sysyn, eds., *Concepts of Nationhood in Early Modern Europe,* Cambridge, Mass.: Ukrainian Research Institute, 1986, 383–392; Michał Łesiów, "The Polish and Ukrainian Languages," in Zvi Gitelman et al., eds., *Cultures and Nations of Central and Eastern Europe,* Cambridge, Mass.: Ukrainian Research Institute, 2000. 397–398. On Protestants in particular: George Williams, *Protestants in the Ukrainian Lands of the Polish-Lithuanian Commonwealth,* Cambridge, Mass.: Ukrainian Studies Fund, 1988, 190, 205.

7. Sofiia Senyk, "Beresteis'ka uniia i svits'ke dukhovenstvo," in Borys Gudziak, ed., *Beresteis'ka uniia ta vnutrishniie zhyttia Tserkvy v XVII stolitti,* L'viv: L'vivs'ka bohoslovs'ka akademia, 1997, 55–66.

8. Jerzy Boręcki, "Unia lubelska jak czynnik kszałtowania się ukraińskiej świadomości narodowej," in Jerzy Kłoczowski et al., eds., *Unia lubelska i tradycje integracyjne w Europie środkowo-wschodniej,* Lublin: IESW, 1999, 60–78; Natalia Jakowenko, "Rus' iak tretii chlen Rechi Pospolytoi 'Dvokh Narodiv' v ukrains'kii dumtsi pershoi polovyny XVII st.," ibid., 84–88; Henyk Samsonowicz, "Mieszczaństwo Rzeczypospolitej wobec Unii Brzeskiej," in Jan Sergiusz Gajek and Stanisław Nabywaniec, eds., *Unia brzeska z perspektywy czterech stuleci,* Lublin: KUL, 1998, 73–80; David Saunders, "Ukrainians since 1600," *Ethnic Studies,* 10 (1993), 113.

9. For this to happen, the Uniate Church had to be transformed from a Polonophone to a Ukrainophile institution, a nineteenth-century story to which we shall return. On the Reformation and peasants in Poland, Wacław Urban, *Chłopi wobec Reformacji w Małopolsce,* Cracow: PWN, 1959.

10. 1570 is the modal year in Jan Rotkowski, *Histoire economique de la Pologne avant les partages,* Paris: Champion, 1927. For a critique of political interpretations of the "second serfdom," Andrzej Kamiński, "Neo-serfdom in Poland-Lithuania," *Slavic Review,* 34, 2 (1975), 253–268.

11. N.M. Iakovenko, *Ukrains'ka shliakhta,* Kyiv: Naukova Dumka, 1993, 265; see also Kamiński, "Szlachta of the Polish-Lithuanian Commonwealth," 31; Frank Sysyn, *Between Poland and the Ukraine,* Cambridge, Mass.: Harvard University Press, 1985, 20–32.

12. Hanover's *Abyss of Despair* cited after Henry Abramson, *A Prayer for the Government,* Cambridge, Mass.: Harvard University Press, 32. On the magnates consult Henryk Litwin, *Napływ szlachty polskiej na Ukrainę 1569–1648,* Warsaw: Semper, 2000; Iakovenko, *Ukrains'ka shliakhta,* 206–207, 219; Rosman, *The Lords' Jews,* 1990, 40, 85, and passim.

13. Ewa Wolnicz-Pawłowska, "Antroponimia polska na kresach południowo-wschodnich," in Janusz Rieger, ed., *Język polski dawnych Kresów Wschodnich,* Warsaw: Semper, 1999, 211–212; Martel, *Langue polonaise,* 200. On the education of women, Andrzej Karpiński, *Kobieta w mieście polskim,* Warsaw: IH PAN, 1995, 285–313; also Maria Bogucka, *Białogłowa w dawnej Polsce,* Warsaw: Trio, 1998, 167–201.

14. On the mismatch in 1569: Vitalii Shcherbak, *Ukrains'ke kozatstvo: Formuvannia sotsial'noho stanu,* Kyiv: KM Akademia, 2000, 42 and passim. On war-fighting: Wiesław Majewski, "The Polish Art of War in the Sixteenth and Seventeenth Centuries," in J.K. Federowicz, ed., *A Republic of Nobles,* Cambridge: Cambridge University Press, 1982, 188.

15. Zenon Kohut, *Russian Centralism and Ukrainian Autonomy,* Cambridge, Mass.: Harvard University Press, 1988, 24–64; Agnieszka Biedrzycka, "Złoty pokój," *Prace Historyczne,* 127 (2000), 27–38.

16. Ivan Butych, ed., *Universaly Bohdana Khmel'nyts'koho,* Kyiv: Al'ternatyvy, 1998, 45, 46, 50, 53; Volodymyr Serhiichuk, "Kozatstvo i Uniia," in Ryszard Łuzny, Franciszek Ziejka, and Andrzej Kępinski, eds., *Unia brzeska,* Cracow: Universitas, 457; Borys Floria, "Natsional'no-konfesiina svidomist' naselennia skhidnoi Ukrainy," in Gudziak, *Beresteis'ka uniia,* 132; Antoni Mironiwicz, "Projekty unijne wobec Cerkwi prawosławnej w dobie ugody hadziackiej," in Gajek and Nabywaniec, eds., *Unia brzeska,* 95–139.

17. Mykhailo Hrushevs'kyi, *Istoriia Ukrainy-Rusy* vol. 10, New York: Knyhospilka, 1958, 346–359; Tetiana Iakovleva, *Hetmanshchyna v druhii polovyni 50-kh rokiv XVII stolittia,* Kyiv: Osnovy, 1998, 305–350; Andrzej Kamiński, "The Cossack Experiment in Szlachta Democracy," *Harvard Ukrainian Studies,* 1, 2 (1977), 178–187.

18. To follow one important trend away from toleration, see Zenon Guldon and Jacek Wijaczka, "The Accusation of Ritual Murder in Poland, 1500–1800," *Polin,* 10 (1997), 119–131.

19. J. H. Elliot, *Europe Divided 1559–1598,* Oxford: Blackwell 2000 [1968], 154–163 and passim.

20. On finances: Larysa Hvozdyk-Pritsak *Ekonomichna i politychna viziia Bohdana Khmel'nyts'koho ta ii realizatsiia v derzhavi Viis'ko Zaporoz'ke,* Kyiv: Oberehy, 1999, 101–102 and passim; on language, Omeljan Pritsak and John Reshetar, "Ukraine and the Dialectics of Nation-Building," *Slavic Review,* 22, 2 (1963), 18–19). On Cossack history and Ukrainian identity: Frank Sysyn, "The Reemergence of the Ukrainian National and Cossack Mythology," *Social Research,* 58, 4 (1991), 845–864; Orest Subtelny, *Ukraine,* Toronto: University of Toronto Press, 1988, 94–95.

21. Oskar Halecki, *Przyłączenie Podlasia, Wołynia, i Kijowszczyzny do Korony w Roku 1569,* Cracow: Gebethner and Wolff, 1915, 244. For the biography, Jan Widacki, *Kniaź Jarema,* Cracow: Wydawnictwo Literackie, 1997, 11–20. The throne anecdote from Iakovenko, *Ukrains'ka shliakhta,* 75; the property anecdote from Sysyn, *Between Poland and the Ukraine,* 76.

22. John Basarab, *Pereiaslav 1654,* Edmonton: CIUS, 1982.

23. On collegia: O.I. Travkina, *Chernihivs'kyi Kolehium 1700–1786,* Chernihiv: DKP PVV, 2000, 8–41; Valeriia Nichyk, *Kyievo-Mohylians'ka Akademia i nimets'ka kultura,* Kyiv: Ukrainskyi Tsentr Dukhovnoi Kul'tury, 2001, 53–94. On Kochanowski: Paulina Lewin, "Jan Kochanowski: The Model Poet in Eastern Slavic Lecture of Poetics in the Seventeenth and Eighteenth Centuries," in Samuel Fiszman, ed., *The Polish Renaissance in Its*

European Context, Bloomington: Indiana University Press, 1988, 429–443. On translations: Thomson, "Slavonic Translations," 191.

24. Bushkovitch, "The Formation of National Consciousness in Early Modern Russia," in Banac and Sysyn, *Concepts of Nationhood,* 355–377; Riccardo Picchio, "Guidelines for a Comparative Study of the Language Question among the Slavs," in Riccardo Picchio and Harvey Goldblatt, eds., *Aspects of the Slavic Language Question,* 2 vols., Columbus, Ohio: Slavica, 1984, Vol. 1, 12–29; I.K. Grot, *Filologicheskiie razyskaniia,* St. Petersburg, 1899, 464–467.

25. Paul Bushkovitch, *Religion and Society in Russia,* Oxford: Oxford University Press, 1992; K.V. Kharlampovych, *Malorossiiskoe vliianie na velikorusskuiu tserkovnuiu zhizn',* Kazan: Golubeva, 1914. For a special instance of a Ukrainian churchman's influence on the historiography of Russia, Edward Keenan, *The Kurbskii-Groznyi Apocrypha,* Cambridge, Mass.: Harvard University Press, 1971, 21–44.

26. Orest Subtelny, *The Mazepists,* Boulder, Colo.: East European Monographs, 1981, 28. See also Zenon Kohut, "Ukrainian Nationbuilding," in Banac and Sysyn, *Concepts of Nationhood,* 566–567.

27. Daniel Beauvois, *Polacy na Ukrainie, 1831–1863,* Paris: Instytut Literacki, 1987, 29–141.

28. Daniel Beauvois, *La bataille de la terre en Ukraine,* Lille: Presses Universitaires, 1993, 22–27.

29. Fr. Rawita-Gawroński, *Rok 1863 na Rusi,* Vol. 2, L'viv: H. Altenberg, 1903, 266.

30. For a revealing map, Norman Davies, *God's Playground,* Vol. 1, New York: Columbia University Press, 1982, 355.

31. A.I. Baranovych, *Magnatskoe khoziaistvo na iuge Volyni v XVIII v.,* Moscow: Akademiia nauk SSSR, 1955, 105–166.

32. Beauvois, *La bataille de la terre,* 68–71, 94. On Shevchenko's historical vision, George Grabowicz, *The Poet as Mythmaker,* Cambridge, Mass.: Harvard University Press for Ukrainian Research Institute, 1982; also very insightful is Oksana Zabuzhko, *Shevchenkiv mif Ukrainy,* Kyiv: Abrys, 1997, 97–142.

33. David Saunders, *The Ukrainian Impact on Russian Culture, 1750–1850,* Edmonton: CIUS, 1985.

34. Michael Hamm, *Kiev,* Princeton, N.J.: Princeton University Press, 55–81.

35. Witold Rodkiewicz, *Russian Nationality Policy,* Lublin: Scientific Society of Lublin, 192–204.

36. The text is reproduced in Paul Robert Magocsi, *A History of Ukraine,* Seattle: University of Washington Press, 1996, 369–370.

37. See for example P.N. Batiushkov, *Volyn',* Saint Petersburg: Obshchestvennaia pol'za, 1888.

38. Pavlo Zaitsev, *Taras Shevchenko,* trans. George Luckyj, Toronto: University of Toronto Press, 1988.

39. Max Rosenfeld, *Die polnische Judenfrage,* Vienna: Löwit, 1918, 68; Józef Bushko, "The Consequences of Galician Autonomy after 1867," *Polin,* 12 (1999), 86; Stanisław Grodziski, "The Jewish question in Galicia," *Polin,* 12 (1999), 62.

40. Mykhailo Vozniak, *Iak probudylosia ukrains'ke narodne zhyttia v Halychyni za Avstrii,* L'viv: Dilo, 1924, 6–14.

41. Stepan Shakh, *O. Markiian Shashkevych ta halyts'ke vidrodzhennia,* Paris: Ukrainian

Christian Movement, 1961, 36; Stefan Zabrowarny, "Dzieło biskupa Jana Śnigurskiego," in Stanisław Stępień, ed., *Polska—Ukraina: 1000 lat sąsiedztwa*, Przemyśl: Południowo-Wschodni Instytut Naukowy, 1996, 169–171.

42. Vozniak, *Iak probudylosia*, 175–176; Antony Polonsky, "The Revolutionary Crisis of 1846–1849 and Its Place in the Development of Nineteenth-Century Galicia," in Gitelman et al., *Cultures and Nations*, 443–469; Jarosław Hrycak, *Historia Ukrainy, 1772–1999*, Lublin, IEWS, 2000, 90ff.

43. Paul Robert Magocsi, "The Language Question in Nineteenth Century Galicia," in Picchio and Goldblatt, eds., *Aspects of the Slavic Language Question*, Vol. 2, 56–57. See also Hugo Lane, "State Culture and National Identity in a Multiethnic Context," Doctoral dissertation, University of Michigan 1999, 231–234.

44. John-Paul Himka, "The Construction of Nationality in Galician Rus'," in Ronald Suny and Michael Kennedy, eds., *Intellectuals and the Articulation of the Nation*, Ann Arbor: University of Michigan Press, 1999, especially 128–129, 143–145; John-Paul Himka, *Religion and Nationality in Western Ukraine*, Montreal: McGill-Queen's University Press, 1999, 130–134; Lane, "State Culture and National Identity," 294–296.

45. Mieczysław Adamczyk, "Szkolnictwo ludowe w greckokatolickiej diecezji przemyskiej," in Stępień, ed., *Polska—Ukraina*, 162–163.

46. Jiří Kořalka, *Češi v habsburské říši a v Evropě 1815–1914*, Prague: Argo, 1996, 16–82. Ukrainians were concerned with Polish culture in L'viv, while Czechs wished to overcome the German language in Prague. Using the reliable Austrian mails, a Czech could write to a Ukrainian in 1900 that "You have the same problems in L'viv as we do in Prague." František Pastrnek to Kyryl Studnyts'kyi, 5 July 1900, in *U pivstolitnykh zmahanniakh*, Kyiv: Naukova dumka, 1993, 54. See also Vozniak, *Iak probudylosia*, 48–54; *Sto padesát let česko-ukrajinských literárních styků*, Praha: Svět Sovětů, 1968, 5–52.

47. Józef Chlebowczyk, *On Small and Young Nations in Europe*, Wrocław: PAN, 1980, 126. Consult Roman Rozdolski, *Engels and the "Nonhistoric" Peoples*, trans. John-Paul Himka, Glasgow: Critique Books, 1986; compare Erica Benner, *Really Existing Nationalisms*, New York: Oxford University Press, 1995.

48. Thomas Prymak, *Mykhailo Hrushevsky*, Toronto: University of Toronto Press, 1987, 41.

49. The Canadian Institute of Ukrainian Studies is publishing an English edition of *History of Ukraine-Rus'*.

50. Czesław Partacz, "Przyczyny i przebieg konfliktu ukraińsko-polskiego w Galicji," *Przegląd Wschodni*, 2, 4 (1992–1993), 843; Ivan Rudnytsky, "The Ukrainians in Galicia under Austrian Rule," in Andrei Markovits and Frank Sysyn, eds., *Nationbuilding and the Politics of Nationalism*, Cambridge, Mass.: Ukrainian Research Institute, 1982, 60–65; Victor Hugo Lane, "Class Interest and the Shaping of a 'Non-Historical' Nation," in Gitelman et al., *Cultures and Nations*, 383; Ivan Rudnytsky, *Essays in Modern Ukrainian History*, Cambridge, Mass.: Harvard University Press, 1987.

51. Iaroslav Hrytsak, *Dukh, shcho tilo rve do boiu*, L'viv: Kameniar, 1990; Prymak, *Mykhailo Hrushevsky*, 56–57; Solomiia Pavlychko, *Dyskurs modernizmu v ukrains'kii literaturi*, Kyiv: Lybid': 1997, 9–38.

52. Valentyna Petrova, "Utvorennia natsional'no-demokratychnoi partii v Halychyni," *Naukovi Zapysky*, 5, 2 (1996), 15; Kerstin Jobst, *Zwischen Nationalismus und Internation-*

alismus, Hamburg: Dölling und Galitz Verlag, 1996, 32–51; Roman Szporluk, "Polish-Ukrainian Relations in 1918," in Paul Latawski, ed., *The Reconstruction of Poland, 1914–1923*, London: Macmillan, 1992, 46.

53. The poem itself, not to mention its publication in St. Petersburg, reveals a more subtle understanding of tactics than that with which Mickiewicz is usually credited.

54. Compare Yaroslav Hrytsak, "A Ukrainian Answer to the Galician Triangle," *Polin*, 12 (1999), 142–145, and Oksana Zabuzhko, *Filosofiia ukrainskoi idei ta ievropeis'kyi kontekst*, Kyiv: Osnovy, 1993, 22–53.

CHAPTER 7. GALICIA AND VOLHYNIA AT THE MARGIN (1914–1939)

1. Robert Kann, *A History of the Habsburg Empire*, Berkeley: University of California Press, 1977, 406–467; Serhii Popyk, *Ukraintsi v Avstrii 1914–1918*, Kyiv: Zoloti Lytavry, 1999.

2. This and above and below figures and interpretations after Piotr Eberhardt, *Polska ludność kresowa*, Warsaw: PWN, 1998, 180, citing *Die Ergebnisse der Volkszählung vom 31.XII.1900*, Vienna, 1902.

3. As a characteristic Polish appeal to Ukrainians had it, "So, you are by sheer mass more numerous than we, but everything which is the spirit and culture of these Carpathian lands is ours and ours alone." Kazimierz Saysse-Tobyczek, *Dość już ignorancji w kwestii Kresów Południowych!* Warsaw, 1919, cited after Jacek Kolbuszewski, *Kresy*, Wrocław: Dólnośląskie, 1999, 236.

4. Maurycy Horn, *Żydzi na Rusi Czerwonej*, Warsaw: PWN, 1975, 75–77; Rachel Menekin, "The Galician Jewish Vote in the 1873 Austrian Elections," *Polin*, 12 (1999), 119; John-Paul Himka, "The Polish-Ukrainian-Jewish Relations in Austrian Galicia," ibid., 37; Edward Dubinowicz, *Stanowisko ludności żydowskiej w Galicyi*, L'viv: Polonia, 1907, 16–17.

5. Oleksandr Pavliuk, *Borot'ba Ukrainy za nezalezhnist i polityka C.Sh.A.*, Kyiv: KM Akademia, 1996, 40–66. See also Mark Baker, "Lewis Namier and the Problem of Eastern Galicia," *Journal of Ukrainian Studies*, 23, 2 (1998), 59–104.

6. John Reshetar, *The Ukrainian Revolution*, Princeton, N.J.: Princeton University Press, 1952. The pertinent novel is Bulgakov's *White Guard*.

7. Antony Polonsky, "A Failed Pogrom," in Yisrael Gutman, Ezra Mendelsohn, Jehuda Reinarz, and Chone Smeruk, eds., *The Jews of Poland Between the Two World Wars*, Hanover, Mass.: Brandeis University Press, 1989, 113.

8. Bogdan Horbal, *Działalność polityczna Łemków na Łemkowszczyźnie 1918–1921*, Wrocław: Arboretum, 1997,

9. Other lands inhabited by speakers of Ukrainian remained in Romania (Bukovina) and Czechoslovakia (Subcarpathian Ruthenia). On Bukovina, Irina Livezeanu, *Cultural Politics in Greater Romania*, Ithaca, N.Y.: Cornell University Press, 1995, 63–68.

10. Richard Pipes, *The Formation of the Soviet Union*, Cambridge, Mass.: Harvard University Press, 1954, 249.

11. We are concerned with the interwar Polish palatinates of Lwów, Stanisławów, Tarnopol, Wołyń, and the southern part of Polesie palatinate, which (with the exception of the far west of Lwów palatinate) were incorporated into Soviet Ukraine in 1945, and which now

constitute the Lviv, Ivano-Frankivsk, Ternopil', Volhynia, and Rivne provinces of independent Ukraine. The parts of the interwar Polish Lublin and Cracow palatinates inhabited by Ukrainian speakers remained part of Poland after the Second World War and are part of Poland today. The linguistic proportions on the basis of 1939 Polish statistics by palatinate: Wołyń 68.4 percent Ukrainian and 16.2 percent Polish, Stanisławów 68.9 percent Ukrainian and 22.4 percent Polish, Lwów 34.1 percent Ukrainian and 57.7 Polish, Tarnopol 45.5 percent Ukrainian and 49.3 percent Polish. These figures inflate the Polish presence, and falsely suggest that every census respondent possessed a clear national identity. The Lwów palatinate was stretched to the west, thereby conveying the false impression that Poles were a majority around the city of Lwów. An imperfect but useful corrective is Volodymyr Kubiiovych, *Heohrafiia ukrains'kykh i sumezhnykh zemel'*, Cracow: Ukrains'ke vydavnytstvo, 1943, 13–14, 20–29.

12. Robert Conquest, *Harvest of Sorrow,* New York: Oxford University Press, 1986.

13. One example to stand for an entire class of people: Valer'ian Pidmohyl'nyi, whose novel *Misto* reveals much about the 1920s policy of Ukrainization, was executed in 1941. Our account now returns to Galicia and Volhynia, or "Polish Ukraine," as the heartland of the Ukrainian national idea in the last three quarters of the twentieth century. Helpful in the reconstruction of the history of prewar Soviet Ukraine are sources cited here and in chapters 6 and 9, as well as Iuri Shapoval, *Ukraina XX stolittia,* Kyiv: Heneza, 2001; Iuri Shapoval, Volodymyr Prystaiko, and Vadym Zolotar'ov, *Ch.K.-H.P.U.-N.K.V.D. v Ukraini,* Kyiv: Abrys, 1997; P.P. Bachyns'kyi, *Dokumenty trahichnoi istorii Ukrainy (1917–1927),* Kyiv: Okhorona pratsi, 2000.

14. Robert Potocki, "Polska a DC UNR," in Iurii Slivka, ed., *Deportatsii Ukraintsiv ta Poliakiv,* Lviv: Misioner, 1998, 65–66.

15. The failure of Galician Ukrainians to win a state, and the influence of dynamic movements such as Italian fascism, changed the views of Dmytro Dontsov (1883–1973). The geopolitician of the pre-1914 era became the philosopher of Ukrainian integral nationalism of the 1920s, with a fetish for organization. Dontsov, born a Russian subject, tended to oppose Russian barbarism to European civilization, to regard Ukraine and Poland as part of Europe, and even to present Poland as a model for Ukraine.

16. Alexander Motyl, *The Turn to the Right,* Boulder, Colo.: East European Monographs, 1980, 43. On Dontsov see Tomasz Stryjek, *Ukraińska idea narodowa okresu międzywojennego,* Wrocław: Funna, 2001, 110–190; Vasyl' Rudko, "Dontsov i Lypyns'kyi," *Harvard Ukrainian Studies,* 9, 3–4 (1985), 477–494.

17. Petro Mirchuk, *Narys istorii orhanizatsii ukrains'kykh natsionalistiv,* Munich: Ukrains'ke Vydavnytstvo, 1968, 93.

18. As UPA Colonel Vasyl' Kuk recalled, reformers such as Hołówko (assassinated in 1931) "divided us ideologically" and "blurred divisions"—and thus had to be destroyed. Motyka, *Tak było w Bieszczadach,* 35. Numbers from Alexander Motyl, "Ukrainian Nationalist Political Violence in Inter-War Poland, 1921–1939," *East European Quarterly,* 19, 1 (1985), 50.

19. Stephan Horak, *Poland and Her National Minorities,* New York: Vantage Press, 1969, 149. Newspapers also preserved contact with the literary language. Mariia Nedilia, "Ukrains'ka presa na zakhidnoukrains'kykh zemliakh," *Naukovi Zapysky,* 7 (1998), 265–270.

20. For photographs, Emil Revyuk, ed., *Polish Atrocities in Ukraine*, New York: United Ukrainian Organizations, 1931; V.J. Kushnir, *Polish Atrocities in the West Ukraine*, Prague: Nemec, 1931.

21. Witold Rodkiewicz, *Russian Nationality Policy*, Lublin: Scientific Society of Lublin, 1998, 35. During the war, Volhynian Germans rather than Volhynian Poles were regarded as a serious threat. Before 1914 Germans had been favored at the expense of Poles. Eric Lohr, "Enemy Alien Politics Within the Russian Empire During World War One," Doctoral dissertation, Harvard University, 1999.

22. Beauvois, *La bataille de la terre*, 137.

23. One Pole from Volhynia recalled the feudal obligations which Polish landholders forced upon Ukrainian peasants as late as the 1930s. II/1362/2k, Archiwum Wschodnie, Ośrodek Karta, Warsaw.

24. Włodzimierz Mędrzecki, *Województwo wołyńskie*, Wrocław: Ossolineum, 1988, 25, 63, 93. Figures drawn from Jan Kęsik, "Województwo wołyńskie 1921–1939 w świetle liczb i faktów," *Przegląd Wschodni*, 4, 1 (1997), 99–136.

25. George Jackson, *Comintern and Peasant in East Europe*, New York: Columbia University Press, 1966, 22, 182, 189, 209. On Soviet raids, Mykoła Kuczerepa, "Polityka II Rzeczypospolitej wobec Ukraińców na Wołyniu w latach 1921–1939," *Przegląd Wschodni*, 4, 1, (1997), 141–146.

26. Janusz Radziejowski, *The Communist Party of Western Ukraine*, Edmonton: CIUS, 1983, 96–97. On demonstrations, see the secret count by the Polish interior ministry's nationality division: Biblioteka Uniwersytetu Warszawskiego, Dział rękopisów (BUWR), syg. 1550.

27. Shmuel Spector, *The Holocaust of Volhynian Jews*, Jerusalem: Yad Vashem, 1990, 20–21; Ezra Mendelsohn, *The Jews of East Central Europe*, Bloomington: Indiana University Press, 1983, 20.

28. Józewski's reports in *Przegląd Wschodni*, 4, 1, (1997), 172–173; election results in Radziejowski, *Communist Party of Western Ukraine*, 174–175; on Józewski's origins, Jan Kęsik, *Zaufany komendanta*, Wrocław: Wydawnictwo Uniwersytetu Wrocławskiego, 1995, 1–36; on his attitudes to Ukraine, Henry Józewski, "Opowieść o istnieniu," BUWR, syg. 3189, Vol. 2.

29. Kęsik, "Województwo wołyńskie 1921–1939," 99–136; Czesław Partacz, "Polacy i Ukraińcy na Wołyniu," *Ukrainia-Polska*, Koszalin: BWSH, 1999, 240–241; Ksawery Pruszyński, *Podróż po Polsce*, Warsaw: Czytelnik, 2000, 123–136; Ksawery Pruszyński, *Niezadowoleni i entuzjaści*, 339–341, 360–368. On Stalin's fears, Terry Martin, "The 1932–33 Ukrainian Terror," presentation at Ukrainian Research Institute, Cambridge, Mass., 5 February 2001.

CHAPTER 8. THE ETHNIC CLEANSING OF WESTERN UKRAINE (1939–1945)

1. Omer Bartov, *The Eastern Front 1941–1945*, New York: St. Martin's, 1986, 103 and passim; Truman Anderson, "Incident at Baranivka," *Journal of Modern History*, 71 (1999), 585–623; for a guide to this literature, Rolf-Dieter Müller and Gerd Ueberschar, *Hitler's War in the East*, Providence, R.I.: Berghahn Books, 1997.

2. Jan Gross, *Revolution from Abroad,* Princeton: N.J.: Princeton University Press, 1988, 31; Volodomyr Kubiiovych, *Ukraintsi v Heneralnii Hubernii,* Chicago: Denisiuk, 1975, 17. Other citizens of interwar Poland, including Belarusians and some Polish peasants, also welcomed Poland's invaders at first. Jan Gross, *Polish Society under German Occupation,* Princeton, N.J.: Princeton University Press, 1979, 140; Marek Wierzbicki, *Polacy i Białorusini w zaborze sowieckim,* Warsaw: Volumen, 2000, 51. On the Jews, Ben-Cion Pinchuk, *Shtetl Jews under Soviet Rule,* Oxford: Blackwell, 5–27; David Engel, "The Wartime Journal of Calel Perechodnik," *Polin,* 12 (1999), 320–321.

3. Kubiiovych, *Ukraintsi v Heneralnii Hubernii,* 49, 197, 280 and passim; I. I. Il'iushyn, *OUN-UPA i ukrains'ke pytannia v roky druhoi svitovoi viiny,* Kyiv: PAN Ukrainy, 2000, 35.

4. Ryszard Torzecki, *Polacy i Ukraińcy,* Warsaw: PWN, 1993, 259–260.

5. Wołodymyr Trofymowicz, "Role Niemiec i Związku Sowieckiego w konflikcie ukraińsko-polskim," in *Polska—Ukraina: Trudne pytania,* vol. 5, Warsaw: Karta, 1999, 193–220; Grzegorz Mazur, "Rola Niemiec i Związku Sowieckiego w polsko—ukraińskim konflikcie narodowościowym," ibid., 221–234.

6. Gross, *Revolution from Abroad,* 146 and 69.

7. Kubiiovych, *Ukraintsi v Heneralnii Hubernii,* on the character of the Committee, 102–103; on the proposal to resettle Poles and Jews, 422–423.

8. Czesław Madajczyk et al., eds., *Zamojszczyzna: Sonderlaboratorium SS,* Vol. 2, Warsaw: Ludowa Spółdzielnia Wydawnicza, 1977, 125, 224, and passim; Grzegorz Motyka, *Tak było w Bieszczadach,* Warsaw: Volumen, 1999, 134–137.

9. Grzegorz Hryciuk, *Polacy w Lwowie 1939–1944,* Warsaw: KiW, 2000, 59.

10. On Nazi ethnic cleansing: Christopher Browning, *Nazi Policy, Jewish Workers, German Killers,* Cambridge: Cambridge University Press, 2000, 1–25. On the German model: Il'iushyn, *OUN-UPA i ukrains'ke pytannia,* 48.

11. O.A. Gorlanov and A.B. Roginskii, "Ob arestakh v zapadn'ykh oblastiakh Belorussii i Ukrain'y v 1939–1941 gg.," *Repressii protiv poliakov i pol'skykh grazhdan,* Moscow: Memorial, 1997, 96 and passim; Piotr Eberhardt, *Między Rosją a Niemcami,* Warsaw: PWN, 1996, 180. On the percentages of Jews, Poles, and Ukrainians, see Jan Gross, *Upiorna dekada,* Cracow: Universitas, 1998, 83. For higher estimates, "Sprawozdanie z dyskusji dotyczającej liczby obywateli polskich wywiezionych do Związku Sowieckiego w latach 1939–1041," *Studia z Dziejów Rosji i Europy Środkowej,* 30, 1, (1996), 117–148. A minimum figure of 330,000 is now certain on the basis of Soviet documents; the question remains as to how many more tens or hundreds of thousands were deported outside the major actions, as prisoners of war, forced labor, etc.

12. On Nazi propaganda, Dieter Pohl, *Nationalsozialistische Judenverfolgung in Ostgalizien,* Munich: Oldenbourg, 1996, 55–60. On the number of Jews in the NKVD (declining in 1938–1939), Nikita Petrov, *Kto rukovodil NKVD, 1934–1941,* Moscow: Zven'ia, 1999. See also Gross, *Upiorna dekada,* 80–93; Hryciuk, *Polacy w Lwowie,* 204–205. On the murder of Jews by Poles in another part of eastern Poland, Jan Gross, *Neighbors,* Princeton, N.J.: Princeton University Press, 2001; on Ukrainian pogroms, Shmuel Spector, *The Holocaust of Volhynian Jews,* Jerusalem: Yad Vashem, 1990, 64–69.

13. For a sensitive treatment of the consequences of Nazi racial categories in Ukraine, Kate

Brown, "A Biography of No Place," Doctoral dissertation, University of Washington, 1999.

14. John Armstrong, *Ukrainian Nationalism*, Englewood, N.J.: Ukrainian Academic Press, 1990, 162; Peter Potichnyj, "Ukrainians in World War II Military Formations," 1999, accessed as www.infoukes.com/upa/related/military.html; and sources cited below.

15. A Volhynian Pole recalled that the Holocaust "brought out the humanity in Poles, or the lack thereof." II/1328/2k, 20, AWKW.

16. Spector, *Holocaust of Volhynian Jews*, 358.

17. Martin Dean, "The German Gendarmerie, the Ukrainian Schutzmannschaft, and the 'Second Wave' of Jewish Killings in Occupied Ukraine," *German History*, 14, 2 (1996), 179.

18. Paul Robert Magocsi, *A History of Ukraine*, Seattle: University of Washington Press, 1996, 632.

19. On the Final Solution in Ostróg: Spector, *Holocaust of Volhynian Jews*, 115, 371. On Hanover and Ostróg: Gershon Hundert, "The Love of Learning among Polish Jews," in Lawrence Fine, ed., *Judaism in Practice*, Princeton, N.J.: Princeton University Press, 2001, 215.

20. Spector, *Holocaust of Volhynian Jews*, 172–187. See also Martin Dean, *Collaboration in the Holocaust*, New York: St. Martin's, 2000. Compare Browning, *Nazi Policy*, 152.

21. "Dii UPA v 1943 rotsi," *Litopys UPA*, Vol. 2, 225; Herasym Khvylia, "V lavakh UPA na Volyni," in Petro Mirchuk and V. Davidenko, eds., *V riadakh UPA*, New York: Dnipro, 1957, 30–32; Ryszard Torzecki, *Polacy i Ukraińcy*, Warsaw: PWN, 1993, 235, 258.

22. Andrzej Paczkowski, *Pół wieku dziejów Polski*, Warsaw: PWN, 1996, 25–26.

23. Motyka, *Tak było w Bieszczadach*, 89.

24. O.S. Sadovyi, "Kudy priamuiut' poliaky?" *Litopys UPA*, Vol. 2, 52; Il'iushyn, *OUN-UPA i ukrains'ke pytannia*, 107.

25. Motyka, *Tak było w Bieszczadach*, 109.

26. See Gross, *Polish Society under German Occupation*, 133–139.

27. This split was precipitated by the NKVD's assassination of OUN leader Konovalets' in 1938. According to the assassin, Pavel Sudoplatov, dividing the OUN was Stalin's intention. Pavel and Anatoli Sudoplatov, *Special Tasks*, Boston: Little, Brown, and Co., 1995, 7–29. See also Wolodymyr Kosyk, *L'Allemagne national-socialiste et L'Ukraine*, Paris: Publications de l'Est Européen, 1986, 74–79, 290; Alexander Motyl, *The Turn to the Right*, Boulder, Colo.: East European Monographs, 1980, 138ff.

28. Compare Mykola Lebed', *Ukrains'ka povstans'ka armiia*, Drohobych, 1987, 53; Taras Bul'ba, *Armiia bez derzhavy*, L'viv: Poklyk sumlinnia, 1993, 272; and Petro Balei, *Fronda Stepana Bandery v OUN 1940 roku*, Kyiv: Tekna A/T, 1996, 141.

29. Consider a report from the UPA's security service, categorizing the people it executed in one small Volhynian military district over the course of one month. It spoke of 110 total victims, of whom at the very least 68 were Ukrainian. *Litopys UPA*, Vol. 2 (new series), 312.

30. Proposal of Lebed' cited after Balei, *Fronda Stepana Bandery v OUN 1940 roku*, 141. See also *OUN-UPA v roky viiny*, 289.

31. On recruitment, Armstrong, *Ukrainian Nationalism*, 126–132; Kosyk, *L'Allemagne national-socialiste et l'Ukraine*, 369; Torzecki, *Polacy i Ukraińcy*, 247. On Sheptyts'kyi,

Stanisław Stępień, "Stanowisko Metropolity Szeptyckiego wobec zjawiska terroru politckiego," in Andrzej Zięba, ed., *Metropolita Andrzej Szeptycki,* Cracow: Polska Akademia Nauk, 1994, 110–118; Iwan Hirnyj, "Moje świadectwo," ibid., 207–210; Bohdan Budurowycz, "Sheptyts'kyi and the Ukrainian National Movement after 1914," in Paul Robert Magocsi, ed., *Morality and Reality,* Edmonton-CIUS, 1989, 63–64; Hansjakob Stehle, "Sheptyts'kyi and the German Regime," ibid., 127, 137; Shimon Redlich, "Sheptyts'kyi and the Jews," ibid., 145–164.

32. Władysław Filar, Michał Klimecki, and Mychalo Szwahaluk, "Chronologia wydarzeń na Wołyniu i Galicji w latach 1939–1945," unpublished, Warsaw 1999; Il'iushyn, *OUN-UPA i ukrains'ke pytannia,* 124–126.

33. Torzecki, *Polacy i Ukraińcy,* 252.

34. "Postanovy III. Konferentsii Orhanizatsii Ukrains'kykh Natsionalistiv Samostiinikiv Derzhavnikiv, 17–21 livtoho 1943 r.," *OUN v svitli postanov Velykykh Zboriv,* 81–83, 88. Polish observers could see the shift: II/1321/2k and II/1328/2k, AWKW.

35. M. Omeliusik, "UPA na Volyni w 1943 rotsi," *Litopys UPA,* Vol. 1, 23–26; Rostyslav Voloshyn, "Na shliakakh zbroinoi borot'by," ibid., Vol. 2, 19–24; Mykola Lebed', *Ukrains'ka povstans'ka armiia,* Drohobych, 1987, 53; Oleksandr Vovk, "Preface," *Litopys UPA,* Vol. 2 (new series), xxxix–xl. See also Taras Bul'ba, *Armiia bez derzhavy,* L'viv: Poklyk sumlinnia, 1993, 272; *Eksterminacja ludności polskiej na Wołyniu,* 37, 71; "Niemcy a UPA: Dokumenty," *Karta,* 23, 1997, 54–73; Tadeusz Piotrowski, *Poland's Holocaust,* Jefferson, N.C.: McFarland & Co., 1998, 246–247.

36. From the beginning, UPA commanders in Volhynia grouped Germans, Bolsheviks, and Poles as "the enemies of Ukraine." Volodymyr Makar, "Pivnichno-zakhidni ukrains'ki zemli" (May 1943), *Litopys UPA,* Vol. 5, 15.

37. On political aims: "Chas ne zhde," reprint from UPA organ *Samostiinist',* 22–29 January 1944; "Politychna deklaratsia UPA," September 1943; "Za shcho boret'sia Ukrains'ka povstancha armiia?", August 1943; all three documents in *Litopys UPA,* Vol. 1, respectively 105–110, 121–126, 126–130; also "U voiennomu krutizhi," ibid., Vol. 2, 77–81. For strategic justifications of the cleansing of Poles, *Eksterminacja ludności polskiej na Wołyniu,* 85. The Ukrainian attitude that "the Germans might leave, but the Poles will stay," was known to the Polish Home Army command. Grzegorz Motyka, "Od Wołynia do akcji 'Wisła'," *Więź* 473 (1998), 110; Armstrong, *Ukrainian Nationalism,* 158.

38. *Armia Krajowa w Dokumentach,* Vol. 2, 8 and 202–203.

39. Ibid., Vol. 1, 318; "Przynależność ziem wschodnich do Rzeczypospolitej Polskiej," zesz. A.9.V., tecz, 39; "Tajne," 3 August 1943," zesz. A.9.V., tecz. 34, MSW, AMPN. On the Polish Left in Galicia, *Dzieje Konfliktów,* Vol. 2, 231–240.

40. Meldunek 89, Radiogram No. M.89, L.dz. 78/42, "Meldunek specjalny—Sprawa Ukraińska," Rówecki to Sikorski, 15 November 1941, Oddział VI, sygn. 3.2.2.2.2, SPPL. The version of this report in volume 2 of *Armia Krajowa w Dokumentach* is missing important lines on page 142.

41. *Armia Krajowa w Dokumentach,* Vol. 2, 277–278, 328–330, 337–338.

42. *Dzieje Konfliktów,* Vol. 2, 29–230; Michael MacQueen, "The Polish Home Army and the National Minorities, 1939–1943," Master's thesis, University of Michigan, 1983, 56, 60ff.; Ryszard Torzecki, "Kontakty polsko-ukraińskie w polityce polskiego rządu

emigracyjnego i podziemia (1939–1944)," *Dzieje Najnowsze,* 13, 1–2, 1981, 332 and passim.

43. Kosyk, *L'Allemagne national-socialiste et l'Ukraine,* 333–339.

44. The 1931 Polish census recorded 396,200 people with Polish as first language and 356,300 people of Roman Catholic religion in Województwo Wołyńskie. The reduction during the war was due to deportations in 1939–41, forced labor in Germany in 1941–43, Soviet and German executions, combat deaths, and disease.

45. It is contended that this ethnic cleansing was a response to Polish actions connected to the German attempts to colonize the former Lublin palatinate, then part of the *General-gouvernement.* The cleansing of Volhynia was a coordinated action on a massive scale which killed tens of thousands of Poles, whereas the Chełm/Kholm killings in the former Lublin palatinate involved hundreds of deaths.

46. One member of the UPA's security services (SB) recalled the general guideline under Soviet interrogation: "Kill all Poles, Czechs, and Jews on the spot." Protokol Doprosa for I.I. Iavorskii, 14 April 1944, GARF, fond R-9478, opis 1, delo 398.

47. For Polish recollections: II/36, II/2110, II/1142, II/594, II/1146, II/1172, II/2353, II/2660, II/2667, II/2506, II/2451, II/2451/3–8, II/2373, II/1914, II/1338/kw, II/1216, II/265, II/1875, AWKW. On the massacres of July 1943, see II/737, II/1144, II/2099, II/2650, II/953, II/775, AWKW. For Polish reports: Poselstwo RP to MSZ in London, 24 February 1944, Zespoł A.9.V., tecz, 8B, AMPN. For German reports: *Eksterminacja ludności polskiej na Wokyniu,* 34, 74; see also Torzecki, *Polacy i Ukraińcy,* 262–263. For Soviet reports: *Represyvno-Karal'na Systema,* 383; *OUN-UPA v roky viiny,* 31, 55.

48. Protokol Doprosa for V.E. Stupak, 30 September 1944, GARF, fond R-9478, opis 1, delo 398.

49. Ewa and Władysław Siemaszko, "Mordy ukraińskie w czasie II wojny światowej," in Krzysztof Jasiewicz, ed., *Europe nie prowincjonalna,* Warsaw: Rytm, 1999r, 1047.

50. *Litopys UPA,* Vol. 2 (new series), 284ff.; Torzecki, *Polacy i Ukraińcy,* 238.

51. Examples of Ukrainians saving Poles in both Volhynia and Galicia: II/17, II/63t, II/1914, II/2110, II/106t, II/1286/2k, II/209, II/1350/2k, II/2650, II/996, II/1216, II/1328/2k, II/737, AWKW.

52. For the estimates of UPA troop strength, Władysław Filar, "*Burza*" *na Wolyniu,* Warsaw: Rytm, 1997, 35.

53. "Za shcho boretsia UPA," *Do zbroii,* 1, 1 (July 1943), in *Litopys UPA,* Vol. 1 (new series), 7–8.

54. This estimate from the calculation of Grzegorz Hryciuk, "Straty ludności na Wołyniu w latach 1941–1944," *Polska—Ukraina: Trudne pytania,* Vol. 5, Warsaw: Karta, 1999, 278. A researcher who wished to learn the names of murdered Polish civilians in Volhynia and Eastern Galicia could begin with the Archiwum Wschodnie Ośrodku "Karta," Archiwum Głównej Komisji Badania Przeciwko Narodowi Polskiemu, Stowarzyszenie Upamiętnienia Polaków Pomordowanych na Wołyniu, Stowarzyszenie Upamiętnienia Ofiar Zbrodni Ukraińskich Nacjonalistów, and the Archiwum Środowiska Żolnierzy 27 Wołynskiej Dywizji Armii Krajowej, as well as the archival and printed sources cited above and below.

55. Spector, *Holocaust of Volhynian Jews,* 250–251.

56. Compare the reaction of Polish Jews to the liquidation of ghettoes in other cities. Calel Perechodnik, *Czy ja jestem mordercą?* Warsaw: Znak, 1995.

57. II/2451/4, II/2451/5, II/2451/6, II/2451/7, AWKW; relations of witnesses also collected in *Śladami ludobojstwa,* 350–367, 379–381; and *Świadkowie mówią,* Warsaw: Światowy Związek Żołnierzy AK, 1996, 45–48.

58. Motyka, *Tak było w Bieszczadach,* 164.

59. On self-defense, II/13562/kw, II/1350/2k, II/1363, II/737, AWKW. On Polish attacks on Ukrainians: Il'iushyn, *OUN-UPA i ukrains'ke pytannia,* 88–90. On Jews in Pańska Dolina, memoir of Olgierd Kowalski, AWKW. See also the articles by Klimecki and Striłka cited below, note 67.

60. This episode is forgotten in Poland and was denied by Khrushchev to Stalin. It is documented by recollections of Poles in the AWKW (II/1328/2k) and in AK reports in Studium Polskiej Podziemnej in London, and will be discussed on the basis of Soviet sources by Jeffrey Burds in his forthcoming book, *A Sea of Blood and Tears.* The estimate is from Mazur, "Rola Niemiec i Związku Sowieckiego," 224.

61. II/1877, AWKW. Sometimes the Poles got the weapons they asked for, sometimes they did not. Compare II/737, II/996, II/1371/2k II/1350/2k, II/1356/2k, AWKW.

62. Grzegorz Motyka, "Polski policjant na Wołyniu, *Karta,* 24, 1998, 126–128.

63. "Zvit pro boiovi dii UPA na Volyni," [April 1943], *OUN-UPA v roky viiny* 309–312, at 311.

64. Vasyl' Makar, "Do pochatkiv UPA—list z Volyni," *Litopys UPA,* Vol. 2, 44. Reports from the same volume (173–174) make clear that the UPA's intelligence was quite aware that it was incorrect to treat Poles in Volhynia as German agents. On the cycle, Il'iushyn, *OUN-UPA i ukrains'ke pytannia,* 68.

65. Ministerstwo Obrony Narodowej, Biuro Ministra—Wydział Polityczny, L.dz. 1900/WPol/44, London, 8 January 1944, Oddział VI, sygn. 3.3.3.13.2 (36); Sztab Naczelnego Wodza, Oddział Specjalny, L.dz.719/Tjn.44, London, 28 January 1944, Oddział VI, sygn. 3.3.3.13.2 (37); Sztab Naczelnego Wodza, Oddział Specjalny, L.dz.2366/tjn.43, 17 May 1943, Oddział VI, sygn. 3.1.3.3.2 (34); Sztab Naczelnego Wodza, Oddział Specjalny, L.dz.108/Tjn.44, London, 8 January 1944, Oddział VI, sygn. 3.1.1.13.2 (22), SPPL. See also Stefan Korbonski, *The Polish Underground State,* New York: Columbia University Press, 1981, 155; Mykola Syvits'kyi, "Pol's'ko-ukrainskyi konflikt 1943–1944 rr.," in *Pol's'ko—Ukrains'ki studii,* Kyiv: Lybid', 1993, 241–248; Agnieszka Cieślowska, *Prasa okupowanego Lwowa,* Warsaw: Neriton, 160–162.

66. One of the division's soldiers is clear on this point: II/737, AWKW. Conversations with other veterans have confirmed me in this view.

67. Michał Klimecki, "Geneza i organizacja polskiej samoobrony na Wołyniu i w Małopolsce Wschodnej podczas II wojny światowej," in *Polska—Ukraina: Trudne pytania,* Vol. 4, Warsaw: Karta, 1998, 70; Roman Striłka, "Geneza polskiej samoobrony na Wołyniu i jej roli w obronie ludności polskiej," in ibid., 82; *Litopys UPA,* Vol. 2, 192–194.

68. Political Resolution 13, Third Extraordinary Congress of the OUN, 21–25 August 1943, in *OUN v svitli postanov Velykykh Zboriv,* 117–118.

69. For respective examples, see II/1350/2k and II/737, AWKW.

70. Gross, *Polish Society under German Occupation*, 141.

71. For a sense of the density, see *Litopys UPA*, Vol. 2 (new series), 283–289, 296–299. The argument adapts Karl Deutsch, *Nationalism and Social Communication*, Cambridge, Mass.: M.I.T. Press, 1966.

72. Waldemar Lotnik, *Nine Lives*, London: Serif, 1999, 59.

73. Villages in the area later petitioned Khrushchev to be joined to the USSR. *Etnichni mezhi i derzhavnyi kordon Ukrainy*, 147–151.

74. The estimate from Motyka, *Tak było w Bieszczadach*. For Ukrainian recollections and lists of victims, *Dzieje Konfliktów*, Vol. 3, 249–250.

75. "Niemcy a UPA: Dokumenty," 71.

76. For estimates, Gregorz Hryciuk, "Straty ludności w Galicji Wschodniej w latach 1941–46," *Polska—Ukraina: Trudne pytania*, Vol. 6, Warsaw: Karta, 2000, 294; see also Ryszard Kotarba, "Zbrodnie nacjonalistów ukraińskich w województwie tarnopolskim," ibid., 267. For recollections of the Galician cleansing see II/17, II/1758/j, II/2266/p, II/94/t, II/1286/2kw, II/1322/2kw, AWKW. See also Il'iushyn, *OUN-UPA i ukrains'ke pytannia*, 113.

77. Sadovyi, "Kudy priamuiut' poliaky?" *Litopys UPA*, Vol. 2, 49, 57.

78. Hryciuk, *Polacy w Lwowie*, 256–257.

79. Motyka, *Tak było w Bieszczadach*, 125–126; *Povstans'ki mohyly*, 144–162.

80. Korbonski, *Underground State*, 158–159; Władysław Filar, "27 WDP AK w Operacji Kowelskiej," *Przegląd Wschodni*, 4, 1 (1997), 217–218.

81. Serhii Tkachov, *Pol's'ko-Ukrains'kii transfer naselennia 1944–1946rr*, Ternopil': Pidruchnyky i Posibnyky, 1997, 123–155.

82. *NKWD o Polsce i Polakach; Vostochnaia Evropa*, Vol. 1, 426 and passim; *Teczka specjalna J. W. Stalina*, 248, 492, and passim.

CHAPTER 9. THE ETHNIC CLEANSING OF SOUTHEASTERN POLAND (1945–1947)

1. "Zagadnienie Ukraińskie," BUWR, syg. 155; *Dzieje Konfliktów*, Vol. 2, 124–130, 229–230, 234, 251–252, 279, 297–298; Ryszard Torzecki, "Kontakty polsko-ukraińskie w polityce polskiego rządu emigracyjnego i podziemia (1937–1944), *Dzieje Najnowsze*, 13, 1-2 (1981), 335–336. On the interwar background, Włodzimierz Mich, *Obcy w polskim domu*, Lublin: Wydawnictwo Uniwersytetu Marii Curie-Skłodowskiej, 1994.

2. Krystyna Kersten, "The Polish—Ukrainian Conflict under Communist Rule," *Acta Poloniae Historica*, 73, (1996), 139. See also Włodzimierz Borodziej, *Od Poczdamu do Szklarskiej Poręby*, London: Aneks, 1990, 32–77.

3. Grabski left the National Democratic party in 1926. He was, however, one of the most eminent thinkers in the National Democratic tradition, and remained very influential on the Polish right.

4. For a Soviet record of Grabski's remarks to Stalin in August 1944, *Sovetskii faktor*, 73–74. The quotations from those conversations are from Stanisław Grabski, *Pamiętniki*, Vol. 2, Warsaw: Czytelnik, 1989, 472–475.

5. On Wasilewska, Eleonora Syzdek, *Działalność Wandy Wasilewskiej w latach Drugiej Wojny Światowej*, Warsaw: MON, 1981, "Dialectic" quotation at 68; treaty reference at 268.

See also Teresa Torańska, *Them,* New York: Harper & Row, 1987, 216–217. Wasilewska was also a novelist.

6. On Grabski in Lwów in September 1945, *Teczka specjalna J. W. Stalina,* 402. For Wasilewska's opinion of Grabski and further analysis of Grabski's mission, Witold Wojdyło, *Koncepcje społeczno-polityczne Stanisława Grabskiego,* Torun: Uniwersytet Mikołaja Kopernika, 1993, 35–39.

7. Key examples of the genre are Andrzej Paczkowski, *Pół wieku dziejów Polski,* Warsaw, PWN, 1996; Krystyna Kersten, *The Establishment of Communist Rule in Poland,* Berkeley: University of California Press, 1991.

8. Amir Weiner, *Making Sense of War,* Princeton, N.J.: Princeton University Press, 2001, 352.

9. Serguei Ekelchik, "History, Culture, and Nationhood under High Stalinism," Doctoral dissertation, University of Alberta, 2000, 49–58.

10. See the reports collected in *Deportatsiia poliakiv z Ukrainy,* 1999, 24–74.

11. The March 1944 report of Khrushchev to Stalin in *OUN-UPA v roky viiny,* 134–144. The OUN-Bandera was not satisfied by the border, but even it had to struggle to portray territorial gains in negative terms. "Ukrains'kyi perets," September 1945, in *Litopys UPA,* Vol. 1 (new series), 300–301.

12. *Vostochnaia Evropa,* 39.

13. Grabski, *Pamiętniki,* Vol. 2, 472–475.

14. *Sovetskii faktor,* 23–24, 30, 41; Vojtech Mastny, *Russia's Road to the Cold War,* New York: Columbia University Press, 1979.

15. Andrzej Paczkowski, *Stanisław Mikołajczyk czyli klęska realisty,* Warsaw: Omnipress, 1991.

16. The Białystok region remained in Poland this time.

17. Ivan Kozlovs'kyi, *Vstanovlennia Ukrains'ko-Pols'koho kordonu,* L'viv: Kameniar, 1998.

18. *Sovetskii faktor,* 208; see also *Vostochnaia Evropa,* 176; Norman Naimark, *Fires of Hatred,* Cambridge, Mass.: Harvard University Press, 2001, 108–112.

19. Czechoslovak-Hungarian transfers were carried out, on a small scale. Hungary's preferences: *Sovetskii faktor,* 238, 504–507; Molotov's urgings: *Vostochnaia Evropa,* 429–430; 519; Stalin on northeastern Europe: *Sovetskii faktor,* 74; Stalin on southeastern Europe: *Vostochnaia Evropa,* 126–129, 275; *Sovetskii faktor,* 133; for what happened next, Ivo Banac, *With Stalin against Tito,* Ithaca, N.Y.: Cornell University Press, 1988.

20. What had been Czechoslovak Sub-Carpathian Rus' was incorporated into Soviet Ukraine, Stalin providing an ethnic justification.

21. *Sovetskii faktor,* 371.

22. Terry Martin, "Stalinist Forced Relocation Policies," in Myron Weiner and Sharon Russell, eds., *Moving Targets: Demography and Security,* Cambridge: Berghahn Books, 2001. The dissolution of Polish institutions in 1935–36 marked a new awareness of the Poles as a national enemy to the Soviet Union, but the result was not the deportation of every Polish individual. Even the 1937–38 "Polish operations" affected others besides Poles, and were meant to destroy rather than consolidate a national group. In both cases, Poles remained Soviet citizens and remained in the Soviet Union. N. V. Petrov and A. B. Roginskii, "Pol'skaia operatsiia NKVD 1937–1938 gg., in *Repressii protiv poliakov i pol'skykh grazhdan,* Moscow: Memorial, 1997, 35.

23. Terry Martin, "The Origins of Soviet Ethnic Cleansing," *Journal of Modern History*, 70 (1998), 813–861. See also Robert Conquest, *The Nation Killers*, London, Macmillan, 1970.

24. Consult Rogers Brubaker, "Nationhood and the National Question in the Soviet Union and post-Soviet Eurasia," *Theory and Society*, 23 (1994), 47–48; Yuri Slezkine, "The USSR as Communal Apartment," *Slavic Review*, 53, 2 (1994), 414–452; Francine Hirsh, "The Soviet Union as a Work in Progress," *Slavic Review*, 56, 2 (1997), 251–278; Ronald Grigor Suny, *The Revenge of the Past*, Stanford, Calif.: Stanford University Press, 1993. Some of the constructivist account of nationality in the early Soviet Union is anticipated in Hans Kohn, *Nationalism in the Soviet Union*, London: Routledge, 1933. The locus classicus is Richard Pipes, *The Formation of the Soviet Union*, Cambridge, Mass.: Harvard University Press, 1954.

25. Leszek Kolakowski, *Main Currents of Marxism*, Vol. 2, Oxford: Oxford University Press, 1978, 398–405.

26. On the Famine, Andrea Graziosi, *The Great Soviet Peasant War*, Cambridge, Mass.: Ukrainian Research Institute, 1996, 66–67; Terry Martin, "The 1932–33 Ukrainian Terror," presentation at Ukrainian Research Institute, Cambridge, Mass., 5 February 2001; also Terry Martin, *Affirmative Action Empire*, Ithaca, N.Y.: Cornell University Press, 2001.

27. For cases of this, *Pereselennia poliakiv ta ukraintsiv*, 2000, 425–430, 679–687.

28. Ibid., 93–102.

29. Gomułka cited in Piotr Madajczyk, "Polska polityka narodowościowa po 1945 roku," *Nashe Slovo* (Warsaw), 15 August 1999. The day before Gomułka's speech, a local party organ published a poem entitled "Poland: Only for the Poles." *Gazeta Robotnicza* (Katowice), 19 May 1945, in Dariusz Baliszewski and Andrzej Kunert, eds., *Ilustrowany przewodnik po Polsce stalinowskiej*, Warsaw: PWN 1999, 300.

30. II/2266/p, II/1914, II1286/2kw, II/1328/2k, AWKW. See also "Biuleteny—No. 62," Związki Ziem Wschodnich Rzeczypospolitej, 15 September 1947, zesz. A.9.V., tecz, 10, MSW, AMPN. For figures, *Deportatsii*, Vol. 1, 25.

31. Compare *Pereselennia poliakiv ta ukraintsiv*, 251–261 and 495–497.

32. On the UPA, *Przesiedlenie ludności polskiej*, 316. The NKVD lost important agents when Poles left the the Soviet Union. Jeffrey Burds, "AGENTURA: Soviet Informants' Networks and the Ukrainian Rebel Underground in Galicia," *East European Politics and Societies*, 11, 1 (1997), 89–130; and *Pereselennia poliakiv ta ukraintsiv*, 747, 789, 877, 914–917.

33. *Deportatsii poliakiv z Ukrainy*, 102; *Pereselennia poliakiv ta ukraintsiv*, 627.

34. These Polish officials were themselves pawns in a much larger game. They were treated ruthlessly by the Soviet NKVD, often arrested and imprisoned. *Przesiedlenie ludności polskiej*, 201–203.

35. Tkachov, *Pol's'ko-Ukrains'kyi transfer naselennia* 51–53, 99–122; *Przesiedlenie ludności polskiej*, 384–385 and passim.

36. *Przesiedlenie ludności polskiej*, 342.

37. Ibid., 214.

38. Within the borders envisioned by the agreement of July 1944, six hundred thousand or so speakers of Ukrainian constituted less than 3 percent of the Polish population. *Repa-*

triacja, Vol. 1, 17–18. A week before the secret agreement, Khrushchev wrote to Stalin asking that territories around Chełm/Kholm be added to the Ukrainian SSR. This would have brought Khrushchev's wife's birthplace into the Soviet Union.

39. In these regions Soviet authorities noted the nationalism of the Poles they installed. *Trahedia Ukraintsiv Pol'shchi,* 128–132; *Pereselennia poliakiv ta ukraintsiv,* 183.

40. II/2196p., AWKW; "Informacja z prasy ukraińskiej nr. 2," zesz. A.9.V., tecz. 9, MSW, AMPN; also the appeals cited below.

41. Quotation from *Pereselennia poliakiv ta ukraintsiv,* 923. On re-repatriants, *Repatriacja,* Vol. 2, 19, 125, 160; *Deportatsii,* Vol. 2, 16.

42. *Pereselennia poliakiv ta ukraintsiv,* 797; *Repatriacja,* Vol. 2, 160, 180.

43. *Repatriacja,* Vol. 2, 262.

44. Ibid., 103–104.

45. Ibid., 81–82, 94, 104–105; estimates from Rafal Wnuk, "Wierzchowiny i Huta" *Polska 1944/5,* 4 (1999), 87; and Grzegorz Motyka, *Tak było w Bieszczadach,* Warsaw: Volumen, 1999, 238–241.

46. *Repatriacja,* Vol. 1, 85–87.

47. Antoni Szcześniak and Wiesław Szota, *Droga do nikąd,* Warsaw: MON, 1973, 257. This extremely useful study suffers from a weakness associated with its publication in People's Poland. Despite the evidence the book presents, the authors reduce Ukrainian nationalism to a variety of Nazism. There are reasons why this assertion is plausible, but it is impossible to understand the motivations of Ukrainian partisans in Poland without liberating oneself from it.

48. On the Lemko region see *1947: Propam'iatna Knyha* 13, 19, 32–33, 61, 123. Almost all of the respondents describe service in or perceptions of the UPA. The volume mentions about 371 local UPA soldiers by name. See also the 507 biograms in *Povstans'ki mohyly;* and the list of UPA soldiers sentenced to death in 1947 in *UPA v svitli pols'kykh dokumentiv,* 567–573.

49. *Trahedia Ukraintsiv Pol'shchi,* 151. For Ukrainian recollections, *1947: Propam'iatna Knyha,* 87, 110, 190, 246.

50. *Pereselennia poliakiv ta ukraintsiv,* 621–625.

51. According to the 507 biograms of UPA soldiers collected by Misylo, 21 had served in the SS-Galizien, 24 in the German police, 6 in the Wehrmacht, and 1 in the Ukrainian Legions. Given the limited nature of the information available to Misylo, it is certain that these numbers were higher: *Povstans'ki mohyly,* 29–218. For Ukrainian recollections of *SS-Galizien* veterans joining the UPA, *1947: Propam'iatna Knyha,* 42–43, 122; also Ivan Dmytryk, *U lisakh Lemkivshchyny,* Munich: Suchasnist, 1977, 115.

52. *Povstans'ki mohyly,* 85–86, 65–69, 180–181.

53. The UPA ran schools for recruits and officers on the territory of southeastern Poland, teaching them that their plight was part of the larger national struggle. Szcześniak and Szota, *Droga do nikąd,* 153–154. *Povstans'ki mohyly* records, where such information is available, that a given local recruit received such training.

54. *Deportatsii,* Vol. 2, 54–59.

55. Order of UPA-West commander Vasyl' Sydor, in Ukrainian Central State Archive in Kyiv, 3833/2/3, cited after Grzegorz Motyka, "Ukraińskie 'powstanie'," *Karta,* 29 (1999), 65.

56. *Repatriacja,* Vol. 1, 64–66; *Deportatsii,* Vol. 1, 471–473; *Trahedia Ukraintsiv Pol'shchi,* 125–128, 156–159.

57. On burning villages, *1947: Propam'iatna Knyha,* 165–168; II/1771, AWKW. On engagements with the army, *Repatriacja,* Vol. 2, 84–87, 110–114, 170–174, Szcześniak and Szota, *Droga do nikąd,* 226–227; and Motyka, *Tak było w Bieszczadach,* 296ff. For repatriation officials, *Repatriacja,* Vol. 2, 140.

58. There was some cooperation against Soviet forces. Grzegorz Motyka and Rafał Wnuk, *Pany i rezuny,* Warsaw: Volumen, 1997, 76–193. For UPA recollections of cooperation with the AK, *1947: Propam'iatna Knyha,* 144, 236; *Povstans'ki mohyly,* 213–214; for Polish reports, *Pereselennia poliakiv ta ukraintsiv,* 733, 911.

59. The meeting: *Repatriacja,* Vol. 1, 147–154. For similar petitions, *Pereselennia poliakiv ta ukraintsiv,* 523–526.

60. Stanisław Grabski, *Państwo narodowe,* L'viv: Igla, 1929, 164, for the opposition between "national state" and "state of nationalities."

61. *Trahedia Ukraintsiv Pol'shchi,* 174–175.

62. *Akcja 'Wisła,'* 15. Podgornyi was one of the troika that ousted Khrushchev in 1964. His given name was Mykola Pidhirnyi.

63. On this incident, *Repatriacja,* Vol. 2, 24, 31, 39, 43.

64. This estimate of resettlements is based upon the statistics provided in *Akcja Wisła.* See also the survey of resettled Ukrainians in Halyna Shcherba, "Deportatsii naselennia z pol's'ko-ukrains'koho pohranychchia 40-kh rokiv." in *Pol's'ko-Ukrains'ki studii,* Kyiv: Lybid', 1993, 254. The estimate of Ukrainians killed from Motyka, *Tak było w Bieszczadach,* 364.

65. *Sovetskii faktor,* 388. Dmytro Manuil's'kyi, the Comintern secretary, wrote to Politburo member Lazar Kaganovich that the Ukrainian SSR should not accept more Ukrainians from Poland, since the resettlement apparatus had been disbanded and there were no longer funds available. *Trahedia Ukraintsiv Pol'shchi,* 404–405. (Manuil's'kyi, incidentally, had been a negotiator at Riga, had watched over the Polish Communist Party before its dissolution, and knew Poland and spoke Polish well.)

66. *Akcja 'Wisła,'* 53-54.

67. Ibid., 65. On Świerczewski's death, Tadeusz Pląskowski, "Ostatnia inspekcja Gen. broni Karola Świerczewskiego," *Wojskowy Przegląd Historyczny,* 4 (1983), 96–112. The official account is *Polska Zbrojna,* 21 March 1947, 1.

68. On West Ukraine: *Deportatsii,* Vol. 2, 64–66; *Desiat' buremnykh lit,* 589; Werth, "L'envers d'une victoire," in Stéphane Courtois, ed., *Le livre noir du communisme,* Paris: Robert Laffont, 1997, 254, 264.

69. *Vostochnaia Evropa,* 596–597. The figure in question was Władysław Wolski, at the time vice minister of public administration for repatriation affairs, in 1949 minister of public administration.

70. *Akcja 'Wisła,'* 82–83, 84–85.

71. Ibid., 43.

72. For a statement of OUN-Bandera goals, see the January 1946 "Prohramovi zasady OUN," in *OUN-UPA v roky viiny,* 451–463. With Volhynia and most of Galicia now within the Soviet Union, the territory in question was the bit of Galicia which remained in Poland (in the Rzeszów palatinate) and parts of the Lublin and Cracow palatinates.

73. *Akcja 'Wisła,'* 98–99.

74. Ibid., 93.

75. I take exception to the argument that resettlement was nothing more than part of a plan to destroy the UPA. This is the view taken in the most comprehensive study of these years. Szcześniak and Szota, *Droga do nikąd.* Tadeusz Piotrowski also takes the view I wish to question in *Poland's Holocaust,* Jefferson, N.C.: McFarland & Co., 1998, 244, 379. I am also disagreeing with the opposing view, that the operation had nothing to do with the UPA. The idea that Polish policy would have been exactly the same, and would have enjoyed the same popularity, if the UPA had not existed is not plausible. It is thus odd to discuss "The Tragedy of the Ukrainians of Poland" without mentioning the slaughter in Volhynia. *Trahedia Ukraintsiv Pol'shchi.*

76. One Pole recalled the unfairness of treating Lemkos as traitors: II/1771, AWKW. On *Kennkarten,* Kersten, "The Polish-Ukrainian Conflict," 147.

77. Kossowski returned to the Soviet Union in October 1948. See his "Sluzhebnaia kharakteristika," 15 October 1948; and "Charakterystyka—Służbowa," 31 March 1948, teczka personalna ppłk. Wacława Kossowskiego, CAWR.

78. Motyka, *Tak było w Bieszczadach,* 407.

79. *Akcja 'Wisła,'* 210. For a criticism of Mossor's tactics by his second-in-command, see Lech Kowalski, *Generałowie,* Warsaw: Pax, 1992, 100–103.

80. *Akcja 'Wisła,'* 222–225, 279–282, 285–286. On security services, John Micgiel, "Bandits and Reactionaries," in Norman Naimark and Leonid Gibianskii, eds., *The Establishment of Communist Regimes in Eastern Europe,* Boulder, Colo.: Westview, 1997, 63–111; Andrzej Paczkowski, *Od sfałszowanego zwycięstwa do prawdziwej klęski,* Cracow: Wydawnictwo Literackie, 1999, 36.

81. Motyka, *Tak było w Bieszczadach,* 368 376–377. Of the 507 UPA deaths chronicled by Misylo, 35 or 6.9 percent are listed as suicides. *Povstans'ki mohyly,* 29–218.

82. Perhaps thirty to fifty thousand Ukrainians and Lemkos escaped resettlement: some by bribing officers, others by hiding with Polish families, others by claiming Polish identity, and perhaps a thousand or so by successfully mobilizing local authorities to protect them (Bodaky, Blechnarka, Wysowa). (Conversations in Łemkowszczyzna, 23–25 July 1999). Sometimes the leaders of Operation Groups, at their own discretion and in violation of orders, allowed couples in mixed marriages, Red Army veterans, as well as Ukrainians employed by the railway and in mining, to remain.

83. *1947: Propam'iatna Knyha,* 15, 73, 79, 142–143; *Nashe Slovo* (Warsaw), 3 March 1996, 3; 10 March 1996, 3; Leszek Wołosiuk, "Historia jednej fotografii," in Włodzimierz Mokry, *Problemy Ukraińców w Polsce po wysiedleńczej akcji "Wisła" 1947 roku,* Cracow: Szwajpolt fiol, 1997, 403–414.

84. 35 more were sentenced to death in the Jaworzno camp. According to one calculation, of the 2,810 death sentences between 1944–56, 573 were of Ukrainians. Given that Ukrainians comprised less than 1 percent of the population, this proportion is high indeed. *Akcja 'Wisła,'* 30. Misylo has collected relevant documents in *UPA v svitli pols'kykh dokumentiv.* On Ukrainians executed before 1947, Maria Turlejska, *Te pokolenia żałobami czarne,* London: Aneks, 1989, 331–337. For a list of 582 Ukrainians who perished in connection with resettlement, *Repatriacja,* Vol. 2, 352–394.

85. Polish procurator's report of treatment of Ukrainian prisoners in the Jaworzno concentration camp reprinted in *Nashe Slovo* (Warsaw), 28 January 1996, 1, 3. See also Mokry, *Problemy Ukraińców w Polsce*, 76–82; *1947: Propam'iatna Knyha*, 49–50, 92–93; Jan Popiel, ed., "Rozmowy przeprowadzone w Dobrej," unpublished, 1997; and finally the memoir of a Polish woman, returnee from Siberia, held on the accusation of sheltering a UPA soldier from the Red Army: II/53, AWKW.

86. The end of UPA activity in Poland is dated from 17 September 1947, when OUN commander Iaroslav Starukh perished in his bunker. UPA commander Myroslav Onyshkevich then released his soldiers from their oaths. In late 1947, three small Operation Groups were formed to rout partisans who continued to fight, and over the next few years the army continued to resettle Ukrainians who had escaped or been passed over. In all about 150,000 Ukrainians were resettled from 1947 to 1952.

87. On the UPA in Soviet Ukraine: Grzegorz Motyka, "Bieszczadzkie sotnie UPA na Ukrainie 1947–1948," *Nashe Slovo* (Warsaw), 6 February 2000, 3; Burds, "Agentura," 89–130; Peter Potichnyj, "Pacification of Ukraine: Soviet Counterinsurgency," 1999; *Desiat' buremnykh lit;* D.M. Stickles, ed., *The Beria Affair,* New York: Nova Science, 1992, 54 and 104. On Lebed': Christopher Simpson, *Blowback,* New York: Weidenfeld and Simpson, 1988, 163–171.

CHAPTER 10. EPILOGUE: COMMUNISM AND CLEANSED MEMORIES (1947–1981)

1. Piotr Eberhardt, *Między Rosją a Niemcami,* Warsaw: PWN, 1996, 109, 127.

2. German, Romani, and Czech were also spoken. Most Gypsies were also murdered by the Nazi regime. Most of the Germans of Volhynia and Galicia fled or were expelled at war's end. Many Czechs were killed, and about 53,000 survivors emigrated. On interwar German settlement, Hans-Jörgen Seraphim, *Rodungssiedler,* Berlin: Paul Parey, 1938. Postwar Western Ukraine also embraces Subcarpathian Ruthenia, formerly in Czechoslovakia, and part of Bukovina, formerly in Romania.

3. Volodymyr Kubiiovych, *Natsional'nyi sklad naselennia Radianskoi Ukrainy v svitli soviet-s'kykh perepisiv,* Paris, 1962, 5–9.

4. These last two figures estimated on the basis of Shmuel Spector, *Holocaust of Volhynian Jews,* Jerusalem: Yad Vashem, 1990, 357–358; Dieter Pohl, *Nationsozialistische Judenverfolgung in Ostgalizien,* Munich: Oldenbourg, 1996, 385–387; and Piotr Eberhardt, *Polska ludność kresowa,* Warsaw: PWN, 1998, 214. The other calculations are based on the sources cited in the previous two chapters and Soviet census data from 1959. One reason so few Jews survived in Volhynia is that almost none were deported during the Soviet occupation. Spector puts the number at five hundred (28).

5. See the anthropological research of Grzegorz Babiński, *Pogranicze polsko-ukraińskie,* Cracow: Nomos, 1997, 114; surveys analyzed by the sociologist Antonina Kłoskowska, *Kultury narodowe u korzeni,* Warsaw: PWN, 1996, 188–189; see also the assessment of the political scientist John Armstrong, *Ukrainian Nationalism,* Englewood, N.J.: Ukrainian Academic Press, 219.

6. Conversations at the Lemkovska Vatra (Lemko Congress), Zdynia, Poland, 25 July 1999.

7. Figures from *Teczka specjalna J. W. Stalina,* 544. See also *Deportatsii,* 22–23.

8. II/2110, AWKW; *1947: Propam'iatna Knyha,* 69.

9. Estimates based upon figures cited above. See also the count prepared by the non-governmental organization Karta in Warsaw, presented in *Polska-Ukraina: Trudne pytania,* vol. 8, Warsaw: Karta, 2000, 159, and that of Grzegorz Motyka, "Co ma Wisła do Wołynia," *Gazeta Wyborcza,* 23 March 2001.

10. Lotnik, *Nine Lives,* London: Serif, 1999, 14. A structurally similar memoir makes clear how such escapes were all but impossible for Jews. Michael Skakun, *On Burning Ground,* New York: St. Martin's, 1999. Although Joseph Skakun, a Jew, imitates a Polish Tatar, escapes to Germany as a laborer, and joins the Waffen-SS as a Lithuanian, his impersonations reveal the enormous problems Jews faced. Being Jewish was a death sentence as was nothing else, over vast territories and for years on end. Jews usually looked different, spoke with characteristic accents, knew little of the practice of Christianity, knew little about work on the farm or life in the wilderness, often did not own inconspicuous clothing, and rarely had experience with weapons. Jewish men were circumcised.

11. Agnieszka Cieślowska, *Prasa okupanowego Lwowa,* Warsaw: Neriton, 1997, 163–164.

12. These incidents from Gregorz Motyka, *Tak było w Bieszczadach,* Warsaw: Volumen, 1999, 456, 435 respectively.

13. This comes up repeatedly in recollections of Ukrainians. See for example II/2196/p, AWKW.

14. As in the case of southern whites and southern blacks who migrated to the industrial north of the United States, obvious cultural similarities are overwhelmed by the felt need to deny them, and undercut by the attractions of other identifications. Compare Włodzimierz Odojewski, *Oksana,* Warsaw: Twój Styl, 1999, and William Faulkner, *The Sound and the Fury,* New York: Jonathan Cape, 1929.

15. The anecdote from Grzegorz Motyka and Rafał Wnuk, *Pany i rezuny,* Warsaw: Volumen, 1997, 8. Christmas Eve invitations can be reciprocated because Western Rite and Eastern Rite Christmas fall on different days: 25 December and 7 January. On the importance of Christmas Eve dinner to "Polish" culture in the east, suggestive is Włodzimierz Odojewski, *Zasypie wszystko, zawieje . . .* Paris: Instytut Literacki, 1973. This extraordinary novel about wartime Polish-Ukrainian relations cries out for translation. For our analysis, it is most helpful in drawing attention to choices of individuals during general conflict. Its chief weakness is its underestimation of Ukrainian nationalism as an attractive force. It was banned in communist Poland.

16. As is evident from Padraic Kenney's social history *Rebuilding Poland: Workers and Communists, 1945–1950,* Ithaca, N.Y.: Cornell University Press, 1997.

17. Andrzej Zięba, "Ukraińcy w oczach Polaków," in Teresa Walas, ed., *Narody i stereotypy,* Cracow: Międzynarodowe Centrum Kultury, 1995, 95–104. On state policy, Danuta Sosnowska, "Stereotypy Ukrainy i Ukraińca w literaturze polskiej," in ibid., 125–131; and Józef Lewandowski, "Polish Historical Writing on Polish-Ukrainian Relations During World War Two," in Peter Potichnyj, ed., *Poland and Ukraine,* Toronto: CIUS, 1980, 231–246. See also John Basarab, "Postwar Writings in Poland on Polish-Ukrainian Relations," ibid., 249; Roman Szporluk, "The Role of the Press in Polish-Ukrainian Relations," ibid., 223; Babiński, *Pogranicze polsko-ukraińskie,* 163; Stefan Kozak, "Polsko-Ukraińskie dylematy i dialogi," *Polska w Europie,* 10 (1993), 46. For a different frame-

work, see Philipp Ther, *Deutsche und polnische Vertriebene,* Göttingen: Vandenhoeck & Ruprecht, 1998.

18. Jan Kęsik, "Województwo wołyńskie 1921–1939 w świetle liczb i faktów," *Przegląd Wschodni,* 4, 1 (1997), 107–108.

19. Jan Popiel, "Rozmowy przeprowadzone w Dobrej w czerwcu-lipcu 1997," 1997; Correspondence from Jan Popiel, November 1999; *1947: Propam'iatna Knyha,* 184–194; *Dzieje Konfliktów,* Vol. 3, 249–250; Motyka, *Tak było w Bieszczadach,* 328. See also Babiński, *Pogranicze polsko-ukraińskie,* 101; Krzysztof Ślusarek, *Drobna szlachta w Galicji,* Cracow: Księgarnia Akademicka, 1994, 161.

20. Respectively: *Śladami ludobojstwa,* 351; and II/2451/4, AWKW.

21. II/1758j, AWKW; *Śladami ludobojstwa,* 473–475.

22. See for example II/737; II/1362/kw; II/17, AWKW. A number of Poles also mention being saved by Ukrainians, as is noted in chapter 8.

23. Consult Anna Strońska, *Dopóki milczy Ukraina,* Warsaw: Trio, 1998.

24. Taras Kuzio, *Ukraine,* London: Routledge, 1998, 111. More generally, consult P.N. Barford, *The Early Slavs,* Ithaca, N.Y.: Cornell University Press, 2001, 278ff.

25. On Polish and Soviet treatments of Ukrainian history, Stephen Velychenko, *Shaping Identity in Eastern Europe and Russia,* New York: St. Martin's, 1993; Andrew Wilson, *The Ukrainians,* New Haven, Conn.: Yale University Press, 2000.

26. Personal experience in L'viv, July 1999 and June 2000. There is a Polish song about Volhynia with similar words, recorded in the memoirs of Poles who fled in 1943.

27. The Eskimo remark: Babiński, *Pogranicze polsko-ukraińskie,* 109. The tale of St. Teresa's/St. John the Baptist is presented in Chris Hann, "Postsocialist Nationalism," *Slavic Review,* 57, 4 (1998), 840–863. The leader of the committee to "protect the Polish Church" gives his views in *Pogranicze* (Przemyśl), 24–28 (1991).

28. *Przesiedlenie ludności polskiej,* 27.

29. Krystyna Kersten, "Forced Migration and the Transformation of Polish Society in the Postwar Period," in Philipp Ther and Ana Siljak, eds., *Ethnic Cleansing in East Central Europe, 1944–1948,* Boulder, Colo.: Rowman and Littlefield, 2001, 75–87.

30. On ethnic purity and communist legitimation, Jan Gross, "A Tangled Web," in István Deák, Jan Gross, and Tony Judt, eds., *The Politics of Retribution in Europe,* Princeton: Princeton University Press, 2000, 107–114; Lukasz Hoirszowicz, "The Jewish Issue in Post-War Communist Politics," in Abramsky et al., *The Jews in Poland,* 199–208; Feliks Tych, *Długi cień Zagłady,* Warsaw: Żydowski Instytut Historyczny, 1999, 74; Eugeniusz Mironowicz, *Białorusini w Polsce, 1944–1949,* Warsaw: PWN, 1993, 146–151; Andrzej Paczkowski, *Od sfałszowanego zwycięstwa do prawdziwej klęski,* Cracow: Wydawnictwo Literackie, 1999, 224.

31. The survey was entitled "Przemiany Polaków," and the thirty replies appeared in the 9 November, 16 November, 23 November, 30 November, 7 December, and 14 December 1968 numbers of *Polityka.* Tadeusz Kotarbiński was the only one to mention the benefits of variety. Józef Chałabiński was the only one to mention the Jews explicitly, in the construction "not to mention the Jews." Several respondents, it should be added, argued that the very notion of a Polish society or a Polish type only made sense in the postwar period, which is consistent with my argument here.

32. Mirosław Czech, *Ukraińcy w Polsce,* Warsaw: Związek Ukraińców w Polsce, 1993, 12, 269; Stefan Zabrowarny, "Polityka narodowościowa polskich władz komunistycznych w kwestii ukraińskiej," in Jacek Pietraś and Andrzej Czarnocki, eds., *Polityka narodowościowa państw Europy Środkowowschodniej,* Lublin: IEWS, 1993, 147; Boris Bej, "Ukraińcy w Polsce," *Kultura,* 429 (1983), 123–126. See also Marcin Król, "Komentarz," *Nowa Respublica,* 54 (1993), 39.

33. Manfred Berger, *Jaruzelski,* Düsseldorf: EconVerlag, 1990, 245–248; Timothy Garton Ash, *The Polish Revolution: Solidarity,* London: Penguin, 1999, 356–363. Jaruzelski's account is *Stan wojenny dlaczego,* Warsaw: BGW, 1992.

CHAPTER 11. PATRIOTIC OPPOSITIONS AND STATE INTERESTS (1945–1989)

1. Observers were hardly sanguine about relations among Poland and its eastern neighbors in 1989. See Daniel Nelson, "Europe's Unstable East," *Foreign Policy,* 82, 1991, 137–158; John Mearsheimer, "Back to the Future," *International Security,* 15, 1 (1990), 5–56; Andrew Michta, *East Central Europe after the Warsaw Pact,* Westport, Conn.: Greenwood Press, 1992, 82; Józef Lewandowski, "Między Sanem a Zbruczem," *Kultura* 519 (1990), 128–134; Józef Darski, *Ukraina,* Warsaw: Sorograf, 1993, 69; Yaroslav Bilinsky, "Basic Factors in the Foreign Policy of Ukraine," in S. Frederick Starr, ed., *The Legacy of History in Russia and the New States of Eurasia,* Armonk, N.Y.: M. E. Sharpe, 1994, 174, 186.

2. There was then a chair in Ukrainian history at Warsaw University, and an Institute of Ukrainian Studies in Warsaw: small reminders of the Polish-Ukrainian alliance of 1920. This institute published the first Ukrainian translation of *Pan Tadeusz,* by Maksym Ryl's'kyi.

3. A large share of the London emigration hailed from eastern territories lost to the Soviet Union, so their revanchism was personal. Of course, Giedroyc's native Minsk was freely given to Bolshevik Russia by Polish nationalists negotiating at Riga in 1921. This perhaps influenced his attitude toward Polish nationalists campaigning for Lwów and Wilno after 1944.

4. Facts drawn from Jerzy Giedroyc, *Autobiografia na cztery ręce,* Warsaw: Czytelnik, 1996; interview with Jerzy Giedroyc, Maisons-Laffitte, France, 7 November 1998. On his influence, Andrzej Friszke, *Opozycja polityczna w PRL,* London: Aneks, 1994, 242, and the treatments of *Kultura* cited below.

5. In the 1950s, concern with the Soviet Union yielded to a plan to create a Central European Federation. After the 1968 Soviet invasion of Czechoslovakia, however, *Kultura* began to concentrate on the geopolitics of Europe after the failure of communism and the collapse of the Soviet Union. Janusz Korek, *Paradoksy paryskiej Kultury,* Stockholm: Almqvist & Wiksell, 1998, 93–96; Marek Suszko, "*Kultura* and European Unification, 1948–1953," *Polish Review,* 45, 2 (2000), 183–195.

6. The paragraphs to follow deal with Juliusz Mieroszewski, "Polska 'Ostpolitik,'" and "Rosyjski 'Kompleks Polski' i ULB," in *Materiały do refleksji i zadumy,* Paris; Instytut Literacki, 1976, 110–122, 175–186. See also his "ABC polityki Kultury," in Zdzisław Kudelski, *Spotkania z paryską Kulturą,* Warsaw: Pomost 1995, 131–144; Krzysztof Kopczyński, *Przed przystankiem niepodległości,* Warsaw: Więź, 1990, 11; and Rafał Habielski,

"Realizm, wizje, i sny romantyków," in Juliusz Mieroszewski, *Finał klasycznej Europy,* Lublin: Wydawnictwo Uniwersytetu Marii Curie-Skłodowskiej, esp. 50. Compare Adam Bromke, *Idealism vs. Realism,* Cambridge, Mass.: Harvard University Press, 1967.

7. The historian Roman Szporluk drew attention to this same concatenation at about the same time: see the 1971, 1973, and 1975 articles reprinted as the first three chapters of *Russia, Ukraine, and the Breakup of the Soviet Union,* Stanford, Calif: Hoover University Press, 2000.

8. Timothy Snyder, "The Polish-Lithuanian Commonwealth since 1989: National Narratives in Relations among Belarus, Lithuania, Poland, and Ukraine," *Nationalism and Ethnic Politics,* 4, 3 (1998), 1–24.

9. On the realists, Stanisław Bieleń, "Kierunki polityki wschodniej III Rzeczypospolitej," in *Patrząc na wschód,* Warsaw: Centrum Badań Wschodnich, 1997, 12. On the government in exile, *Radio Free Europe Report,* 7 September 1990.

10. On the period before Solidarity, Friszke, *Opozycja;* Andrzej Paczkowski, *Pół wieku dziejów Polski,* Warsaw: PWN, 1996; Grzegorz Ekiert, *The State against Society,* Princeton, N.J.: Princeton University Press, 1995. On Solidarity, Timothy Garton Ash, *The Polish Revolution,* London: Penguin, 1999; Roman Laba, *The Roots of Solidarity,* Princeton, N.J.: Princeton University Press, 1991; Jan Kubik, *The Power of Symbols against the Symbols of Power,* University Park: University of Pennsylvania Press, 1994; Michael Bernhard, "Reinterpreting Solidarity," *Studies in Comparative Communism,* 24, 3 (1991), 313–330; David Mason, "Solidarity as a New Social Movement," *Political Science Quarterly,* 101, 1 (1989), 41–58.

11. For the PPN program and KOR publications, Friszke, *Opozycja,* 423, 491–493. On the open letter, Jan Lózef Lipski, *KOR,* Berkeley: University of California Press, 1985, 387. See also Antoni Kamiński and Jerzy Kozakiewicz, *Stosunki Polsko-Ukraińskie,* Warsaw: ISP PAN, 1997, 5; Ilya Prizel, "The Influence of Ethnicity on Foreign Policy," in Roman Szporluk, ed., *National Identity and Ethnicity in Russia and the New States of Eurasia,* Armonk, N.Y.: M.E. Sharpe, 1994, 108; *Polityka* (Warsaw), 7 March 1998, 42.

12. Jacek Kurón, *Wiara i wina,* London: Aneks, 1989, 347–349.

13. On censored (legal) historiography, I.T. Lisevych, "Ukrains'ko-pols'ke kulturne spivrobitnytstvo v 70-kh rokakh," *Mizhnarodni zv'iazky Ukrainy,* 4 (1993), 58–68; L.O. Zashkil'niak, "Ukraina i ukrains'ko-pols'ki vidnosyny u pisliavoiennii pols'kii istoriohrafii," ibid., 145–156. Key uncensored (illegal) texts were Kazimierz Podlaski [Bohdan Skaradziński], "Bialorusini—Litwini—Ukraińcy: Nasi wrogowie czy bracia?" and Tadeusz Olszański, "Notatnik bieszczadzki."

14. On Ukrainian questions during the Solidarity period, Iurii Zaitsev, "Pol's'ka opozytsiia 1970–80 rokiv pro zasady ukrains'ko-pols'koho porozuminnia," in Iurii Slivka, ed., *Deportatsii ukraintsiv ta poliakiv,* L'viv: NAN Ukrainy, 1998, 54; Taras Kuzio, "The Polish Opposition and the Ukrainian Question," *Journal of Ukrainian Studies,* 12, 2 (1987), 51; Friszke, *Opozycja,* 321; Mirosław Czech, *Ukraińcy w Polsce,* Warsaw: Związek Ukraińców w Polsce, 1993, 269; Garton Ash, *Polish Revolution,* 133.

15. See the recollections of Bohdan Osadczuk, Iaroslav Hrytsak, Myroslav Popovych, Ivan Dziuba, Mykola Zhulyns'kyi, Mirosław Czech, and Roman Szporluk in *Nashe Slovo* (Warsaw), 8 October 2000.

16. On the KPN see below. The declaration of Wolność i Pokój in *Stosunki Polsko-Ukraińskie 1917–1947*, Warsaw: Perturbancii, 1990, 122–123. Publications which took up these questions included *Karta, Znak, Spotkania, Obóz, Międzymorze*, and *Nowa Koalicja*. An important document was [Zdzisław Najder et al.], "Polska-Ukraina," internal position paper, Polskie Porozumienie Niepodległościowe, November 1981. See generally Krzysztof Łabędź, *Spory wokół zagadnień programowych w publikacjach opozycji politycznej w Polsce*, Cracow: Księgarnia Akademicka, 1997, 181–187; Jerzy Pomianowski, *Ruski miesiąc z hakiem*, Wrocław: Wydawnictwo Dolnośląskie, 1997, 47; Józef Darski, "Kronika białoruska," *Kultura*, 471 (1986), 96; Jan Widacki, "Stosunki polsko-litewskie," *Kultura*, 602 (1997), 37–38.

17. Antoni Dudek and Maciej Gawlikowski, *Leszek Moczulski bez wahania*, Cracow: Krakowski Instytut Wydawniczy, 1993, 268; *Życie Przemyskie*, 29 April 1992, 1, 3; *Sprawozdanie Stenograficzne z 25 posiedzienia Sejmu Rzeczypospolitej*, 6 July 1994, 13–14 (hereafter session (25) in parentheses); ibid. (31), 13 October 1994, 113.

18. Stefan Kozak, "Polsko-Ukraińskie dylematy i dialogi," *Polska w Europe*, 10 (January 1993), 47.

19. Milada Vachudová and Timothy Snyder, "Are Transitions Transitory?" *East European Politics and Societies*, 9, 1 (1997), 1–35.

20. This reversed an older East and Central European pattern. Most outstanding interwar fascists and nationalists were former socialists. Most outstanding postcommunist fascists and nationalists were former communists.

21. Interview with Aleksander Kwaśniewski, Warsaw, Poland, 17 May 1999; interview with Jerzy Giedroyc, Maisons-Laffitte, France, 7 November 1998; also *Gazeta Wyborcza*, 3–4 January 1998, 10.

22. Anna Grzymała-Busse, "The Regeneration of Communist Parties in East Central Europe after 1989," Doctoral dissertation, Harvard University, 1999.

CHAPTER 12. THE NORMATIVE NATION-STATE (1989–1991)

1. For the legal stance of the Federal Republic of Germany, *Documentation Relating to the Federal Government's Policy of Détente*, Bonn: Press Office of the FRG, 1974, 16, 27. For the views of expellee leaders, Herbert Hupka, *Unruhiges Gewissen*, Vienna: Langen Müller, 1994, 433ff.; Herbert Czaja, *Unterwegs zum kleinsten Deutschland?* Frankfurt am Main: Josef Knecht, 1996, 753ff. Polish public opinion polls are cited below.

2. Quotation from *Gazeta Wyborcza*, 27 November 1989, 1. See also *Rocznik Polskiej Polityki Zagranicznej 1991*, 80. Consult Jacques Lévesque, *The Enigma of 1989*, Berkeley: University of California Press, 1997, 110–119.

3. On the Kohl visit to Warsaw, Horst Telchik, *329 Tage*, Berlin: Siedler, 1991, 13–15; Helmut Kohl, *Ich wollte Deutschlands Einheit*, Berlin: Ullstein, 1996, 125–127; Bronisław Geremek, *Rok 1989*, Warsaw: Plejada, 1990, 327; Philip Zelikow and Condoleezza Rice, *Germany Unified and Europe Transformed*, Cambridge, Mass.: Harvard University Press, 1995, 102. Waigel's remarks cited after Krzysztof Skubiszewski, *Polityka zagraniczna i odzyskanie niepodległości*, Warsaw: Interpress, 1997, 16 n. 1.

4. Timothy Garton Ash, *In Europe's Name*, New York: Random House, 1994, 230, 353–354;

Zelikow and Rice, *Germany Unified,* 132–133, 220–221; Telchik, *329 Tage,* 132, 184, 296–297; *Gazeta Wyborcza,* 8 February 1990, 7; 9 February 1990, 7; 22 February 1990, 1; 2 March 1990, 1; 15 March 1990, 1; Krzysztof Skubiszewski, "Poland and the North Atlantic Alliance 1989–1990," in Jörn Ipsen, ed., *Recht—Staat—Gemeinwohl,* Cologne: Heymann, 2001; Skubiszewski, *Polityka zagraniczna,* 29–34; *Sprawozdanie Stenograficzne,* (28), 26 April 1990, 8–10.

5. Włodzimierz Derczyński and Robert Draczyk, *Stosunek Polaków do innych narodowości,* Warsaw: CBOS, August 1996, 29.

6. On the initiation of negotiations, Antoni Dudek, *Pierwsze lata III Rzeczypospolitej 1989–1995,* Cracow: Geo, 1997, 70; Grzegorz Kostrzewa-Zorbas, "The Russian Troop Withdrawal from Poland," in Allan Goodman, ed., *The Diplomatic Record, 1992–1993,* Boulder, Colo.: Westview Press, 1995, 122–123. On Vilnius aflame, Grzegorz Kostrzewa-Zorbas, "Imperium kontratukuje," in Jacek Kurski and Piotr Semka, interviewers, *Lewy czerwcowy,* Warsaw: Editions Spotkania, 1993, 159–162.

7. On Polish fears of Germany, "Security for Europe Project Final Report," Providence, R.I.: CFPD, 1993, 15. For a May 1992, survey, *Życie Warszawy,* 1 August 1992, 23. Hupka's query in Skubiszewski, *Polityka zagraniczna,* 75. On German diplomats, ibid., 140.

8. Communication from Krzysztof Skubiszewski, 7 December 2000, 8–9. This is clear in Skubiszewski, *Polityka zagraniczna,* 379–395. See also Ilya Prizel, "Warsaw's Ostpolitik," in Ilya Prizel and Andrew Michta, eds., *Polish Foreign Policy Reconsidered,* New York: St. Martin's, 1995, 96–98.

9. Respectively: *Sprawozdanie Stenograficzne* (14), 8 May 1992, 193; Skubiszewski, *Polityka zagraniczna,* 29.

10. In 1968 Skubiszewski had criticized Polish participation in the invasion of Czechoslovakia and the anti-Semitic policy of the Polish régime; in 1980 he had joined Solidarity. Nevertheless, he participated in a Consultative Council to General Wojciech Jaruzelski from 1986 to 1989. Jaruzelski stayed on as president of Poland until 1990, and so Skubiszewski's career made him an acceptable choice for both sides as foreign minister in 1989.

11. On Skubiszewski, *Polityka* (Warsaw), 27 October 1990. On logistics, *Gazeta Wyborcza,* 9–10 June 1990; communication from Krzysztof Skubiszewski, 7 December 2000, 10.

12. The exception is the Hungarian engagement of the Ukrainian SSR, a result of Hungary's concerns about its minority there. Skubiszewski quotation: *Polityka zagraniczna,* 74. Skubiszewski's characterization of the policy: *Sprawozdanie Stenograficzne* (51), 14 February 1991, 22; *Polityka zagraniczna,* 271; and the sources cited in the next note. The two-track memorandum: Grzegorz Kostrzewa-Zorbas, "Tezy do polskiej polityki wschodniej u progu lat dziewięćdziesiątych," 22 March 1990. On its relation to policy: Communication from Grzegorz Kostrzewa-Zorbas, 27 February 1998. See also Geremek, *Rok 1989,* 338; *Gazeta Wyborcza,* 13–14 January 1990, 5–6; *Rzeczpospolita,* 14 January 1994, 22.

13. *Sprawozdanie Stenograficzne* (28), 26 April 1990, 15; and 65, 27 June 1991, 20.

14. Grzegorz Kostrzewa-Zorbas, "Stosunki polsko-litewskie," submitted to the Polish Senate's Foreign Affairs Committee and to the Obywatelski Klub Parlamentarny, Warsaw, 23 October 1989.

15. Skubiszewski, *Polityka zagraniczna,* 71, 96. For criticism, see Adam Chajewski, "Polityka polska wobec Litwy w latach 1989–1994," *Arcana,* 1, 7, (1996), 97.

16. Timothy Snyder, "The Poles," in Charles King and Neil Melvin, eds., *Nations Abroad,* Boulder, Colo.: Westview Press, 1998, 186–187.

17. On contacts with Sąjūdis, Chajewski, "Polityka polska wobec Litwy," 95; Jan Widacki, "Stosunki polsko-litewskie," *Kultura,* 602 (1997), 46; "Materiały okrągłego stołu litewsko-polskiego," *Lithuania,* 9–10 (1993–1994), 16; Jerzy Marek Nowakowski, "Polska—Litwa, *Polska w Europie,* 2 (1990), 64.

18. "Rukh" and "Sąjūdis" mean "movement" in Ukrainian and Lithuanian, which makes translation senseless and precision hard.

19. Myroslav Shkandrij, "Literary Politics and Literary Debates in Ukraine 1971–1981," in Bohdan Krawchenko, ed., *Ukraine after Shelest,* Edmonton: CIUS, 1983, 55–68; Roman Solchanyk, "Politics and the National Question in the Post-Shelest Period," ibid., 14–17.

20. *Kultura,* 436–437 (1984), 143–145; Taras Kuzio, "The Polish Opposition and the Ukrainian Question," *Journal of Ukrainian Studies,* 12, 2 (1987), 48; Stephen Burant, "Poland's Eastern Policy, 1990–1995," *Problems of Post-Communism,* 43, 2 (1996), 48–57; "Informacja o założeniach i dotychczasowej działalności Instytutu Polsko-Ukraińskiego," 1997.

21. Michnik quotation from Mirosław Czech, *Ukraińcy w Polsce,* Warsaw: Związek Ukraińców w Polsce, 1993, 16; the reaction from Roman Solchanyk, *Ukraine: From Chernobyl to Sovereignty,* New York: St. Martin's Press, 1992, 59; Ivan Drach, Roman Szporluk, and Mark Kramer discussed the Michnik speech with me.

22. Interview with Jerzy Kozakiewicz, Warsaw, 4 March 1997; Iurii Zaitsev, "Pol's'ka opozytsiia 1970–80 rokiv pro zasady ukrains'ko-pols'koho prozuminnia," in Iurii Zaitsev, ed., *Deportatsii ukraintsiv ta poliakiv,* L'viv: NAN Ukrainy, 1998, 56–63; Antoni Kamiński and Jerzy Kozakiewicz, *Stosunki polsko-ukraińskie,* Warsaw: Instytut Spraw Publicznych, 1997, 20; Czech, *Ukraińcy w Polsce,* 18 22; Gazeta Wyborcza, 8 May 1990, 6.

23. Interview with Jacek Czaputowicz, Warsaw, 9 September 1997; Stephen Burant, "International Relations in a Regional Context: Poland and its Eastern Neighbors," *Europe-Asia Studies,* 45, 3 (1993), 409; *Gazeta Wyborcza,* 18 October 1990, 6.

24. Interview with Jerzy Kozakiewicz, Warsaw, 4 March 1997; Skubiszewski, *Polityka zagraniczna,* 273–274; *Sprawozdanie Stenograficzne* (14), 8 May 1992, 196; Jan de Weydenthal, "Polish-Ukrainian Rapprochement," *RFE/RL Research Report,* 28 February 1992, 26; Czech, *Ukraińcy w Polse,* 47; Kamiński and Kozakiewicz, *Stosunki polsko-ukraińskie,* 21–22; *Nashe Slovo* (Warsaw), 13 December 1992, 1–2.

25. Andrew Wilson, *Ukrainian Nationalism in the 1990s,* Cambridge: Cambridge University Press, 1997.

26. Alexander Motyl and Bohdan Kravchenko, "Ukraine," in Ian Bremmer and Ray Taras, eds., *New States New Politics,* Cambridge: Cambridge University Press, 1997, 235–249; Roman Szporluk, "Reflections on Ukraine after 1994," *Harriman Review,* 7, 7–9 (1994), 1–10; Wiktor Nebożenko, "Ukraińska opinia publiczna o polityce zagranicznej," *Polska w Europie,* 15 (1994), 149–162.

27. Poland also received assurances that the Russian Federation would not settle Germans in the Baltic province of Kaliningrad, taken from Germany and kept by the Soviet Union after the Second World War. Skubiszewski, *Polityka zagraniczna,* 272–273.

28. Kostrzewa-Zorbas, "Russian Troop Withdrawal," 121–125; *Rocznik Polskiej Polityki Za-*

granicznej 1991, 80–81; *Rocznik Polskiej Polityki Zagranicznej 1992,* 189; Dudek, *Pierwsze lata III Rzeczypospolitej,* 255.

29. Yitzhak Brudny, *Reinventing Russia,* Cambridge, Mass.: Harvard University Press, 2000, 262 and passim.

30. Wojciech Roszkowski, "Polska," in Marek Beylin, ed., *Europa środkowo-wschodnia 1992,* Warsaw: ISP, 1993, 273; on the May 1992 treaties see Kostrzewa-Zorbas, "Russian Troop Withdrawal," 132.

31. *Kultura,* 512 (1990), 87–88; Stephen Burant, "Belarus and the Belarusian Irredenta in Lithuania," *Nationalities Papers,* 25, 4 (1995), 645; Alfred Erich Senn, *Gorbachev's Failure in Lithuania,* New York: St. Martin's, 1995, 73, 115.

32. On 1989, Algimantas Prazauskas, "The Influence of Ethnicity on the Foreign Policy of the Western Littoral States," in Roman Szporluk, ed., *National Identity and Ethnicity in Russia and the New States of Eurasia,* Armonk, N.Y.: M.E. Sharpe, 1994, 165. On 1990, *Kultura,* 517 (1990), 120.

33. On the visit: interview with Jacek Czaputowicz, 9 September 1997, Skubiszewski, *Polityka zagraniczna,* 272; Tadeusz Gawin, *Ojcowizna,* Hrodna: Fundacja Pomocy Szkołom Polskim, 1993, 65; *Gazeta Wyborcza,* 16 October 1990, 1; 18 October 1990, 6; 22 November 1990, 6; *Kultura,* 519 (1990), 102–106; ibid., 560 (1994), 19. On territory and minorities: "Interview with Vintsuk Vyachorka," *Uncaptive Minds,* fall 1991, 39–49; *Kultura,* 505 (1989), 106–107; *RFE/RL Research Report,* 1, 37 (18 September 1992), 41–45.

34. *Gazeta Wyborcza,* 4 September 1991, 6; *Kultura,* 560 (1994), 19; Moscow Interfax in English, 10 October 1991, in *FBIS-SOV,* 11 October 1991, 63; Moscow *Tass* in English, 11 October 1991, ibid., 17 October 1991, 76; *Le Monde,* 8–9 March 1992, in *FIBS-EEU,* 10 April 1992, 25–28; Jan Zaprudnik, *Belarus,* Boulder, Colo.: Westview, 1993, 216.

35. Zdzisław Winnicki, "Polacy na Białorusi," in Jacek Pietraś and Andrzej Czarnocki, eds., *Polityka narodowościowa państw Europy Środkowowschodniej,* Lublin: IEWS, 1993, 199.

36. Juozis Lakis, "Ethnic Minorities in the Postcommunist Transformation of Lithuania," *International Sociology,* 10, 2 (1995), 179–180. In 1953, 27,000 students studied in Polish schools or studied Polish in non-Polish schools. By 1987 this number had fallen to 10,133. Grzegorz Błaszczyk, "Polacy na Litwie," *Przegląd Wschodni,* 1, 1 (1991), 156.

37. Eberhardt, "Przemiany narodowościowe na Litwie," 478.

38. Thomas Szayna, "Ethnic Poles in Lithuania and Belarus," Rand Report, August 1993, 35.

39. Jacek Kuśmierz, "Między 'wschodem' a 'zachodem,'" *Przegląd Wschodni,* 1, 3 (1991), 512–513; Lech Mróz, "Problemy etniczne w Litwie wschodniej," ibid., 496; Szayna, "Ethnic Poles in Lithuania and Belarus," vii.

40. Senn, *Lithuania Awakening,* 99; Vesna Popovski, *National Minorities and Citizenship Rights in Lithuania,* Houndmills: Palgrove, 2000, 132–133; Piotr Łossowski, "The Polish Minority in Lithuania," *Polish Quarterly of International Affairs,* 1, 1–2 (1992), 83; *Kultura,* 499 (1989), 106–112; Chajewski, "Polityka polska wobec Litwy," 96; *Gazeta Wyborcza,* 27 September 1989, 6.

41. Widacki, "Stosunki polsko-litewskie," 41–44; *Gazeta Wyborcza,* 5 October 1990, 6.

42. As Ernest Renan put it, "to have forgotten, to commit historical errors, this is crucial to the creation of a nation." *Qu'est-ce qu'une nation?* Paris: Calmann-Levy, 1882. But see Benedict Anderson, *Imagined Communities,* rev. ed., London: Verso, 1991, 199–201.

43. Grzegorz Kostrzewa, "Stare i nowe," *Gazeta Wyborcza*, 22 September 1989, 6.
44. The letter in *Gazeta Wyborcza*, 15–17 September 1989, 2. Vladivostok mockery ibid., 8–10 September 1989, 1. See also ibid., 11 September 1989, 6; 5 June 1990, 6.
45. "Aide Mémoire w sprawie potrzeb mniejszości polskiej w Republice Litewskiej," Polish Ministry of Foreign Affairs, 26 November 1990. This campaign for territorial autonomy received no attention in the West precisely because it lacked (in Rogers Brubaker's terms) a "nationalizing external homeland" which supported its claims. *Nationalism Reframed*, Cambridge: Cambridge University Press, 1994. For the voices of the autonomists: *Nasza Gazeta* (Vilnius), 22 October 1989, 3; 22 October 1989, 1; 8 November 1989, 1, 3; 4 December 1989, 2; 8 April 1990, 1–2; 23 April 1990, 2; 13 May 1990, 1; 3 June 1990, 2; 15 October 1990, 2.
46. Senn, *Gorbachev's Failure*, 145; see also the sources cited in note 31.
47. *Gazeta Wyborcza*, 23 May 1991, 7; 18 January 1992, 1; *Rzeczpospolita*, 11–12 April 1992, 7; Chajewski, "Polityka polska wobec Litwy," 102.
48. *Sprawozdanie Stenograficzne* (49), 11 January 1991, III.
49. Timothy Snyder, "National Myths and International Relations: Poland and Lithuania, 1989–1994," *East European Politics and Societies*, 9, 2 (1995), 318–319; *Gazeta Wyborcza*, 14 January 1991, 3.
50. *RFE Daily Report*, 20 February 1992.
51. *Gazeta Wyborcza*, 12–13 January 1991, 1; 15 January 1991, 1; 21 January 1991, 11.
52. Ibid., 14 January 1991, 1; 15 January 1991, 1; 18 January 1991, 3; Leszek Jesień, personal communication, 9 April 2000.
53. Ibid., 12–13 January 1991, 1; 14 January 1991, 3.
54. Compare F. Stephen Larrabee, *East European Security after the Cold War*, Santa Monica, Calif: RAND, 1993, 11–12.

CHAPTER 13. EUROPEAN STANDARDS AND POLISH INTERESTS (1992–1993)

1. The EU was called the EC (European Communities) until 1993. To avoid confusion, I will use "EU" throughout. Poland's desire to join NATO was not made explicit before 1992, and was always more freely discussed by Prime Ministers Jan Olszewski and Hanna Suchocka than by Skubiszewski. It was the subject of conversations with Western partners as early as 1991 (if not before).
2. Krzysztof Skubiszewski, *Polityka zagraniczna i odzyskanie niepodległosci*, Warsaw: Interpress, 1997, 205.
3. Ibid., 29.
4. For basic statements of policy: *Sprawozdanie Stenograficzne* (14), 8 May 1992, 152–159; Skubiszewski, *Polityka zagraniczna*, 274, 282, 299–308. See also the views of the Polish ambassador from 1992 to 1997 in Jan Widacki, "Stosunki polsko-litewskie," *Kultura*, 602 (1997), 46; Žilvinas Norkunas, "Steering the Middle Course," *Lithuania in the World*, 4, 2 (1996), 18–23; and the address of the next foreign minister, Andrzej Olechowski: *Sprawozdanie Stenograficzne* (20), 12 May 1994, 27.
5. "Polska—Ukraina—Białorus," *Polska w Europie*, 12 (1993), III–II2.
6. The latter explicitly referred to the 1990 Copenhagen statement on minority rights. Ver-

trag zwischen der Bundesrepublik Deutschland und der Republik Polen über gute Nachbarschaft und freundschaftliche Zusammenarbeit, 17 June 1991, article 20, available at www.auswaertiges-amt.de.

7. *Polityka* (Warsaw), 3 February 1996, 40. See also Skubiszewski, *Polityka zagraniczna,* 126, 206; Mirosław Czech, *Ukraińcy w Polsce,* Warsaw: Związek Ukraińców w Polsce, 1993, 278.

8. Hans-Dietrich Genscher, *Rebuilding a House Divided,* New York: Broadway Books, 1998, 525; Helmut Kohl, *Ich wollte Deutschlands Einheit,* Berlin: Ullstein, 1996, 446–447. On the "European" character of the 1991 German-Polish treaty, Dieter Bingen, *Die Polenpolitik der Bonner Republik von Adenauer bis Kohl,* Baden-Baden: Nomos, 1998, 292–306. Consult generally Timothy Garton Ash, *In Europe's Name,* New York: Random House, 1994.

9. Czech, *Ukraińcy w Polsce,* 34; Andrew Wilson, *Ukrainian Nationalism in the 1990s,* Cambridge: Cambridge University Press, 1997, 85. But see also *Kultura,* 542 (1992), 119–122. Sources on Polish fears of their neighbors are cited below.

10. Czech, *Ukraińcy w Polsce,* 130–131, for the Polish apology and the Ukrainian reply.

11. *Rocznik Polskiej Polityki Zagranicznej 1992,* 140.

12. Remarks of Dmytro Pavlychko in *Holos Ukrainy* (Kyiv), 13 February 1992, 5; interview with Ivan Drach, Kyiv, 27 May 1997.

13. Quotations from Burant, "International Relations in a Regional Context: Poland and its Eastern Neighbors," *Europe-Asia Studies,* 45, 3 (1993), 410.

14. "Shosta sesiia Verkhovnoi Rady Ukrainy, 12 sklykannia," *Biuletyn* 5, 1992, 36–56.

15. Hanna Suchocka, Dmytro Pavlychko, Hennadii Udovenko cited after, respectively: Władysław Gill and Norbert Gill, *Stusunki Polski z Ukrainą,* Toruń: Marszałek, 1994, 28; *Kultura,* 547 (1993), 92–93; *Życie Przemyskie,* 17 March 1993, 1, 3. See also *Holos Ukrainy* (Kyiv), 14 January 1993, 2.

16. See the resolution "Kontseptsiia Derzhavotvorennia v Ukraini," from the Rukh congress of 4 December 1992; also *Literaturna Ukraina,* 17 December 1992; *Kultura* 528 (1991), 80–81.

17. *Holos Ukrainy* (Kyiv), 20 May 1992, 1–2; Warsaw Radio Warszawa Network, 18 May 1992, in *FBIS-EEU,* 19 May 1992, 8; *Izvestia,* 19 May 1992, 5, in *Current Digest of the Post-Soviet Press,* 49, 20 (1992), 24–25; Bohdan Osadczuk, "Od Belwederu do Kamieńca Podolskiego," *Kultura,* 538–539 (1992), 140.

18. See for example the collection of statements in *A Russia That We . . .,* Kyiv: UCIPR, 1993.

19. "To strengthen Regional Security in Central and Eastern Europe," Ukrainian Embassy in Warsaw, 22 April 1993; [Dmytro Pavlychko], "Oświadczenie," *Kultura,* 537 (1992), 90–91. See also Ivan Drach, *Polityka,* Kyiv: Ukraina, 1997, 197; Larrabee, *East European Security,* 19, 108–109; Antoni Kamiński and Jerzy Kozakiewicz, *Stosunki polsko-ukraińskie* Warsaw: Instytat Spraw Publicznych, 1997, 30–31; Wilson, *Ukrainian Nationalism,* 177.

20. Reactions to the pact: Stephen Burant, "Ukraine and East Central Europe," in Lubomyr Hajda, ed., *Ukraine and the World,* Cambridge, Mass.: Harvard University Press, 1998, 42. Polish explanations of Ukrainian policy: *Kultura,* 568–569 (1995), 41; Skubiszewski, *Polityka zagraniczna,* 282. Equal distance: Jan de Weydenthal, "Economic Issues Dominate Poland's Eastern Policy," *RFE/RL Research Report,* 2, 10 (5 March 1993), 24; Warsaw TVP, 13 January 1993, in *FBIS-EEU,* 14 January 1993, 28; *RFE Daily Report,* 4 February 1993.

21. Warsaw later reversed its position and reneged on its deal with Moscow in order to support Ukraine. In 2000 Polish energy policy was more pro-Ukrainian than was Ukrainian energy policy; such a posture proved difficult to sustain in 2001. These issues were unresolved when this volume went to press, and will remain a key dimension of European security for decades. Fear of gas dispute: *RFE Daily Report,* 3 April 1992; on Ukrainian energy problems and foreign policy, Arkady Toritsin, "Political Economy and Foreign Policy in Post-Soviet Successor States," Doctoral dissertation, Rutgers University, 1999. "Anti-Ukrainian act": Stephen Burant, "Poland's Eastern Policy, 1990–1995," *Problems of Post-Communism,* 43, 2 (1996), 52. Major Lysenko: Burant, "Ukraine and East Central Europe," 55.

22. On Krauchanka: *Gazeta Wyborcza,* 28 July 1997, 16; Jacek Gorzkowski, "Litwa," in Marek Beylin, ed., *Europa Środkowo-Wschodnia 1992,* Warsaw: ISP, 1993, 252; *Kultura,* 535 (1992), 102–106; on the intellectuals, Stephen Burant, "Belarus and the Belarusian Irredenta in Lithuania," *Nationalities Papers,* 25, 4 (1995), 646–647.

23. On Shushkevich: Siergiej Owsiannik and Jelena Striełkowa, *Władza i społeczeństwo,* Warsaw: Presspublica, 1998, 64–96; on Lithuania: Gorzkowski, "Litwa," 253.

24. Tadeusz Gawin, *Ojcowizna,* Hrodna: Fundacja Pomocy Szkołom Polskim, 1993, 127–128; Stanisław Bieleń, "Kierunki polityki wschodniej III Rzeczypospolitej," in *Patrząc na wschód,* Warsaw: Centrum Badań Wschodnich, 1997, 35; "Polska—Ukraina—Białorus," 140; Thomas Szayna, "Ethnic Poles in Lithuania and Belarus," Rand Report, August 1993, 42.

25. By redrawing diocese boundaries to reflect the contemporary Belarusian border, and by selecting an archbishop who was more sensitive to Belarusian concerns.

26. There was some early discussion of national minorities as such: *Narodnaia gazeta* (Minsk), 4 January 1992, 1; 12 February 1992, 1. The estimate of the Belarusian minority in Poland in 1992 is from Piotr Eberhardt, *Między Rosją i Niemcami,* Warsaw: PWN, 1996, 131. The Polish minority in Belarus is calculated according to the 1989 Soviet and 1999 Belarusian censuses.

27. Kathleen Mihailisko, "Security Issues in Ukraine and Belarus," in Regina Owen Carp, ed., *Central and Eastern Europe,* Oxford: Oxford University Press, 1993, 229–230; Burant, "Belarusian Irredenta," 645–648.

28. Warsaw PAP, 24 April 1992, in *FBIS-EEU,* 28 April 1992, 15.

29. Burant, "International Relations," 407; *Rocznik Polskiej Polityki Zagranicznej 1992,* 147.

30. Quotation from Tadeusz Kosobudzki, "Stracone szansy," *Kultura,* 560 (1994), 20; see also Warsaw PAP, 19 November 1992, in *FBIS-EEU,* 19 November 1992, 16; RFE Daily Report, 23 November 1992.

31. Interview with Czesław Okińczyc, Vilnius, 7 April 1994; Widacki, "Stosunki polsko-litewskie," 50.

32. *Gazeta Wyborcza,* 14–15 September 1991, 1; 16 September, 17; Landsbergis quotation from 24 September 1991, 6. The two men did meet informally when Landsbergis passed through Warsaw in transit.

33. Tass World Service, 12 January 1992, *SWB/SU,* 14 January 1992; PAP, 14 January 1992, *SWB/SU,* 16 January 1992.

34. Warsaw PAP, 15 January 1992, in *FBIS-EEU,* 22 January 1992, 20.

35. Timothy Snyder, "National Myths and International Relations: Poland and Lithuania, 1989–1994," *East European Politics and Societies,* 9, 2 (1995) 326–331; Widacki, "Stosunki polsko-litewskie," 52, for quotation.

36. Skubiszewski, *Polityka zagraniczna,* 191–193.

37. Vilnius Radio, 3 September 1993, in *FBIS-SOV,* 8 September 1993, 105; *Rzeczpospolita,* 16–17 October 1993, 9; Tallinn BNS, 21 October 1993, in *FBIS-SOV,* 22, October 1993, 88; *Dokumentation Ostmitteleuropa,* 20, 1–2 (April 1994), 116–119.

38. *Gazeta Wyborcza,* 27 April 1994, 1. For his historical views on Polish culture, Barbara Christophe, *Staat versus Identität,* Cologne: Wissenschaft und Politik, 1997, 234–236.

39. Quotations from Warsaw *Słowo Powszechne, FBIS-SOV,* 27 November 1991, 36; RFE Daily Report, 27 July 1993. See also Audrius Butkevicius, "The Baltic Region," *NATO Review,* 41, 1 (1993), 7–11. He seems to have changed his mind on NATO enlargement in 1994, after it became Lithuanian policy. His vision of Lithuanian state interests was less clear later in the decade, when he was convicted of taking a bribe while a parliamentary deputy, and when he accused Landsbergis of working for the KGB. The point of naming individuals here is not to create heroes, but to describe the domestic politics of strategic decisions.

40. Snyder, "National Myths," 334. This was after Skubiszewski's term had ended, and was precipitated by a special mission by Wałęsa's aide Andrzej Zakrzewski and the head of the Polish delegation Iwo Byczewski. It should still be seen as an accomplishment of the 1989–93 period.

41. Louisa Vinton, "Domestic Politics and Foreign Policy, 1989–1993," in Ilya Prizel and Andrew Michta, eds., *Polish Foreign Policy Reconsidered,* New York: St. Martin's, 1995, 24; *Rocznik Polskiej Polityki Zagranicznej 1993–1994,* 18.

42. Public opinion on Ukraine and Ukrainians: Grzegorz Babiński, *Pogranicze polsko-ukraińskie,* Cracow: Nomos, 1997, 166–168; Andrzej Zięba, "Ukraińcy w oczach Polaków," in Teresa Walas, ed., *Narody i stereotypy,* Cracow: Międzynarodowe Centrum Kultury, 1995, 97–98; Antonina Kłoskowska, *Kultury narodowe u korzeni,* Warsaw: PWN, 1996, 196; Warsaw PAP, 14 February 1992, in *FBIS-EEU,* 18 February 1992, 31; *Życie Warszawy,* 1 August 1992, 23. See also Marek Skórka, "Wspólne sąsiedztwo czy nie chciani intruzi?" *Więź,* 473 (1998), 70–81.

43. One sign of just how far matters had proceeded is that Battling Solidarity (Solidarność Walcząca), a radical labor union on the right, entered international politics with a pro-Ukrainian little tome including apologies for Operation Vistula. *Stosunki Polsko-Ukraińskie 1917–1947,* Warsaw: Perturbancii, 1990.

44. Jacek Raciborski, *Polskie wybory,* Warsaw: Scholar, 1997, 42; *Kultura,* 520–521 (1991), 145; *Gazeta Wyborcza,* 9 September 1991, 1; *Rocznik Polskiej Polityki Zagranicznej 1992,* 20; Prizel, "Warsaw's Ostpolitik," in Prizel and Michta, *Polish Foreign Policy Reconsidered,* 112; *Rzeczpospolita,* 15 January 1994, 22; *Gazeta Wyborcza,* 11 January 1994, 3.

45. The other major exception to the consensus was the Polish Senate's funding of an organization, Polish Community, which opposed Skubiszewski's policy by materially supporting organizations claiming to represent the Polish minority in Lithuania regardless of their political aims. From this group came Polish activists who argued that Poland should place the interests of Polish minorities above those in good relations with the

nation-states to the east. Interview with Agnieszka Panecka, Warsaw, 27 February 1998; Andrzej Stelmachowski, "O debacie," *Wspólnota Polska*, 58 (April 1997), 39. See also Widacki, "Stosunki polsko-litewskie" and Natalla Piatrowicz, "Katolicyzm na Białorusi," *Więź*, 467 (1997), 83.

46. This assertion is based upon a reading of the parliamentary record for 1989–94. On the right, see *Sprawozdanie Stenograficzne* (51), 14 February 1991, 15–54; (14), 8 May 1992, 152–199; (31), 13 October 1994, 108–114.

47. A role for which he was later recognized with the Order of Prince Iaroslav the Wise by Ukraine. *Polityka i kul'tura* (Kyiv), 10–16 September 1999, 38–39.

48. As he put it to the Senate: "Let us recall what various politicians have forgotten and still forget, that a Poland which lacks regulated, good and friendly relations with its eastern neighbors stops counting as a partner for the West." Skubiszewski, *Polityka zagraniczna*, 247.

49. Lech Wałęsa, "List do wyborców," 27 April 1989; *Literaturna Ukraina* (Kyiv), 3 June 1993, 1; 27 May 1993, 2; *Lithuania*, 11–12 (1994), 140–141; Moscow *Itar-Tass*, 29 June 1993, in *FBIS-SOV*, 30 June 1993, 64; *Kultura*, 550–551 (1993), 106–113.

50. "Security for Europe Project Final Report," 15; and Kłoskowska, *Kultury narodowe u korzeni*, 386.

CHAPTER 14. ENVOI: RETURNS TO EUROPE

1. On East European domestic politics and EU leverage, Milada Anna Vachudová, "The Systemic and Domestic Determinants of East European Foreign Policies," Doctoral dissertation, University of Oxford, 1997.

2. Klaus Bachmann, "Nasza i wasza wolność," *Rzeczpospolita*, 6 January 2001.

3. Foreign Minister Andrzej Olechowski tried to reengage the eastern neighbors in 1994, but was thwarted by Prime Minister Waldemar Pawlak.

4. *Gazeta Wyborcza*, 3 January 1994, 2.

5. Ibid., 6 March 1998, 3; 15 March 1998, 6; 1 July 1998, 1; *Segodnia*, 30 June 1998, 2; *Kommersant Daily*, 30 June 1998, 2; *Russkii Telegraf*, 30 June 1998. On the consequences of NATO enlargement, Stephen Burant, *Problems of Post-Communism*, 48, 2 (2001), 25–41.

6. Opinion poll data in Yuri Levada, "After the Thaw," *Wilson Quarterly*, 55, 2, (2001), 78.

7. *Gazeta Wyborcza*, 26 June 1998, 1.

8. Ustina Markus, "Belarus: You Can't Go Home Again?" *Current History*, 113, 585 (1994), 337–341.

9. *Minsk News*, 2 November 1997, 1.

10. The quotations: (IMF) Marek Karp, *Gazeta Wyborcza*, 26–27 July 1997, 16–17 *Rzeczpospolita*, 2 January 1997, 6; (wives) *Rzeczpospolita*, 6 August 1996, 23. See also *Gazeta Wyborcza*, 17 August 1995, 9; *Minsk News*, 22 December 1997, 3; *Gazeta Wyborcza*, 18 July 1997, 12; Siarhej Ausiannik and Ałena Strałkowa, "Białoruś," in *Europa Środkowo-wschodnia*, Warsaw: ISP PAN, 2000, 27. See also David Marples, *Belarus*, Amsterdam: Harwood, 1999, 90–91.

11. M. Koszelew, "Polacy w oczach Białorusinów," *Dzieje Najnowsze*, 27, 2 (1995), 81–93;

Natalla Piatrowicz, "Katolicyzm na Białorusi," *Więź*, 467 (1997), 81–92; Ryszard Radzik, "Ruski i Pan—asymetria stereotypu," *Europa Środkowo-wschodnia*, 63–80; Uładzimier Padhol, "W oczach 'sowka,'" ibid., 53–62; *Minsk News*, 17–23 March 1998, 3. Belarusians do see Poland as part of the capitalist West. Marek Śliwiński and Valerijus Čekmonas, "Świadomość narodowa mieszkańców Litwy i Białorusi," *Przegląd Wschodni*, 4, 3 (1997), 572.

12. Interview with Stanislau Shushkevich, 8 December 1996; "Chronicle, March 1995–February 1997," Polish Ministry of Foreign Affairs; *Minsk News*, 10–16 February 1998, 1; *Gazeta Wyborcza*, 6 February 1998, 8; *Głos znad Niemna* (Hrodna), 16–22 January 1995, 1.

13. *Itogi perepisi naseleniia Respubliki Belarus 1999 goda*, Minsk: Ministerstvo Statistiki, 2000. About 15 percent of "passport Belarusians" claimed in surveys that they are Russians, but then again about 10 percent of "passport Russians" in Belarus say that they are Belarusians. Śliwiński and Čekmonas, "Świadomość narodowa mieszkańców Litwy i Białorusi," 574.

14. A theme pursued by Roman Szporluk: consult chapters 4 and 9 of *Russia, Ukraine, and the Breakup of the Soviet Union* (Stanford, Calif., 2000).

15. On wartime losses: Marceli Kosman, *Historia Białorusi*, Wrocław: Ossolineum, 1979, 350; Piotr Eberhardt, *Między Rosją a Niemcami*, Warsaw: PWN, 1996, 185. On Neo-Uniates, Siarhej Abłamiejka, "Problem statystyki parafii neounickich na terenie Zachodniej Białorusi," in Jan Sergiusz Gajek and Stanisław Nabywaniec, eds., *Unia Brzeska z perspektiwy czterech stuleci*, Lublin: KUL, 1998, 213. On urbanization, Chauncy Harris, *Cities of the Soviet Union*, Chicago: McNally, 1970, 322. On Pazniak see Jan Zaprudnik, *Belarus*, Boulder, Colo.: Westview, 1993, 168; also Włodzimierz Pawluczuk, "Białoruś i sprawa polska," *Kultura*, 634 (2000), 112–13.

16. Steven Guthier, "The Belorussians: National Identification and Assimilation," *Soviet Studies*, 29, 2 (1977), 281; Nicholas Vakar, *Belorussia*, Cambridge, Mass.: Harvard University Press, 1956, 216–219; David Marples, *Belarus*, London: Macmillan, 1996, 30–31; Zaprudnik, *Belarus*, 107; Lilia Diamieszka, "Takie książki powinny być trzymane w wyjątkowo dobrze zamkniętych szafach," in *Inna Białoruś*, Warsaw: CSM, 1999, 29.

17. *Gazeta Wyborcza*, 28 April 1998, 4. See also "Polska polityka zagraniczna w 1996 roku," Polish Ministry of Foreign Affairs, 1997; Józef Oleksy, "Toast at the Official Dinner Given in his Honour by Mr. Adolfas Slezivicius," 16 September 1995; *Gazeta Wyborcza*, 28 January 1998, 2, 5.

18. Minority organizations' demands for territorial autonomy continued to go unheeded by Warsaw, and were considered less threatening in Vilnius. Wanda Marcinkiewicz, "Kronika litewska 1997," *Lithuania*, 26–27 (1998), 234.

19. *Rzeczpospolita*, 12 April 1996, 6; 15 January 1996, 6; *OMRI Daily Digest*, 7 January 1997.

20. Address at Harvard University, 14 November 2000.

21. On the right, *Ukrains'ka Respub'likans'ka Partia*, Kyiv: Fond Demokratii, 1996; *Narodnyi Ruch Ukrainy*, Kyiv: Fond Demokratii, 1996; *Ukraina: Stanovlennia Demokratii*, Kyiv: Ahentsvo Ukraina, 1997, 292; *Ukrains'ka Natsional'na Asambleia*, Kyiv: Ahentsvo Ukraina, 1998, 23. On Ukrainians generally, compare Wiktor Nebożenko, "Ukraińska opinia publiczna o polityce zagranicznej," *Polska w Europie*, 15 (July–August 1994), 159, and Evhen Golovakha and Ilko Kucheriv, "NATO and Public Opinion in Ukraine," *Politi-*

cal Portrait of Ukraine, 8 (1997), 63. For analysis, Jarosław Hrycak, "Jeszcze raz o sto-
sunku Ukraińców do Polaków," *Więź,* 473 (1993), 15–32; Olga Iwaniak, "Zamożniejsi
kuzyni," *Rzeczpospolita,* 22 May 1997, 6.

22. Interview with Anton Buteiko, 9 March 1999, Cambridge, Mass.; *Polityka i kul'tura*
(Kyiv), 10–16 December 1999, 10.

23. *Holos Ukrainy* (Kyiv), 29 June 1996, 1.

24. *Kultura,* 586–587 (1996), 153–157; Antoni Kamiński and Jerzy Kozakiewicz, *Stosunki
polsko-ukraińskie,* Warsaw: Instytut Spraw Dublicznych, 1997; Wladisław Gill and Norbert Gill, *Stusunki Polski z Ukrainą,* Toruń: Marszałek, 1994, 33; *Rocznik Polskiej Polityki
Zagranicznej 1995,* 123; *Rocznik Polskiej Polityki Zagranicznej 1996,* 136; *Rzeczpospolita,* 26
March 1997, 7.

25. For the text, *Rzeczpospolita,* 22 May 1997, 6; in English in Tadeusz Piotrowski, ed., *Genocide and Rescue in Wołyn,* Jefferson, N.C.: McFarland, 2000, 255–256. See also *Den'*
(Kyiv), 24 May 1997, 4; *Nashe Slovo* (Warsaw), 14 April 1996, 2.

26. Anatolii Martsynovs'kyi, "Prymyrennia davno prymyrenykh," *Holos Ukrainy* (Kyiv), 22
May 1997, 7; also worth consulting are essays by Iuri Andrukhovych. The most articulate
critic writing in Polish is the German Klaus Bachmann. *See Polska kaczka—europejski
staw,* Warsaw: CSM, 1999, 106 and passim.

27. The Ukrainian parliament was less important, and parliamentary ties never matched
Lithuanian-Polish levels. Interview with Borys Andresiuk, Cambridge, Mass., 25 September 2000.

28. Interview with Aleksander Kwaśniewski, 17 May 1999, Warsaw, Poland.

29. Włodzimierz Derczyński and Robert Draczyk, "Stosunek Polaków do innych narodowości," Warsaw: CBOS, August 1996, 29.

30. *Gazeta Wyborcza,* 13–14 September 1997, 12–13.

31. See Chris Hann, "Postsocialist Nationalism," *Slavic Review,* 57, 4 (1998), 840–863; *Polityka* (Warsaw), 14 December 1996, 87; *OMRI Daily Digest,* 10 October 1996.

32. The first seven volumes in Polish are *Polska—Ukraina: Trudne pytania,* Warsaw: Karta,
1998–2000; in Ukrainian as *Ukraina—Pol'shcha: Vazhki pytannia.* I was present at the
sixth and eighth conferences, in 1999 and 2000.

33. Peter Andreas and Timothy Snyder, eds., *The Wall Around the West,* Lanham, Md.: Rowman and Littlefield, 2000.

34. The relevant EU document: Treaty of Amsterdam, Conference of the Representatives of
the Governments of the Member States, Brussels, 23 September 1997; on German concerns: *Gazeta Wyborcza,* 4 February 1998, 6; 5 February 1998, 1.

35. *Minsk News,* 3–9 February 1998, 3; 10–16 March 1998, 1; *Gazeta Wyborcza,* 11 March
1998, 7.

36. *Den'* (Kyiv), 2 February 1999, 7; Yaroslav Hrytsak, "National Identities in Post-Soviet
Ukraine," in Zvi Gitelman, et al., eds., *Cultures and Nations of Central and Eastern Europe,* Cambridge, Mass.: Ukrainian Research Institute, 200, 274.

37. *Gazeta Wyborcza,* 15–16 November 1997, 6. His Ukrainian counterpart's comparison of
the EU external border to a new "Iron Curtain" is overdrawn, but it does call attention
to the consequences of EU policy for the EU's eastern neighbors and for Europe itself.

Ukrainian Foreign Minister Borys Tarasiuk at the inaugural meeting of the Ukrainian-Polish conference on European integration, Warsaw, 29 March 1999.

38. *Gazeta Wyborcza*, 28 April 1998, 7; Macieja Falkowska, *Społeczeństwo polskie wobec wschodniej polityki wizowej, gospodarczej, i kulturalnej*, Warsaw: CBOS, February 1995, 19–31.

39. *Vysokyi zamok* (L'viv), 9–16 January 1999, 1.

Acknowledgments

I wrote the introduction to this book in a carrel by a window. As I was writing, I heard bits of familiar birdsongs, one after the other. I turned to see a brown thrasher, perched on the sill outside, looking at me through the glass. Thrashers are mimics, and this one knew half a dozen songs. Repeating phrases from each song exactly twice, he moved through his songbook from beginning to end, drawing together strains from forest and seashore. He stood a foot away from my hand. When I raised my pen to record his songs, he made a grave little bow and flew away.

This is my grave little bow. A few people have followed this project from its genesis at Oxford to its conclusion at Yale, among them Timothy Garton Ash and Thomas W. Simons Jr. My initial approach was influenced by Leszek Kołakowski and the late Isaiah Berlin. Early efforts to connect history, myth, and policy were encouraged by Stephen Peter Rosen and the late Richard Smoke. Roman Szporluk, Andrzej Walicki, and Piotr Wandycz offered steady critique over several years. Several friends and colleagues read full drafts, among them Stephen Burant, Jeremy King, Eric Lohr, Stuart Rachels, Oxana Shevel, and Kieran Williams. Andrzej Paczkowski, Mary Elise Sarotte, Milada Anna Vachudová, and Tomas Venclova offered useful criticisms of large parts of the manuscript. For their attention to particular chapters I thank Chris Boyer, David Brandenberger, Kate Brown, Peter Holquist, Yaroslav Isaievich, Victor Hugo Lane, Terry Martin, Grzegorz Motyka, Richard Turits, Nerijus Udrenas, Theodore Weeks, Rafał Wnuk, and Larry Wolff. On questions of special difficulty I turned to Laura Belin, Audrey Helfant Budding, Michael Flier, Yaroslav Hrytsak, Katarzyna Jesień, Joshua Katz, Edward Keenan, and Mark Kramer. Keith Darden, Władysław Filar, Chris Hann, Ihor Il'iushyn, Jeffrey Kopstein, Grzegorz Kostrzewa-Zorbas, Dmitry Koublitsky, Leszek Jesień, Michael Mac-Queen, Paweł Świeboda, and Jason Wittenberg supplied me with ideas and sources. Jeffrey Burds and Jagoda Hernik Spalińska deserve special mention for their generosity with their own research. Fruitful directions of inquiry were suggested by Peter Andreas, Aaron Belkin, John Czaplicka, Norman Davies, Volodymyr Dibrova, the late Jerzy Giedroyc, Jerzy Jedlicki, Tony Judt, Charles Maier, Sean Pollack, Antony Polonsky, Peter Potichnyj, and Veljko Vujačič.

I benefited from the reactions of my seminar students Serhyi Bilenky, Steven Seegel, Anna Sluz, and Steven Swerdlow. In general, my ideas improved enormously after public presentation, and I feel very fortunate to have had the opportunity to discuss this work with interested audiences. I would like to thank participants of twelve seminars at Harvard University; three at the Institut für die Wissenschaften vom Menschen in Vienna; three at the University of Oxford (one at All Souls, two at St. Antony's); and two at the University of Virginia. I would also like to thank those who attended lectures at the Institute of History of the Polish Academy of Sciences, Central European University, the University of Colorado at Boulder, Columbia University, Georgetown University, the Massachusetts Institute of Technology, the University of North Carolina at Chapel Hill, Stanford University, and Yale University; as well as those who attended policy conferences organized by the Kolegium Europejskie in Warsaw, the EastWest Institute in Kyiv, the Euro-Atlantic Center in Chisinau, and the Wilson Center in Washington. The International Union of Home Army Soldiers and the Union of Ukrainians in Poland kindly allowed me to observe Polish-Ukrainian conferences at the Polish Military Academy in Rembertów. The people who agreed to be interviewed, recorded in the notes, were very gracious. Jonathan Brent, Larisa Heimert, and Margaret Otzel courageously undertook the production of this book; I am particularly grateful to Gavin Lewis for careful editing. For the accuracy of fact and the totality of interpretation of this book I alone take responsibility.

The project would have been unthinkable in its present form without the open stacks of the Widener Library at Harvard and the Sterling Library at Yale. I am also grateful to the institutions that made available the illustrations. Figures 15, 16, 17, 18, 19, and 25 are courtesy of Reference Library of the Ukrainian Research Institute, Harvard University. The photograph reproduced in Figure 19 is found in the Stephania Halychyn Collection, the others in the Bohdan Krawciw Collection. Thanks are due to Robert De Lossa, Daria Yurchuk, and Ksenya Kiebuzinski for help in reproducing these photographs. Figures 10, 11, 12, 20, 21, 23, and 24 appear courtesy of the United States Holocaust Memorial Museum, Washington, D.C. Of these, figures 10, 20, and 24 originate from the YIVO Institute for Jewish Research, 23 from the Muzeum Wojska Polskiego, 10 from the Lithuanian Central State Archives, and 12 from George Kaddish. I thank those who made their photographs available to the Museum, and the Museum for facilitating their further use. Figures 3, 4, 5, 9, 14, and 22, by the American photographer Louise Arner Boyd, are courtesy of the American Geographical Society in New York. Photographs of interwar Vilnius by Jerzy Hoppen (figure 6) and Edmund Zdanowski and Bolesława Zdanowska (figures 7 and 8) are used by permission of the Muzeum Narodowe in Warsaw. Figure 26 was reproduced from Jerzy Giedroyc and Krzysztof Pomian, *Autobiografia na cztery ręce*, Warsaw: Czytelnik, 1996, and is used by permission of the Instytut Literacki, Paris. Figure 1, a reproduction of a woodcut by Frantsysk Skaryna, was executed by Liavon Tsimafeevich Barazna; Jan Zaprudnik and Adam Maldzis answered questions about its reproduction. Figure 13, a photograph of an Ostroh Bible, was taken by the author with the permission of the Chernihiv Museum of History, Ukraine. The maps were drawn by Jonathan Wyss of Topaz Maps.

This book was conceived in Oxford, Paris, Vienna, and Prague; researched in Warsaw, Vilnius, Minsk, Kyiv, L'viv, and along state borders; composed in Cambridge, Massachusetts; and completed in New Haven, Connecticut. For financial support I am grateful to the International Research and Exchange Board, the Institut für die Wissenschaften vom Menschen, the American Council of Learned Societies, the Olin Institute for Strategic Studies, and the Harvard Academy for International and Area Studies. Samuel Huntington directed the latter two institutions during my time at Harvard, and it is to his courtesy and toleration that I owe three fruitful years. Thanks are also due to Chet Haskell, Beth Hastie, and Ira Kukin for their work for the Harvard Academy. Occasional expenses were subsidized by the EU Center of Harvard University, the MIT-Mellon Project on Forced Migration, and the Ukrainian Research Institute. This project would have been impossible without travel and thus without hospitality, in particular that of Larysa and the late Serhyi Shevel in Kyiv, and Agnieszka and Andrzej Waśkiewicz in Warsaw. It also required public places in which to read, write, and rephrase. A nostalgic cup of late-night black coffee is raised to Cafés Pamplona in Cambridge, Museum in Vienna, Slavia in Prague, Nowy Świat in Warsaw, and Au St. Michel in Paris (now, I believe, defunct).

Index